WITHDRAWN

D1518378

# A Vulnerable System

# A Vulnerable System

## The History of Information Security in the Computer Age

Andrew J. Stewart

Cornell University Press

Ithaca and London

First published 2021 by Cornell University Press

Printed in the United States of America

Library of Congress Cataloging-in-Publication Data

Names: Stewart, Andrew, 1975– author.
Title: A vulnerable system : the history of information security in the
    computer age / Andrew J. Stewart.
Description: Ithaca [New York] : Cornell University Press, 2021. | Includes
    bibliographical references and index.
Identifiers: LCCN 2021013834 (print) | LCCN 2021013835 (ebook) |
    ISBN 9781501758942 (hardcover) | ISBN 9781501759048 (pdf) |
    ISBN 9781501759055 (epub)
Subjects: LCSH: Computer security—History. | Computer networks—
    Security measures—History.
Classification: LCC QA76.9.A25 S755 2021 (print) | LCC QA76.9.A25
    (ebook) | DDC 005.8—dc23
LC record available at https://lccn.loc.gov/2021013834
LC ebook record available at https://lccn.loc.gov/2021013835

To the Memory of Rose Lauder

# CONTENTS

# A Vulnerable System

# INTRODUCTION

## *Three Stigmata*

At the end of the 1990s, Julian Assange was living in Australia and spent his time developing free software.[1] It was six years before he would launch WikiLeaks, but his knowledge of information security was already well established. In the previous five years he had been convicted of computer hacking and helped to publish a book that described the exploits of a group of young computer hackers.[2] Assange had also cofounded a company with the goal of creating commercial computer security products.[3]

Because of his interest in information security he was subscribed to several email discussion lists. One of those mailing lists was called "Information Security News," and it carried news articles from the mainstream press on the topic of information security.[4] The members of the list would also post various other items of interest and discuss information security among themselves.[5]

On June 13, 2000, a message was posted to the mailing list that contained a link to one of the earliest published pieces of research on the topic of computer security.[6] It was titled "Security Controls for Computer Systems," and the posting described it as "the paper that pretty much started it all." Seeing this, Assange shot back a reply: "And what a sad day for humanity that was. A mechanized scheme for anal retentive paranoids with which to live out their authoritarian dream of automatically crushing any acts of unauthorized, unforeseen creativity."[7] This reply—histrionic, acerbic, and perhaps facetious—was a small contribution to his later legacy in support of the idea within hacker culture that "information wants to be free."[8]

But Assange was wrong. The study of information security has in fact provided tremendous value to society. It is security technologies and techniques that enable private and anonymous communications online. Dissidents can organize and protect themselves from snooping. Whistleblowers can more safely expose the corrupt and illegal practices of corporations and governments. WikiLeaks itself could not operate without the use of technologies and operational practices that have emerged directly from the study of information security.

Assange was wrong to portray efforts to study information security in purely black-and-white terms, because there are clearly both benefits and costs. Leon Trotsky is reputed to have said, "You might not be interested in war, but war is interested in you." What he meant was that people should not ignore matters that might affect them, and information security concerns now pervade the fabric of everyday life. The creation of the first digital computers marked the beginning of the modern era of both computing and information security. As the information in the world becomes increasingly digitized, the ability to secure that information becomes paramount. The importance of information security will only increase, but the challenge of delivering information security has not yet been met. Severe failures of information security are endemic, and these failures have their root cause in profound structural problems.

Billions of dollars are spent on commercial security products and services with the goal of protecting intellectual property and confidential customer data and to demonstrate compliance with laws that govern information security practices.[9] But even after spending billions, data breaches continue to be numerous and widespread. In 2005, hackers were able to acquire the debit and credit card information for more than one hundred million customers of the US-based department store TJ Maxx.[10] In 2013, a data breach at Yahoo! caused information from three billion user accounts to become compromised.[11] The theft of personal information in data breaches harms individuals and the organizations that have been breached.

On the world stage, computer hacking has been researched, developed, and employed by nation-states to steal intellectual property, influence elections, and carry out espionage. The "Stuxnet" computer virus that was discovered in 2010 was created with the goal of infecting and damaging Iranian centrifuges used in the production of nuclear material.[12] That same year, there was strong evidence presented that the Chinese government used industrial-scale hacking of computers to steal intellectual property from US companies.[13] This was followed by revelations regarding the use of computer hacking techniques to enable widespread international snooping on computers and electronic communications by the National Security Agency (NSA) and Government Communications Headquarters (GCHQ) in the United Kingdom.[14]

The twin problems of data breaches and computer hacking are compounded by a modern-day field of information security that has become trapped in a cycle of addressing the symptoms of security problems rather than attempting to fix the underlying causes. This is not only because there is a constant torrent of new technologies and new security vulnerabilities to keep up with but also because of a human bias toward the New. The New is fashionable, and so the New is desirable. But the desire to stay on top of things can block the opportunity to get to the bottom of things. The types of vulnerabilities used to compromise the security of computer systems in the current day such as buffer overflows, phishing, and SQL injection are not in fact new. Buffer overflows were written about in 1972, phishing in 1995, and SQL injection in 1998.[15] This "epistemic closure" within the field of information security—a term used to describe the situation in which a group retreats from reality into a make-believe world—has caused the past to be forsaken for the present. The unfortunate consequence has been the creation of massive opportunity costs.

These three profound failures—data breaches, the use of computer hacking by nation-states, and epistemic closure—are visible stigmata that mark the field of information security. It is only by confronting causes, not symptoms, that the three stigmata can be addressed, and this requires an understanding of how they came to exist.

Assange was quick to dismiss the early research into information security, but the challenges that exist within the field of information security have their roots in the foundational work that was carried out in the 1970s. It was during that period that a small number of academics and researchers developed ideas that laid the path to the future. They came together from think tanks such as the RAND Corporation, from government agencies such as the Central Intelligence Agency (CIA) and NSA, and from defense contractors such as Lockheed Missiles and Space Co.

They were technocrats, united in a belief that computer systems could be secured according to rational, scientific laws. To this effort they brought an intellectual purity. Their vision was one that promised security and order. But what they did not realize was that from the beginning there was a dangerous oversight at the very heart of their project. That imperfection would have a dramatic effect on the development of information security and on the ability to deliver information security in the modern day.

Chapter 1

# A "New Dimension" for the Security of Information

In the late 1960s and early 1970s, a small group of academics and researchers developed ideas that would have profound effects on the modern world. Their dream was to create a future for computing where information could be protected. They believed that human beings would function as cogs in a rational machine that could then be operated by the United States military. The results of their efforts would indeed change the world but not in the way that they had intended.

That history is the provenance of information security today. Their work established the board on which the game of information security is played. The players are the organizations struggling to defend against computer hackers, the governments attempting to prevent leaks by insiders, and every person trying to protect their personal information. On the opposite side of the board are computer hackers, spies, and terrorists, but they are players too.

The academics and researchers were brought together by the US military—an organization with a long history of embracing new technologies, including the earliest computers. The influence of the US military on the development of information security is tightly coupled to the influence that they had over the development of computing itself. Beginning in 1943, the US Army financed the design and development of the ENIAC—the world's first "electronic calculator."[1] The designers of the ENIAC were J. Presper Eckert and John William Mauchly. Eckert was an electrical engineer and Mauchly a physicist, and both worked at the Moore School of Electrical Engineering at the University of Pennsylvania, a center for wartime computing. They formed the Eckert-Mauchly Computer Corporation in 1948 so that they could sell their ENIAC computers.[2]

The army used the ENIAC to calculate firing tables for artillery guns.[3] The ENIAC was a machine well-suited for this task because the work involved having to repeatedly perform the same type of complex mathematical equations.[4] Understanding and predicting the ballistics of shells fired from artillery guns was of great interest to the army due to the large number of new types of guns that were being developed to fight World War II.

The ENIAC was an impressive installation. It weighed thirty tons and filled an entire room with eighteen thousand vacuum tubes, noisy Teletype machines, and whirring tape drives.[5] It used a vast amount of cables—cables that were vulnerable to hungry mice. When the ENIAC was being designed, Eckert and Mauchly conducted an experiment in which they put several mice into a box with various types of cable insulation. The insulation that the mice chewed the least was selected to be used in the machine.[6]

The operators of the ENIAC, who were arguably the first ever computer programmers, were six pioneering women who had been recruited by the US Army from the University of Pennsylvania.[7] They were given the task of configuring the ENIAC by using their mathematical knowledge to wire different parts of the computer together. This would enable the requested calculations to be carried out.[8] The contributions that they made to the ENIAC and to the field of computing have been recognized only in more recent years.[9]

In 1950, the Eckert-Mauchly Computer Corporation was acquired by the conglomerate Remington Rand. This organization was no stranger to the military market—they manufactured and sold conventional weapons including the now-iconic 1911 handgun.

After the end of World War II, the US military was facing a new set of challenges not directly related to war fighting. Many of those challenges involved logistics: how to most efficiently move around personnel and equipment and how to supply the large number of newly created US air bases around the world. To assist with these tasks, they looked to employ a successor to the ENIAC named the UNIVAC. The UNIVAC had also been designed by Eckert and Mauchly and sold for around a million dollars at the time.[10] UNIVAC stood for Universal Automatic Computer, a name that was carefully chosen to indicate that the UNIVAC could solve general problems and was not limited to performing particular types of calculations.[11] This flexibility was a valuable innovation and made the UNIVAC especially attractive to the US military because they had many different types of problem to solve.

Three of the first ten UNIVAC computers to be manufactured were installed at US military facilities. The US Army, Navy, and Air Force each received a UNIVAC that they would use for their own specific needs.[12] The UNIVAC delivered to the air force was installed at the Pentagon in June 1952.[13] It was used on an initiative code named Project SCOOP—the Scientific Computation of Optimal Problems. Project SCOOP used the UNIVAC to help solve logistics problems by performing mathematical calculations that involved almost one thousand variables. Unlike human mathematicians, the UNIVAC could deliver the answers to those calculations quickly. The project was considered so successful within the air force that the UNIVAC machine was still in use in 1962, at which time there were several other more sophisticated computers available. In the words of one of the Project SCOOP team members, "the digital computer triggered a vision of what could be accomplished."[14]

That vision was expansive. The US military wanted computers to help break encrypted messages, to assist in the development of new weapons, to solve logistics problems, and for hundreds of other tasks large and small.[15] They even speculated about using computers to support technologies that had not yet been built, such as for calculating the trajectories of satellites.[16] The US military understood the benefits that computers provided, and so they expected the world at large to become increasingly computerized. Indeed, at the end of the 1950s and the beginning of the 1960s, there was a growing dependence on computers. This was also a period of great upheaval and advancement in computing, and those developments would have far-reaching effects on the security of information.

The computers of the late 1950s were baroque by today's standards. Like an organist playing a pipe organ within a cathedral, a single operator would sit at the controls, surrounded by the machine. The computer did only what it was told to do, and when the operator stopped to think, the computer waited obediently. This created an inefficiency; computers were extremely expensive and ideally there would be no downtime where the computer wasn't performing some calculation. The solution to this problem came in the form of a brilliant technical innovation: the development of computers with the ability to perform time-sharing. In a time-sharing computer the pauses taken by a user could be used to service other tasks. Even the minuscule gaps between keystrokes could be put to productive use. Several people could now use a computer at the same time, and the computer could operate in a manner where each user felt that they had the machine's undivided attention.[17] The experience of using a computer was transformed from one that was individual and solitary into one that was shared and collaborative. This change created entirely new categories of security risk. Because a computer could now have multiple simultaneous users, those users could potentially interfere with each other's programs or perhaps see classified data that they should not see.

The idea of "classification" is at the heart of how the US military secures information. Documents are given a classification level such as Top Secret, Secret, or Confidential. A person is not permitted to view information that has a classification higher than their level of clearance. For example, a person who has only Confidential clearance cannot view information that is classified as Top Secret. One user of a time-sharing computer might have Top Secret clearance and another user might not. How could Top Secret information be stored and processed on that computer without exposing it? Before time-sharing, a computer could be locked in a room and a guard posted at the door. But a time-sharing system could have multiple terminals that users could use to interact with the computer, and those terminals could be spread around a building. This made the physical security of a time-sharing computer and the monitoring of its users much more difficult.[18]

The economic advantages that time-sharing computers delivered made it highly likely that their use would become widespread, and so time-sharing computers were expected to bring about a revolution in computing. The potential dangers to the security of information stored on computers would increase exponentially, and the fear of those dangers was felt by the US military and the defense contractors they employed. They saw these developments as a "new dimension" for the task of securing information.[19] It was a problem the US military had to solve. They did not believe that they could accomplish the task alone, and so they enlisted partners. Those partners were other US government agencies such as the Central Intelligence Agency (CIA) and National Security Agency (NSA), alongside large defense contractors and think tanks. Preeminent among the think tanks was the RAND Corporation—the name being a contraction of "research and development." RAND was a factory of ideas, a think tank that was already advising the US government on how to wage and win wars.

RAND was conceived in 1942 by Henry "Hap" Arnold, an air force general.[20] At the end of World War II, there was deep concern that the scientists and academics who had been gathered together for the war effort would disperse and that the US military would lose access to their expertise.[21] Arnold pledged ten million dollars from unspent war funds to form RAND as a group that would provide a home for those researchers.[22] In the decades to come, the air force would essentially provide RAND with unlimited funds—a blank check for attempting to solve some of the trickiest problems faced by the US military.[23]

RAND researchers were initially housed in offices inside an aircraft plant at the Cloverfield Airport in Santa Monica, California.[24] In 1947, RAND moved to a building in downtown Santa Monica, just five minutes' walk from the white sand of the beach.[25] The interior of their new facility was designed to maximize chance encounters between RAND staff members and thereby promote collaboration.[26] This is an approach to building design that is still used by companies today, including by Apple.[27] The RAND building was innocuous-looking, but it was formally a Top Secret US government research facility, with armed guards twenty-four hours a day. Every RAND employee had to receive a government security clearance, and until they received that clearance they were escorted everywhere inside the building—even to the bathroom.[28]

RAND would initially report into the part of the air force hierarchy that dealt with research and development, and this placed RAND under the auspices of General Curtis LeMay.[29] If any person could be considered the historical heart and soul of RAND, it is LeMay. He played a key role in the development of the organization and imbued it with his mind-set and his approach to the world. Looking at LeMay with modern eyes, he appears to be a parody of the archetypal Cold War general. He had a gruff manner and a "never surrender" attitude and held court over his subordinates while chewing on the end of a cigar.[30] But behind this self-cultivated image was a deadly serious individual. During World War II, LeMay oversaw the bombing campaign against Japan, including the firebombing of Tokyo on March 10, 1945. LeMay ordered the defensive guns to be removed from 325 B-29 Superfortress bombers so that they could hold more bombs, napalm, and other munitions that were then dropped on Tokyo—almost two thousand tons in total. The attack killed nearly one hundred thousand civilians, and the larger bombing campaign against Japan that was also led by LeMay is estimated to have killed up to five times that number.

LeMay's take-no-prisoners attitude was a constant throughout his life. During the Cold War he supported a massive preemptive strike against the Soviet Union. His plan was to drop the entire US stockpile of nuclear weapons onto seventy Soviet cities in an attack he referred to as the "Sunday punch."[31] The film director Stanley Kubrick would later use LeMay as the inspiration for the unhinged air force general in the film *Doctor Strangelove*, which also features an organization called the Bland Corporation.[32] When LeMay was confronted with the accusation that he only focused on the practical goal of winning at the expense of all other considerations, he was unrepentant, saying, "All war is immoral. If you let that bother you, you're not a good soldier."[33] LeMay saw war as a problem to be solved in a rational, scientific manner. The more bombs that could be dropped increased the probability of defeating the enemy. A preemptive nuclear strike that wiped out your opponents was a rational decision because it gave the enemy no chance to retaliate. It was a supremely unemotional, analytical approach. This philosophy would come to permeate the work that RAND would carry out over many decades and over which LeMay had dominion. Thomas Schelling, a RAND analyst and future winner of the Nobel Prize in Economics, wrote in his book *Arms and Influence* that wars are won with bargaining power and that bargaining power "comes from the capacity to hurt."[34]

Analysts at RAND were attracted to abstract theory and to what they considered to be the largest, most challenging problems. They took an amoral approach to the policies that they designed and advocated and to the side effects of those policies.[35] RAND employed their numbers-driven, technocratic approach in their attempts to tackle the most pressing challenges of the US military. In doing so, they developed entirely new analytical apparatus.

A simple game in which two players compete against each other can be used as a model for more complex conflicts, even a nuclear war between countries. The use of mathematics to study such games is known as game theory, and many of the major figures in the field of game theory worked for RAND at some point during their careers.[36] RAND analysts used game theory to model the nuclear standoff between the United States and the Soviet Union and used their models to try to predict the best moves in the game.[37]

Building on their research in game theory, RAND developed a new technique that was entirely their own invention. First conceived by Edwin Paxson in 1947, "systems analysis" enabled a problem to be broken down into its constituent parts.[38] Each part would then be analyzed and all of that analysis brought together to generate a high-level conclusion. This was a useful tool for organizations such as the US military who needed to make decisions about complex systems that have lots of moving parts and many open questions. An example that was close to General Curtis LeMay's heart was the topic of strategic bombing. What is the most effective way to deploy a bomber fleet of aircraft against an enemy? At what altitude should the bombers fly in order to maximize the damage of the dropped bombs but also minimize the number of bombers that are shot down? What is the cost of the logistics effort required to carry out such a bombing campaign? Systems analysis was designed to be able to answer these types of question.[39]

Systems analysis required a lot of mathematical heavy lifting and computers to carry it out. In 1950, RAND analysts were using two early computers designed by IBM, but they decided that substantially more computing power was required.[40] They visited several different computer manufacturers in order to survey the state of the art. These included IBM and the Eckert-Mauchly Computer Corporation, but RAND deemed their work "too whimsical" and not sufficiently forward-thinking, so they made the decision to build their own computer in-house.[41]

The machine they built was named the JOHNNIAC, and it became operational in 1953.[42] RAND did not do things by half measures—for several years the JOHNNIAC would be among the most sophisticated computers in the world.[43] The JOHNNIAC demonstrated a number of firsts: it could support multiple users, it had the first rotating drum printer and the largest core memory, and it was said to be able to run for hundreds of hours.[44] This was a considerable feat, given that the ENIAC could run for only between five and six hours before it had to be reset.[45] One of the innovations implemented within the JOHNNIAC was a powerful air-conditioning system that was used to keep the machine cool. When the machine was opened for maintenance, the cold air would escape into the room in which the computer operators worked, requiring them to don ski jackets. For this reason, one of the JOHNNIAC's nicknames became "the pneumoniac."[46]

The development of systems analysis and the creation of the JOHNNIAC were significant accomplishments, but RAND would become best known for an influential piece of work that the US military has kept partially classified even today.[47] In the 1950s, a RAND analyst named Kenneth Arrow devised a theory based on the assumption that people will act in their own rational self-interest.[48] The premise is intuitive: people will make choices to maximize the things they want and minimize the things they do not want. Arrow's goal was to build a mathematical model that would allow the Russian leaders' decisions to be predicted. The US government wanted to be able to anticipate how those leaders would behave in international affairs and in war. They wanted to answer questions such as which neighboring country the Soviet Union might invade, or what actions they might take during a conflict.[49] Before Arrow's work, the ability to predict the decisions of the Soviet apparatus was essentially nonexistent. "Sovietologists" would try to infer which officials were in favor by analyzing how close each person stood to Stalin in propaganda photographs released by the Kremlin.[50]

Systems analysis, game theory, and the other analytical techniques developed and employed by RAND were perceived to be very successful. They enabled a numbers-driven approach to be applied to problems. They reduced the chaotic complexity of the world to something manageable, such as a mathematical model or equation. The allure of this method that appeared to enable both the world to be understood and the future to be predicted was comforting for analysts and the US military brass when confronting situations where one possible outcome was nuclear war. These qualities were so attractive that RAND would use this kind of approach for decades to come when they began to study other complex problem domains such as social planning, health care, and education policy.[51]

At the end of the 1950s and the beginning of the 1960s, with the increasing growth in the number of time-sharing computers and on the cusp of an anticipated explosion in computing capabilities, RAND analysts began to study the problem of information security.[52] They brought to bear their analytical acumen and the rational approach that they had developed in their studies of nuclear war. Their efforts would kick-start the study of information security in the modern age.

# Chapter 2

# The Promise, Success, and Failure of the Early Researchers

Willis Ware was born in Atlantic City, New Jersey, on August 31, 1920.[1] Ware was an electrical engineer by training. He first studied at the University of Pennsylvania, where one of his classmates was J. Presper Eckert, and then attended the Massachusetts Institute of Technology (MIT).[2]

During World War II, Ware was exempt from military service because he was working on designing classified radar detection tools for the US military.[3] In spring 1946, at the end of the Pacific War, he learned about the work at Princeton University to build a computer for John von Neumann.[4] Von Neumann had devised a computer architecture in which the data and the program are both stored in the computer's memory in the same address space. This is the design used by most computers today and is based on the work of Eckert and Mauchly and their ENIAC.

Ware applied to Princeton University and accepted a job offer at the Institute for Advanced Study (IAS).[5] He worked on the IAS computer project while he studied for his doctorate, receiving free tuition because of his work on the computer.[6] The IAS machine was a pioneering project—one of the first electronic computers—and it led to Ware joining RAND in Santa Monica to help construct their JOHNNIAC.[7] Ware's opportunity to join RAND came partly from the fact that the primary person who was building the JOHN-NIAC, Bill Gunning, had broken a leg while skiing, and Gunning's supervisor realized that the company "had all their eggs in Bill Gunning's head, and if he got hit by a truck, RAND was in trouble."[8] Ware was brought onto the JOHN-NIAC project to provide redundancy for Gunning, and he started work as a bench engineer in spring 1952.[9]

Like other computers of that era, the JOHNNIAC was a substantial machine, so Ware was prescient in that as early as the 1960s he predicted the ubiquity of personal computing. He wrote that "a small computer may conceivably become another appliance" and that "the computer will touch men everywhere and in every way, almost on a minute-to-minute basis. Every man will communicate through a computer wherever he goes. It will change and reshape his life, modify his career, and force him to accept a life of continuous change."[10]

At RAND, Ware served on a number of committees that advised the US government, including the Air Force Scientific Advisory Board.[11] As part of that work, he assisted the air force with various projects, including the design of the computer software for the F-16 fighter jet.[12] As a result of these assignments, Ware and his colleagues began to realize how heavily the air force and the Department of Defense were beginning to depend on computers. They would talk among themselves in the hallways at conferences, and gradually there emerged a concern among them that they ought to do something to find out how to protect military computer systems and the information stored within them. Those conversations were the first organized efforts in what would become the study of information security in the computer age.[13]

A practical example of the need for computer security would soon present itself. A US defense company named McDonnell Aircraft had an expensive computer that they used for classified work as part of their defense contracts with the US military. McDonnell Aircraft had a long history of working on such projects. They had built the *Mercury* space capsule used for the United States' first human spaceflight program and had also designed and built the US Navy's FH-1 Phantom fighter jet, which was the first jet-powered aircraft to land on an American aircraft carrier. They wanted to rent their computer to commercial customers when it wasn't being used for classified work. This would allow them to recoup some of the high cost of the computer and enable them to establish new business relationships with other local firms.[14]

The Department of Defense received the request from McDonnell Aircraft and realized that they had never considered the possibility of a computer being used in a situation where some users of the computer would have security clearances, but others would not. Because this was an entirely new idea, the Department of Defense had no official policy on the matter.[15] As a result of the request from McDonnell Aircraft, a committee was established in October 1967 by the Department of Defense to investigate computer security in multi-user time-sharing computer systems.[16] The committee was also tasked with investigating the topic of computer security more broadly. Willis Ware was made the chairperson, and the committee included representation from various think tanks, military contractors, US government agencies, and academic institutions, including the RAND Corporation, Lockheed Missiles and Space Co., the CIA, and the NSA.[17]

The committee's report was delivered in 1970.[18] It was titled *Security Controls for Computer Systems* but came to be known colloquially as the Ware report.[19] It was the first structured and in-depth investigation of the topic of computer security that examined the subject from both a technology and governmental policy perspective. Due to the affiliations of its authors, the Ware report was primarily focused on military security rather than the commercial world. Ware wanted the report to be made public on its publication because he wanted its findings to influence commercial industry and not just military thinking. However, it took five years for the report to become declassified and made available to all in 1975.[20]

The Ware report predicted that as computers became more complex, the technical abilities of the users of those computers would also increase, but then so would the difficulty of implementing security measures that could control users.[21] The report notes that computer operating systems—the programs that control the computer hardware and the other software running on the computer—are both large and complex. Because of their size and complexity, it was likely that "inadvertent loopholes exist in the protective barriers [that] have not been foreseen by the designers."[22] As a consequence, "it is virtually impossible to verify that a large software system is completely free of errors and anomalies," and "it is conceivable that an attacker could mount a deliberate search for such loopholes with the expectation of exploiting them."[23] These words, published in 1970, were a remarkable achievement. They correctly and concisely predicted how events would unfold within the field of information security over the next fifty years.

To counter the threat of security loopholes, the Ware report recommended that computer vendors should "build security in" rather than waiting to add security features after the computer had already been designed.[24] The report also proposed fundamental principles on which the authors believed that a secure computer system could be built. Because the Ware report was created with military sponsorship, those principles were focused on how to secure classified documents inside computers. This led to recommendations that were impractical for commercial computer installations, such as the recommendation that the computer system should shut down immediately and entirely if any security failure was detected so that no information could be subsequently received or transmitted to any user.[25]

This extreme approach to computer security was the result of adopting the same rules that the military applied to handling classified information in paper form. After World War II, a RAND analyst named Roberta Wohlstetter spent several years writing a study on the surprise attack on Pearl Harbor by the Japanese.[26] She completed her report in 1957, and it was immediately classified as Top Secret by the air force. Because Wohlstetter did not have Top Secret clearance, she did not have the ability to keep a copy of her own work, and the only two paper copies were locked away in a vault at an air force facility.[27]

The classification of information in the United States began in 1940 after an executive order from President Franklin D. Roosevelt.[28] The purpose of classification is to enable appropriate security measures to be put in place.[29] But despite the best of intentions, the use of classification has led to a number of unintended consequences.

"Overclassification" occurs when a document is classified at a level that is higher than it should be or when information is kept classified for longer than necessary. This is harmful because it stops government workers from sharing information with each other, it prevents oversight of government actions, and the security measures that are required to protect classified information impose a cost.[30]

One of the reasons why overclassification occurs is because different government agencies create separate guides describing when information should be classified. This creates a morass of conflicting guidance. A 2017 report by the Information Security Oversight Office—a US government entity responsible for providing oversight over the classification system—identified 2,865 different security classification guides.[31]

There are also powerful incentives to overclassify. Only a limited number of people can see classified information, and so classification can be used to hide information that might be embarrassing or reveal incompetence.[32] There are legal penalties that can be imposed on US government workers for not classifying information that it is subsequently discovered should have been classified. But there is no such incentive in the other direction, as there are no penalties for overclassification.[33]

These factors combine to create an incentive structure in which there is essentially no reason to refrain from classifying information. As a result, it is believed that somewhere between 50 percent and 90 percent of classified documents do not need to be classified and that the information contained in those documents could be safely released.[34]

A second problem emerges with the use of "code word" classifications. Although Top Secret is formally the highest level of classification, code word classifications enable information within any particular level to be compartmentalized.[35] This is useful in situations where the government needs to limit access to information so that not everyone who holds the same level of clearance can access it. Such information is known as sensitive compartmented information (SCI). The problem is that some intelligence agencies have over a million code words, and the management of these is a difficult and complex task.[36]

A security clearance is a privilege, and so it can be taken away. In 1948, the Eckert-Mauchly Computer Corporation had been investigated by the Army Intelligence Division and five employees including John Mauchly declared to have "subversive tendencies or connections."[37] That investigation was the result of growing anticommunist sentiment within the United States, which ultimately led to the second Red Scare. The five employees had their security clearances revoked, and the company was banned from bidding on military contracts.[38] A Federal Bureau of Investigation (FBI) investigation eventually cleared Mauchly, finding that he was not a communist sympathizer and guilty only of being eccentric.[39]

The Ware report had been created partly due to the request from McDonnell Aircraft that both military and commercial customers be able to use its computer. After investigating the request, the report ultimately concluded that it would be unwise to provide McDonnell Aircraft with permission to do so unless a significant risk of accidental disclosure of classified information could be accepted.[40] The request from McDonnell Aircraft was denied, but the idea had created interest, so the air force established a second committee to propose a road map for computer security research.

The Computer Security Technology Planning Study, also known as the Anderson report, was commissioned in February 1972 by Major Roger Schell of the Air Force Electronic Systems Division.[41] Schell was a major who had also earned a PhD from MIT. He viewed the Ware report as having described a number of problems but not offered many solutions.[42] The goal for the Anderson report was therefore to propose solutions and lay out a road map for how they could be accomplished.[43]

The report was written by representatives from US government agencies such as the air force and NSA. The Anderson report name came from James P. Anderson who was the report's primary author. Anderson's first job was working for John Mauchly, who had hired him to create programs for processing meteorological data.[44] He later served in the US Navy as a gunnery officer and as a radio officer. As a radio officer he had worked with cryptography—the study of how to secure information and communications using codes and cyphers—and this had created his broader interest in information security.[45]

The Anderson report committee began work in February 1972 and issued their report in September of that same year.[46] Prior to publication, Schell experienced an uncomfortable feeling that the NSA would want to classify the report in the same way that the Ware report had been classified, which would greatly restrict its impact. He asked for three hundred copies to be printed and sent out "to everybody."[47] The next day, he received a call informing him that the NSA were exercising their classification authority over the document, but because he had already arranged for the report to be mailed out to hundreds of people—some of whom did not hold security clearances—the cat was already out of the bag, and the report would remain unclassified.[48]

The report states that "at first glance, the problems of providing security in resource-shared systems seems ridiculously simple." It then deadpans, "Unfortunately, that is not the case." The report goes on to wrestle with the same fundamental problem that the Ware report had documented, which was how to create a computer that can simultaneously service users who have a security clearance and who are handling highly classified data alongside users who hold a lesser security clearance or no security clearance at all. If all of the users of a computer hold a clearance level that is the same as the highest classification of the information contained on the computer, then the problem does not exist.[49] But that situation was unlikely to occur. It was far more likely that there would be multiple users with different clearance levels.

The authors of the Anderson report highlighted a new threat that they described as the "malicious user." A malicious user might attempt to find vulnerabilities—the loopholes that the Ware report had described—in the design or implementation of the computer or the programs running on it. Those vulnerabilities might allow the malicious user to take control of the computer and access information that they should not be able to access. The malicious user problem was made more difficult if users were able to program the computer rather than just use the computer to view information. A malicious user could carry out programming "to help his penetration and subsequent exploitation of the system" because, in the thinking of the Anderson report authors, "vulnerability increases with increased user control."[50]

The Anderson report also reiterated key findings from the Ware report, that as a computer system becomes more complex the security risk is increased and that a computer system should be designed to be secure in the first place rather than for security measures to be added as an afterthought.[51]

Because there were no computers available that could enable users with different clearance levels to work on the same time-sharing system, the authors of the Anderson report estimated that the air force was losing one hundred million dollars per year due to the resulting inefficiencies.[52] They recommended that at least one secure operating system be created.[53] That operating system could then be used as a real-world example to aid in the creation of other computer systems. They estimated that to create such a computer would take eight million dollars—a relatively small price to pay for the benefits and cost savings that would be received.[54]

To create a secure operating system would require a new way of thinking about computer security. Their idea, as described in the Anderson report, was the "reference monitor."[55] This would be a program that made authorization decisions—the task of determining "who can access what"— inside the computer operating system. The reference monitor would receive requests from users and other programs to access files and other resources on the computer. It would evaluate those requests and either permit or deny them. Through this mechanism, a user with Top Secret clearance would be permitted to read a file that was classified as Top Secret, but if a second user who held only Secret clearance attempted to read the same file, they would be denied access. Within the operating system a "security kernel" would implement the reference monitor. The security kernel would need to work correctly all of the time, and it would also have to be resistant to tampering, otherwise a malicious user could bypass it or stop it from working.[56] The security kernel would also have to be proven to work correctly, otherwise there was no guarantee that it would enforce security as expected.[57]

The authors of the Anderson report envisioned that the security kernel concept would play a central role in delivering the security of computers, and a security kernel was incorporated into the design of Multics, the first major operating system that was designed with a strong emphasis on security.[58] Multics was a cooperative project between MIT, General Electric, and Bell Labs, with the Department of Defense providing the funds that enabled MIT to participate.[59] The design and implementation of the security measures within Multics would have a strong ripple effect on the future of operating system design and on the approach to operating system security generally. Multics implemented a ring structure, like the rings on a dartboard, where the inner rings numbered zero through three were used by the operating system itself, and the outer rings beginning with ring four would contain user programs. Programs in the outer rings could not, in theory, harm programs in the inner rings, which enabled programs and the information they processed to be kept separate.[60]

In 1974, two years after the Anderson report was published, the computer scientist Jerome "Jerry" Saltzer wrote an analysis of Multics security. In that paper, he described a list of five design principles that he saw as being represented by the Multics implementation.[61] The following year, Saltzer teamed up with a fellow computer scientist named Michael Schroeder, who had been Saltzer's doctoral student, to publish an updated version. The title of the new version of the paper was "The Protection of Information in Computer Systems," and it would come to be known as a classic work in the field of information security.[62]

In their paper, Saltzer and Schroeder describe three fundamental goals for information security. Confidentiality is the goal of preventing people from reading data unless they have permission to do so, integrity is the goal of preventing people from changing data unless they have permission to do so, and availability is the goal of preventing people from stopping those who should be able to access data from being able to do so.[63] This formulation—confidentiality, integrity, and availability—would become known as the CIA triad. If confidentiality, integrity, and availability were important goals for security, then each of those goals had opposing forces that could subvert them. Confidentiality could be compromised by stealing the data or eavesdropping on the data as it was being communicated. Integrity could be compromised by surreptitiously altering the data. Availability could be compromised by a "denial of service" attack that stopped the computer from working, either by disrupting the hardware or software. The CIA triad is commonly used today as a way for security practitioners to design and analyze security measures. When the security of a computer system is being designed, the designers might ask: What are the goals for the system in terms of its ability to deliver the confidentiality, integrity, and availability of the information contained within it? What might a malicious party do to try to compromise each of those three aspects?

In addition to describing the CIA triad, Saltzer and Schroeder's paper also provided several design principles. These were novel and insightful ideas for how computer systems could be designed to deliver security. They described why the security mechanism, such as a reference monitor, should check every access request and only permit access when explicit permission is present. These are the principles of "complete mediation" and "fail-safe defaults." When combined, they are akin to a maître d' at a restaurant ensuring that only those parties with reservations are able to enter the restaurant and be seated. Two other important design principles described by Saltzer and Schroeder are the principles of "least privilege" and "separation of duties." Least privilege is the principle that the security mechanism should force every piece of the system, including users, to function with the minimum privileges required to accomplish their assigned tasks. An example of least privilege implemented in a hospital setting would be for nurses to be able to view the information contained in the medical records of only the patients to which they are assigned. Separation of duties means requiring more than one person to perform a task. The teller at a bank cannot unlock a safe-deposit box by themselves because they also need the second key that is kept by the owner of the box.

These design principles described by Saltzer and Schroeder in their paper would continue to be useful as the decades passed and new technologies rose and fell in popularity. Although their work is a significant milestone in the history of information security, the paper itself would become known as one of the most quoted but least read. This was largely because of the dense and rather impenetrable language in which the paper is written. The writing is so obtuse in parts that efforts were undertaken in later years to reframe the design principles using simpler language and examples from the Star Wars film franchise.[64]

Saltzer and Schroeder's work propelled the field of information security in a positive direction, but an unsettling discovery was about to be made. In June 1974, the air force published a paper that described the results of a "tiger team" security assessment of the latest version of the Multics operating system.[65] A tiger team is a group of people who are employed to attempt to break the security of a system, essentially simulating the likely actions of an attacker. The purpose of a "penetration test" carried out by a tiger team is to identify vulnerabilities in the system that can then be "patched," meaning fixed. This approach of finding vulnerabilities, fixing them, and repeating the process over and over would become known as penetrate and patch.[66]

RAND had itself carried out a number of tiger team assessments on behalf of the US government in the 1960s, and their success rate against those early computers had been spectacular.[67] The operating systems of the 1960s were said to be "Swiss cheese in terms of security loopholes," and one tiger team was able to penetrate the security of a computer made by Honeywell on the very first day that it was put on public display.[68] After successfully compromising the security of a computer system, a tiger team would use the knowledge and techniques that they had acquired in that assessment to attack the next system that they were tasked with evaluating, often finding that many of those techniques would be effective across different types of system.[69]

But Multics was expected to be far more secure than those earlier computers. The security features within Multics had been "built in" from the beginning—exactly as the Ware and Anderson reports had recommended. Multics also implemented the security kernel concept, although the Multics implementation did not fully satisfy the strict definition of a security kernel because Multics was considered to be too large and too complex to have a formal proof of its implementation. The air force carried out their assessment of Multics precisely because it was the most sophisticated implementation of the thinking at that time regarding how a computer should be designed and built in order to be secure.[70]

The high hopes for the security of Multics would soon be dashed. After expending "a relatively low level of effort," the tiger team found three major vulnerabilities. One of those vulnerabilities enabled all of the passwords stored on the system to be read.[71] The tiger team declared Multics to be "in some sense significantly more secure than other commercial systems" but "not currently a secure system," because "the system cannot be depended upon to protect against deliberate attack."[72]

These findings influenced the thinking of those working on computer security in two significant ways. The first was that they began to view the tiger team approach as ultimately futile.[73] If a tiger team completed a security assessment of a piece of software and found vulnerabilities in that software, it could not be known whether there were other vulnerabilities present that the team had simply not discovered. If a computer system were to survive a tiger team assessment, it might just mean that the tiger team members had not been sufficiently skilled or imaginative. The report describing the Multics security assessment stated that "without a doubt, vulnerabilities exist that have not been identified."[74] The second shift in thinking was that they began to believe that security controls such as passwords were no more than "security blankets" as long as the fundamental security controls surrounding the hardware and software of the computer did not work as desired.[75] They became convinced that in order to create a secure system they would need a formal way to prove that the system was secure, and two researchers would soon claim to be able to provide a way to obtain that proof.[76]

David Elliot Bell received his PhD in mathematics from Vanderbilt University in 1971.[77] After graduating, he visited the placement office at the university to ask for their assistance in finding a job. They provided him with a folder the size of a phone book that was filled with information regarding companies, and he reviewed that book looking for organizations that might want to employ someone with his qualifications. He owned a manual typewriter, and he would type and then send five job application letters each day. Months passed until he received a telegram from a company based in Boston named MITRE. And so, Bell, in his own words, cut his hair, put on his best suit, and went to Boston to interview.[78]

What he found at MITRE was something like a university campus with sprawling buildings that had walkways between them, and people milling around, some of whom had long hair and were wearing sandals.[79] MITRE was a think tank like RAND, and it employed intellectuals who were sometimes idiosyncratic.[80] One of the people who interviewed Bell at MITRE was Len LaPadula.[81] He was a mathematician and electrical engineer who had worked as a software engineer, and after Bell was hired they became office mates. At that time, MITRE employed around twenty-five hundred people, but only around twenty were working on information security.[82] MITRE was reviewing US government contracts that had begun to be created as a result of the Anderson report. Every year, the air force came to MITRE and described the work that they wanted think tanks to carry out.[83] One of those pieces of work was to find a way to prove the security of a computer system, and so Bell and LaPadula set to work. They examined the existing academic literature but found those papers to be either too theoretical or too specific to certain computer operating systems.[84] They decided to first focus on general principles and then later think about how those general principles could be applied to computers.[85] The first question that they had to answer was fundamental: what did it mean to say that something was secure? The US military wanted "multilevel secure systems" that could isolate users with different clearance levels, and so Bell and LaPadula began to work on a mathematical theory for such a system.

Their initial efforts incorporated the idea that the classification assigned to a piece of information could change, so a document that was classified as Secret could be reclassified as Top Secret, perhaps as the result of some world events. But when they showed this to the air force major who was supervising their work, they were told to assume that the classification of documents would never change. This was unexpected—it meant that they could simplify their approach. They decided to call their mathematical model the basic security theorem and later joked that this was in comparison to the "complex and extremely sophisticated security theorem" that they had originally envisioned.[86]

The feedback from the air force major had caused their original plans to be disrupted, and so they decided to stay circumspect about their work from that moment onward. MITRE conducted annual salary reviews, but because Bell and LaPadula had been keeping their work to themselves, it did not appear that they were being productive. The management team at MITRE had put in paperwork that would give them both a bad annual review, with a corresponding hit to their financial compensation. The head of their department told the pair that they needed to make a presentation describing what they had accomplished in their research, with the implicit suggestion that they needed to shape up or risk being fired.[87]

Bell and LaPadula quickly organized a presentation for MITRE management where they explained their work on their basic security theorem. They described what they had created as "a mathematical framework within which to deal with the problems of secure computer systems."[88] They were confident in their model, saying that "at the present time we feel that the mathematical representation . . . is adequate to deal with most if not all of the security problems one may wish to pose."[89] They claimed that using their definition of security, a computer system that implemented their model could be guaranteed to be secure in its operation.[90] As they made their presentation, the audience of MITRE managers became increasingly agitated.[91] They began to see the potential for the basic security theorem, but they also knew that the paperwork containing the critical annual reviews for Bell and LaPadula had already been filed. A decade later, Bell's manager at MITRE told him that ever since that meeting his intent had been to pay him so much money that he would never leave the company.[92]

The basic security theorem has as its premise the idea that a system can only be secure if it begins in a secure state, and then when the system changes state it can only move to a different state that is also secure. By policing the state transitions there was no possibility that the system could ever move into an insecure state, only an endless procession of secure states. The mathematical model was described in such a manner that it could be applied to real-world situations, such as the design of the security measures within a computer operating system. Because of the military's desire for multilevel secure systems, the basic security theorem focused on mandatory access control (MAC). Under MAC, the computer would check whether a user was authorized to carry out a requested action against a resource such as a file and that authorization decision would involve the consideration of the classification of the file and the clearance level of the user.

Bell and LaPadula's model appeared to solve the problem of penetrate and patch. There would never be unknown vulnerabilities lurking in the system that a tiger team might be unable to find during a penetration test because the system could be guaranteed to be secure. Roger Schell, the air force major who had commissioned the Anderson report, stated that he believed that the "foundation of mathematical completeness" would enable the creation of computers that were "penetration-proof—in particular to all those clever attacks that the . . . designers never contemplated."[93] If a computer system was mathematically proven to be secure, then there would be no concern regarding hidden security vulnerabilities. The provenance of the system would also be irrelevant. As long as it was proven to be secure, the US government could use a computer system that had been designed and built by the KGB, the security agency of the Soviet Union.[94]

But there was a problem. A researcher named John McLean who worked for the Center for High Assurance Computer Systems at the Naval Research Laboratory had learned about the Bell-LaPadula model through his employer's relationship with the NSA.[95] He reviewed their model and identified what he believed were fundamental concerns. The Bell-LaPadula model was based on the idea of a system moving from one secure state to the next, but what if those states were absurd? He developed an example of a computer system that implemented the Bell-LaPadula model he named System Z.[96] In System Z, every piece of information in the system was downgraded to the lowest possible level of classification. Any user could read any piece of information, and so the system could not possibly be considered secure.

McLean wrote that the Bell-LaPadula model provided "little help to those who design and implement secure systems" and that "what is captured by the Basic Security Theorem is so trivial that it is hard to imagine a realistic security model for which it doesn't hold."[97] He also expressed the view that there was a disconnect between the theoretical, academic world out of which the Bell-LaPadula model had emerged and the physical, real world in which organizations such as the air force wanted to build and use secure computers. Bell and LaPadula had created their model as "primarily a research tool developed to explore the properties of one possible explication of security."[98] But the air force and others wanted to evaluate real-world computers against their model. These were different objectives, and the two communities were failing to understand each other because of differing assumptions.[99] McLean's System Z and his broader critique challenged the basic premise that a theoretical mathematical model could be used in a formal way to prove that a real computer system was secure.

David Bell's response to McLean's work was that the mathematics of System Z were correct and that there was nothing wrong with having a computer system that implemented System Z if that was the goal for the system.[100] But in response to System Z, the Bell-LaPadula model was updated to include the "tranquility principle" where the security levels within the system could not change in a way that violated the security goals of the system. McLean's response to that change was that if the tranquility principle was included in the Bell-LaPadula model, then the model would be so strong that it could never be implemented in the real world. But if the tranquility principle was not included, then System Z could exist, which was absurd. In McLean's view, the Bell-LaPadula model was caught in a catch-22 situation.[101]

Those who believed in using mathematics to prove the security properties of a computer system needed a way to overcome these criticisms, and they turned to a new discipline within computer science named formal verification. By using formal verification, it appeared to be possible to provide a mathematical proof that a specific computer correctly implemented a particular security model. Both aspects, the model and the implementation of the model in the computer, could be mathematically proven to be correct, and this would create a perfectly secure system.[102]

The US government provided grants to organizations to investigate the use of formal verification for the purpose of delivering computer security.[103] One of the organizations that received a grant was SRI International, based in Menlo Park, California. SRI began a project in 1973 named the Provably Secure Operating System (PSOS) with the goal of creating an operating system and formally verifying its security properties.[104] The underlying security model used in PSOS was the Bell-LaPadula model. The formal specification for PSOS was four hundred pages long, and this made for slow progress in its formal verification.[105] Seven years later in 1980, a report on the PSOS project described it not as a "provably secure" operating system but instead as a "potentially secure" operating system that "might someday have both its design and implementation subjected to rigorous proof."[106] SRI was not alone in experiencing such challenges with the formal verification of security. The University of California, Los Angeles (UCLA), attempted to formally verify the security of an operating system but ended that project having verified only between 35 percent and 40 percent.[107]

There appeared to be some benefits to using formal verification for the purpose of improving the quality of software. But formal verification ran into the same problem that had been warned about in the Ware report and that had existed within Multics, that operating systems appear to be too large and too complex to have a complete formal proof of their implementation. As the process of formal verification is carried out, the benefits diminish and the costs become too great. In theory, the challenge of completing the formal verification of an entire operating system could be overcome with sufficient resources. But a far more subtle and insidious problem was about to be discovered—one that could not be overcome through brute force alone.

The primary security objective for a multilevel secure system was to keep different users with different security clearances separated. If two users with different security clearances were not separated, a user with Top Secret clearance could pass Top Secret information to another user who did not have Top Secret clearance. To their horror, security researchers discovered that there was a relatively straightforward way for users with different clearance levels to communicate with each other inside the computer.[108] That communication channel also did not rely on needing to find a vulnerability because it bypassed the security controls entirely.

Communication between two users could be accomplished by the first computer user writing a program that would increase the computer's utilization of its central processing unit (CPU). This could be achieved by having the program perform a complicated calculation that would tax the CPU. A second user could then write their own program that would detect those spikes in CPU utilization. A spike within a certain time window would indicate a binary 1. The absence of a spike would indicate a binary 0. Over time, the first user could generate a string of binary 1s and 0s—0110100001101001— that would communicate information that the second user could see and then decode. In this way, the first user could communicate with the second.[109] The two users who wanted to communicate within the computer might agree to this scheme in advance. They might also never communicate outside of the computer and be able to infer that the other user was signaling to them. If two people agree to meet in Manhattan on a certain day but they haven't had the opportunity to discuss a meeting time or location, they might both independently guess that a good place and time to meet would be underneath the clock in Grand Central Station at midday. The same kind of tacit collusion could be used to establish the means of communication within the computer.

This idea of passing information in a manner that circumvents security controls is called a covert channel. Using the computer's CPU was one way to implement a covert channel, but many other ways began to be found.[110] One researcher with a PhD in mathematics had spent years attempting to prove "with mathematical exactitude" that the kernel of the Multics operating system satisfied the Bell-LaPadula model. He was shown how one Multics user could communicate with another by consuming all of the space on the computer's hard disk, which the other user could detect. He found this profoundly disturbing, asking, "How could this happen?"[111] Forty years later, the problem of covert channels—known as the confinement problem—is present in entirely new domains of computing such as mobile computing and cloud computing.[112]

The cost and time required to provide a formal verification of security and the problem of covert channels combined by the end of the 1970s to cause the Department of Defense to reassess their strategy. Instead of the ideal that every computer would have its security formally verified, they began to take a more pragmatic tack. Security requirements would form various levels. The highest levels would require formal verification, but the lower levels would not. The highest levels would require greater controls to protect against covert channels, but the lower levels would not.[113] The various levels would be described in a set of "evaluation criteria" written by the Department of Defense.[114] The evaluation criteria would describe the security features that would be required to exist at each level, and commercial technology companies would build computers that would be evaluated and certified according to the criteria. This scheme would enable the Department of Defense to buy commercial computers "off the shelf" that came with certain guarantees regarding the level of security that they implemented.[115] Commercial vendors would also benefit because they could use the evaluation criteria to identify the security features that they should incorporate into their products. The vendors could also use the certification process to prove that their computers implemented a certain level of security.

The Department of Defense developed a set of evaluation criteria named the Trusted Computer Security Evaluation Criteria, which quickly became known as the Orange Book because of the color of the cover on the official printed copies.[116] (The earlier drafts had progressed from white to what was described as a "sickly shade of olive green" and finally orange.[117]) The Orange Book was issued on August 15, 1983, and was 117 pages long.[118]

Some of the key authors of the Orange Book had also worked on the Multics project, so the requirements described in the Orange Book had a "strong

Multics flavor."[119] The Multics project used the idea of security rings, and the Orange Book had levels or, more formally, divisions. There were four levels, with only the highest named A1 requiring a formal proof. The A level required the use of an automated verification system endorsed by the National Computer Security Center, but that proof would have to cover only the design of the system and not also the implementation.[120] Below level A was level B. Computers that were certified at level B were judged to be suitable for implementing multilevel security. If McDonnell Aircraft could have purchased a computer that was certified at level B, they could have serviced both their military and commercial customers on that computer. To receive certification at level B, the designers of a computer had to make a "convincing argument" that the security model was consistent with its implementation.[121] Below level B were levels C and D. Level C softened the security requirements of level B, and level D was reserved for computers that had been evaluated but had failed to satisfy the requirements of a higher level.[122]

The expectation of the authors of the Orange Book was that commercial vendors would move quickly to get their products evaluated at the lower levels and then work to add more security features to enable them to achieve the higher levels.[123] But this was slow going. By 1991, only two systems had received A1 certification: Honeywell's Secure Communications Processor (SCOMP) and the Department of Defense's Blacker system.[124]

Evaluation and certification were a slow process, whereas the rest of computing was speeding up. The personal computer (PC) revolution was popularizing computing through the miniaturization of components. A computer could now fit on a desktop and came equipped with a user-friendly graphical user interface, keyboard, and mouse. The home users and organizations that were buying the new PCs had no need for security features such as multilevel security and mandatory access control. They were on the whole commercial companies that did not store or process classified data, and they did not even think about their data in the same way as the US military with its classification scheme.[125] The US military was focused on keeping information confidential, but a commercial business was more likely to care about making sure that information such as customer records were not modified and therefore retained their integrity, which was a different security goal.

The SCOMP computer that achieved A1 certification sold fewer than thirty units and never broke even.[126] Microsoft's Windows NT operating system for PCs achieved a C2 rating, but that rating was dependent on the installation of Windows NT being run on a stand-alone computer with no computer networking and with the floppy disk drive disabled.[127] It would be highly unlikely for a computer running Windows NT to be used with that configuration in a real-world setting. Roger Schell described the C2 rating as being for computers that could protect themselves from only "the pure rank amateur," such as a "bored college student" who had "no real resources at all."[128]

The cost of implementing a multilevel secure system within a computer operating system was estimated to double the development costs.[129] Implementing the security features required to satisfy one of the higher levels of the Orange Book and then having that computer evaluated could also take years, and by the time those products came to market they would be more expensive and outdated in comparison to competing products that had not received certification.[130]

The Orange Book was a failure.[131] It may have raised the awareness of commercial vendors with regard to the security requirements of the US military, but it diverted the effort of those vendors that did participate into a scheme that divorced them from the new realities of the commercial market.[132]

RAND and the other early researchers who began the study of information security in the early 1960s believed that they could unlock the gates to a new world where classified information could be protected. But their dream was overpowered by the concerns of the market. In that regard, RAND had been proven correct, that rationality did indeed reign supreme. It was entirely rational for the new computer companies to forsake the creations of the early researchers such as multilevel security, formal verification, and the Orange Book.

By the mid-1990s, the field of information security was adrift. There was no clear path forward. But at the very same time that this was happening, a new and wondrous idea was beginning to change computing. And that idea would lead to a profoundly different approach to information security.

Chapter 3

# THE CREATION OF THE INTERNET AND THE WEB, AND A DARK PORTENT

The launch of the *Sputnik* satellite on October 4, 1957, created an intense panic within the US military.[1] The Soviet Union had demonstrated a capability that the United States could not yet achieve, and as a result, the US government began to invest a massive amount of money in research and development.[2]

The Advanced Research Project Agency (ARPA) was founded in 1958 with $500 million in seed funds and a $2 billion annual budget.[3] The organization was given the goal of directing the US space program and all strategic missile research.[4] ARPA did not directly employ any scientists or researchers. Instead, it employed managers who directed the work of scientists and researchers working in academic institutions and commercial organizations.[5] Because of this arrangement, ARPA was intensely interested in fostering collaboration between research scientists at academic sites such as MIT, Berkeley, and Stanford.[6] ARPA was vexed by the problem of the academics at those separate sites having to establish their own computers, programming languages, computer programs, and processes. This duplication of effort was a waste of resources, and ARPA was convinced that the various research sites could be joined together using a computer network, even though the task of connecting distant computers together had never been attempted.[7]

The idea that would enable their vision would come from a researcher working at RAND named Paul Baran. Baran had graduated from the Drexel Institute of Technology in 1949 with a degree in electrical engineering.[8] His first job was working at the Eckert-Mauchly Computer Corporation as a technician, testing computer parts that would be used in the UNIVAC. In 1959, Baran joined the RAND Corporation in their computer science department, and in the early 1960s, he became interested in how a military communications network could be built that could survive a nuclear attack.[9]

*Sputnik* had initiated the space race between the Soviet Union and the United States, and the threat of nuclear-tipped intercontinental ballistic missiles and the possibility of nuclear weapons being launched from space was now an existential threat to both countries. The game theory that was beloved of RAND analysts described how the United States and the Soviet Union were held in a stable equilibrium. Neither side could start a nuclear war because the other side would retaliate. This was the theory of mutually assured destruction, which was also known by its pertinent acronym MAD. But that equilibrium could only hold if the United States retained the ability to return fire after receiving an initial attack. If the first wave of Soviet missiles destroyed the ability of the commanders in the US military to pass orders down the chain of command, the counterattack could not be carried out. This was the problem that Baran wanted to solve. He would later describe his work as being undertaken "in response to the most dangerous situation that ever existed."[10]

Baran drew inspiration from the ability of the human brain to recover from physical damage.[11] Inside the brain there is no specific piece of gray matter without which the brain cannot function. This means that a brain is sometimes able to fully recover, even though a part of it has been irrevocably damaged. The remaining parts of the brain can learn to function without the damaged piece—adapting and compensating automatically over time. Baran applied this same idea to the problem of how to make a communications network continue to function if a part of it had been destroyed by a nuclear missile. Just as in a brain, the communications network would recognize where it had been damaged and route communications around the damaged areas.[12]

Baran worked to develop a plan that contained two key elements. The first element would be the construction of a communications network that functioned in a similar decentralized manner to the brain, with many individual smaller pieces connected together to form a larger whole.[13] The second element was the design for how information would be transmitted across that network. Information would be broken up into message blocks, also known as packets.[14] Those packets would travel via packet switching—meaning from one part of the network to the next until they reached their destination. If a part of the network was destroyed, the packets could be routed around that damage.[15] The term *packet* came from the idea of a small package because, like a small package, the outside of each packet would contain an address that would enable it to be routed through the network.[16] This was a fundamentally different approach to how telecommunications networks were implemented at that time. In those networks, a connection was established between a person making a telephone call and the person receiving the call, and that connection would have to be maintained over the entire duration of the call between the two parties.

By 1965, Baran had completed development of his plan. He made a pitch to his colleagues at RAND, who recommended to the US Air Force that a communications network be built that incorporated Baran's ideas for decentralization and packet switching.[17] The telecommunications network in the United States was owned and operated by AT&T, and on hearing Baran's proposal, they were skeptical. His approach was radically different to their current business and their existing technology. As a result, AT&T refused to consider implementing a packet-switching network even after the air force told AT&T that they would pay for them to build and operate the network.[18] The air force decided to proceed without the help of AT&T, but the Pentagon decided to give responsibility for building the network to the Defense Communications Agency instead of the air force; like AT&T, the Defense Communications Agency did not understand or believe in Baran's vision. Despondent but pragmatic, Baran recommended to the air force that they wait until an organization came along that would properly commit to his ideas.[19]

Baran would have to wait only two short years. In 1967, ARPA allocated $500,000 for a project that would begin work on developing a packet-switching network.[20] A small group of researchers and engineers, which included Paul Baran, began meeting to sketch out the initial design.[21] The group submitted their proposal to the management team at ARPA in

June 1968.[22] That proposal was approved by ARPA, and permission was granted to solicit bids from companies using an initial budget of $2.2 million.[23] Special computers would be built to enable the various ARPA research centers to be connected. These computers would be named Interface Message Processors (IMPs).[24] The team at ARPA sent out a request for proposal to 140 companies to submit bids describing how they would propose to build the IMPs.[25] Some large companies that received the request from ARPA declined to send a proposal. IBM decided not to participate because they believed that there were no computers small enough to make the network cost-effective.[26] ARPA did receive bids from a dozen companies, however, including Digital and Raytheon. Stacked on top of each other, the responses formed a six-foot-tall monolith of paper.[27]

ARPA carefully evaluated the bids and decided to award the contract not to one of the giant defense contractors such as Raytheon but instead to a small consulting company based in Cambridge, Massachusetts, named BBN (Bolt, Beranek, and Newman).[28] BBN had submitted an extremely detailed proposal to ARPA that described exactly how they planned to build the IMPs. The level of detail that BBN provided to ARPA gave them the confidence to pick them over the other bidders.[29]

The contract between ARPA and BBN specified that the first IMP should be delivered on Labor Day 1969, followed by one additional IMP per month through December of that year.[30] The first IMP was delivered and installed at UCLA in September 1969, the second at SRI International in October, the third at UC Santa Barbara in November, the fourth at the University of Utah in December, and the fifth at BBN itself in early spring 1970.[31] During summer 1970, the sixth, seventh, eighth, and ninth IMPs were installed at MIT, RAND, System Development Corporation, and Harvard University, respectively.[32] The ARPANET began to take shape. The first connection between two sites was established between IMPs at UCLA and SRI.[33] Less than a year after BBN had won its contract to build the IMPs, there were four sites attached to the network, at UCLA, SRI, UC Santa Barbara, and the University of Utah.[34]

Just as ARPA had intended, the early users of the ARPANET were almost exclusively computer scientists, but the growth of the network would be accelerated by a new "killer app" that appealed to scientists and nonscientists alike.[35] The ability to exchange messages between users on a single stand-alone computer had existed since the early 1960s, but the ARPANET enabled users at different sites using different computers to communicate using a new system of communication called email. Email provided a way for electronic messages to be sent between computers quickly and efficiently. The use of the @ symbol helped to make email addresses easy to understand, and a special effort was made to create email clients that were easy to use.[36] Email began to be used in earnest around 1972 and was found to be so compelling that by 1973 three-quarters of all network traffic on the ARPANET was email related.[37]

Each person who joined the network and created an email address for herself could now be contacted by every other person who also used email. The value that was received by a person from having an email address increased with every new person who joined the network, creating an ever-increasing momentum. This same phenomenon has been observed in the exponential growth of other communication technologies such as telephones and fax machines and would later become codified as Metcalfe's law.

The egalitarian nature of email was its great strength but over time would also become a weakness. The first spam email message would arrive in electronic mailboxes in 1978, although the use of the word *spam* to refer to unsolicited email would not enter common parlance until the 1980s.[38] The dubious honor of being the first person to send a spam email went to an employee in the marketing department at Digital Equipment Corporation, who sent an email advertising Digital's DEC-20 family of computers.[39] The email was sent to around six hundred email addresses and asked the recipients to "PLEASE FEEL FREE TO CONTACT THE NEAREST DEC OFFICE FOR MORE INFORMATION ABOUT THE EXCITING DECSYSTEM-20 FAMILY."[40] That email was described by commentators as a "flagrant violation" of the ARPANET, which on paper was still intended to be used only for official US government business.[41] It also kicked off a debate about what constituted the appropriate and inappropriate use of email—a debate that was itself carried out over email.[42]

The IMP machines and the connections between them provided the physical matter of the network, but network protocols were required to enable the computers connected to the network to communicate with each other. In the general sense, a protocol is an agreement between parties regarding how to communicate. A handshake is an example of a protocol. The first person knows to extend his hand and the second person knows to grasp the outstretched hand and shake it. After a short time, both people know to stop shaking. Another example of a protocol is a student in a classroom raising her hand to gain the attention of the teacher, who can then choose to call on the student to speak.

The network protocols for the ARPANET were described in documents called Request for Comments (RFCs).[43] This name was chosen to imply an open and collaborative process of creation.[44] Any person could provide feedback on an RFC and also write and propose an RFC describing a network protocol of her own design.[45] RFCs were not only used to describe network protocols but also to provide guidance to users of the network, present new ideas, and occasionally for humorous purposes. An RFC published on April Fool's Day in 1990 proposes a network protocol for the transmission of network packets using carrier pigeons. The "avian carriers" are described as having "an intrinsic collision avoidance system," but the reader is warned that "storms can cause data loss."[46]

Once an RFC is approved, it is added to the common law created by the corpus of other approved RFCs. A new version of an RFC can replace an older version, and in this way the RFCs can keep up with changing times and new technologies. The key network protocols that were some of the first to be designed were the Internet Protocol (IP) and the Transmission Control Protocol (TCP), known together as TCP/IP.[47] A larger set of related protocols form the TCP/IP protocol suite, and it is the protocols within this suite that enable packets to be routed around interruptions, exactly as Paul Baran's design had described.[48] The first two application-layer protocols to be created enabled computer users to interact using the computer network and so be productive. The Telnet protocol enables a user to connect to a remote computer and operate it as if the user was physically sitting in front of it.[49] A user at the RAND offices could use Telnet to work on a computer at, say, Harvard University or the University of Utah. The File Transfer Protocol (FTP) enables a user to transfer files from one computer to another.[50]

None of these protocols were designed with security in mind. The initial RFC that describes the Telnet protocol does not contain the word *security*, and there was no RFC examining the security of FTP until 1999.[51] The initial lack of consideration for security features was likely due to the desire to make the network as useful as possible as quickly as possible, and adding security features would have been, at least to some extent, a distraction from that goal. As a consequence, RFCs were only required to include a section that discussed security considerations beginning in 1993.[52]

By 1988, the network consisted of around three hundred sites, with each of those sites having hundreds or in some cases thousands of computers that were connected.[53] The total number of computers connected to the network at that time was believed to be around sixty thousand.[54] The number of computers connected to the network was growing at an exponential rate, however, in large part because of a new type of computer that had become available in the 1980s known as a workstation. A workstation could fit on a desk and typically ran the Unix operating system.[55]

The ARPANET had been the product of central planning by ARPA, but the unstructured way that computers were being attached to local networks represented organic growth. This was the fuzzy line that represented the transition between the ARPANET and the internet as the network is known today. A person who connected her computer to the internet could connect to other computers, but those computers could also connect to them. In this way, every computer that was connected to the internet was now connected to every other computer that was also connected to the internet.[56] That connectivity opened up a world of possibilities for collaboration and for productivity but also created security risks, and there would soon be a dramatic demonstration of those risks.

On the afternoon of Wednesday, November 2, 1988, system administrators at Cornell University detected what they thought was a virus infecting some of their computers.[57] The term *computer virus* was first used in a formal way in 1983 by the computer scientist Fred Cohen.[58] As a graduate student at the University of Southern California, Cohen was attending a class that happened to make him think about how a computer program could copy itself and self-replicate. He spoke about the idea with his PhD advisor, Len Adleman, who suggested that he call such a self-replicating program a computer virus.[59] Cohen wrote his doctoral dissertation on the topic of computer viruses and also wrote what he claims was the first ever computer virus program.[60] That program was born on November 3, 1983.[61] By coincidence, the virus that was believed to be infecting the computers at Cornell University was detected almost exactly five years later.[62]

The infection at Cornell was unusual because up until that moment viruses had tended to be spread by being transferred between computers via floppy disks. But at Cornell, the virus was spreading from computer to computer across the computer network. This was not, then, a virus but rather a worm—a name taken from parasitic tapeworms that live inside other creatures and sap their resources to maintain themselves.[63]

By nine o'clock that evening, RAND and Stanford University had also detected the worm on their computers.[64] The worm was now spreading rapidly, and just like a biological pandemic, the number of infections began to grow exponentially. A mere twelve hours after the worm had first been detected at Cornell, more than one thousand computers were infected.[65] These included computers at major sites such as MIT, Harvard, and NASA Ames.[66] Word spread among system administrators who attempted to warn each other about the worm. One wrote: "IF YOU WANT TO PROTECT YOUR MACHINE . . . JUST TURN YOUR MACHINE OFF, OR UNPLUG IT FROM THE NETWORK!!!!"[67]

The worm was able to infect two types of Unix computer: VAX computers made by Digital Equipment Corp and Sun-3 workstations.[68] It did not appear to have a malicious payload that would delete files, but it did consume a large amount of system resources on the infected machines, which slowed them down and in some cases used up all of their available hard disk space.[69] The rate at which the worm was attempting to infect other computers was also causing so much network traffic that the network became overloaded at times.[70]

System administrators and security personnel at various sites worked to capture instances of the worm and then to disassemble them to try and understand how it worked. It quickly became clear that the worm used several different techniques to infect remote computers. This was discovered after system administrators would identify one technique, block it, purge the worm from their computers, only to find that the worm would reinfect those same computers using a different technique and thus establish itself again.[71] The system administrators shared their findings with each other over email, often on a special email list that they set up to discuss the worm called phage.[72] One of the techniques used by the worm to infect systems employed email. This caused some sites to shut down their ability to send and receive emails, but since email was only one of many techniques employed by the worm, those sites would get reinfected anyway.[73] Shutting down email also had the negative effect of stopping communication and information sharing regarding how to stop the worm.

Connections between the military's dedicated network, MILNET, and the internet were severed in response to the worm but only after the worm infection had already spread to computers on MILNET.[74] It took a week for the worm to be dissected and fixes to be developed that could be applied to the Unix operating systems. Those fixes stopped the worm from infecting computers, and so the worm was able to be slowly purged from the network.[75] The worm had ultimately been successful at infecting around three thousand computers—approximately 5 percent of all computers connected to the internet at the time.[76] The question was now where the worm came from, who created it, and what was their motivation? Suspicion fell on the unknown author of an email that had been sent on Thursday, November 3, at 3:34 a.m. EST, just a few hours after the first worm infections had been reported. The email had been sent anonymously by connecting directly to an email server at Brown University from a computer at Harvard University. The body of the email began with the statement "I'm sorry" and then described how a virus might be loose on the internet and that system administrators could take three steps to avoid infection.[77] Those steps could only have been written by the author of the worm or someone who had a very good understanding of the design of the worm. Unfortunately, the spread of the worm slowed down the delivery of email, and the warning message was not seen until over a day later.[78]

The investigation into the mysterious email led investigators to a graduate student named Robert T. Morris.[79] Morris was a first-year graduate student in computer science at Cornell after having graduated from Harvard. Morris had telephoned two friends at Harvard University—Andrew Sudduth and Paul Graham—and asked Sudduth to send the anonymous email containing the warning.[80] The computer code for earlier versions of the worm were found on backup tapes taken by system administrators at Cornell University, and Graham had also sent an email to Morris in the previous month in which he asked him was there "any news on the brilliant project?"[81]

Morris was the first person to be arrested and tried for releasing a malicious computer program.[82] The trial took place in the US District Court in Syracuse, New York. At trial, Morris did not deny that he had written and released the worm, but he pled not guilty with the argument that he did not intend to cause any damage and that the damage did not meet the threshold described in the applicable law. The jury deliberated for five and a half hours and returned a verdict of guilty on January 22, 1990.[83] Establishing its place in history, the ruling was the first court decision in the United States to refer to the internet.[84]

Morris was sentenced on May 4, 1990. The sentencing guidelines recommended fifteen to twenty-one months in prison, but Morris received three years of probation, four hundred hours of community service, and a fine of $10,000.[85] The decision was appealed by Morris and his legal team, but the US Court of Appeals upheld the trial court's decision, and the US Supreme Court declined to hear a further appeal. In addition to the punishment dictated by the court, Morris was suspended from Cornell University for a year and subsequently refused readmission. But Morris did go on to earn his PhD at Harvard University in 1999 and then became a professor of computer science at MIT. He also became a partner in Y Combinator, a start-up incubator that has helped to birth successful technology companies including Airbnb and Dropbox.

Morris has never publicly explained his goals for the worm. He has stated that he did not intend to release it, but the worm was clearly designed with features that were intended to help it to evade detection.[86] After the worm had infected a Unix computer, it would change its name to "sh," which is the name of a common program in Unix.[87] Changing its name in this way would help the worm to avoid being noticed by system administrators. The worm was also programmed to periodically restart so that it would not show up in a list of long-running programs.[88] If the worm program crashed for some reason, it was designed so that it would not leave any digital remains, known as a core dump, for investigators to examine.[89] But if Morris intended the worm to evade detection, why did the worm make its existence so obvious by spreading so quickly that it overloaded computers and even overloaded the network itself? The answer appears to be that Morris did not intend for the worm to spread as quickly as it did. Each copy of the worm was supposed to check that it was not infecting a computer that had already been infected, but because of a programming error, that piece of computer code inside the worm only worked correctly on one out of every fifteen occasions.[90]

Some felt that the quality of the computer code that comprised the worm was "mediocre, and might even be considered poor" and that the worm code seemed to be the product of an "inexperienced, rushed, or sloppy programmer."[91] But there were two areas of the code that appeared to have been written by a different programmer entirely. One of the techniques that the worm used to spread from computer to computer was by attempting to guess passwords. To accomplish this, the worm needed to duplicate the encryption algorithm that was used to encrypt passwords in Unix systems. The code that performed that encryption within the worm was discovered to be nine times faster than the standard implementation of the algorithm within the Unix operating system.[92] The worm's code also supported both encryption and decryption even though the worm only used encryption, and these observations suggested that the encryption code had been cut and pasted by Morris into the worm from elsewhere.[93]

The second piece of code within the worm that seemed to have not been written by Morris was another of the techniques used to break into computers. The technique was called a buffer overflow. A program that is vulnerable to a buffer overflow expects to receive no more than a certain amount of data, such as AAA. But instead of sending AAA, the attacker sends AAAX. The X represents code that overflows the buffer and is executed by the computer—meaning run. Since that code is provided by the attacker, it can be anything that the attacker would like it to be, such as code that grants the attacker's program the highest level of privilege within the computer operating system. The concept of buffer overflows had first been written about in the Anderson report in 1972, but the worm was a very public demonstration of the technique.[94] The worm contained code that could exploit a buffer overflow in one of the two popular flavors of Unix systems that existed at that time but not the other. This seemed to imply that Morris had acquired the buffer overflow code from somewhere and had integrated it into his worm but that he did not know how to write a buffer overflow himself.[95]

If Morris did not write either the password encryption algorithm or the buffer overflow, then where did he obtain that code? One possibility is his father.[96] Robert T. Morris's father was Robert Morris, a computer security researcher who began working at Bell Labs in 1960. Bell Labs is the research company that invented the laser, the transistor, and the Unix computer operating system. Like at RAND, the scientists working at Bell Labs carried out research on information security. While at Bell Labs, Robert Morris was personally responsible for developing the password encryption scheme used in Unix.[97] In 1986, he left Bell Labs to join the NSA and become their chief scientist for the fledgling National Computer Security Center.[98] If Robert T. Morris obtained the code from his father or from the NSA indirectly through his father, this would mean that the NSA knew how to break into Unix systems but were keeping that knowledge secret. The particular code that the buffer overflow exploited was described as being present in Unix "from the dawn of time," so if the NSA had discovered it, they would have been able to compromise essentially any Unix computer.[99] After his son's arrest, Robert Morris provided a quote to the *New York Times*, telling them that the worm was "the work of a bored graduate student."[100] That statement could have been a father being protective of his son, but it could also simultaneously have been an attempt by a senior figure in the NSA to downplay the involvement of the NSA in the creation of the worm.

The number of computers that the Morris worm was able to infect came as a shock to the internet community.[101] Although the effects were felt widely, the damage could have been much worse. The worm could have been programmed to delete information from computers or to copy information and transmit it elsewhere. The fact that the Morris worm had spread primarily by taking advantage of security vulnerabilities in the Unix operating system also caused the security of Unix to be examined more closely.

Unix was first developed in 1969 by Ken Thompson and Dennis Ritchie, both researchers at Bell Labs in New Jersey.[102] Thompson and Ritchie were Multics programmers, and the Unix name was a pun on Multics and intended as "a backhanded slap at the project."[103] By 1972, the number of Unix installations had grown to ten, with the famously understated "more expected."[104]

Thompson and Ritchie gave the source code for Unix away for a nominal fee, and although Unix was originally written on DEC hardware, it was relatively straightforward to alter the code so that it could run on different types of computers.[105] The fact that Unix was inexpensive and could be easily modified made it attractive to universities, and by the mid-1970s, Unix had become widely used on college campuses.[106] Those who studied Unix at university took that knowledge and experience into the commercial world. Unix was the operating system that they had the most experience with and that they preferred, and this led to Unix increasingly being used in commercial settings.[107] ARPA (which gained a "D" for "Defense" when it was renamed DARPA in 1972) favored Unix because it implemented the TCP/IP protocol suite, and recommended Unix as a preferred operating system in 1980.[108] By the mid-1980s, Unix had become the most prevalent operating system.[109] It was so popular and so dominant that on one occasion Ken Thompson was approached by a professor who told him, "I hate you. Unix has stopped all research in operating systems."[110]

Unix was originally written in assembly language and then in a programming language that Ken Thompson and his colleagues created named B. Between 1969 and 1973, the B language evolved into a language named C.[111] Unix was rewritten in C and is still written in C today. C is a language that was designed to enable the type of low-level programming that would equip programmers to write operating systems such as Unix. It provides the programmer with the ability to create programs that are fast, efficient, and can completely control the computer. But C also imposes enough structure that it can be used to write large programs such as an operating system. Ritchie has described C as a language that is "close to the machine" and "quirky, flawed, and an enormous success."[112] The C programming language gives programmers a lot of power to control the computer, but they have to be careful not to write code that contains security vulnerabilities. Because C requires the programmer to explicitly manage the memory used by the program, mistakes can lead to buffer overflows such as the one that the Morris worm exploited. In this regard, C has been criticized as being "too easy to slice your fingers off."[113] But the absence of a strong focus on security within the initial design of the C programming language partly reflects the era in which it was designed. Criticizing the designers of C for not implementing security measures that would prevent vulnerabilities such as buffer overflows has been described as being akin to criticizing Henry Ford for not also inventing antilock brakes.[114]

In addition to the fact that it is written in C, the Unix operating system was not developed with a strong focus on security. In the late 1970s, Ritchie stated that "this fact alone guarantees a vast number of holes."[115] Much of early Unix was written by students or as quick projects by programmers working in research labs. The rigorous testing that would be expected within a commercial piece of software was typically not present, and the result was "a large collection of tools that usually work, but sometimes fail in spectacular manner."[116] A 1981 academic study of the security of Unix identified twenty-one new vulnerabilities of six different types.[117] The report was circulated among computer security researchers but only published decades later as part of a retrospective.[118] A five-hundred-page book on Unix security was published in 1991.[119] One of the authors of the book, Gene Spafford, had taken a central role in the response to the Morris worm and had started the phage mailing list that was used to investigate the worm and identify how to stop it.

Unix vulnerabilities were also widely discussed in hacker circles. The online *Phrack* magazine—the name of which derives from a combination of "phreak" and "hack"—posted several articles examining Unix security including "Unix Nasties" by "Shooting Shark," "An In-Depth Guide to Hacking Unix" by "Red Knight," and "Unix Hacking Tools of the Trade" by "The Shining."[120] These articles described Unix vulnerabilities and topics such as how hackers could hide on Unix systems once they had gained access to them. USENET newsgroups and the Bugtraq mailing list also served as popular forums to discuss Unix vulnerabilities. Bugtraq was established for the purpose of discussing computer security topics such as the technical details of vulnerabilities.[121] The types of Unix vulnerabilities that were discussed on Bugtraq were "remote vulnerabilities"—vulnerabilities that could grant access to a Unix computer from a different computer—and "local vulnerabilities"—ways to become the most powerful user on a Unix system. A remote vulnerability could be used to gain access to a distant computer, and then a local vulnerability could be used to take control of that computer.

It was not only the details of Unix vulnerabilities that were being discussed in these various forums. The exploits that could take advantage of the vulnerabilities were also being made widely available. An exploit is a computer program that enables the person who uses it to take advantage of a vulnerability without having to understand the technical details of that vulnerability. For example, a person could run an exploit for a buffer overflow vulnerability without having to understand the technical details of how a buffer overflow works.

The increasing number of security vulnerabilities that were being found in Unix and the easy availability of exploits led to jokes that "Unix security" had become an oxymoron such as "instant classic" or "military intelligence."[122] The expectation began to take root that Unix could *never* be made secure, that there would always be a new security vulnerability to be found. This was the same criticism that had been leveled at tiger teams and the "penetrate and patch" paradigm, and which originates from a feeling of hopelessness. The effort that system administrators had to expend to secure Unix computers was increasing as the number of vulnerabilities found in Unix increased. How could an organization that had hundreds or even thousands of Unix computers keep all of those computers secure? A fundamentally new approach was needed, an approach that could compensate for the insecurity of individual computers. And some believed they had found it.

Their inspiration was taken from the design of certain automobiles and buildings that incorporated a firewall. The purpose of a firewall is to protect the occupants by stopping the fire from spreading through the physical structure. The firewall idea could be applied to the task of providing security to a group of computers, such as might be owned by an organization. Instead of trying to secure every individual computer, a firewall would sit between the computers and the internet. All communications between the computers and the internet would pass through the firewall. Only network traffic that was explicitly permitted by the firewall administrator would be allowed to pass—an approach that is described as default deny.[123] As long as the firewall held, the computers that it protected would not have to each be secured individually.[124] The concept of a firewall is sometimes explained with the example of a medieval village. The occupants of the village can protect themselves from barbarians by building a tall wall that has a single gate manned by guards. The guards ensure that only villagers and other people with permission can enter or leave, and the only way into the village is through the gate. In this metaphor, the villagers' homes are the computers that the firewall is protecting, the barbarians that threaten the village are the threats that exist on the internet such as internet worms and hackers, and the firewall is the security that is provided by the combination of the wall, the gate, and the guards. Because the security of the computers protected by a firewall is dependent on the security of the firewall itself, the firewall would require a special focus to make it as secure as possible.[125] This hardening process would strip the firewall down to only the bare minimum of functionality that it requires in order to function. Making the firewall as simple as possible reduces complexity that could lead to the presence of a vulnerability.

Firewalls represented a paradigm shift from the host security model, where security efforts were focused on the security of individual computers, to the perimeter security model, where security efforts were focused on using a firewall to create a defensible perimeter. But the firewall was in fact a new implementation of the reference monitor idea from the 1970s. The reference monitor as originally conceived would function by policing activity in an operating system, and a firewall functions by policing activity on a computer network. The Anderson report had even used the term *firewall* in the context of operating system security to wit: "if we can build better 'firewalls' between users we can limit the extent of security compromise in multi-user, multi-level security."[126] Time-sharing forced a consideration of the security risks that resulted from having multiple people using a computer at the same time. Computer networking created a similar pressure in that it forced a consideration of the security risks that resulted from having multiple people using multiple computers on the same computer network.

The firewall was the apparent solution to the problem of how to secure a large number of computers within an organization from security threats on the internet, but in the early 1990s not everyone viewed firewalls in a favorable light. Some described those who chose to use a firewall as "too lazy" to improve the security of individual computers.[127] Others viewed firewalls as an unfortunate partitioning and balkanization that was anathema to the open spirit of the internet.[128] These criticisms fell largely on deaf ears. For organizations, the benefits of using a firewall were too compelling. Organizations with hundreds or thousands of computers knew that they could not secure those computers individually, and a firewall appeared to be a relatively simple and straightforward solution.[129]

Much of the early work on firewalls was carried out by Bill Cheswick and Steve Bellovin when they worked together at Bell Labs. Cheswick created a firewall in 1987, one year before the Morris worm.[130] As the worm spread, his firewall was able to stop the computers on the Bell Labs network from being infected.[131] After the worm, Cheswick examined the Bell Labs network and found that over three hundred of the computers on the network contained at least one of the security vulnerabilities that the worm had exploited. This meant that if Bell Labs had not had a firewall in place, it would have suffered a major infection.[132]

Cheswick published the first paper on the topic of firewalls titled "The Design of a Secure Internet Gateway" in 1990.[133] He knew that the idea was novel and that by publishing the paper and referencing Bell Labs it would perhaps attract computer hackers. Because of this, he concluded his paper with a warning that stated, "This paper is not an invitation to come test the security of our gateway. It is management's policy to call the authorities when intruders are detected."[134]

Steve Bellovin's contribution to the study of firewalls began when he examined the network traffic that was being received at the Bell Labs firewall. He found examples of attempted attacks and other suspicious network traffic that he described as ranging from "simple doorknob-twisting to determined assaults."[135] His work showed that the open internet was becoming an increasingly dangerous place, which supported the value proposition of firewalls.

Cheswick and Bellovin collaborated to write the first book on the topic of internet firewalls, which was published in 1994.[136] Because of the high level of interest in firewalls, the book sold out of its initial ten-thousand-copy print run within a week.[137] The first edition alone would go on to sell one hundred thousand copies and be translated into a dozen languages.[138]

Firewalls provided clear benefits for the organizations that deployed them, but they were also a single point of failure. Cheswick himself described the perimeter security model as "the armadillo model; a sort of crunchy shell around a soft, chewy center."[139] If a firewall were to fail by being bypassed or by being compromised, then the computers inside the firewall could also become compromised. Each firewall had to be configured according to the particular needs of the organization, and creating that configuration could be a difficult task. The firewall "rules" that described what network traffic the firewall would permit or deny were written in custom languages that could be difficult to understand.[140] A 2004 study of the firewall configurations at thirty-seven organizations found that more than 90 percent contained errors—a finding that the report authors described as "dismal."[141] A follow-up study in 2010 examined more than twice as many organizations and found that those firewalls were also poorly configured.[142]

Computer hackers and internet worms were a threat, but a firewall was not a panacea. Firewalls and the perimeter model of security would soon be challenged by a newly emerging technology called the World Wide Web.

The person who played the most central role in the invention of the web was the English engineer and computer scientist Tim Berners-Lee.[143] In 1990, Berners-Lee worked at the European Organization for Nuclear Research, known as CERN.[144] He wanted to close the gap between application-layer internet protocols such as Telnet and FTP that were text based, and the experience of using a PC that could deliver images, sound, and video.[145] He was also interested in the problem of how people could discover information on the internet, because to download a file using FTP would require knowing the specific computer that contained the file and the path to the file on that computer.[146] Berners-Lee pictured a way for internet users to build "a pool of human knowledge."[147] To accomplish this task, he imagined that a system could be created that would enable links to be created to files on computers around the world. Those links could be shared, and that sharing would enable the creation of a web of information. The files that would be shared using links could contain not only text but also pictures, video files, or any other kind of media.[148]

For the web to be successful it would have to work seamlessly with the existing internet, and this meant compatibility with the TCP/IP protocol suite.[149] But to build the web would also require the creation of a number of new application-layer protocols that would sit conceptually on top of TCP/IP. Hypertext Transfer Protocol (HTTP) was created to enable information to be shared between web servers, which are the publishers of information on the web, and web clients, which are the consumers of information on the web, such as web browsers.[150]

The first web server came online at CERN in December 1990, and CERN began distributing the software for that web server over the internet the following summer.[151] By 1992, several other research sites had established web servers, with one of those sites being the National Center for Supercomputing Applications (NCSA) at the University of Illinois.[152] The NCSA had been established as a supercomputing facility, but the need for supercomputers had diminished with the rise of workstation computers that could provide sufficient computing power to satisfy many research tasks. The staff at the NCSA were looking for a new purpose, and the idea of the web appeared to be promising.[153]

In 1993, a team at NCSA led by Marc Andreessen began work on developing a new web browser named Mosaic.[154] It included innovative features such as the ability for an image to act as a web link, where clicking the image would send the web browser to the linked page, and it could run on most PCs and Unix workstations. Mosaic was made available for free in November 1993.[155] It took only ten minutes for the first copy to be downloaded, and within thirty minutes the number of downloads numbered in the hundreds.[156] More than forty thousand copies of Mosaic were downloaded in the first month, and by spring 1994, it was estimated that more than one million copies were in use.[157] The number of web servers increased from sixty in April 1993 to more than twelve hundred in May 1994.[158] The web was growing exponentially due to Metcalfe's law—the same effect that had powered the growth of email and the internet. As more websites were brought online, more people began to use web browsers such as Mosaic, and this in turn caused more people to build websites.

In 1994, Andreessen and his team left the NCSA to begin work on a commercial version of Mosaic.[159] That product was the Netscape web browser. Netscape provided several advantages over Mosaic, such as being easier to use and having increased performance. It also supported the Secure Sockets Layer (SSL), a protocol that would encrypt information sent between the web browser and the web server so that activities such as online shopping using credit cards could take place. SSL was the predecessor to today's equivalent of Transport Layer Security (TLS). All of these features were attractive to the users who switched from Mosaic to Netscape.

The growth of the web posed a challenge for firewalls. In order for an organization to offer a website, they would need to permit web traffic such as HTTP to pass through their firewall. If the web server software being used by the organization contained a vulnerability, the firewall would be unlikely to be able to stop a hacker from exploiting that vulnerability. A common response was to move web servers into their own partitioned part of the network near to the firewall called a DMZ.[160] The term *DMZ* came from "demilitarized zone," a neutral territory between nations. In a DMZ, a web server would typically be surrounded by two firewalls: one between the web server and the internet and another between the web server and the other computers within the organization. This configuration would provide the organization with more of an opportunity to stop or detect a hacker, but if a hacker could hack into the web server, they could then attempt to pivot into the internal network.

By 1995, the web was becoming mainstream, and companies were rushing to establish an online presence. How would information security fare in this new period? One person was about to find out.

Dan Farmer is an ex-marine who obtained conscientious objector status for the first Gulf War.[161] His postmilitary career would have been difficult to predict. He advised the US Department of Defense regarding network security after the attacks of 9/11, testified before Congress, and served as an expert witness for the Recording Industry Association of America in their legal case against the peer-to-peer file-sharing service Napster.[162] The recording industry viewed Farmer's contribution to that case as so valuable that they gave him an honorary gold album.[163] But he is also an iconoclast with a self-described "pathological contrariness."[164]

Farmer's introduction to the field of information security was the Morris worm with which he became captivated. He would later thank Robert T. Morris for writing the worm and thereby starting his career in the field.[165] After the Morris worm, an organization named the Computer Emergency Response Team (CERT) was formed to serve as a clearinghouse for security information.[166] CERT established a hotline that was available twenty-four hours a day that anyone in the world could call if they had a question or concern related to computer security.[167] CERT would also issue security advisories highlighting and describing vulnerabilities that were being publicized on mailing lists such as Bugtraq.[168] Farmer joined CERT and used his time there to build his knowledge about how hackers broke into computers.[169] In 1993, he coauthored an article titled "Improving the Security of Your Site by Breaking into it."[170] This was intended as a guide for system administrators to use so that they could look for possible vulnerabilities in their computers.[171] He then used his knowledge of computer security to coauthor a computer program that would automatically scan a remote computer for vulnerabilities. This idea for a network vulnerability scanner was powerful because such a tool could enable a single person using that computer program to determine whether tens, hundreds, or even thousands of computers were vulnerable. What had previously been a manual process could be automated and therefore scale to a much higher degree. The program that he coauthored was named the Security Administrator Tool for Analyzing Networks (SATAN).[172] The name was provocative, but for those who were offended, Farmer provided a separate program named "repent" that would change the name to the more friendly SANTA.

The idea of a network vulnerability scanner was not new. William Gibson's 1984 science fiction novel *Neuromancer* describes a "Chinese-made Kuang Grade Mark Eleven penetration program" that would automatically break through the "ICE," which was a type of firewall that protected the corporate networks in the dystopian future described within the book. SATAN was also not the only network vulnerability scanner to be created, as some commercial network vulnerability scanners were being sold during the same period as SATAN.[173] But at that time, SATAN was the most comprehensive network vulnerability scanner in terms of the number of vulnerabilities that it could detect. It was also straightforward to use because it was one of the first pieces of software to use a web browser as its user interface.

A few months before SATAN was due to be released, Farmer had taken a job as the security czar of Silicon Graphics, a Silicon Valley manufacturer of computer hardware and software with a focus on products that enabled the creation of 3D computer graphics.[174] He informed Silicon Graphics of his work on SATAN and was subsequently invited to a meeting with a vice president of the company and two lawyers.[175] Farmer was given three choices: to let Silicon Graphics turn SATAN into a commercial product, to not release SATAN publicly, or to leave the company.[176] Farmer chose to leave.[177]

SATAN was released on Dan Farmer's birthday in 1995.[178] The reaction from the press was hyperbolic. The *Oakland Tribune* described SATAN as "like randomly mailing automatic rifles to five thousand addresses." The *San Jose Mercury* used a similar metaphor, saying that releasing SATAN was "like distributing high-powered rocket launchers throughout the world, free of charge, available at your local library or school, and inviting people to try them out by shooting at somebody." The *Los Angeles Times* claimed that "SATAN is like a gun, and this is like handing a gun to a twelve-year-old."[179] On a security mailing list, an anonymous poster said that "the authors of the recently released SATAN package for probing internet sites have shown a level of amorality that should gladden the hearts of arms merchants around the world."[180] Within the field of information security, however, it was understood that any threat that SATAN created was not as great as the mainstream press was portraying it. An email was circulated among security professionals describing the "Top 10 Ways You Can Tell SATAN Has Invaded Your Network," which included "your monitor starts spinning around in circles" and "your firewall turns into a ring of flame."[181]

In 1996, Farmer was curious about the security of organizations that were rushing to establish their own websites, so he decided to carry out a bold experiment. He used a specially modified version of his SATAN program to examine the security of thousands of high-profile internet sites including online banks, newspapers, credit unions, government institutions, and one of the earliest and most profitable internet ventures, online pornography. The government institutions that he examined included the sites for the US executive and judicial branches, Congress, the Federal Reserve, and some intelligence agencies.[182] What he discovered was, in his own words, both startling and depressing.[183] Over 60 percent of the sites could be "broken into or destroyed," and an additional 9 percent to 24 percent could be broken into if a single new security vulnerability was found in either of two widely used programs. (Within a month, vulnerabilities were discovered in both of those programs.) Farmer estimated that an additional 10 percent to 20 percent of the sites that he tested could be broken into or "rendered unusable" relatively easily by using more advanced techniques. The overall result was that three-quarters of the sites could have their security compromised "if significant force and effort were to be applied."[184]

Farmer made no attempt to hide his SATAN scans, even running them from a domain he owned named trouble.org. But out of the two thousand–

plus sites that he tested, only three sent an email to his domain asking what he was doing.[185] The number of sites that detected the SATAN scans but did not attempt to contact Farmer is unknown, but the number of sites that were able to detect a network vulnerability scan appeared to be very low. This meant that not only were sites unprotected, but they were also flying blind.

These were important findings, but some of the details were peculiar. The security of the sites offering online pornography was found to be *higher* than the security of the sites owned by US government institutions, banks, credit agencies, and newspapers.[186] The explanation might have been that the pornography sites were designed for the purpose of making online financial transactions whereas the other sites were not and that functionality required more security measures. The American bank robber Willie Sutton is said to have answered the question of why he robbed banks by answering, "because that's where the money is." In the mid-1990s, the money was being made online in pornography. Pornography websites had led the way in using various technological innovations such as instant messaging, chat rooms, streaming video, and the ability to make online purchases, which may have driven them to consider security earlier and to a greater degree than other sites.[187] Indeed, in 1996, half of all chat rooms provided by the internet service provider America Online were sex related, with those chat rooms generating more than $80 million per year in revenue.[188]

Farmer then compared the results for the sites that he had scanned during his experiment to a random sampling of computers on the internet. He found that the sites he had scanned for his experiment had more than *twice* as many security vulnerabilities as the randomly selected computers. Even though many of the sites that were scanned for the experiment used firewalls and other security measures, their security was less effective overall.[189] What was the reason for this counterintuitive result? Farmer believed that the organizations that were racing online were doing so without understanding the security risks involved. Simply installing a firewall would not provide protection because a firewall was not a turnkey solution that provided "security in a box." A company might use a security guru to install a firewall, but then that security guru might "disappear for a year or more" and the firewall would not receive the care and feeding over time that it required, leading to a state of insecurity.[190]

The stage was set. The ARPANET had evolved to become the internet, an important new medium for communication and commerce. The difficulty of securing networks of individual computers led to the invention of the firewall and the transition from the host security model to the perimeter security model. Organizations embraced this new way of thinking as they rushed to do business online. But Dan Farmer had shown that the level of information security was not what it seemed. His experiment was a dark foreshadowing of what would soon take place.

Chapter 4

# THE DOT-COM BOOM AND THE GENESIS OF A LUCRATIVE FEEDBACK LOOP

The dot-com boom was a speculative bubble wherein the value of internet stocks rose for an extended period beyond anything that could be justified on economic grounds.[1] Like other speculative bubbles, the dot-com boom was caused by an invention that created inflated hopes of financial profits.[2]

When Netscape Communications—the company that had developed the Netscape web browser—went public on the US stock exchange on August 9, 1995, the price of one share in the company rose from $28 when the market opened to $71 at market close. The founder of Netscape, Jim Clark, saw his net worth increase by $663 million in a single day, instantly making him one of the wealthiest people in the United States. Within eighteen months, Netscape would be valued at more than $2 billion, nearly the same value as long-established companies such as the gigantic defense contractor General Dynamics.[3]

This economic bounty was the result of an innovation in the form of the World Wide Web. The web provided people with the ability to consume entertaining content, to communicate in new ways, and to purchase products and services online. The web browser was the software used to interact with the web, and a fierce battle was about to take place for the hearts and minds of web browser users. Both Netscape and Microsoft believed that whoever could create the most popular web browser would be in the best position to promote the interests of their company.[4]

The web was a recently created set of technologies and protocols. The study of web security was therefore new by definition. There were no experts in web security and little research findings that companies such as Netscape and Microsoft could draw on when implementing security within their products. The nature of the intense competition between Netscape and Microsoft also affected security. Both companies wrote their web browser and web server products using the C programming language.[5] It was the C language that enabled the buffer overflow vulnerabilities to be created that were exploited by the Morris worm. Netscape and Microsoft knew that it was difficult to write programs using C that did not contain these types of vulnerabilities, but they chose to use C because it enabled them to quickly create software that was fast and efficient; from their perspective those benefits were judged to outweigh the security risks.[6] As a result of these choices, both the Netscape web browser and the Internet Explorer web browser created by Microsoft suffered from a raft of security vulnerabilities, including buffer overflows.[7] One month after Netscape Communications went public, a security vulnerability was found in the Netscape web browser that could reveal the details of online transactions.[8] In 1997, Microsoft posted patches for four security vulnerabilities in Internet Explorer in a single thirty-day period.[9]

Both Microsoft and Netscape struggled with how to secure mobile code, which was also known as applets, controls, or scripts. These were programs that were downloaded from websites in the process of browsing the web. Mobile code provided a richer experience for the user beyond the capabilities of the web browser alone, such as by providing embedded chat rooms or games. Mobile code was attractive to web developers and companies that wanted to attract web surfers to their websites. The security challenge presented by mobile code was how to stop it from escaping from the web browser and carrying out malicious actions on the user's computer. A piece of mobile code that was written with nefarious intent might attempt to read information from the user's computer or even delete files.[10]

The two popular types of mobile code were Java and ActiveX, and each approached security differently. Java attempted to constrain the mobile code inside a sandbox from which it would not be able to escape.[11] But due to implementation errors and design flaws, various vulnerabilities were found in Java that permitted malicious mobile code to read any file on the computer, run any command, modify or delete data, and insert programs that could, for example, spy on the user.[12] The approach taken within ActiveX was to sign the mobile code in order to identify the author and then present that authorship information to the user.[13] The person using the web browser would then be able to use the author information that was being presented to them to decide whether to run the mobile code or not.[14] But a number of vulnerabilities were found in ActiveX, including ways to trick a user into accepting the mobile code or that enabled mobile code to be run without the user's explicit permission.[15]

These security vulnerabilities in Java and ActiveX were examples of a new kind of vulnerability that was intrinsic to the architecture of the web. The Morris worm had exploited server-side vulnerabilities, meaning that the worm reached out across the network to other computers and tried to break into them. But the web enabled a new pattern in which malicious web servers could sit and wait for web browsers (clients) to contact them, and when those web browsers did so, the server could attempt to compromise them. This was a new era of client-side vulnerabilities where the simple act of browsing to a web server could cause the security of a user's computer to become compromised.[16] Numerous client-side vulnerabilities were found in web browsers, including vulnerabilities that enabled a website to read any file on the user's computer or execute any code.[17]

Client-side vulnerabilities began to proliferate during the early days of the web, but there were also classical server-side vulnerabilities in web servers. When a web browser makes a request to a web server, it sends information to the web server that the web server then has to process. For example, a person might enter the word *laptop* into a form on a website in order to search for laptop computers. That "laptop" string is used by the web server to search for a list of matching products. But because the text that is entered into the form on the website is under the complete control of the user, an attacker can deliberately enter text that might confuse and thereby subvert the processing of that text by the web server. This can result in the web server performing arbitrary actions that the attacker can embed in whatever text he enters into the form. This is referred to as the problem of command injection. The solution is for the web server to sanitize the text to remove anything that would be harmful to the web server. But if that sanitization is not implemented flawlessly, then the problem of command injection would remain.[18] A notable type of command injection attack against databases, called SQL injection, began to be used prolifically by hackers and continues to be used in the current day.[19]

The task of installing and configuring a web server also created the possibility of introducing vulnerabilities. A misconfiguration could cause all of the information on the computer to be made available to web browsers, rather than just the information that the system administrator intended. This information leakage could result in a hacker being able to obtain information from the computer on which the web server was installed, such as the list of encrypted passwords.[20] Those passwords could then be cracked—meaning guessed—and used to access the computer. The problem of unintended information leakage from web servers was compounded by search engines such as Yahoo! and Google that would index all of the available information on the web and make it available to anyone who searched for it.

The SSL protocol developed by Netscape Communications enabled communications between web browsers and web servers to be encrypted, but this was of little benefit if web browsers and web servers contained security vulnerabilities that could be exploited. This situation was described by Gene Spafford as being "the equivalent of heavily armored cars being used to transfer money between a person who sleeps on a park bench and a person who sleeps in a cardboard box underneath a highway bridge (further: the roads are subject to random detours, anyone with a screwdriver can control the traffic lights, and there are no police)."[21]

These security problems combined to make it difficult for organizations to secure their websites. Consequently, many of the largest and most popular websites were hacked or were found to contain security vulnerabilities, including eBay, Yahoo!, and Hotmail.[22] US government sites also suffered security incidents, with the websites of the US Senate and the FBI both being hacked and temporarily shut down.[23] Security companies were not immune, with the websites of security product vendor Verisign and security services provider the SANS Institute both being defaced.[24]

Defacement was the digital equivalent of spray-painting graffiti on a wall or a billboard. A hacker would replace the hacked website's content with his own message or with content that promoted his ideology or political point of view.[25] The CIA's website was defaced to say "Welcome to the Central Stupidity Agency."[26] Hackers also defaced websites for the purpose of self-aggrandizement and to participate in the larger community of hackers, such as when a website was defaced by a hacker to protest the arrest of a fellow hacker.[27] Another defacement was used to send a birthday greeting from one hacker to another.[28] When presidential candidate George W. Bush's website was defaced by hackers, they replaced his picture on the site with an image of a bright red hammer and sickle.[29] The text on the site was replaced with a passage that read, "We must take the Marxist doctrine of proletarian revolution out of the realm of theory and give it reality."[30] It seems unlikely that visitors to Bush's website would have believed that these statements represented a change in Bush's political position. However, a more subtle attack could have taken place: the hackers could have altered the description of Bush's policy objectives, and unlike the calls for a Marxist revolution, those changes might have gone unnoticed by the administrators of the website.

The early days of web security were the Wild West. But the web was itself dependent on the underlying TCP/IP protocols, and one hacker was about to prove how unstable the foundations created by those protocols were.

"Route" is the handle used by a hacker who was active during the 1990s. His interest in computers began in 1982, when he was given a Commodore 64 computer.[31] He would program his own adventure games on the computer and save them to a tape drive.[32] As he grew older his interest in computers increased and became what he described as a "tireless thirst."[33] He purchased more and more computers until his room was alive with "a myriad of blinking and flashing lights, several humming fans, and hundreds of feet of fire-hazard-inducing cables."[34] The computers generated so much heat that he had to cover his windows with aluminum foil to keep the sun out to maintain a tolerable room temperature.[35] On his back he sported a large black tattoo of a die used to create computer chips.[36]

By 1996, route had established himself in the field of information security. He had made more than two thousand posts to the alt.2600 forum that was dedicated to discussing security topics.[37] He had also become one of three coeditors of *Phrack* magazine.[38] *Phrack* had first been published in 1985 and had a long history of publishing articles in the areas of telecommunications and computer security.[39] Route had particular expertise in network security, and between January 1996 and November 1997, he used *Phrack* to publish his research. That sequence of articles was a virtual rampage through the TCP/IP protocol suite.

In January 1996, route published an article in *Phrack* that he titled "Project Neptune." In his article he described an attack against the TCP protocol called SYN flooding.[40] In the TCP protocol, when a computer wants to connect to another computer it sends a packet asking, "Can I connect?" If the other computer is willing and able to accept the connection, it sends back a reply packet that says, "Yes, you can connect." The first computer then completes the protocol by sending a packet that says, "OK, I am connecting." The attack described by route involved the first computer sending the first packet asking, "Can I connect?" The second computer would then reply saying, "Yes, you can connect," but then the attacker would deliberately not send the third packet in the protocol.[41] The second computer would wait for the third packet, and after a while it would assume that the first computer no longer wanted to talk and so would stop waiting. But what route described in his article was that on many operating systems, if there were more than a certain number of these half-open connections, the computer would not accept any additional requests to talk. An attacker could exploit this vulnerability to stop a program such as a web server from accepting any connections from web browsers.[42]

The vulnerability existed because the programmers who wrote the vulnerable code made certain assumptions. They assumed that no one would try to use TCP to connect several times over but not complete the entire protocol used to establish a connection. This pattern, whereby a person such as a programmer makes assumptions and then those assumptions are violated in some way, is a common cause of security vulnerabilities.

SYN flooding was not an attack that could be used to directly hack into a computer. Nor was it an attack that could cause sensitive information to be revealed to the attacker. It was a denial-of-service attack that affected availability by denying the ability of users to use the computer.[43] Security weaknesses in TCP/IP had been written about during the period of the Morris worm.[44] Steve Bellovin, the coauthor of the first book on internet firewalls, had anticipated SYN flooding attacks in 1989.[45] But Bellovin and his coauthor, Bill Cheswick, did not describe the attack technique in their book because there was no known way at that time to defend against it.[46] This was a decision that Bellovin would later say that he regretted.[47]

The SYN flooding attack had not been invented by route, but route had investigated and documented the effectiveness of the attack against different types of operating system and then popularized the existence of the technique. In his *Phrack* article he also provided a program named Neptune that could be used to perform a SYN flood.[48] Eight months after route had published his article on SYN flooding, an internet service provider in Manhattan named Panix (Public Access Networks Corporation) was knocked offline for several days by a SYN flood attack.[49] A few months later, a large website provider named WebCom was also affected by a SYN flood attack that took more than three thousand websites offline for forty hours.[50]

The next issue of *Phrack* would come out in August 1996, and in that issue, route published two new articles. The first was named "Project Hades." It introduced two programs that would exploit vulnerabilities in the implementation of TCP/IP protocols within computer operating systems.[51] "Avarice" would stop all TCP connections between computers on a network, and "Sloth" would cause network traffic to slow down.[52] The second article was named "Project Loki," after the trickster god of Norse mythology.[53] In Project Loki, route brought the confinement problem into the domain of computer networking. The classic formulation of the confinement problem as it related to operating system security is concerned with the difficulty of stopping two users on the same computer from communicating using a covert channel. Route described how the same confinement problem can exist on a computer network. For example, if a firewall sits between two users that blocks their communications, those users might want to establish a covert channel in order to be able to communicate.[54]

His research focused on a protocol within the TCP/IP protocol suite named the Internet Control Message Protocol (ICMP).[55] ICMP is used to send information between computers and network infrastructure such as routers that route packets around the network.[56] ICMP traffic is usually considered to be benign by system administrators and network administrators since it would not be considered unusual for two computers to exchange ICMP messages.[57] This makes ICMP attractive for creating a covert channel.[58] The RFC that describes the specification of the ICMP protocol allows for a certain amount of data to be included in each ICMP packet.[59] Those data are used by the protocol in certain situations, but normally that space in each packet is left empty.[60] Route's Loki program used the empty space to store information so that it could be passed surreptitiously between two computers. The ICMP packets would ostensibly look like normal ICMP packets, but secretly they would contain information.[61] Although route did not publish the source code for his Loki program in the August 1996 issue of *Phrack*, he did subsequently make it available in a later issue in September 1997.[62]

In April 1997, route released Juggernaut, which was a program that enabled the user to spy on network connections, stop them, and even hijack them.[63] In November 1997, he released Teardrop—a denial-of-service program that could crash Windows computers.[64] Teardrop worked by exploiting a vulnerability in the implementation of the IP protocol. IP splits large pieces of data into separate packets that are reassembled at the destination computer. Each packet includes a number that allows the packets to be reassembled by the destination computer in the correct order. Teardrop sent two packets where the numbers overlapped—a situation that shouldn't happen—causing the computer that received those packets to crash.[65] Teardrop was the first of a number of denial-of-service programs that exploited vulnerabilities in TCP/IP, which included Land and the dramatically named ping of death.[66] Land would send a packet to a computer that pretended to come from that same computer, causing the computer to freeze. The ping of death caused a computer to crash by sending a packet that was larger than the permitted size described in the RFC.

Vulnerabilities in web browsers and web servers, high-profile website defacements, and route's tear through the TCP/IP protocol suite painted a sorry picture of internet and web security in the late 1990s. Commercial companies riding the wave of the dot-com boom wanted to protect their websites from attack. Suffering a denial-of-service attack, having their computers hacked, or having their website defaced were all bad for business. But those companies did not typically have the expertise or the desire to implement their own security technologies—just as Dan Farmer had demonstrated with his experiment. Into this void would step the bourgeoning commercial information security industry. They would build and commercialize security products with the goal of finding security vulnerabilities and detecting hackers, and they would sometimes portray those products as absolute solutions. In one print advertisement for a security product named Proventia, the CEO of the company holds aloft a gun bullet with the tagline "Proventia: Security's Silver Bullet?"[67]

The first broad category of security products to gain prominence in this new commercial market was network vulnerability scanners. Dan Farmer's SATAN was the first widely publicized network vulnerability scanner, and the fact that SATAN was made available for anyone to download and use was a major factor in the hysteria that occurred within the media around its release. The dot-com boom created the opportunity to create and sell commercial network vulnerability scanners, and several commercial products would soon begin to emerge. Prominent network vulnerability scanner products were created by Internet Security Systems—an Atlanta-based security company founded by a student from the Georgia Institute of Technology—and Cisco—a manufacturer of network devices such as routers and switches.[68]

Organizations could use a network vulnerability scanner product as a kind of "tiger team in a box." A network vulnerability scanner enabled an organization to identify vulnerabilities in their computers without having to employ a team of experts to accomplish that task. The automation provided by a network vulnerability scanner also scaled much better than human efforts because a scanner could identify vulnerabilities in computers at a much faster rate than a human. And unlike a human, it would never tire. The creators of network vulnerability scanner products condensed their security expertise into those products, which could then be operated by someone with less knowledge of security. But because a network vulnerability scanner was a computer program, it had no creativity; it could not find novel vulnerabilities as a human member of a tiger team could. If finding vulnerabilities is both an art and a science, a network vulnerability scanner could duplicate the science but not the art.

Organizations used network vulnerability scanners to scan the computers behind their firewalls and would also scan the outside of their firewall from the internet side in order to get the same view of their web servers and other internet-facing computers that a hacker on the internet would have. After a scan was completed, a network vulnerability scanner product would produce a report listing the vulnerabilities that had been detected. That report would rank the vulnerabilities using a scheme such as high, medium, or low to indicate their severity. A system administrator at the organization could then take the report and apply the necessary security patches for any vulnerabilities that had been found. In this way, network vulnerability scanners enabled the automation of a portion of the penetrate-and-patch cycle.[69]

The second significant category of security product to emerge during the early dot-com years was network intrusion detection systems. If a firewall was like having a wall around a village with a gate and a guard, then an intrusion detection system was like installing a burglar alarm on a house. The

Ware report had discussed the need for audit trails—records of activity on a computer system—that could be used to "permit reconstruction of events that indicate an unsuccessful attempt to penetrate the system or that clearly resulted in a compromise of information or a security violation."[70] The Anderson report recommended that computers should contain a "surveillance system" that would collect data and report attempted or successful security violations.[71] James P. Anderson—the principal author of the Anderson report—wrote a paper in 1980 that described how security audit trails could be used by security personnel whose job it was to maintain security on a computer system.[72] That report was highly influential for much of the work to develop intrusion detection systems that was carried out during the 1980s. Notable work carried out during that decade includes the Intrusion Detection Expert System (IDES) created by Dorothy Denning and Peter Neumann at SRI and Denning's 1987 paper "An Intrusion Detection Model."[73] Intrusion detection was not, then, a novel idea in the 1990s, but the existence of commercial intrusion detection products that an organization could purchase, plug into their network, and use relatively easily was new.

A network intrusion detection system would watch the network traffic passing across the part of the network where it was installed and attempt to detect evidence of attacks taking place. This was an attractive proposition for organizations because it seemed to compensate for the weaknesses of firewalls, where network traffic that was permitted to pass through the firewall such as web traffic could contain attacks. If an attack was able to pass through the firewall, then the intrusion detection system would be triggered, enabling the organization to respond. An intrusion detection system could also be installed in front of a firewall to see what attacks were hitting the firewall from the internet side.

Intrusion detection products had two main methods for attempting to detect attacks. In the first method the intrusion detection system would look for particular signatures—meaning patterns—in the network traffic.[74] Simplistically, if a known attack used the string "HACK," then the intrusion detection system would look for packets that contained that string. The second method involved creating a baseline of expected behavior and then detecting anomalies that occurred outside of that baseline.[75] The signature-based method was more common than the anomaly detection method during the 1990s. This was partly because of the training problem where it was difficult to generate a clean baseline of network traffic that could then be used to train an anomaly detection system. If the training data contained attacks, then through the process of training the system it would learn to ignore those same attacks.[76]

Network intrusion detection products were similar to firewalls in that one single instance of each could be used to protect many computers within an organization. Both network intrusion detection system products and firewall products therefore aligned with the perimeter model of security, and this made them attractive to purchasers. In 1997, the President's National Security Telecommunications Advisory Committee recommended that as a matter of national policy there should be a "federal vision" for intrusion detection technologies with federal research objectives, targets, and priorities.[77] The market for intrusion detection products was $20 million in 1997 but $100 million just two years later in 1999.[78]

For the companies that were establishing their online presence and online businesses on the web during the years of the dot-com boom, the security products that were available amounted to a kind of formula: use a firewall to separate the computers on the company's internal network from the internet, use a vulnerability scanner to identify vulnerabilities in those computers, and use an intrusion detection system to detect attacks. But behind that apparent simplicity was a more complex and problematic reality. Companies lacked expertise in security, so they wanted the capabilities that the security products would provide. But because they lacked security expertise, they had no ability to evaluate the products that were being offered to them. They could not determine that a particular firewall or a network intrusion system was effective.[79]

This situation has been characterized as the fundamental dilemma of computer security.[80] The fundamental dilemma was the same problem that the Orange Book had tried to solve in the 1980s by assessing and then certifying the security of operating system products. That model had fallen apart because the world was moving too quickly for the evaluation process to keep up, and during the years of the dot-com boom events were unfolding even faster. Testing an intrusion detection system was a challenge even for those who had security expertise. A physical gate can be tested by attempting to break through it, but testing a burglar alarm is not so simple. Activating a burglar alarm cannot determine whether the alarm would have caused an appropriate response.

Like their customers, vendors of commercial security products also suffered from incomplete information. Security vendors could build intrusion detection products to detect attacks, but attackers could modify their attacks in unknown ways in order to avoid detection, and consequently the security vendors could not know that their products would be able to continue to function effectively.[81] Gene Spafford described testing an intrusion detection like this: "You're proposing to build a box with a light on top of it. The light is supposed to go off when you carry the box into a room that has a unicorn in it. How do you show that it works?"[82] The CEO who posed for the advertisement holding a silver bullet was more correct than he knew but for the wrong reasons. He presumably expected the audience to interpret the silver bullet in the popular sense of the phrase: as a simple solution to a complex problem. But software engineers use the phrase in a different way: to refer to something that is presented as a solution without any rational means to justify that claim.[83] The CEO was correct only in the second sense of the expression.

These problems did not dissuade many organizations from purchasing commercial security products, either because they were unaware of these aspects or because they accepted the claims made by the commercial vendors regarding their products. There may also have been what economists refer to as a herding effect, where managers inside organizations with the responsibility for purchasing decisions buy products sold by big-name suppliers.[84] Choosing a big-name supplier provides a certain justification for the purchase. This phenomenon was known by security professionals, some of whom discussed how the market share of security products was not representative of how effective a product was but instead the result of how effective the vendor's sales and marketing efforts were.[85]

The evidence of the dysfunction in the commercial market for information security products that was created by the fundamental dilemma would soon become clear. In 1998, two researchers decided to investigate whether they could sneak attacks past widely used network intrusion detection systems.[86] They observed that a network intrusion detection system can see the packets passing by on the network but cannot know with certainty that those packets will actually reach the destination computer or how that computer will interpret those packets. In other words, an intrusion detection system can observe what is happening on the part of the network to which it is connected, but it is not omniscient regarding all activity throughout the entire network.[87] The two researchers used this insight to develop various techniques that could be used to evade network intrusion detection systems. If an intrusion detection system was looking for the word "HACK," an attacker could send the word "HXACK," knowing that the packet containing the *X* would reach the intrusion detection system but not the target computer. The target would receive "HACK," but the intrusion detection system would see "HXACK" and therefore not trigger an alert.[88] They also developed other evasion techniques that took advantage of the fact that when operating system vendors implemented the TCP/IP protocols in their products, there was enough wiggle room in the descriptions of the protocols within the RFC documents that slight variations in the implementation within each operating system would creep in. This meant that an attacker could send network packets to a target computer and the intrusion detection system could not know how that computer would interpret them: would that computer interpret them as "HAKC" or "HACK"?[89] At best, an intrusion detection system might be able to detect that an evasion was taking place, but instead of being able to report that it saw an attack, it would be reduced to only being able to say that there might be an attack and could not specify what type of attack it was.[90]

Every network intrusion detection system that was tested by the researchers could be evaded using these types of techniques.[91] Worse, the problems appeared to be elemental to the way that the systems functioned. The researchers described their work as showing that network intrusion detection system products were "fundamentally flawed" and that the entire class of products "cannot be fully trusted until they are fundamentally redesigned."[92] In 2017, a different group of researchers revisited these findings and tested ten commercial network intrusion detection products. They found that the majority were vulnerable to evasions and that the techniques described in the 1990s were still effective.[93]

The evasions study exposed the practical reality of the fundamental dilemma. There was no good way for organizations to determine whether the security products that were available for sale were truly effective. The trade press reviewed security products but tended to evaluate them based on their stated features and ease of use.[94] Because of this, vendors would compete not on the basis of technical matters such as their product's ability to avoid evasions but rather on superficial aspects such as the number of vulnerability signatures built into them. If one intrusion detection product contained signatures to detect eight hundred vulnerabilities but a different vendor's competing product had one thousand signatures, this was a difference that a purchaser could easily grasp.[95] The effect was to create a perverse incentive for security product vendors to game the number of signatures built into their products. They implemented as many signatures as they could, sometimes stretching the definition of a vulnerability to include minor problems, and this in turn increased the workload on the security staff within organizations that used those products.[96]

Perverse incentives also manifested in other ways. DARPA started a project with the goal of enabling network intrusion detection products to exchange information.[97] This would be useful because an organization could buy products from two different vendors and use them together. If one product failed to detect an attack, then perhaps the other might succeed. But DARPA's effort failed because vendors of network intrusion detection products had no incentive to make their products interoperate with those of their competitors. In fact, they had the opposite incentive. Every vendor was seeking to defeat their competitors in the marketplace and become the dominant provider.

The research that revealed the ability to evade network intrusion detection system products would soon be compounded by a second important piece of work. But in this case, the findings would fly under the radar for several years. In 1999, a student from Chalmers University of Technology in Sweden named Stefan Axelsson presented a paper at one of the earliest conferences dedicated to the topic of intrusion detection.[98] In his paper, Axelsson described his research on the topic of false alarms. False alarms, also referred to as false positives or type I errors, are those cases where an intrusion detection system believes that it detected an attack, but in fact an attack did not take place.[99] False alarms could occur for various reasons, such as a signature that was looking for the string "HACK" and happened to see a network packet containing a harmless reference to the string "HACKERS."[100] What he discovered was that the limiting factor in the operational performance of an intrusion detection system is the number of false alarms that it generates. This is because false alarms can swamp the security staff at an organization and make it impossible for them to find the needle in the haystack that is a real attack.[101]

At the heart of Axelsson's work was the base-rate fallacy. In his paper he uses the example of a medical test used to detect a disease in a patient. If such a test is 99 percent accurate, that means that if the test population are entirely free of the disease, only 1 percent of tests will generate a false alarm. A hypothetical doctor gives a patient the test and informs him that unfortunately he has tested positive for the disease. The good news for that patient, however, is that in the entire population only one in ten thousand people have the disease. Given this information, what is the probability of the patient having the disease?

Even though the test is 99 percent accurate and the patient has tested positive for the disease, the chance of his having the disease is actually only one in a hundred. This is because the population of healthy people is much larger than the population of people with the disease. This result can be surprising because it defies intuition. The reason is that it is difficult to take the base rate of incidence into account when reasoning about false alarms. The implication for intrusion detection was that using an intrusion detection system in a realistic operational setting would be much more difficult than expected. The factor limiting the performance was not the ability of an intrusion detection system to correctly identify intrusions but rather the ability to correctly suppress false alarms.[102] In subsequent years, this problem would be demonstrated with a number of spectacular real-world examples. In a 2014 hacking incident at clothing retailer Neiman Marcus, hackers caused intrusion detection systems to generate more than sixty thousand alerts. But those alerts represented only 1 percent of the total number of alerts generated each day, and so they were not acted on by security staff.[103] In 2015, a retrospective on Axelsson's paper commented that although his research was by then almost fifteen years old, "these kinds of problems might actually be getting worse."[104]

There were now two realities. One reality was inhabited by the attendees of academic conferences where the analysis of intrusion detection systems such as Stefan Axelsson's work was presented. In the other reality, intrusion detection systems were proclaimed as "the future."[105] One month after the research was published that demonstrated the fundamental problems with intrusion detection system products that caused them to be vulnerable to evasions, Cisco, a multinational technology conglomerate, purchased the intrusion detection vendor WheelGroup for $124 million.[106]

The disconnect between those two worlds was caused in large part by the inexorable rise in the financial markets caused by the dot-com boom. But another major factor was the influence of computer hackers.

What it means to be a hacker might appear to be self-evident: a person who intentionally compromises the security of a computer system. But the popular meaning of the term has changed over time and especially so within certain groups. The earliest uses of "hack" in the modern era used the word to describe working with or altering a machine in a creative way.[107] The minutes for the April 1955 meeting of the Tech Model Railroad Club at MIT state that "Mr. Eccles requests that anyone working or hacking on the electrical system turn the power off to avoid fuse blowing."[108] MIT was one of the earliest centers for digital computing, and the term was adopted by the computer scientists there. In those days, the terms *hack* and *hacker* did not have a negative connotation. A creative or inspired piece of programming would be referred to as a "good hack."[109] The word *hacker* has been used to refer to a person who attempts to intentionally compromise the security of a computer system since at least November 1963, when the MIT student newspaper noted that "many telephone services have been curtailed because of so-called hackers, according to Prof. Carlton Tucker, administrator of the Institute phone system. The hackers have accomplished such things as tying up all the tie-lines between Harvard and MIT or making long-distance calls by charging them to a local radar installation."[110]

Over time, the term *hacker* bifurcated into the notion of "white hat" and "black hat" hackers. White hat hackers are said to use their skills ethically, such as by working as members of a professional tiger team. In contrast, black hat hackers skirt or break the law. In the earliest motion pictures that told stories about cowboys, the protagonist would often wear a white cowboy hat, whereas the antagonist would wear a black cowboy hat. The different color hats would serve as a helpful narrative aid for the viewer and would also symbolize the intrinsic battle between good and evil. George Lucas would use a similar device in his *Star Wars* movies to distinguish between two aspects of a mysterious "Force": a "light side" and a "dark side." From an early age, children can also be seen to separate the characters in their imaginary play world into "goodies" and "baddies." A simplifying binary separation such as this is appealing to the human psyche. But "white hat" and "black hat" are merely labels, and labels can be slippery since they can be applied and used in ways that seek to contradict the reality of a person's actions. The sociologist Erving Goffman wrote about why people might act differently in different social contexts.[111] They might wish to present themselves as a white hat in certain situations, such as to a prospective employer, but as a black hat to their social group of like-minded hackers.

Was Dan Farmer a black hat, given that some claimed that writing SATAN and making it available for anyone on the internet to download was "like handing a gun to a twelve-year-old"? Or was Farmer an altruistic white hat who had spent his personal time to create a program that could be used to help system administrators identify vulnerabilities in their computers? Was route a black hat for releasing his Neptune program that enabled less-skilled hackers to carry out SYN flood denial-of-service attacks and that potentially led to the attacks that brought down Panix? Or was route a prescient white hat who brought attention to an important vulnerability, as demonstrated by the later attacks against Panix?

The security software that was created and made available by Dan Farmer and route was inherently dual use. A rocket can fly a person to the moon but can also carry a nuclear warhead to another country. SATAN could be used by a system administrator to find vulnerabilities in the computers that she administered but could also be used by a hacker to find vulnerabilities in computers across the internet. The Neptune SYN flooding tool that was written by route could be used to test a computer to determine if it was vulnerable to a SYN flooding attack but could also be used to launch a denial-of-service attack.

There is no clear measure by which a person can be definitively categorized as either a black hat or a white hat. Being convicted of a computer crime might seem to be such a method, but the US Congress did not enact the Computer Fraud and Abuse Act until 1984.[112] In the United Kingdom, the Computer Misuse Act was not put into law until 1990.[113] The conviction rate for computer hacking is also extremely low, and publishing articles and distributing software as Dan Farmer and route did is not against the law. The reality of the situation was that both hackers and the commercial security industry benefited from the pretend notion of a clean separation between black hats and white hats. Hackers had developed skills and knowledge that was not easily acquired and for which there was considerable demand.[114] There were only a handful of universities that offered bachelor's degree courses in information security, and those universities produced a limited number of graduates each year. There were not many publicly available materials that could be used for the self-study of information security, with only a handful of books having been published. A person with expertise in security was almost certainly self-taught and likely learned in part from so-called underground resources such as *Phrack* magazine.

The commercial security industry needed employees with security expertise. They needed their knowledge to build commercial products such as network vulnerability scanners and intrusion detection systems. A company would be unlikely to hire a self-confessed black hat, and so some hackers were secretly nonbinary: "black hat by night and white hat by day." Other hackers viewed this as two-faced and akin to sleeping with the enemy. In 2002, a group of black hat hackers published a document online that was intended to out a number of hackers who had day jobs as white hats but who also used hacker handles and mixed in social circles with black hats.[115]

This, then, was the beginning of a new phase: the idolatry of computer hackers and their secret knowledge and the creation of a powerful feedback loop. Hackers would research vulnerabilities and then publish their findings on public mailing lists such as Bugtraq. This would serve the surface goal of putting the information into the public domain so that organizations could learn about vulnerabilities and then patch their computers. But the public, performative aspect of those online posts also enabled hackers to satisfy their desire to demonstrate their expertise to their peer group and to the world at large.[116] The stream of new vulnerabilities that the hackers created fed commercial security companies who would take the information that was being posted online by the hackers and create signatures for those vulnerabilities in their products.

Because the hackers were posting information regarding vulnerabilities to open mailing lists such as Bugtraq, other hackers could learn from their discoveries. If a hacker posted a working exploit that demonstrated a vulnerability, less-knowledgeable hackers called script kiddies could use those exploits to hack vulnerable computers.[117] The term *script kiddie* was used in a derogatory way to refer to hackers who would use exploits without understanding the details of how they functioned.[118] Because script kiddies could use the exploits that were being made public to carry out attacks, organizations needed more defenses, which meant buying security products. For the hackers who worked for security companies, this created the absurd situation where they would spend their nights researching and publishing information about vulnerabilities and their days writing signatures and other defenses for the attacks that they themselves had created.[119] The gamekeeper was also the poacher; the firefighter simultaneously the arsonist.

This feedback loop that was created between hackers and the commercial security industry was a powerful engine that caused the size of the market for information security products to skyrocket. The arrangement worked so well precisely because it served the interests of everyone involved. Hackers were able to satisfy their intellectual curiosity, signal their expertise to their peers, and earn a living. Commercial security companies could build and sell security products for which a growing market was being created. Even companies that participated in the feedback loop in an ancillary way could profit handsomely. By 2001, there was so much interest in security vulnerabilities that CERT was able to commercialize their production of security advisories and create an aggregation service as a commercial offering. Membership in that service cost up to $75,000 per organization.[120]

The strange symbiotic relationship between hackers and the commercial security industry was an unspoken but mutually beneficial arrangement. As Karl Marx said, "A philosopher 'produces' ideas, a poet poems, a preacher sermons, a professor text-books, and so forth. A criminal 'produces' crimes. It is not crimes alone that the criminal 'produces'; he also 'produces' criminal legislation, and, as a consequence, he is also the first mover in the 'production' of the professors who 'produce' lectures thereon, along with the inevitable text-books in which these professors cast their lectures as 'goods' on the markets of the world."[121] Further, "the criminal breaks the monotony and humdrum security of bourgeois life, he thereby insures it against stagnation, and he arouses that excitement and restlessness without which even the spur of competition would be blunted. Thus, the criminal furnishes the stimulants to the productive forces."[122]

The stimulant to the productive forces created by the hackers was new vulnerabilities, but the underlying currency was fear. Organizations feared that they would be hacked using those new vulnerabilities, and so they purchased security products. Fear is such a well-developed currency within the field of information security that it has its own acronym, FUD, which stands for fear, uncertainty, and doubt. Both hackers and the commercial security industry knew that FUD was a great motivator and wielded that power in flagrant ways. Symantec, one of the largest commercial security companies, created an antivirus product named Norton Internet Security. When the product license expired, the user was presented with a pop-up message that read, "Time's up, your Norton Internet Security has expired. Your protection is history. Any second now a virus may infect your computer, malicious malware might be installed, or your identity may be stolen. Maybe things will be OK for a while longer. Then again, maybe cyber-criminals are about to clean out your bank account. The choice is yours; Protect yourself now, or beg for mercy."[123]

One of the most well-known security conferences is the Black Hat Briefings, which is known within the field of information security simply as Black Hat. Tickets to Black Hat cost thousands of dollars, which reflect its intended corporate audience.[124] The first Black Hat Briefings conference was promoted with an advertisement that read, "It's late. You're in the office alone, catching up on database administration. Behind you, your network servers hum along quietly, reliably. Life is good. Life is secure. Or is it? A wave of unease washes over you. The air seems cold and frighteningly still. Your hands turn clammy as a sixth sense tells you, suddenly, you're not alone. They're out there. Worse, they're trying to get in. But who? And how? And what can you do to stop them? Only the Black Hat Briefings will provide your people with the tools and understanding they need to thwart those lurking in the shadows of your firewall. The reality is they are out there. The choice is yours. You can live in fear of them. Or, you can learn from them."[125] Someone who came upon this advertisement and happened to experience FUD as a result of reading it would no doubt have been surprised to discover that the founder of the Black Hat Briefings conference was also the founder of Defcon, the largest annual convention for hackers. Both Black Hat and Defcon were begun by Jeff Moss, who is also known by the handle "Dark Tangent."[126] Moss, just like the broader commercial security industry, was able to successfully monetize both the white hat and black hat sides of hacking.

The lucrative feedback loop that had been created by the hackers and the commercial security industry was being operated with little consideration for the possible side effects. But there was about to be a very public declaration of discontent.

Marcus J. Ranum describes getting involved with the field of information security as being like "getting your neck tie caught in powered machinery— it sucks you in and never lets you go."[127] Ranum was involved in the early firewall movement and is credited with creating the idea of a proxy firewall, also known as an application-layer firewall. A proxy firewall functions as a middleman for network connections, re-creating those connections on the other side of the device. This approach was thought to provide more security than a firewall that either permitted or denied individual packets. Ranum also played a central role in the creation of the first commercial firewall product named the DEC SEAL.[128]

In 1993, Ranum was working at a security company named Trusted Information Systems (TIS), when they received a call from DARPA.[129] DARPA was contacting TIS on behalf of the White House, who wanted to establish the first ever White House website. Bill Clinton had recently been inaugurated, and the Clinton administration was eager to embrace the new technology of the web.[130] A meeting between representatives from DARPA and TIS was set for the following day. Seeing the opportunity presented by the circumstance, Ranum stayed up all night to write a proposal.[131] DARPA and the White House liked his proposal so much that Ranum became the project leader for a DARPA-funded research project for a secure White House website.[132] As part of building the site, Ranum registered the whitehouse.gov domain name, which is the same domain name that is used by the White House website today.[133] A few days later, Ranum was meeting with government personnel in Washington, DC, and he suggested that they also acquire the whitehouse.com domain. The reply from the government officials was that they were unconcerned—that if anyone took that domain name, the government could simply send a cease-and-desist letter. But someone did register the whitehouse.com domain name, and it would later be sold for $2 million.[134]

Later in his career, Ranum would live in an 1820s farmhouse in Morrisdale, Pennsylvania, with two dogs, three barn cats, and two horses.[135] The open space on the farm would enable him to carry out various creative arts including soap making and glamour photography.[136] He would also pursue idiosyncratic projects and experiments, such as learning how to shoot a Mongolian bow while riding on horseback, attempting to re-create Lee Harvey Oswald's rifle shot that killed John F. Kennedy, and attempting to open a locked safe by shooting it with a large-caliber sniper rifle.[137]

Ranum held strong opinions regarding the embrace of hackers and hacking by the field of information security. In his view, if hacking on the internet was to be discouraged, that could not possibly be accomplished if the field promoted training courses and lectures led by hackers, bought books written by hackers, and paid hackers tens of thousands of dollars to carry out tiger team assessments.[138] Ranum deplored the notion that "hacking is cool," calling it "one of the dumbest ideas in computer security."[139]

An invitation to give a keynote address at the Black Hat Briefings conference in summer 2000 provided Ranum with the opportunity to speak his mind. The conference was being held inside the Caesars Palace casino in Las Vegas. Ranum would deliver his talk to thousands of conference attendees inside a vast ballroom. The title of his talk that was listed in the conference program was the innocuous-sounding "Full Disclosure and Open Source," but when he began his presentation, he revealed that he would instead be delivering a talk that he titled "Script Kiddies Suck."[140] In the talk, Ranum decried how the actions of the hackers and the commercial security industry were creating hordes of script kiddies. He described how security vulnerabilities were being researched solely for the purpose of being disclosed in order for hackers and commercial security companies to market themselves.[141] Ranum criticized the tolerance within the field for what he described as the "very large gray area between white hats and black hats." He stated that "there are too many people who fight on both sides of the battle" and that this had the effect of creating an environment in which people felt "completely comfortable carrying out extremely irresponsible actions." Too much credit was being given to people—hackers—who only knew how to break things but did not know how to build them.[142] He proposed that the field take a "counterterrorism" approach to defeat the "amateur terrorism" of hackers and "take the battle to the enemy where they live" with a scorched-earth, zero-tolerance approach to "reduce that comfortable gray area" and "stop hiring ex-hackers as security consultants." As he put it, "selling reformed wolves as shepherds is an insult to the sheep."[143] Ranum ended his talk with a challenge. He asked those conference attendees who were sitting in the audience and who currently spent their time researching vulnerabilities to instead use their knowledge to build something useful, such as a better firewall or a more secure operating system—to "do something productive and worthwhile to benefit the community."[144]

The effect of the talk, in Ranum's words, was "as if the pope gave a sermon wearing Moonies' robes."[145] The stated goal of the Black Hat conference was to have hackers present their knowledge and techniques to the conference attendees, and so for the conference attendees, Ranum's talk generated massive cognitive dissonance. They were attending a conference to hear from hackers while simultaneously being told that this was unproductive.

Ranum's talk had the potential to alter the direction of the field of information security, at least to some degree. But his talk had been delivered within a few months of the beginning of the dot-com crash. On a day that would become known as Black Friday, a massive sell-off of technology stocks took place. When the closing bell rang, the Nasdaq had dropped by more than 350 points—the biggest drop ever recorded by the index.[146] The Dow Jones Industrial Index also dropped by more 600 points that day.[147]

The dot-com boom was over. The market crash would have the same effect on the field of information security as it did on the capital markets: a retrenchment that would shift the focus from short-termism back to fundamentals. In doing so, it would shine a light on one of the largest companies in the world.

Chapter 5

# Software Security and the "Hamster Wheel of Pain"

The feedback loop that emerged during the dot-com boom had created profitable security companies and provided lucrative employment to hackers. But it had also created an ever-increasing number of new vulnerabilities that organizations needed to respond to by applying security patches. For such organizations, "penetrate and patch" had become "patch and pray": patch new vulnerabilities and pray that further vulnerabilities would not be discovered. But new vulnerabilities would always be discovered, and new vulnerabilities meant yet more patches. This situation created what one security professional described as a "hamster wheel of pain."[1] In this analogy, the hamster represented the organizations that were always running by installing patches but never really moving forward.

The security technologies that had become popular during the dot-com boom had to some extent exacerbated the problem. At the heart of the perimeter model of security was the firewall, but an organization's firewall had to permit web traffic to reach the organization's web server. If the web server had a vulnerability, which it almost certainly would experience over time, a hacker could compromise its security and likely then compromise the security of the operating system on which the web server was running.

The idea that security could be provided by web servers and other applications without a solid foundation of support provided by the underlying operating system began to be seen as a flawed assumption.[2] Because the operating system sat conceptually below applications such as web browsers and web servers, it could in theory stop an application with a vulnerability from causing the security of the entire computer to become compromised. A 1998 paper written by NSA staff members stated that "the computer industry has not accepted the critical role of the operating system to security, as evidenced by the inadequacies of the basic protection mechanisms provided by current mainstream operating systems."[3] The paper also said that any security effort that ignored operating system security could only result in a "fortress built upon sand."[4]

A desire for the focus of security efforts to be placed on operating system security was a curious return to the thinking of the 1970s and 1980s. The Ware report, the Anderson report, the work on provable security, and the development of the Bell-LaPadula model were all operating system focused. But operating system security had been somewhat neglected after the failure of the Orange Book and the excitement created by the emergence of the internet.

The two dominant operating systems at the beginning of the twenty-first century were Unix and Windows. By this time, Unix was being used less as a desktop operating system and more for the purpose of providing servers such as web servers. Unix came in many different flavors created by different nonprofit groups and commercial vendors. The various flavors of Unix tended to be open source, meaning that the source code to the software was publicly available. With open source software, people can take the software and modify it for their own purposes.

The Windows product line was developed by Microsoft, based in Redmond, Washington. Windows was closed source, meaning that the source code could be seen and modified only by Microsoft employees. Microsoft created different versions of Windows for different types of customers and markets, such as home users and large companies. New versions of Windows were released over time and branded with different product names, such as Windows NT, Windows 2000, Windows XP, and Windows Server. The Windows operating system was widely used around the world, as was Microsoft's database software named SQL Server and Microsoft's web server software named Internet Information Server (IIS). In the early 2000s, these Microsoft products experienced several well-publicized security failures.[5] The number and types of vulnerabilities being found in Microsoft products pointed to what appeared to be systemic problems with the way that Microsoft created software. This was because the vulnerabilities being discovered ranged from low-level vulnerabilities in the implementation of the TCP/IP protocols within Windows to application-level vulnerabilities in applications that ran on top of Windows, such as IIS.[6] A vulnerability discovered in SQL Server enabled hackers to gain full control of the computer on which it was running by sending a single packet.[7] There were so many vulnerabilities found in Internet Explorer that it gained the nicknames Internet Exploiter and Internet Exploder.[8]

Counting the number of vulnerabilities was not a straightforward task. The number of vulnerabilities being recorded could vary by a factor of two, depending on which public vulnerability database was used. This was because different vulnerability databases counted vulnerabilities according to different criteria.[9] There were also various biases baked into public vulnerability statistics. A hacker or security researcher might look for vulnerabilities in the products created by a particular software vendor because he perceived that vendor to be an easy target or because he disliked that company and wanted to harm it by creating bad press.[10] Software that could be freely obtained or that was open source might also attract more vulnerability research in part because it could be easily acquired. A particular hacker or security researcher might specialize in finding a specific type of vulnerability and so search for that type across many different pieces of software. This could result in his finding hundreds of separate instances of that one type of vulnerability, which would cause the count for that type of vulnerability to spike upward.[11] One researcher who specialized in vulnerability statistics referred to them as "worthless" because the underlying issues such as these could lead to poor analysis.[12]

If these problems with the quality of vulnerability statistics were causing a misleading impression of the insecurity of Microsoft products, a very public demonstration would soon put the matter beyond doubt.

On July 19, 2001, an internet worm used a buffer overflow in Microsoft's IIS to infect more than three hundred thousand computers.[13] Those infections occurred in less than fourteen hours.[14] At the peak rate more than two thousand new computers were being infected every minute.[15] Unlike the Morris worm, this new worm did contain a malicious payload. After the worm had infected a web server running on a computer, it would deface the web page to say "Hacked by Chinese!"[16] It would then make the infected computer carry out a denial-of-service attack once per month against certain targets, including the web server of the White House.[17] The worm was coined Code Red because the two researchers who first discovered it happened to be drinking a highly caffeinated soft drink called Code Red Mountain Dew at the time.[18] The Code Red worm could have deleted all the data from the infected machines, and therefore its impact could have been substantially worse. Even so, the worm was speculated to have caused damages of more than $2.6 billion and was described as a "wake-up call" for "the need to keep computers up-to-date with security developments."[19]

Just two months after Code Red, another internet worm named Nimda took advantage of vulnerabilities in Windows. The Nimda name was Admin spelled backward—a reference to the administrator account on Windows systems that has the highest level of security privileges. Nimda began to spread across the internet on September 18, 2001.[20] It could infect five different types of Windows operating system: Windows 95, Windows 98, Windows ME, Windows NT, and Windows 2000.[21] Unlike Code Red, which exploited a single vulnerability, Nimda spread using "every trick in the book."[22] It exploited vulnerabilities in email and in open network shares and exploited both client-side and server-side vulnerabilities.[23] Once it had infected a computer, Nimda would reconfigure it so that the contents of the computer's hard drive would be exposed to the internet.[24] On Windows NT and Windows 2000 systems, it would also add a guest account to the computer and add that guest account to the administrators group.[25] Any person who subsequently connected to the computer using that guest account would then be able to carry out any action he desired on the computer.[26]

Researchers who investigated the Nimda worm found that the source code within the worm contained the text "Concept Virus(CV) V.5, Copyright(C)2001 R.P.China."[27] The reference to China might indicate that the worm was created in China, or it might have been the author of the worm trying to deflect attention from himself by casting aspersions onto China.

Nimda infected computers around the world. The countries with the highest number of infected machines were Canada, Denmark, Italy, Norway, the United Kingdom, and the United States.[28] For the organizations that had been infected, removing the worm was a time-consuming and expensive proposition. The worm was an "infuriating program" and in some cases caused organizations to "ground to a halt."[29] Even the timing of the Nimda worm was problematic. Nimda began to spread just one week after the attacks on the United States on September 11, 2001. The close proximity of the two events caused the attorney general of the United States, John Ashcroft, to issue a statement saying that there was no known connection between them.[30]

In response to the Code Red and Nimda worms, the research advisory company Gartner recommended to companies that "enterprises hit by both Code Red and Nimda immediately investigate alternatives . . . including moving web applications to web server software from other vendors."[31] They added, "Although these web servers have required some security patches, they have much better security records . . . and are not under active attack by the vast number of virus and worm writers. Gartner remains concerned that viruses and worms will continue to attack . . . until Microsoft has released a completely rewritten, thoroughly and publicly tested, new release."[32]

Code Red, Nimda, and the escalating costs created by the need to apply a seemingly never-ending procession of security patches caused companies to begin to reconsider their use of Microsoft products. The Office of Management and Budget (OMB) stated that all US government agencies would have to report their security costs for all of their computer systems.[33] The air force then met with Microsoft and told them that they were "raising the bar" on their level of expectation for secure software.[34] At that time, the air force had an annual technology budget of $6 billion, and Microsoft was their biggest supplier. The chief information officer of the air force, John Gilligan, told Microsoft that "we just can't afford the exposures, and so those who give us better solutions, that's where we're going to put our business."[35]

Other organizations went even further. The University of California at Santa Barbara banned Windows NT and Windows 2000 computers from its residential network, citing "hundreds of major problems" such as vulnerabilities and infections by Code Red and Nimda.[36] Newnham College within the University of Cambridge banned the use of two Microsoft email clients, Outlook and Outlook Express, because it was "tired of having to allocate resources to clean up virus infections."[37] As if to place an exclamation mark on the security issues plaguing Microsoft, over the course of 2001, thirteen websites owned by Microsoft were defaced, including the website for Microsoft

UK and the Windows Update Server website that Microsoft used to issue security patches.[38]

The defacement of Microsoft websites, internet worms that took advantage of vulnerabilities in Microsoft products, and companies fleeing Microsoft products combined to lead to an increasing amount of bad press for Microsoft.[39] Some raised the question of whether Microsoft should be held liable in the courts for the costs associated with security vulnerabilities.[40] The Computer Science and Telecommunications Board of the US National Research Council recommended to legislators that they should consider increasing the liability of software manufacturers for the cost of security breaches—an amount that was speculated to be in the billions of dollars.[41]

Public opinion of Microsoft with regard to security was changing for the worse. The security requirements of Microsoft customers were also changing. The Windows XP operating system that was released in 2001 had been designed to give users easy connectivity to computer networking equipment and to other applications. But this led to Windows XP having several open network ports that a hacker could use to try and compromise the security of the computer.[42] This approach of opening ports by default was described as like parking a car "in a bad part of town, with the doors unlocked, the key in the ignition and a Post-It note on the dashboard saying, 'Please don't steal this.'"[43] It had been rational for Microsoft to create Windows XP with those features because customers had demanded ease of use. It had also been rational for Microsoft to write software and create products without much consideration for security vulnerabilities because that enabled them to bring those products to market quicker than their competitors. Shipping a product with bugs and correcting them in a later version was rational behavior, and whichever company had won in the PC business—as Microsoft had done—would necessarily have done the same.[44] But customers were now increasingly demanding security, and Microsoft would have to respond to those demands.

Bill Gates, the chairman of Microsoft, knew that he had to act, in part because he had personal experience with the dangers of hacking. In the late 1960s, while working as a student at the University of Washington, Gates hacked into a nationwide network of computers called Cybernet that was owned by a company named Control Data Corporation.[45] While attempting to insert his own program, he accidentally caused all of the computers to crash simultaneously.[46] For this, Gates was caught and reprimanded.[47]

On January 15, 2002, Gates sent a memo in the form of an email to every full-time Microsoft employee.[48] The subject of the email was "Trustworthy Computing," and in the memo he described how security should be, in his words, "the highest priority for all the work we are doing."[49] He acknowledged the damaging effects of security failures on Microsoft, saying that Microsoft "can and must do better" and that "flaws in a single Microsoft product, service or policy not only affect the quality of our platform and services overall, but also our customers' view of us as a company."[50] Gates then described the paradigm shift that he believed needed to take place within Microsoft. He described how in the past Microsoft had focused on "adding new features and functionality," but that "now, when we face a choice between adding features and resolving security issues, we need to choose security."[51] He stressed that "this priority touches on all the software work we do."[52] Gates confronted the difficulties that organizations faced with vulnerability patching, saying that the new approaches to security taken within Microsoft "need to dramatically reduce the number of such issues that come up in the software that Microsoft, its partners and its customers create."[53] He also challenged Microsoft employees to "lead the industry to a whole new level of Trustworthiness in computing."[54]

Five years earlier, in response to criticism regarding the security of its products, Microsoft had attempted to defend itself by stating that Microsoft products were "fundamentally secure."[55] The Trustworthy Computing memo was an admission that its products were not in fact fundamentally secure, nor anything even approaching fundamentally secure. Microsoft was now committed to security at the highest levels within the organization. The world would have the opportunity to discover whether it was possible for a major software company to improve the security of its products in a meaningful way.

In the year before the Gates memo, two Microsoft employees—Michael Howard and David LeBlanc—had written a book titled *Writing Secure Code*.[56] That book had been published by Microsoft Press, and in his memo, Gates had recommended the book to Microsoft employees.[57] In a sign that they had heard the message within Gates's memo loud and clear, in the weeks following the publication of the memo, the book would jump to the top of the Amazon best-seller list.[58]

The program of work that Microsoft began as a result of the Gates memo was named the Trustworthy Computing initiative.[59] Microsoft began the initiative by having its Security Assurance group lead more than eight thousand Windows programmers, testers, and program managers through a four-hour-long training course on the topic of secure programming.[60] That effort was expected to take one month but in fact took two, at a total cost of $200 million.[61] After those initial training courses were completed, every team within Microsoft that contributed software code to any part of the Windows operating system had to create a written plan for how they intended to remove security vulnerabilities from that code.[62] Those plans had to emphasize a new philosophy: that Microsoft software had to be "secure by design and secure by default."[63] If a particular feature would not be used by 90 percent of Windows users, then it had to be turned off by default.[64] This new philosophy was fundamentally different from the previous approach that Microsoft had taken with Windows XP. The goal was to reduce the attack surface of the software, such as by closing open ports, which would decrease the opportunities for hackers to exploit vulnerabilities.

In every product group within Microsoft a designated person was made responsible for software security.[65] The financial compensation that Microsoft software engineers received, including their raises and bonuses, would also be tied to the security of their products.[66]

To reduce the number of vulnerabilities that were being created in software code, Microsoft introduced a number of technical innovations. A stack protection mechanism was built into their Visual Studio .NET compiler product.[67] This would help to mitigate the risk of stack-based buffer overflows. Crucially, that stack protection would be activated by default so that all programs created by the compiler would receive the protection.[68] The design of this technology was similar to an existing product named StackGuard.[69] Microsoft also deployed a number of other technologies for the purpose of identifying possible vulnerabilities, such as static analysis and fuzzing. Static analysis involves having a computer program examine source code to detect patterns that might indicate that a vulnerability is present.[70] Fuzzing is the process of inputting invalid and unexpected random data into a computer program in an attempt to make it crash or behave in unexpected ways. This can duplicate the type of techniques that a hacker might use when trying to find security vulnerabilities.[71]

But just as those efforts were beginning to gain momentum, a new and highly virulent internet worm dubbed Slammer began to infect computers that used two types of Microsoft database product. Slammer began to infect computers at around 05:30 UTC on Saturday, January 25, 2003.[72] Whereas the Code Red worm had taken over fourteen hours to infect the population of vulnerable computers on the internet, Slammer infected more than seventy-five thousand computers in less than ten minutes.[73] At the peak rate, the number of computers being infected by Slammer doubled every eight and a half seconds.[74] Just three minutes after it had been released, Slammer had infected so many computers that those infected computers were generating fifty-five million packets per second in an attempt to infect other computers.[75] The number of Slammer infections generated so much network traffic that parts of the internet temporarily ran out of carrying capacity.[76]

Slammer was able to spread so quickly because the entire worm could be contained in a single network packet.[77] Because of this, the worm did not have to establish a separate network connection to each prospective target computer—it could simply spray copies of itself across the internet. Slammer was described as the first fast worm.[78] A fast worm spreads so rapidly that no human could ever act quickly enough to respond. Attempting to block a fast worm such as by manually making a change to a firewall would be futile since a fast worm will infect every possible vulnerable computer on the internet within minutes or even seconds.

Slammer did not contain a malicious payload, but some internet connections became clogged because of the rate at which it spread, and this affected a number of organizations. The website of American Express was knocked offline for days.[79] Some Bank of America customers could not withdraw cash from automated teller machines.[80] The computer systems used by the Seattle police and fire services were impacted to the extent that they had to fall back on using pencil and paper.[81]

The source code for Slammer did not contain any information that might have identified who had created it because the author had taken precautionary measures to remove information that might have revealed the country of origin.[82] However, it was quickly discovered that Slammer exploited a known vulnerability—a vulnerability that had first been revealed at the Black Hat Briefings conference.[83]

Slammer would be followed by another internet worm that exploited Microsoft products. On August 11, 2003, the Blaster worm began to exploit a vulnerability in Windows XP and Windows 2000.[84] The source code for Blaster contained the message "billy gates why do you make this possible?

Stop making money and fix your software!!"[85] (In a later interview, Gates said that he did not take the message personally.[86])

On August 18, just one week after Blaster, an internet worm named Welchia began to spread.[87] Welchia had an interesting twist. It was designed to infect computers that had been infected with Slammer, then it would attempt to remove the Slammer infection, patch the vulnerability so that Slammer could not reinfect the computer, and then delete itself in 2004.[88] Welchia appears to have been written with good intentions, but it used a new vulnerability in Microsoft Windows to spread where it was not wanted.[89] When the US State Department discovered Welchia on its network, they shut down access for nine hours.[90]

Welchia was followed by Sobig, which infected millions of Windows computers by sending emails with enticing subject lines such as "Re: Approved" and "Re: Your application."[91] Microsoft offered a reward of $250,000 for information leading to the arrest of the creator of Sobig, but that person was never caught.[92]

Sobig was followed by yet another worm, named Sasser. Sasser began to spread in late April 2004 by exploiting a vulnerability in Windows XP and Windows 2000.[93] Sasser crashed computers in hospitals in Hong Kong, caused Delta Airlines in the United States to cancel forty flights, and stranded thousands of rail travelers by infecting computers used by the Australian rail network.[94] As they did with Welchia, Microsoft offered a reward of $250,000 in an attempt to catch the creator of Sasser, and on this occasion they received multiple tip-offs.[95] On May 7, 2004, eighteen-year-old Sven Jaschan was arrested by German police.[96] Jaschan was a computer science student in Rothenburg, Germany. Some of the tip-offs may have come from his classmates, to whom he had bragged about his activities. Jaschan was reportedly an introvert who spent most of each day in front of the computer in his family's home.[97] He admitted to having launched the worm on April 29, which was his eighteenth birthday.[98] Because he had been seventeen years old when he had created and released the worm, he was tried by the German courts as a minor and received a twenty-one-month suspended sentence.[99]

The Code Red, Nimda, Slammer, Blaster, Welchia, Sobig, and Sasser internet worms were portents of a possible bleak future. A group of academic researchers began to calculate the possible cost of a worst-case internet worm. Such a worm would spread using a vulnerability in Microsoft Windows and would carry a highly destructive payload. Their estimation regarding the damage that such a worst-case internet worm could create was $50 billion in direct economic damages, and they found that this level of harm could be achieved with just a small team of experienced programmers.[100] The same researchers also investigated the idea that a hacker could create a worm that infected millions of computers on the internet and then control those computers to carry out various attacks, such as by launching denial-of-service attacks.[101] Such a network of infected computers could be wielded as a weapon by a nation-state and could be used to battle other networks of infected computers controlled by competing nations.[102]

High-profile and damaging internet worms gave the impression that Microsoft's security initiatives were not succeeding, with pundits quick to claim that the Trustworthy Computing initiative had been a failure.[103] This caused some to wonder whether Microsoft had too much of a dominant role as the provider of the world's most popular software. In July 2003, the US Department of Homeland Security announced that Microsoft had been awarded a $90 million contract to supply Microsoft Windows desktop and server software.[104] A Washington, DC–based nonprofit organization named the Computer & Communications Industry Association (CCIA) took note. The CCIA had previously been involved in the 2001 antitrust case against Microsoft regarding the bundling of Microsoft's Internet Explorer web browser with the Windows operating system and whether that bundling constituted a monopoly.[105] The CCIA asked the secretary of the Department of Homeland Security to reconsider awarding Microsoft the contract, and a few months later in September 2003, the CCIA published a position paper titled "CyberInsecurity: The Cost of Monopoly."[106] The authors were a group of information security professionals, and their paper examined the risk of a technology monoculture.[107] Monoculture is a term that is used in the field of agriculture, specifically regarding biodiversity. When a farmer grows only a single crop, their costs are reduced because they need to tend to and harvest only that one specific type of plant. But a monoculture increases the risk that a single disease might wipe out the entire crop. The Morris worm was able to spread because many of the computers on the internet used a Unix operating system, and therefore those computers contained the same buffer overflow vulnerability. In a similar way, the internet worms that affected Microsoft products were each able to exploit a vulnerability that was present in many different installations of the same Microsoft product.

The authors of the paper described what they believed to be a "clear and present danger" created by the widespread use of Microsoft software.[108] If nearly all of the computers in the world ran a single type of operating system, namely Microsoft Windows, and Microsoft Windows contained security vulnerabilities, then most computers would be vulnerable to any internet worm or hacker that could exploit those vulnerabilities. The sales figures for computer software seemed to support their argument. The paper quotes sources that state that at that time, the market share for Microsoft Windows exceeded 97 percent and that Microsoft Windows represented "94 percent of the consumer client software sold in the United States in 2002."[109] The authors further developed their argument by describing how a software vendor that is in a dominant position within the market for operating systems can entrench that position. Vendor lock-in can be created by increasing switching costs for users—the costs that a user would incur from moving to a competitor. The vendor can accomplish this in various ways, such as by perpetuating custom file formats. If a computer owner uses Microsoft Word for word processing and that program saves files in a specific file format, then to convert those documents to a different file format creates costs. Those switching costs lock the computer owner into the use of Microsoft Word and therefore into the Microsoft Windows operating system. For two users to share documents, they both need to have word processing programs that can understand at least one shared file format, and so it becomes increasingly attractive for a person to purchase Microsoft products if all of her friends with whom she wants to exchange files also happen to use Microsoft products. Software vendors want to create these kinds of network effect in order to increase their market share, but this has the side effect of increasing the likelihood of a monoculture.[110]

The authors of the monoculture position paper suggested that the only way to truly mitigate the risk of widespread vulnerabilities in Microsoft Windows was to take conscious steps to "counter the security threat of Microsoft's monopoly dominance of computing."[111] They recommended that governments force Microsoft to implement Microsoft software such as Microsoft Office and Internet Explorer on other operating systems such as Linux and Mac OS and also force Microsoft to open the interfaces to its products and operating systems in order to improve interoperability.[112] They further advised that governments use regulation to ensure that government facilities did not become technology monocultures.[113] They suggested that this could be accomplished by implementing a rule that required that no more than 50 percent of computer operating systems used in government be sourced from any single vendor.[114]

Technology monoculture was now a hot topic. The National Science Foundation granted Carnegie Mellon University and the University of New Mexico $750,000 to study computer monocultures and the benefits of diverse computing environments.[115] But the counterargument to reducing monoculture is that technological diversity has a cost. An airline does not increase the diversity of its aircraft in order to avoid a flaw in any one type of aircraft grounding its fleet. By standardizing on a single type of aircraft, an airline reduces its costs in terms of the initial purchase cost and the ongoing maintenance, and the same applies to an organization buying and maintaining computer software.[116] Creating a diverse software environment also generates operational security costs because the patches for those multiple types of software need to be monitored and installed on an ongoing basis.

The monoculture position paper described itself as a "wake-up call that government and industry need to hear," but it was pointed out that the paper might have been "a shot across the stern of a ship that's already sailed."[117] Microsoft's dominance in the market for operating systems was by then well established. Other companies had previously taken their turn on top, with IBM having dominated both computer hardware and software before Microsoft's rise, and other companies were sure to follow. There was also a more practical and pressing concern underlying the existence of internet worms that took advantage of vulnerabilities in Microsoft products. Microsoft was identifying security vulnerabilities in its products and then creating and making patches available for those vulnerabilities, but organizations were not installing them quickly enough to avoid the vulnerabilities being exploited.

The Slammer worm used a vulnerability for which a patch had been available for six months, and yet there were still tens of thousands of computers that had not installed the patch that Slammer was able to infect. Microsoft was infected with Slammer because by their own acknowledgment they, "like the rest of the industry, struggle to get 100% compliance with . . . patch management."[118] In the case of the vulnerability used by the Blaster worm, a patch had been available for one month. For Code Red, a patch had been available for sixteen days and for Sasser, seventeen days. An academic study of sites that had suffered security incidents showed that patches for the vulnerabilities that were exploited in those incidents were typically available for at least a month before each incident took place.[119] That study described the speed at which patches were being applied for known vulnerabilities as "woefully inadequate."[120] A second study showed that in the general case, two weeks after the announcement of a vulnerability, more than two-thirds of computers had not yet installed the related patch.[121]

Microsoft was carrying out a massive effort to find security vulnerabilities in its products and issue patches so that its customers could close those vulnerabilities. But organizations were not installing the patches that were being made available to them, and this was happening even in the presence of large-scale internet worms and organizations such as the US government telling companies that effective patch management was "critical."[122] The reason was that for organizations, the day-to-day reality of patching was not straightforward. Every organization had to track the security advisories and patches that were being issued by software vendors. Simply being able to understand which patches needed to be applied was itself a time-consuming task.[123] There would also need to be a plan for how to remove the patch from computers if the patch caused a problem after installation. Even after an organization had decided to apply a particular patch, they would typically not want to deploy it to all of the computers within the organization at once in case it conflicted with a second piece of software that was installed on those computers, or in case it was subsequently discovered that the patch did not function correctly. On a number of occasions, Microsoft had to withdraw security patches because they conflicted with other software, such as in the case where a security patch for Windows XP stopped six hundred thousand computers from being able to connect to the internet, or where a security patch caused computers to crash with the so-called blue screen of death.[124]

Each organization therefore had to decide when to install each and every patch.[125] Patch too early, and the organization risked installing a patch that could cause harm or would subsequently be withdrawn by the vendor. Patch too late, and there was an increased risk of a hacker exploiting the vulnerability that the patch addressed. To mitigate these problems, organizations would first install patches on a small group of computers within their environment and test if the patch was working correctly, then extend that testing to progressively larger groups of computers. This meant that it could take several weeks for a patch to be installed on all of the computers that needed it within a large organization. This provided a window of opportunity for hackers to exploit vulnerabilities.[126] The question of by which mechanism patches would be installed was also complex. A popular method for patch deployment was Microsoft's Software Update Services (SUS) program, but Microsoft also provided seven other patching tools.[127]

Microsoft recognized these challenges relating to patching and made several key decisions. They committed to reducing the number of patching mechanisms from eight to two.[128] Instead of issuing multiple individual patches, they began to bundle patches together into service packs. Those service packs would be cumulative so that installing the latest service pack would bring a computer up to date on all previous service packs. In September 2003, Microsoft also moved from a model where security patches were released on an ad hoc basis to a monthly schedule where patches were released on the second Tuesday of each month.[129] The goal for this fixed schedule was to reduce the burden on system administrators who, up until that point, would have to scramble to respond to patches as they were announced.[130] Microsoft named the new monthly schedule Update Tuesday, but it became more commonly known as Patch Tuesday.[131]

An unfortunate but predictable by-product of issuing security patches was the effort that was undertaken by hackers to reverse engineer those patches and identify the vulnerabilities that were being patched. A patch would change a piece of code in a program, and typically that code would contain the vulnerability or be closely related to the cause of the vulnerability. A patch could therefore serve as a beacon directing hackers where to look. Once they had identified the details of the vulnerability that was being patched, hackers could write an exploit and then use that exploit against organizations that had not yet installed the patch. For this reason, the day following each Patch Tuesday began to be referred to as Exploit Wednesday.[132]

The challenges that organizations experienced with installing patches for vulnerabilities was in one sense a by-product of Microsoft's security efforts. Microsoft was responding to the increasing number of security vulnerabilities being found in its products, but patches were the result. If vulnerabilities were the yin, patches were the yang. Only by removing vulnerabilities from the source code of their products *before* they were released could Microsoft reduce the number of patches, and this meant improving their ability to create secure software.

Microsoft concentrated their software security efforts on what they called pushes to improve the security of each product.[133] But those pushes were intense and time consuming for the software developers involved.[134] By late

2003, there was the realization that they needed a more formal approach that could be implemented in a way that would avoid the constant pushes.[135] In mid-2004, Steve Lipner, a key figure in the Microsoft Trustworthy Computing group and a contributor to the Orange Book two decades earlier, had organized the existing security training materials into a process that could be integrated into the very fabric of the way that Microsoft created their products.[136] That new process was named the Security Development Lifecycle (SDL).[137] With the approval of Microsoft CEO Steve Ballmer, the SDL went into production in July 2004.[138] All software written at Microsoft would now have to integrate security efforts into every phase of the process by which that software was created, from project inception through the definition of requirements, design, implementation, and release.[139] Even after software products had been introduced to the marketplace, there would be a structured approach to addressing the vulnerabilities that were discovered in those products over time.[140] The Trustworthy Computing initiative at Microsoft that led to the creation of the SDL was the most comprehensive and well-funded approach to software security that had ever been attempted by a major software vendor.

Representatives of Microsoft had on occasion claimed that the goal of Microsoft's security efforts was to reduce the number of patches that customers needed to install to zero, although those statements were likely made for the purpose of marketing their security efforts.[141] It was more likely that Microsoft had the pragmatic goal of making their products secure enough such that security problems did not jeopardize their market dominance. Improving the security of their software could also be seen as a kind of cost reduction. Bad press imposed costs, as did the need to respond to vulnerabilities. It is well-known within the field of computer science that finding and fixing bugs earlier in the software development life cycle is less costly than having to address them later, such as by issuing a patch.[142] In that regard, reducing the number of security vulnerabilities could be viewed as an effort to improve software quality. After all, a vulnerability is simply a software bug with a security implication.

Microsoft's security efforts would take years to pay large-scale dividends. A year after Bill Gates's Trustworthy Computing memo, an informal survey of information technology managers, analysts, and information security professionals gave the security of Microsoft products letter grades ranging from B+ to D–.[143] Over the following years, concerns about the effectiveness of the Trustworthy Computing initiative slowly abated, and the overall progress became viewed as having a positive effect on the internet.[144] Commentators praised Microsoft as a "security leader" and for having created the "gold standard" in software security programs.[145] Microsoft's SDL became a widely used template for how organizations approach the task of implementing software security. Companies that were influenced by the SDL include Adobe and Cisco.[146] Since its first release in 2004, the documentation that Microsoft produced that describes the SDL has been downloaded more than one million times and has reached more than 150 countries.[147]

The decision taken by Bill Gates to focus Microsoft on building more secure software and the significant and far-reaching changes that were implemented within Microsoft as a result of that decision stand in stark contrast to some other notable major corporations. Oracle Corporation is the exemplar of such an organization that decided to employ a very different approach.

Oracle was founded in 1977 in California. The company primarily produces database software. Those products have been so successful that Larry Ellison, the CEO and cofounder of Oracle, has become a billionaire many times over and one of the richest people in the world. Ellison has developed a reputation for extravagant purchases due to his ownership of a fighter jet, a California estate modeled after a feudal-era Japanese village, and his purchase of the Hawaiian island of Lanai, for which he paid $300 million.[148]

On November 13, 2001, four months after the Code Red worm began to spread, Ellison gave a keynote speech at a computer trade show in Las Vegas. In that speech he made the bold claim that Oracle software was "unbreakable."[149] Ellison had been warned before his talk by Oracle employees not to call the software unbreakable because it would attract hackers, but he decided to ignore those warnings and went further, stating that even though the number of attacks against Oracle software had increased recently, every attempt had failed.[150] That same month, Oracle issued four patches for security vulnerabilities.[151] Those patches were followed by seven more in December and twenty in February.[152]

Perhaps in response to the skeptical reaction from information security practitioners that Oracle software was as "unbreakable" as Ellison had said, Oracle released a white paper that attempted to reframe the claim.[153] That document reads as if it were attempting to retroactively construct a marketing campaign around Ellison's use of the word. The document asks in a seemingly pained manner, "How can anyone claim to be unbreakable?" and "Why would anyone claim to be unbreakable?"[154] The authors attempted to answer these questions by asserting that the "unbreakable" claim rested specifically on the fourteen security evaluations of Oracle products that had been carried out by independent security evaluators over the previous ten-year period.[155] Those evaluations are described in the white paper as having cost one million dollars, and the authors suggest that the two nearest competitors to Oracle "have 0 and 1 evaluations, respectively."[156] During the early 2000s, when Ellison made the "unbreakable" comment and the subsequent white paper was written, Microsoft was issuing large numbers of security patches for vulnerabilities that were being found in its products. The authors of the Oracle paper criticize Microsoft for this, although they do not refer to Microsoft by name, by saying that security that is achieved "once you have applied the latest twelve security patches" is "a disgrace."[157] The paper also decries "one of our competitors" that "issues a security alert every two and a half days."[158]

These comments would not age well. In February 2002, a paper was published that demonstrated how to hack into Oracle database products.[159] That paper described a "vast" number of attacks that could be carried out, including buffer overflows, techniques to bypass authentication, and the presence of easily guessed passwords for privileged accounts.[160] A press article published in response to the paper sarcastically described it as "required reading for anyone who owns or administers an unbreakable Oracle box."[161]

Between March and October 2002, Oracle released patches for twenty-two security vulnerabilities.[162] The following month, Ellison doubled down, making the claim that it had been more than ten years since an Oracle database had been hacked.[163] He also claimed that Oracle had invited the "toughest hackers from China, Russia, and all over the world" to attempt to break into Oracle products and that none had been successful.[164]

In the next eighteen months, Oracle released sixty-six patches for security vulnerabilities.[165] In January 2005, a researcher who had found dozens of security vulnerabilities in Oracle products took issue with the quality of those patches.[166] He accused Oracle of creating patches that would stop a specific vulnerability exploit from functioning but that did not fix the underlying issue. If a small modification was made to the exploit, then it would begin to work again, making the patch that had been issued useless. He described the approach taken by Oracle as "slapdash with no real consideration for fixing the actual problem itself."[167]

The number of patches for security vulnerabilities issued by Oracle increased each month, with sixty-nine in April 2005, ninety in October 2005, and one hundred and three in January 2006.[168] By May 2008, a researcher who specialized in tracking vulnerabilities stated that there was "no real statistical evidence to show that Oracle is improving."[169]

The Oracle white paper on the topic of their "unbreakable" marketing campaign stated that through their software security efforts, Oracle would "improve security for the entire industry."[170] But that grandiose claim was revealed over time to be an abject fantasy. For software to be unbreakable, it must not contain bugs, but it is the most basic finding in the field of software development that almost all software contains bugs.

The bravado with which Oracle described its security was not married to the kind of practical efforts undertaken by Microsoft. Software security could not simply be asserted or wished into existence. The claims made by Ellison and Oracle were found to be continually at odds with the reality of the types and quantity of security vulnerabilities that were discovered in Oracle products. In the single month of October 2018, Oracle would issue more than three hundred security patches.[171]

The possibility does exist that Oracle was carrying out some unspoken grand strategy. They had perhaps made the opposite calculation to Microsoft and determined that it would be in their best interests to pay lip service to security but not to invest to the same degree. If this was their plan, it contained substantial downside risk. In 2015, Oracle was charged by the US Federal Trade Commission (FTC) with promising customers that by installing security patches they would be "safe and secure."[172] However, certain Oracle patches did not uninstall the old versions of the software, meaning that the insecure software remained on users' computers and was vulnerable to being hacked. The FTC complaint stated that Oracle was aware of this fact and failed to inform consumers.[173] Oracle agreed to settle with the FTC and under a consent order was prohibited "from making any further deceptive statements to consumers about the privacy or security of its software."[174]

Where Oracle failed, Microsoft succeeded. The Trustworthy Computing group within Microsoft was broken up in 2014, twelve years after the Bill Gates memo. Other initiatives that were begun by Microsoft as part of the Trustworthy Computing initiative are still maintained to this day. These include the publication of an annual *Security Intelligence Report* that describes security trends, the creation of security guides that help system administrators to configure Windows systems, and the creation of a hub for responding to security vulnerabilities and security incidents named the Microsoft Security Response Center (MSRC).[175] A book published in June 2006 that describes the SDL also continues to be influential.[176]

Microsoft's focus on software security that began in the early 2000s contributed to the broader field of information security beginning to orient itself to the challenge of approaching software security in a structured way, and for software security to be recognized as a clearly defined discipline. The use of techniques such as static analysis and fuzzing has become increasingly common. More open source and commercial tools to programmatically analyze software have also become available and have been improved over time.[177] Defensive programming practices have gained popularity. Such practices attempt to ensure that a particular program or piece of code will continue to function as expected, even when the surrounding code does not. There has also been an increasing recognition of the benefits that stem from using new programming languages that are designed to avoid certain types of security vulnerability entirely. The designers of programming languages such as Rust and Microsoft's C# (pronounced "C sharp") made the deliberate decision to design them in such a way that they would not produce code that was vulnerable to buffer overflows and certain other types of security vulnerability. A focus on software security also helped to balance the heavy emphasis on commercial security products that occurred during the dot-com boom. Vulnerability scanners could to some degree automate the process of identifying vulnerabilities in computers, and an intrusion detection system could possibly detect a hacker exploiting a vulnerability, but software security held the promise of avoiding vulnerabilities in the first place. As Phil Venables, the chief information security officer at Goldman Sachs, has put it, "We need secure products, not security products."[178]

Apple is notable in having embraced this philosophy in its approach to the design of both software and hardware. Microsoft Windows dominated the market for computer operating systems in the early 2000s and drew the attention of hackers and security researchers who wanted their efforts to have the greatest possible impact.[179] Apple benefited during this period from the attention that was being placed on Windows. In 2007, the US Army chose to replace some Windows computers with Apple machines, stating that the small number of security patches being released by Apple was a "good sign."[180] It was likely the case, however, that at that time there were simply fewer hackers and security researchers investigating the security of Apple products. By the end of the decade, Apple was releasing a steady number of patches for security vulnerabilities.[181]

The release of the first iPhone in 2007 received substantial attention from the media because of its touch-screen and user-friendly interface, but some organizations were distrustful regarding the security capabilities of the revolutionary device. One such organization was NASA, who deemed the iPhone "not enterprise ready" because of, in part, a lack of available security software.[182] These concerns regarding the security of the iPhone were validated by a security consulting firm that performed an investigation and found what they described as "serious problems with the design and implementation of security."[183] Apple responded by making significant investments in security, and those efforts have led to a powerful synthesis of hardware and software security measures.

Mobiles devices such as phones can be easily lost or stolen, and so they can fall into the wrong hands. An unscrupulous individual might attempt to guess the password on a phone. A sophisticated attacker can go further and attempt to "image" a phone, meaning create a copy of the data on the phone and read it on a separate computer, thereby bypassing the need to guess a password entirely. Apple's solution to this problem is the Secure Enclave, which was introduced in the iPhone 5s in 2013. The Secure Enclave is a piece of hardware that is distinct from the main processor.[184] Its purpose is to store a secret key that is unique to each device and which is used to encrypt the data on the device.[185] The Secure Enclave is designed in such a manner that the software running on the device cannot extract that secret key, even if that software has been completely overtaken by an attacker.[186] Attempts to image the phone will fail because reading the data requires the secret key, and the secret key cannot be extracted from the physical Secure Enclave.[187] The practical result is that the only way to access an iPhone is to know the password that has been set by the owner. The iPhone can be configured to erase all of the data on the device after ten failed password guesses, and even if unlimited password attempts are permitted, the Secure Enclave slows down those attempts, which makes it too time consuming to guess a sufficiently long password.[188]

In 2014, a year after the release of the iPhone 5s that contained the Secure Enclave functionality, a US Justice Department official described the device as "the equivalent of a house that can't be searched, or a car trunk that could never be opened."[189] After the San Bernardino shootings in 2015, in which fourteen people were killed and twenty-two others were seriously injured, a federal judge ordered Apple to provide the FBI with "reasonable technical assistance" in unlocking the iPhone owned by one of the perpetrators.[190] Apple refused the request, saying that it would not create technology that would threaten the security of its customers.[191] Apple lawyers also argued that the judge's orders were an "unprecedented use of the All Writs Act of 1789 to justify an expansion of its authority."[192]

Apple is a consumer electronics company, and so its security efforts have primarily been focused on physical products such as the iPhone. Microsoft is best known for its computer software, and so its security efforts have historically been focused on software security. Microsoft was successful in reducing the number of security vulnerabilities in its software, in contributing to the creation of software security as a discipline, and in raising the profile of software security generally. The first dedicated software security workshop was held in 2003 with attendees from Microsoft, DARPA, AT&T, IBM, and various universities.[193] Since then, an increasing number of workshops and conferences relating to software security have taken place, and many academic research papers on the subject of software security have been published. As Microsoft's software security efforts began to pay increasing dividends, it became more and more difficult to find vulnerabilities that could be exploited in Microsoft products. The cost in terms of the time and effort required to find a remote exploit in Windows priced out the average hacker. Windows had become difficult to hack.[194] Hackers would begin to look for greener pastures elsewhere, and in doing so they would find a target for their efforts for which there could be no software patches: the human brain.[195]

Chapter 6

# Usable Security, Economics, and Psychology

Every computer has a processing limit, and so does every brain. Those limits are reached more quickly if a person is impaired, tired, or experiencing stress.[1] It was not engineering flaws but rather human errors that were the primary factor in catastrophes such as the space shuttle *Challenger* disaster and the Chernobyl nuclear accident, to give just two examples.

If the software running on computers was becoming increasingly difficult to hack, then it was rational to look elsewhere for vulnerabilities. The human users of computers were a logical target. The user of a computer is in a prime position to act in ways that could compromise the security of the entire system, such as by revealing a password or by carrying out actions that weaken security measures. Within the field of information technology there exists a long history of disdain for the seemingly endless fallibility of users. Terms such as PEBCAK (problem exists between chair and keyboard) have been used by technologists in a derogatory manner to refer to the misunderstandings of people with less knowledge of computers. Information security professionals have also long decried the lack of security knowledge held by the typical user. In 1999, the Princeton professor of computer science and public affairs Edward Felten coined an aphorism that has been frequently repeated: "Given a choice between dancing pigs and security, users will pick dancing pigs every time."[2]

This propensity for users to not understand the security implications of their actions has been exploited since the early days of telephony.[3] Hackers would place calls to telephone company employees and convince them to provide information that would enable them to gain access.[4] These social engineering attacks did not require any knowledge of technology, merely the ability to convince a person.[5] The growing number of households that owned a computer that was connected to the internet created the situation where an increasing number of security decisions were being put into the hands of everyday people. But those people suffered from the fundamental dilemma of computer security: they wanted security, but because they had no security expertise, they could not judge whether they were making good security decisions. An article in a 2008 issue of an information security journal characterized the period beginning with the release of the IBM personal computer in 1981 as creating an environment in which "the majority of computers will be administered by incompetents."[6] This feeling within security practitioners was created in large part because they observed users acting in ways that violated established security norms. In 2004, the *New York Times* reported on the results of a survey in which 172 people encountered on the street were asked if they would reveal the password they used to log onto the internet in exchange for a bar of chocolate.[7] Of those surveyed, 70 percent took the chocolate, although it is doubtful that all of them revealed their real passwords.[8]

The strength of a system has often been described as being like a chain, with the overall resilience being dictated by the strength of the weakest link.[9] If human beings were now the weakest link in the security of computer systems, then there would need to be a new focus on examining, understanding, and strengthening that weakest link.[10]

In the work that was carried out by RAND and the other early researchers, the importance of usability was not a significant consideration. The earliest computers were created as a result of military funding and for military purposes, and military personnel were trained to obey orders, rules, and procedures to the letter—to function as components within the machine.[11] The work that followed on multilevel secure systems and provable security prized the purity of mathematics and largely ignored human factors.[12] The importance of the human operator of the computer was not entirely neglected, though. One of the design principles described by Jerry Saltzer and Michael Schroeder in their classic 1975 paper was the requirement for "psychological acceptability."[13] This was the need for the "human interface" to be designed "for ease of use, so that users routinely and automatically apply the protection mechanisms correctly."[14] They also describe how the implementation of security within the system should be consistent with users' mental model for their security goals.[15] These recommendations are aligned with the two types of errors that human beings tend to make. People *slip* when they try to do the right thing but are not able to accomplish that goal. People make a *mistake* when they accomplish their goal, but that goal was not the right thing to do.[16]

In 1996, a paper by two academic researchers noted the paradox that "usability has yet to greatly influence the security community," but "this lack of impact is not from lack of need, nor from lack of understanding usability's importance in general and to security in particular."[17] That disconnect would continue during the manic period of the dot-com boom because the incentives within the market led companies to focus on developing and selling security products, meaning software. Software has low marginal costs and the opportunity to be the first to market, both of which are highly attractive to entrepreneurs. The promise of new security technologies such as firewalls and network intrusion detection systems was that they could protect all of the users within an organization by isolating them from the threats that existed on the internet.

A concerted focus on what would become known as the study of usable security could arguably be said to have begun in 1999, when an academic paper was published titled "Why Johnny Can't Encrypt."[18] That paper described the results of a usability study of an encryption program named PGP.[19] PGP stands for pretty good privacy.[20] It is a program that can be used to encrypt emails and also to sign them to prove to the recipient that the email was sent by a particular person.[21] PGP took advantage of an innovation in the field of cryptography called public key cryptography, also known as asymmetric cryptography.[22] The public key cryptography scheme solved the problem that had previously existed whereby if two people wanted to communicate securely, they would have to exchange a secret piece of information in advance of that communication. Public key cryptography and its implementation in products such as PGP created the possibility of simple and secure communications for everyone. The marketing materials for PGP made the claim that the "significantly improved graphical user interface makes complex mathematical cryptography accessible for novice users," and the product received highly positive reviews in the trade press.[23]

In the PGP usability study, the researchers gave the test participants ninety minutes to use the PGP software to encrypt and then send an email, an amount of time that should have been more than sufficient to accomplish that task.[24] But the results of that experiment could only be described as catastrophic. Even with ninety minutes, not a single test participant was able to successfully encrypt and then send the email.[25] Seven participants sent an email that was encrypted incorrectly, three thought that they were sending an encrypted email that in reality was not encrypted, and one was unable to encrypt anything at all.[26] The researchers attributed these failures to "inescapably a user interface design problem."[27] They described their belief that effective security required a different set of techniques for user interface design than was being used to create consumer software.[28]

The Johnny paper highlighted the challenge of making security usable for the average person. In 2003, a nonprofit organization named the Computing Research Association published a paper describing "Four Grand Challenges in Trustworthy Computing."[29] Its purpose was to identify the most opportune areas of research within the field of information security. One of the goals the paper identified was to "design new computing systems so that the security and privacy aspects of those systems are understandable and controllable by the average user."[30] The academic community responded to these calls to action by establishing a venue for the publication of research on usability security. The annual Symposium on Usable Privacy and Security (SOUPS) was established in 2005.[31]

SOUPS would serve as one of the principal venues where research on usable security would be published. As a larger group of academics and other researchers began to engage with the topic, they discovered that there were fundamental aspects of usable security that made it a difficult problem.[32] At the heart of these challenges is an apparent contradiction between security and usability. Improving usability involves making a system easier to use, but improving security seems to require making a system less easy to use—by making users perform tasks relating to security that they would not otherwise have to carry out.[33] Computer users want to surf the web, send email, and use software that they have downloaded. Users do not typically set out to perform any specific task with regard to security. Security is at best a secondary goal, and consequently users might be apathetic toward the topic of security or assume that someone else is taking care of security on their behalf.[34]

A second profound problem is that in the physical world, people make conscious choices that increase or decrease their security and privacy, such as by holding a conversation on a delicate matter in private rather than in a busy café where other people can overhear, or by choosing to keep the front door of their house locked rather than unlocked. People can constantly monitor their level of security and alter it according to their perception of the changing circumstances. This is possible because the mental model held by people regarding their security comports to reality. But in the online world, the visible properties that would enable a similar assessment are diminished or nonexistent.[35]

Given these difficulties, it seemed logical to try to simply remove the human in the loop entirely. If users could be unburdened from having to make any security decisions, then they could not possibly make the wrong decision.[36] This was a similar idea to the secure-by-default approach that Microsoft employed in their software security efforts. However, Microsoft knew that they could not remove *every* security decision from users—only the decisions relating to the initial configuration of the software. Once the software was installed and had been configured, it would begin to be used, and it was not possible to anticipate every future decision that the user might need to make. Unless the human user could be replaced entirely with a computer program, there would always be decisions to be made, and those decisions could affect security.[37]

The technologies that the average person used on the internet were email and the web. Whether he realized it, when a person made the decision to open an email or not and when he made the decision to click on a web link or not, he was making security decisions. Those decisions could be exploited by a hacker, and this would be demonstrated by a new and highly effective attack technique called phishing.

A phishing attack begins with a hacker sending an email to the person that he wishes to target. The email is designed by the hacker to compel the person to take some kind of action, such as clicking on a web link in the body of the email or opening a file that is attached to the email.[38] In order to accomplish this, the hacker might entice the person into carrying out those actions by playing on the recipient's fears, such as by making the phishing email appear to come from a financial institution and suggesting that a suspicious transaction was detected. Or the hacker might play on other emotions, such as by making the email state that the person has won a prize or by using a tempting name for a file attachment such as "salaries." When the person clicks the web link in the email or opens the file attached to the email, the security of his computer becomes compromised. This can be accomplished by the hacker exploiting a vulnerability in the person's web browser.[39] Another common type of phishing involves a hacker luring a person using a phishing email to a website that appears to be legitimate but is in fact a fraudulent website created by the hacker. The fraudulent website asks the person to enter his username and password, and if the person does so, then the hacker can use that username and password to connect to the real website.[40]

Phishing was described as a new type of attack in 2003 and rose to prominence around 2005.[41] The number of phishing websites rose dramatically within a short period. A research group detected five thousand new phishing websites created during August 2005, then seven thousand new sites created just three months later during December.[42]

The origins of the term *phishing* reach back as early as 1995, when fishing attacks were employed by hackers against users of America Online, a US-based internet service provider.[43] Over time, "fishing" became "phishing" in a phonetic transformation that is popular with hackers.[44]

The explosive growth in phishing attacks that began in the mid-2000s was the result of various trends. Firewalls blocked hackers from attacking individual computers. Software security efforts had made vulnerabilities in software such as computer operating systems more difficult to find and exploit. But emails passed through firewalls, and a phishing attack does not need to employ any vulnerabilities at all if the victim can be convinced to enter his username and password into a fraudulent website. The task of identifying phishing emails before they reach users is also a difficult problem for organizations. If the filtering is too tight, legitimate emails are blocked, but if the filtering is too lax, phishing emails can reach users. Phishing attacks therefore required relatively little skill and relatively low effort in comparison to breaking through a firewall or finding an exploitable vulnerability in Microsoft Windows. The choice for hackers was to either try to compete with Microsoft's professional programmers or to trick a person into clicking on a web link within a phishing email, and the latter was much easier than the former.

Phishing also created an economy of scale for hackers. Hackers could essentially send an unlimited number of phishing emails, and because of this, they would eventually find success. Several different studies have attempted to identify the success rate of phishing attacks with varying results.[45] But even if just a small percentage of the recipients of a phishing email are fooled, this can translate into a large number of incidents for an organization.[46] The law of large numbers says that a small proportion of a large number will itself be a large number, and so hackers can send millions of emails and likely be successful on tens of thousands of occasions.[47]

Phishing became the perfect battleground for usable security because every user who received an email now had to decide if the email was legitimate or not. Hackers had to create emails and websites that fooled people, and user interface designers and usable security researchers had to create user interfaces and security measures that could defeat those phishing attempts.

The first efforts to defeat phishing focused on "browser indicators."[48] This was information that was presented to the user in their web browser in an attempt to enable them to realize that a web page was not authentic. The idea of the Uniform Resource Locator (URL) is central to the function of the web. The URL for a website such as http://bank.com contains a domain name—in this case, bank.com. To pretend to be that bank, a hacker might register a different domain name such as banc.com or bank.securelogin.com and then include that domain name in the web link within a phishing email. The recipient of the email would need to determine whether the domain name was the legitimate domain name for the bank or a fraud, and browser indicators were intended to help the user make that decision.

In theory, the SSL protocol and the underlying public key infrastructure that had been developed during the early years of the dot-com boom could enable users to determine that they were connected to a legitimate website. In practice, the ability to make that determination relied to a large degree on users having an understanding of those security technologies, which is something that the average user would be very unlikely to know.[49] Web browsers attempted to abstract the complexity of SSL into a visual indicator that the user could understand, such as the presence or absence of a padlock icon near to the URL of the website within the user interface of the web browser. But users still needed to know to look for that padlock. Hackers could also simply place the padlock icon onto their phishing web page in order to confuse users.[50]

These problems with browser indicators led usable security researchers and commercial companies to create plug-ins that could be installed into web browsers. Those plug-ins would present information to the user to help him distinguish between legitimate websites and phishing websites.[51] For example, eBay created a browser plug-in that would inform users when they were connected to the legitimate eBay website.[52] But when those web browser plug-ins were tested, they were found to be ineffective for a large percentage of users, even in cases where the user being tested was primed to pay attention.[53] When the test subjects in these studies were asked why they did not follow the guidance that was being provided to them by the plug-in, they would provide rationalizations such as thinking that a phishing website pretending to be the Yahoo! website in Brazil might be legitimate because Yahoo! might have just opened a new branch office there.[54]

If browser indicators and plug-ins were inadequate to prevent phishing, then perhaps users could be given additional training that could increase their ability to recognize phishing emails. A simulated phishing email could be sent to users, and if users clicked the web link in the email, instead of the security of their computer being compromised they would be presented with a message that provided guidance regarding how to better spot that type of phishing email in the future.[55] Companies that offered this service began to form, and organizations began to use them to train their users. Even simply giving users training materials to read was effective in reducing their susceptibility to phishing.[56] The challenge for such initiatives was how to train users to recognize phishing emails in general rather than training users to recognize specific phishing techniques that hackers could simply change.

Hackers employ phishing attacks in two different ways. If a hacker wishes to target a specific person, then he can tailor the phishing email and the phishing website specifically to that person, such as by addressing the person by name. This approach makes the attack more likely to succeed and is called spear phishing.[57] In contrast to the targeted nature of spear phishing, if a hacker wishes to cast a wide net and ensnare as many victims as possible, the phishing email can be written in a broad way.[58] This type of phishing in which malicious emails are sent to many recipients is similar in approach to other online scams that use email. Many people have received implausible emails that claim to have been sent from temporarily inconvenienced Nigerian princes looking for a Westerner who is willing to accept a generous commission for helping to move funds through the banking system.[59] In these types of scam, the victim is not lured to a website. Instead, they are convinced to provide their banking information in a subsequent email exchange so that their electronic funds can then be stolen.[60]

The Nigerian genre of email fraud is common, with one study finding that 51 percent of email-based scams mention Nigeria and a further 31 percent mention Senegal, Ghana, or another West African country.[61] Why would the scammers behind these schemes use the same Nigerian theme so frequently, especially since "Nigerian scam" is so easily Googled? The answer is that the scammers experience many of the same challenges as the people who are working in the field of information security and trying to stop them. Stefan Axelsson had shown that if the number of false alarms generated by an intrusion detection system becomes too high, the system becomes unusable because too much time is spent responding to those false alarms. Email-based scams have the same structural problem. If the person who responds to a scam email cannot be convinced in the resulting email exchange to hand over his bank account details, this imposes an opportunity cost on the scammer. In other words, it wastes the scammer's time. It is therefore in the interests of the scammer to select the most gullible people with which to engage. By using the extremely well-known and easily identifiable Nigerian scam genre, the scammer can effectively identify the tiny subset of the population who are so gullible as to not first research the topic using a search engine.[62]

It is the combination of two relatively modern technologies, email and the web, that enables phishing to exist. But usable security issues have been present since the use of the earliest security technologies, with the most ubiquitous example of such a technology being the humble password.

Passwords play a central role in the experience of using computers. A password is the near-universal means by which access is gained to computers and websites. Mobile devices such as cell phones and tablets typically use a personal identification number (PIN) rather than a conventional password, but a PIN is itself a type of password. Passwords are an authentication mechanism.[63] Authentication is the task of validating a person's identity to enable her to prove she is who she claims to be.[64] Authentication is typically the first action that takes place when a person begins to use a computer, the act of "logging in."

Passwords are the overwhelmingly dominant method used to carry out authentication because they have several useful properties. Passwords are simple to understand, easy to use, can be memorized, are easily stored by writing them down, and can be shared with another person by simply telling them what the password is.

The first use of passwords in the modern era was in time-sharing mainframe systems, such as in the Compatible Time-Sharing System at MIT in 1961.[65] The purpose of passwords in those early computers was to ensure that each user did not use more than her allotted amount of computer time.[66] But even in those early days, security problems relating to passwords were reported. Those problems included users guessing each other's passwords and leaks of the master password file where passwords were stored.[67] In the security evaluation of Multics that was carried out by the US Air Force in 1974, passwords were identified as a notably weak aspect of that operating system.[68] Unix followed Multics, and Unix implemented its own password scheme. The Unix approach to passwords was documented in a paper by Ken Thompson, one of the cocreators of Unix, and Robert Morris, the father of Robert T. Morris.[69] In the Unix password scheme, passwords are encrypted with a one-way cryptographic hashing algorithm.[70] A hash can only be generated in one direction, from plaintext to ciphertext, meaning from unencrypted form to encrypted form.[71] Given the ciphertext of a password, hackers cannot simply reverse the algorithm to identify the plaintext; they can only repeatedly guess what the password might be and then encrypt each guess and compare the two ciphertexts in an attempt to identify a match.[72] Such a scheme is weakened when users pick easily guessed passwords, however. One of the methods by which the Morris worm was able to spread from computer to computer was by cracking passwords.

Morris and Thompson describe in their paper how every user in Unix has to select a password that conforms to certain rules. If the user enters a password that is comprised of only alphabetic characters and is shorter than six characters or is more complex but shorter than five characters, then the password program would ask him to enter a stronger password.[73] The paper also described the results of the authors' testing of the strength of passwords selected by Unix users. They found that even with the password rules that they had implemented within Unix, users tended to pick weak and easily guessed passwords. Morris and Thompson also experimented with creative methods of password cracking, such as by testing passwords against all valid car license plates in New Jersey, where Thompson's employer, Bell Labs, was based.[74]

In 1985, the US Defense Department published their Green Book, which described the strategies that they recommended for defending against password cracking.[75] Like the Orange Book, the Green Book was named after the color of the cover on the official printed copies. The Green Book provided recommendations regarding password complexity, such as the required length of a password and the characters that should be allowed to be used in a password. It also attempted to eliminate the risk of users selecting weak passwords entirely by recommending that "all passwords should be machine-generated using an algorithm."[76] Because passwords would be generated by an algorithm, the user would have to use a different password for each computer to which she had access. The authors believed that forcing users to use a different password on every computer would remove the risk of one computer being compromised and the passwords from that computer being cracked and then used to compromise other computers.

Following the Green Book, the National Institute of Standards and Technology (NIST) published their password usage guidelines.[77] NIST kept the password complexity requirements recommended in the Green Book but dropped the requirement for user passwords to be generated by an algorithm. Instead, NIST recommended that users "shall be instructed to use a password selected from all acceptable passwords at random, if possible, or to select one that is not related to their personal identity, history or environment."[78] On the surface, this guidance from NIST appears pragmatic since having all users remember computer-generated passwords was not practical. But it was in fact a catastrophic error. The Green Book assumed that complex passwords would be generated by an algorithm, but the NIST guidance transferred that task to the user. This meant that the user was now responsible for devising a different complex password for each of the computers to which she had an account. This has been described as being the equivalent of asking a person to "pick a password that you can't remember and do not write it down."[79]

The availability of relatively inexpensive personal computers and the increasing use of desktop computers within businesses was increasing the number of computers used by the average person. During the dot-com boom, the number of useful websites also increased dramatically, and these factors combined to greatly increase the number of passwords that each person had to remember. Remembering different complex passwords was infeasible for anything other than a small collection, and this led to users reusing the same password across multiple computers and multiple websites.[80] One study on password reuse showed that the average user had six passwords that are frequently reused.[81] A second study found that between 43 percent and 51 percent of users reused the same password across multiple websites.[82]

Reusing passwords was only one of the coping mechanisms employed by users as a result of strict password policies. A password policy that requires passwords to be changed every month can be defeated by essentially using the same password each month but slightly modified each time that a change is required. For example, to conform with a password policy that states that all passwords must be at least six characters long, must contain at least one capital letter, must contain at least one number, and must be changed once per month, a user can choose "Password1" in the first month, "Password2" in the second month, and so on.[83] Requiring that a user put a special character in their password such as "!" or "@" would seem to be a good way to increase the entropy of a password, but using "p@ssword" instead of "password" does not add substantial entropy and is the kind of transformation that can be easily guessed by a hacker.[84]

A common recommendation for a method that can be used to generate a password that will conform to a strict password policy is to create a mnemonic password. In a mnemonic password, the first letter from each word in a sentence is combined. A line from a poem such as "Things fall apart; the center cannot hold" could become the password "TFA;tcch." But research has shown that mnemonic passwords are only slightly more resistant to guessing than other passwords because hackers can create dictionaries of possible mnemonic passwords using phrases found on the internet.[85] After all, as Sherlock Holmes said, "What one man can invent, another can discover."

The research into passwords further showed that the fundamental question of what constitutes a "strong" password has not yet been answered. A password that contains an uppercase letter and a special character such as "P@ssword" is clearly easier to guess than a password that simply uses a string of random lowercase letters.[86] A password such as "Dav1d95" is more difficult to guess than "7491024" in the abstract, but if the user's middle name is David and he is known to have been born in 1995, then it might actually be more straightforward to guess.[87] For these reasons, the strength of a password and the likelihood that it can be guessed are not strongly correlated, even though users typically believe that a more complex password will make them more secure.[88]

Although passwords are by their nature simple and easy to use, the need to use complex passwords on different computers and websites can create a frustrating overall experience. A person trying to log in to a website might first try to remember which of his five or six passwords he used to register on that site, perhaps by trying each password in turn, and then finally resort to using a password reset mechanism. As these usability and security problems with passwords became increasingly apparent, usable security researchers began to try and devise alternative technologies and techniques that could be used to authenticate users and thereby replace passwords. The stakes for these efforts were high, with the potential to improve security and the everyday life of hundreds of millions of password users.

Graphical passwords are based on the idea of having the user authenticate by selecting from a sequence of images rather than typing letters on a keyboard.[89] The user might select from, say, a sequence of human faces or pictures of animals. The problem with graphical passwords is that they are essentially a proxy for many of the same underlying issues that exist with text-based passwords. A user might be just as likely to pick an easily guessable sequence of images as to pick an easily guessable password. Because of this, graphical passwords were found to provide only minimal advantages over passwords and only in certain regards.[90]

Two-factor authentication schemes grant access based on the combination of an initial factor such as a password (something you know) and an additional second factor such as the possession of a mobile phone (something you have).[91] The idea of "something you know and something you have" is compelling because it solves one of the fundamental problems with traditional passwords, which is that if a hacker obtains someone's password, he can use it to access the victim's account. In the case of two-factor authentication, if the hacker does not also have the second factor, such as the user's mobile phone, the compromised password alone is not sufficient to gain access. The challenge with two-factor authentication is that there are now two things that the user needs to possess in order to successfully authenticate. Instead of being "something you know and something you have," the joke is that two-factor authentication is based on "something you've forgotten and something you've lost."

Biometrics such as facial recognition systems and fingerprint scanning offer the possibility of using "something you are" as means to authenticate.[92] These technologies have become commonly used in cell phones with the use of fingerprint readers and facial recognition software. The obvious disadvantage with biometric schemes from a security perspective is that a person can be forced to place a finger onto a biometric device.

The technologies that were proposed as replacements for passwords such as graphical passwords and biometrics typically provided better security than passwords, but this was to be expected since the researchers who worked to invent them were usually researchers who were interested in improving security. But it was not enough to only improve security; improved security was a necessary but not sufficient condition. A successful replacement for passwords would have to deliver the same useful properties as passwords and also be able to be used in all of the different situations in which passwords are currently used. None of the alternative authentication technologies that have been proposed are able to satisfy all of these requirements. From the perspective of the vendors of computer operating systems and website administrators, if they decided to switch from using passwords to using one of the alternative authentication technologies, this would impose a burden on their customers, who might move to a competitor as a result.

This stubborn reality has not stopped public proclamations that the era of the password is over. Bill Gates declared in 2004 that "the password is dead"—a statement that in retrospect could not have been more wrong.[93] Every attempt to provide a widely adopted replacement for passwords has been unsuccessful. Instead, passwords have become increasingly entrenched as the dominant mechanism for authentication.[94] Two-factor authentication is widely used for websites, but two-factor authentication is an enhancement to traditional passwords. Biometric authentication is used in smartphones, but if biometric authentication fails, it is common to default to an underlying PIN.

The failure of the usable security field to replace passwords has been described as a "major embarrassment," and usable security researchers in the round have been criticized for failing to consider real-world constraints.[95] Don Norman, a professor at MIT who specializes in design and usability, has said that "academics get paid for being clever, not for being right." His statement can be applied as a succinct critique of the work by usable security researchers to replace passwords. Passwords continue to be with us because, to paraphrase Winston Churchill, they are the worst form of authentication except for all the others. Because passwords have not yet been replaced, the argument could be made that in many situations they are best fit for the authentication requirements that exist.[96] The use of passwords enabled the web to grow to the point where billions of users can access millions of password-protected websites. Passwords are a simple and low-cost method that websites can use to authenticate users. By implementing passwords, websites can authenticate users while guaranteeing accessibility using any kind of web browser. The internet might not have been able to grow to its current size and influence without the benefits provided by passwords.[97]

Recent research on passwords has focused on correcting the hodgepodge of contradictory advice that has accumulated over the decades and on recasting the conventional wisdom regarding passwords and password policies. One of the key findings within that research is that there has been too much of an emphasis on password strength.[98] A strong password that conforms to a complicated password policy can still be straightforward to guess for other reasons. And even if a strong password is difficult to guess, this is not necessarily a useful property. If the list of encrypted passwords from a system is obtained by a hacker, strong passwords do make it more difficult for the hacker to crack those encrypted passwords. But if the hacker is already able to obtain that list of encrypted passwords from a system, they are unlikely to need to crack those passwords. Having a strong password also does not protect against phishing, and successful phishing attacks are much more common than those cases where a hacker is able to access a list of encrypted passwords.[99] Organizations should instead concentrate on ensuring that their list of encrypted passwords is not compromised.[100] If an organization does detect that their password list has been compromised, they should quickly reset all passwords so that users have to select new passwords.[101]

Strong passwords for websites are ineffective where the security of the user's computer has already been compromised. In that scenario, a hacker can record everything that is typed by the user, revealing the password no matter how strong it might be. A website does not have to require strong passwords in order to stop hackers from successfully guessing user passwords. If a website is configured to lock out or pause access for a user after three failed login attempts, a weak password with only twenty bits of entropy such as a six-digit PIN is enough to make password guessing against a single user account unrealistic.[102]

The historical advice to not reuse passwords across different websites is no longer useful, given the number of accounts held by the average person. More pragmatic advice is to avoid reusing passwords for important accounts but not to worry unduly about reusing passwords on accounts that have little value to a hacker.[103] The people who represent the exception to this rule are public individuals such as politicians and celebrities who require more protection than private individuals.

Password expiration policies that require a password to be changed after a certain amount of time, such as every month, cause many problems. Such policies make it more likely that users will forget their password, causing them to get locked out of their account. The advantage of an expiration policy is that it narrows the window of opportunity that an attacker has to use a compromised password, but a study shows that a hacker who knows an old password for a user can guess the new password selected by that user 41 percent of the time.[104]

These findings demonstrated that it was useful to broaden the analysis of security problems beyond the technology alone. It was possible that by further broadening the analysis, an even more useful set of discoveries could be made.

The person who would play the pivotal role in opening the door to that larger world was Ross Anderson, a professor of security engineering at the University of Cambridge.[105] As a child, Anderson came across a book in a local library that described how a teacher could use ideas from mathematics to inspire schoolchildren. At that moment he became determined to become a mathematician.[106] He was accepted to study mathematics at the University of Cambridge, but in his second year he realized that some of his fellow students could live and breathe mathematics in a way that he could not.[107] He shifted the focus of his studies, and in his third year he began to study the history and philosophy of science.[108] After graduating from Cambridge, he spent a year traveling to Europe, Africa, and the Middle East.[109] He then worked in computing but in his early thirties returned to Cambridge to study for a PhD.[110] His PhD thesis advisor was a computer scientist named Roger Needham, who had many accomplishments in the field of information security, including coauthoring the Needham-Schroeder security protocol.[111] Needham-Schroeder is used in a popular piece of security software named Kerberos that was developed at MIT and used to deliver authentication in computer networks.[112] One of Needham's sayings was that "good research is done with a shovel, not with tweezers."[113] He advised Anderson that "when you find yourself down on your hands and knees with tweezers picking up the crumbs left by two hundred mathematicians that trampled the place flat already, you're in the wrong place. Leave that to the guys from the University of Mudflats and go and find a big pile of muck, a big pile of steaming muck, and drive a shovel into it."[114] Anderson was primed by this advice to look for entirely new ways to address the problems of the day.

In 2000, Anderson was attending a security conference in California known as the Oakland conference, and he began to hold a conversation with an economist named Hal Varian.[115] Varian was a local to Oakland because he was a professor at the University of California, Berkeley. Varian was interested in the question of why people did not seem to purchase antivirus software. Anderson was able to provide him with the answer, which was that people used to pay for antivirus software when viruses would delete data, but since the mid-1990s, hackers had become less interested in deleting data and more interested in using infected computers to launch denial-of-service attacks or to send spam emails.[116] When a hacker compromises a large number of computers and uses them en masse, those computers are said to form a botnet. Because of this new way of using infected computers, consumers had less of an economic incentive to prevent their own computer from becoming infected since the actions of the botnet would probably not affect them directly. A person might spend a hundred dollars to avoid his own data being deleted but might not pay a single dollar to avoid a third party from being harmed.[117]

Varian recognized this situation as an example of the tragedy of the commons, which is a concept created by the British economist William Forster Lloyd in 1833.[118] The classic example of the tragedy of the commons involves a village where farmers live. Those farmers each let their sheep graze in the fields surrounding the village. If a farmer adds another sheep to his flock, then the farmer gets the benefit of an additional sheep that can create wool, and the quantity of grass that the other sheep can eat declines only very slightly. But because any of the farmers can add any number of additional sheep to their flock, the fields surrounding the village turn into a dust bowl.[119] Anderson and Varian had started their conversation while driving back to the conference after visiting a restaurant. They became so captivated by this line of thinking that after arriving in the parking lot for the conference they continued their conversation for an hour while sitting in the car, missing most of the drinks reception that was held that night.[120]

What Anderson and Varian had identified was a key insight regarding the importance of economics to information security and specifically the role of externalities. In economics, externalities are the side effects that are felt by third parties. Externalities can be positive or negative. Scientific research creates positive externalities because scientific discoveries build on each other to a greater good. A power plant that produces environmental pollution creates negative externalities. The owner of the power plant does not experience the full costs of their actions—they profit from them. In a similar way, an individual who does not use antivirus software on their personal computer can create negative externalities for other people on the internet. It is other people who will experience the spam emails or suffer the denial-of-service attacks that are sent from the botnet that is able to infect the person's computer. A botnet named Reactor Mailer that was made up of at least two hundred thousand infected computers was found to have sent more than 180 billion spam emails per day.[121] The reason that hackers use botnets to send such a vast number of spam emails is that quantity is the only way to make the spam business profitable. This was demonstrated when a group of researchers were able to infiltrate a botnet and change the spam emails that were being sent so that they linked to a website that was controlled by the researchers.[122] The researchers could then see how many people would actually complete the sale and buy whatever was being advertised. They found that from 350 million emails sent, only 20 sales were made, which is a conversion rate of 0.00001 percent.[123]

A regulatory solution that the villagers could have employed to stop their grazing fields from turning into a dust bowl would have been for them to create a law where each farmer is permitted to own only a certain number of sheep.[124] For the problem of botnets, the solution was not so clear. Placing liability on the hackers who infect computers to create botnets is unrealistic, given that those hackers are difficult to track down and may live in other countries. Putting the responsibility on the operating system vendor would be the next obvious place, but operating system vendors such as Microsoft have been investing heavily in security for decades and it is not clear what further marginal improvements in security can be made. The method by which computers become infected is also much more likely to be as a result of a hacker exploiting the user, such as with a phishing attack, rather than through the exploitation of vulnerabilities in the operating system. Computer operating systems such as Windows and Unix provide tremendous flexibility to users, who are given the ability to carry out essentially any actions that they wish. If a user decides to perform an action that causes the security of his computer to become compromised, it would seem unfair to make the vendor of the operating system that is installed on that computer responsible for the user's decision.

But making the individual owners of computers responsible for installing and maintaining security tools such as antivirus software would be difficult because many users do not have the sufficient knowledge and technical skills. Attempting to solve the problem by focusing on the hackers, the operating system vendors, and the users all appear to be dead ends. But there is a fourth possibility. Internet Service Providers (ISPs) provide internet access to customers. ISPs are therefore in an ideal location to be able to monitor the network traffic being sent to and from personal computers.[125] If an ISP detects that a computer has been infected and is being used to send spam emails or participate in a denial-of-service attack, the ISP can take actions such as temporarily disconnecting the computer from the internet or blocking the network traffic.[126] ISPs can also use their customer information to identify who owns a computer and communicate with that person, which other people on the internet cannot easily do.[127] This was the type of thinking that provided a fresh outlook on long-standing problems within the field of information security.

Anderson wrote what is considered to be the first paper on the topic of security economics. The paper is titled "Why Information Security Is Hard—An Economic Perspective" and was published in December 2001.[128] In the paper, Anderson describes how ideas from economics such as externalities can be used to explain various problems in information security. After the paper was published, he helped to organize the first Workshop on the Economics of Information Security (WEIS), which was held in June 2002.[129] As Anderson and other researchers began to apply concepts from economics to security problems, some fascinating and useful discoveries began to be made.

During the dot-com boom, a number of for-profit businesses were established that would sell so-called trust certifications to companies. The companies that received certification would be permitted to display a badge on their website to indicate that they met certain privacy and safety standards. The purpose of receiving and displaying the certification was to create more trust in the minds of the people who were browsing the site, who would see the badge and then perhaps be more inclined to feel that they could safely make a purchase from the site. Benjamin Edelman from Harvard Business School examined online trust certifications and found a hidden and powerful case of adverse selection.[130] Adverse selection occurs where participants in a market receive asymmetric information. Edelman looked at the security and privacy of sites that had received a trust certification from a certification company named TRUSTe. TRUSTe advertised itself as "the number one privacy brand" and claimed that its "Certified Privacy Seal" was "recognized globally by consumers, businesses, and regulators as demonstrating privacy best practices."[131] Edelman compared sites that were TRUSTe certified to sites that were not certified. He found that sites with the TRUSTe certification were more than *twice* as likely to be untrustworthy compared to uncertified sites.[132] Two percent of websites without TRUSTe certification were malicious, but 5 percent of websites with TRUSTe certification were malicious.[133] What was happening could be explained by adverse selection. If a certification process, such as the one operated by TRUSTe, did not effectively measure the security of a site, then weak sites had more of an incentive to sign up for certification than strong sites.[134] A site that was untrustworthy could pretend to be trustworthy and would do so for the same reasons that a con artist might wear a Rolex watch. TRUSTe would later agree to settle charges from the US Federal Trade Commission that they deceived customers as well as misrepresented themselves as a nonprofit organization, and paid a $200,000 fine.[135]

Another valuable insight came from the application of economic modeling. In 2004, Hal Varian published a paper based on the work of the economist Jack Hirshleifer, a professor at the University of California, Los Angeles, who had worked at RAND for several years.[136] In his paper, Varian asks the reader to imagine a city with a perimeter wall, where the security of the city depends on the height of that wall. If all of the families that live in the city join together to build the wall, the city's security can be said to depend on the sum of efforts—how high they can make the wall by working as a collective. But if the responsibility for building the wall is spread out among the families who are each assigned a different segment of the wall to build, the security depends on the weakest link—the height of the shortest segment. A third possible scenario is where the city can have multiple walls with each wall being built by an individual family. The security of the city now depends on the best shot—the tallest wall.

The economic model described in Varian's paper showed that sum of efforts provides the best security, with weakest link providing the worst.[137] The same model can be used to analyze the task of building secure software. Software security depends on the weakest link where there is the possibility that a programmer might inadvertently introduce a security vulnerability. There is also a dependency on the sum of efforts where testers have the responsibility to find security flaws. Software security also depends on the best shot where security hinges on the effort of a single person such as the security architect of the software. The lesson for organizations that are attempting to improve the security of their software is to hire fewer, better programmers, hire as many people as possible to test the code, and hire the most skilled security architects to lead projects that they can find.[138]

Shortly after the first Workshop on the Economics of Information Security was held, Daniel Kahneman won the Nobel Prize in Economics for his work on the new field of behavioral economics.[139] (His coauthor, Amos Tversky, died before the prize was awarded, and the Nobel Prize is not awarded posthumously.) Behavioral economics sits conceptually between psychology and economics. It involves the examination of the psychological reasons for why people make systematic errors in their behavior when participating in economic markets. The person, the agent, in classical economics is assumed to be a rational actor whose preferences do not change. Behavioral economics demonstrated that people are not fully rational and that their preferences *do* in fact change. In cases where there is uncertainty, people can be observed to fall back on existing heuristics, meaning rules of thumb. People are also vulnerable to cognitive biases that cause their decisions to separate from what would be considered the economic optimum. Behavioral economics was more speculative than traditional economics; it depended on both the current understanding of economics being correct and the current understanding of psychology being correct. But it held the promise of generating new insights into human behavior—new insights that could illuminate information security problems.[140]

In practical terms, hackers were already far ahead of security researchers in their application of psychology. Phishing and spam emails attempt to lure victims by appealing to base emotions such as fear and greed. Social engineering attacks prey on naivete and psychological inclinations such as the impulse to help someone in need. In Japan, one online scam involves presenting the user who is browsing a pornographic website with a pop-up that states that the user has entered into a binding contract that must be paid. Not coincidentally, the amount that is demanded is typically around ¥50,000, which is normally the amount of monthly pocket money that a Japanese salaryman receives from his household budget.[141] This online scam is found only in Japan because it preys on aspects of the psychology of Japanese people, namely their respect for authority and their desire to avoid embarrassment.[142] Psychology is used in this way by scammers and hackers to craft better attacks, but it can also be used to provide insights into why computer security fails.

When Microsoft ended support for their Windows XP operating system, they publicly announced that no more security patches would be created. But four years after that announcement, the market share for Windows XP was still 6.6 percent.[143] Some of those Windows XP users were no doubt entirely unaware of the lack of new security patches and some others would be unable to afford an upgrade to a more current operating system, but some portion of users must have made the conscious choice to continue to use an operating system that was now insecure.[144] This behavior can be explained by considering psychological factors. An overabundance of advice on security—much of it conflicting and much of it too complicated for the average person to understand—can lead to security fatigue.[145] When discussing security with researchers, users described their feelings using words such as "irritating" and "frustrating" and said they were "tired" and "overwhelmed."[146]

Security fatigue can lead people to throw up their hands in defeat or fall back on flawed mental models. The majority of home computers are operated by users who have little or no security knowledge and who have never had occasion to obtain detailed information about how to defend themselves against computer hacking.[147] What information they do know about security they have likely learned from incidental sources such as web pages, news articles, and personal experiences conveyed to them by friends and family members.[148] As a result, the security decisions made by those users are not made on the basis of sound knowledge regarding information security but rather on "folk models" they have constructed inside their minds using the information they have encountered.[149] Those models provide them with the basis for their decision making.[150] In investigating this, people were discovered to be motivated to take actions to protect themselves against the threats that they believe to exist and that they believe are likely to target them. One study found that if a person believes that hackers are teenage troublemakers, that person is more likely to install security software onto his personal computer to try and keep them out.[151] But if a person believes that hackers are criminals, that person has more of a tendency to believe that he is not important or rich enough to be targeted by those criminals and therefore not make the effort to install security software.[152] A second study identified a similar finding—that some people believe that hackers target "interesting people" and "important computers" such as bank computers or computers owned by major companies.[153] They believed that they were unlikely to be targeted by a hacker because they were normal people who were not "important," "interesting," or "challenging" enough to hack.[154] People who actively seek out information about computer security from informal sources are likely to be exposed to information regarding hacking and how to defend against that hacking but not who the hackers are or why they carry out attacks.[155] Conversely, people who encounter information on security organically are likely to learn information regarding the different kinds of attackers but not how to protect against the types of attack employed by those hackers.[156] If a person has access to only informal sources of information about computer security, then he would need to employ multiple sources of such information in order to get a well-rounded view.[157]

But even in the case where people can acquire good information regarding security that they can understand and act on appropriately, a further finding from the fields of economics and psychology might make those efforts irrelevant. This is the theory of risk compensation, sometimes referred to as behavioral adaptation or risk homeostasis. It is the idea that after a safety or security measure is introduced to an activity, the people participating in that activity will tend to reset the level of risk to the previous level. The introduction of the security measure does not improve the level of security; the level stays the same because the users redistribute the risk around the totality of the system.[158]

Although the idea is counterintuitive, it is borne out by a number of real-world examples. If a skydiver is knocked unconscious during free fall, she will die. That is, unless she is wearing a special device called a CYPRES (Cybernetic Parachute Release System). A CYPRES can detect that a skydiver is still in free fall at a preset altitude, usually 750 feet, at which time it will automatically deploy the skydiver's reserve parachute. Even if the skydiver is unconscious, she will likely survive the subsequent landing under the open reserve parachute canopy. The CYPRES has been widely adopted by skydivers and has saved many lives. Curiously, however, if the number of deaths in skydiving caused by not deploying a parachute is displayed on a graph alongside the number of deaths for other reasons, there is an almost-perfect inverse relationship.[159] After correcting for the number of skydivers participating in the sport over time, the total number of deaths in skydiving can be seen to be roughly the same for each calendar year, but the types of deaths have changed.[160] This result is anticipated by risk compensation theory because it predicts that after a safety measure such as the CYPRES is introduced, skydivers will compensate by taking greater risks in other aspects of the sport.[161]

In the United Kingdom, a law was passed that made the wearing of seat belts mandatory. But after the enactment of that law, the number of fatalities resulting from car accidents actually increased, including the number of pedestrians that were struck by a car and killed.[162] Risk compensation theory suggests that drivers feel safer when wearing a seat belt and therefore drive faster. Arguably, making the use of seat belts mandatory transferred the risk from those people who were participating in the less socially desirable act of driving cars to those who were participating in the more socially desirable act of walking.[163]

Antilock brakes enable cars to brake more aggressively. A study examined the effect of the installation of antilock brakes in cars used by taxi drivers in Oslo, Norway.[164] It found that after antilock brakes had been installed, the taxi drivers drove much closer to the car in front of them, thereby canceling out the safety benefits that the antilock brakes provided.[165] A second study on antilock brakes was carried out in Munich, Germany.[166] Two groups of cars were monitored, with the cars in each group being identical other than the presence or absence of antilock brakes. Taxi drivers were randomly assigned to either a car that had antilock brakes installed or a car that did not. After three years, the number of accidents involving the cars was collected, and it was found that the group of cars with antilock brakes was involved in more accidents.[167]

These studies suggest that attempts to reduce risk will be frustrated if users believe that their current level of risk is already acceptable. In economics, the term *moral hazard* is used to describe this risk compensation effect. When people do not bear the direct cost of their actions, they behave differently to the situation in which they would experience those costs. Insurance companies account for this effect in their models because people with insurance tend to take greater risks. There are many examples of cases where a security measure was relied on too heavily, creating a false sense of security. Firewalls and the perimeter model of security were criticized as leading to the neglect of the security of individual computers.[168] A lamp used in mining called the Davy lamp was described as having saved the lives of miners because it operated at a temperature below the ignition point of methane. But the lamp enabled mining operations to extend deeper underground, which led to an increase in the number of deaths.[169]

The application of ideas from economics and psychology to the study of information security had generated important insights in the areas of externalities, incentives, and mental models of security. But it had also opened a Pandora's box that revealed security could never be achieved by adding more security technologies: more cryptography, more firewalls, more intrusion detection systems, and such like. There were more fundamental challenges that had to be overcome relating to the way that users perceived security and how and why they made security decisions.

It was perhaps ineluctable that the study of information security would make its way to the point where it had to consider these aspects. The linguist Noam Chomsky has said, "Take, say, physics, which restricts itself to extremely simple questions. If a molecule becomes too complex, they hand it over to the chemists. If it becomes too complex for them, they hand it to biologists. And if the system is too complex for them, they hand it to psychologists."[170]

The "Why Johnny Can't Encrypt" paper that marked the beginning of the study of usable security had shown that email encryption software was too difficult for a normal person to use, but its real contribution had been to show that there was a disconnect between the capabilities of software developers and information security practitioners and how they saw the world versus the capabilities of ordinary users and how they viewed the world.[171] Ideally, Johnny would never need to "encrypt"—to carry out various tasks in order to acquire security. This could be accomplished if computers could be made to protect users transparently without any human intervention. But computers are general-purpose devices. Users want the flexibility to be able to tell the computer exactly what to do in order for their specific needs to be met, and it is the very nature of email and the web that those technologies require users to make choices when they use them.

The usable security researchers tried to make it possible for Johnny to encrypt, but they failed. One paper even suggested that Johnny might *never* be able to encrypt—that there should be a consideration of the upper limits on the cognitive abilities of the typical person when dealing with tasks relating to security.[172] Fatalistically, risk compensation theory predicts that even if Johnny was able to encrypt, he would compensate for that newfound ability by introducing more security risk elsewhere. This is a bleak outlook, but there is another way of thinking about Johnny's plight. A security researcher named Cormac Herley has made the case that it is rational for Johnny to ignore the protestations of security experts recommending that he encrypt.[173] Herley's argument is that the security guidance provided to users has the benefit of possibly stopping hacking attempts, but carrying out that security guidance imposes substantial costs on users, and in the aggregate those costs outweigh the benefits.[174] This is especially true where the costs of a successful hack are not borne by the user but instead create an externality. People need not worry unduly about online scams because banks typically refund any losses to the victims.[175] The Federal Reserve in the United States limits the liability of consumers in cases of fraud to $50, but in practice, banks and other financial institutions such as credit unions offer guarantees of zero liability.[176]

If every person who receives a suspicious email spends a minute carefully reading and analyzing the web link within the body of the email to determine if it is a phishing attack, the cost in terms of the time spent would be orders of magnitude greater than all losses created by phishing.[177] There are approximately 180 million adults who go online in the United States. If their time is worth on average twice the minimum wage, then one minute of their collective time per day is $16 billion.[178] The rejection of security guidance by users is therefore rational in the round since the costs that are created by following the security guidance massively outweigh the possible downside. It is Herley's position that the field of information security has not accounted for this calculation, and so it is not users who need to be better informed but rather the security profession itself.[179] In this way, the oft-used aphorism about users picking dancing pigs over security can be seen to have a deeper meaning. On the surface, it represents the lament of the security professional regarding the seeming carelessness of users with regard to their security choices. But it also reveals that security professionals do not understand why users exhibit those behaviors.[180] Security practitioners believe that their goals for security should be adopted by the world at large, but those goals are not what users actually want, nor could they be achieved without creating excessive costs.[181]

Herley's critique of the unrealistic nature of security guidance is most damning where it identifies the harmful technocratic paternalism at the heart of the field of information security. RAND and the early researchers had expected that a computer operating system could impose its will on the users of the computer, in effect forcing them to be secure. That philosophy was adopted by those who worked in the field of information security in the subsequent decades and manifested as a revealed preference for technological solutions. But with the rise of email and the web, the user and her decisions became crucial to the security of the overall system. The possibility that security could be accomplished through technology alone was revealed to be a machine fantasy. The security of a computer is beholden to the whims of the user, and those whims are driven by the chaotic influence of economic motivations and psychological factors.

These revelations were damaging to the interests of a commercial security industry that wanted to portray a simple world in which buying a security product could deliver security. Hackers, security researchers, and all of those working to discover new vulnerabilities and new hacking techniques were also diminished. They needed a new idea that would restore their power and authority, so they set out to prove that the threat of security vulnerabilities was far greater than anyone had ever thought. If they could convince the world that everything could be hacked, their skills would again be in high demand. It was a vision that would become so successful that it would come to possess not just those working in the field of information security but also change how companies, the media, and governments came to view information security.

Chapter 7

# Vulnerability Disclosure, Bounties, and Markets

During the period of British colonial rule in India, bureaucrats in the city of Delhi became concerned with deaths caused by cobra bites. With the goal of reducing the number of deaths, the authorities established a program whereby the skin of a dead cobra could be exchanged for a monetary reward. Initially this plan was successful, and the number of cobras was reduced. But then some enterprising citizens began to game the system by breeding cobras. The government caught wind of the scheme and canceled the program. This meant that the people who had been breeding the cobras no longer had any use for them, so they released them from captivity. As a result, there were now even more of the deadly snakes than ever before.[1]

In the United States in 2012, the Bureau of Alcohol, Tobacco, Firearms and Explosives (ATF) set up a fake surplus shop that would buy guns. Their goal was to reduce the number of guns on the streets and thereby reduce gun violence. To enable them to purchase as many guns as possible, the ATF agents who ran the store decided to pay higher than the market rate. This led to an increase in crimes such as burglary where criminals would look for guns to steal in order to sell them at the store. The store was also burglar-ized and the fully automatic machine guns used by the ATF agents stolen and never recovered.[2] The ATF's plan led to more crime and more guns on the streets.

The perverse incentives created by the bureaucrats in Delhi and by the ATF agents in the United States led in both cases to the opposite outcome than the one they desired. This same pattern would play out in the field of information security at the beginning of the twenty-first century, and it was caused by an obsessive focus on technical security vulnerabilities.

The dot-com boom had created an immense and ever-growing market for computer software. The size and complexity of software crept inexora-bly upward over time as developers added new functionality in order to en-tice and retain users. Web browsers and web servers grew in size to become millions of lines of code. A 2004 book from Microsoft Press suggested that one thousand lines of code would typically contain between two and twenty bugs, although that number would be substantially lower if the code had been created within a process such as Microsoft's SDL.[3] Software security efforts such as Microsoft's Trustworthy Computing initiative, the SDL that they had created, and the increasing use of software security technologies such as static analysis and fuzzing had increased the level of skill required to find vulner-abilities in software. This had the effect of increasing the value of security vulnerabilities discovered in widely used software packages since those dis-coveries were now more rare.

A vulnerability that is not common knowledge and for which no patch has yet been released is referred to as a zero-day vulnerability, sometimes written as "0day" and pronounced "oh-day."[4] The term *zero-day* refers to the fact that there have been zero days' advance warning, meaning no days, re-garding the risk that the security vulnerability represents.[5] If a person can find a zero-day vulnerability in a popular piece of software, this can result in a large number of computers being vulnerable.[6] If a hacker is able to find a zero-day vulnerability in, say, the operating system of a mobile phone, then in theory that hacker can now hack any mobile phone that uses that operat-ing system. That is, until the vulnerability becomes patched. (In practice, there might be other hurdles the hacker would need to overcome in order to carry out those attacks.)

Zero-day vulnerabilities have value in large part because they represent secret knowledge.[7] But zero-day vulnerabilities also provide hackers with special advantages. Security technologies such as intrusion detection systems and antivirus software normally try to detect known patterns of attack and so typically would be unlikely to detect the use of a zero-day vulnerability.[8] A well-prepared organization might be able to detect the use of a zero-day vulnerability through some other means, however, such as by detecting the subsequent actions of the hacker after he has gained access.

A vulnerability that has been discovered but not disclosed in a little-used piece of software could technically meet the definition of a zero-day but is unlikely to be referred to as such. Colloquially, the term *zero-day* is reserved for vulnerabilities that are expected to create a significant impact, such as those that are found in popular software. Within the security community there is also an extent to which a zero-day vulnerability should have a "cool factor," with one researcher describing zero-day vulnerabilities, perhaps in a deliberately ostentatious way, as "totally gnarly."[9] A zero-day vulnerability need not necessarily be a software bug such as a buffer overflow. The knowledge of a novel technique for maintaining access to a computer through a "back door," or a new technique for creating a covert channel could also be thought of as a zero-day.[10]

The etymology of the term *zero-day* is unclear. Winston Churchill, writing in his book *Closing the Ring*, which was published in 1951, described October 20, 1943, as the "zero day" for German V2 rocket attacks to begin on London.[11] The term *zero-day* was used in illegal file sharing circles wherein pirated content such as movies, music, and computer software was shared and traded. Naming a folder with a leading zero such as "0day" would put the listing at the top of the directory and make the files contained in the folder more likely to catch the attention of another person.[12] But quite how the "zero-day" qualifier first began to be used in the way that it is now commonly used to refer to security vulnerabilities is unclear.[13]

The buffer overflow exploited by the Morris worm was the first wide-scale demonstration of a zero-day vulnerability, even though the Morris worm also used other techniques to infect computers such as cracking passwords. After the Morris worm had been decompiled and the source code thoroughly examined by the people who were investigating it, the zero-day vulnerability that it employed was discovered. Patches were issued that would stop subsequent attempts to exploit that particular buffer overflow. This example reveals the paradox of zero-day vulnerabilities—that exploiting a zero-day vulnerability creates the possibility that it will be revealed.[14] A victim that has been hacked by a zero-day vulnerability can potentially reconstruct the technical details of the vulnerability from log files and other artifacts that are created as a by-product of the attack.[15] This is an inversion of the situation faced by Microsoft, where hackers would use the information in the patches issued by Microsoft to identify the underlying vulnerabilities that were being patched. Here, the shoe is on the other foot.

Once the details of a zero-day vulnerability begin to be widely known, its utility begins to decrease. After a patch for the vulnerability is issued by the software vendor, the usefulness of the vulnerability to hackers depends on organizations and individuals not applying the patch. As more and more organizations apply the patch, the value of the vulnerability decreases asymptotically to zero (or near-zero, as it is unlikely that every single organization will install the patch). Because of this, the use of zero-day vulnerabilities is actually quite rare.[16] One study estimates that the use of zero-day vulnerabilities represents just one-tenth of 1 percent of all vulnerabilities that are exploited.[17] But when zero-day vulnerabilities are used, it is usually against targets that have special importance to the hackers involved.

In 2011, hackers sent a phishing email to employees of a company named RSA Security. The email had the subject line "2011 Recruitment Plan," and one of the RSA employees who received the email opened the attached spreadsheet file.[18] That file contained code that exploited a zero-day vulnerability on the person's computer and installed a back door. The hackers then used that back door as a foothold to gain access to sensitive data that they then copied and exfiltrated, meaning stole.[19] The reason that the hackers used a valuable zero-day vulnerability to hack RSA was because RSA is a security company that makes two-factor authentication products. The sensitive data that the hackers copied from RSA was the information that they needed to hack the two-factor authentication system used by Lockheed Martin, the largest defense contractor in the United States and a manufacturer of spy satellites and fighter planes for the US military.[20] The hackers appeared to know that in order to hack Lockheed Martin, they first needed to hack RSA, and so they used a zero-day vulnerability to accomplish that.

Companies such as Microsoft looked for vulnerabilities in their own products so that outside threats such as hackers could not find them and exploit them. But commercial companies would also look for vulnerabilities in popular software packages in order to demonstrate their security expertise by promoting their discoveries.[21] A commercial security company could also use any zero-day vulnerabilities that they had discovered in their commercial penetration testing engagements since the knowledge of a zero-day vulnerability in a piece of software would practically guarantee the ability to penetrate any organization that used that software.[22]

In the early 2000s, the consensus within the field of information security was that disclosing zero-day vulnerabilities was necessary to force software vendors to patch those vulnerabilities.[23] The belief was that vendors would have no reason otherwise to do so.[24] As a consequence, hackers and security researchers who posted the details of zero-day vulnerabilities on mailing lists such as Bugtraq were considered to be increasing social welfare.[25] Only a few voices expressed concern, including Marcus Ranum who made the observation that "nobody appears to consider the less palatable possibility" that the reason vulnerabilities were being disclosed was for the purpose of marketing the person doing the disclosure.[26]

The widespread availability of exploits for zero-day vulnerabilities created the risk that hackers and script kiddies could use those exploits to hack into computers. At that time, exploits for vulnerabilities were typically a relatively small computer program, usually no longer than two or three hundred lines of code, and so those exploits could easily proliferate around the world within seconds by being transferred over the internet. Releasing exploit code or scripts was sometimes justified as providing a proof of concept for the purpose of enabling people to test whether their systems were vulnerable. But the ready availability of exploits that anyone could use to hack into computers was also harmful since it enabled a larger group of people to carry out hacking who would not ordinarily be able to do so.[27] One study found that hackers closely monitored mailing lists such as Bugtraq where information regarding new vulnerabilities was being posted in order to obtain the knowledge of those vulnerabilities and then begin to exploit them.[28] There was clearly a trade-off, and the question being asked was whether looking for vulnerabilities and then publicizing the details of those vulnerabilities in public forums such as Bugtraq was beneficial.

A 2005 study examined that question.[29] Given that there were many hackers and many security researchers looking for security vulnerabilities, the overall quality of software should have noticeably increased as the pool of vulnerabilities became depleted by those efforts. The study found, however, that there was only very weak evidence for the idea of depletion.[30] In fact, the authors found that they could not rule out no depletion taking place at all.[31] This result aligned with the experience of security professionals at that time, which was that it was not unusual for vulnerabilities to be found in software where those vulnerabilities had been present for many years, even after the software had previously received security audits. The study concluded by saying that the apparent lack of evidence to support the value of looking for and publicly disclosing vulnerabilities was "troubling."[32] A second study found that vulnerability depletion caused by software security efforts could not be ruled out but that more investigation was needed.[33]

The question of whether it was useful to look for vulnerabilities was interesting perhaps only in a theoretical, academic sense. If no one looked for vulnerabilities, then the only vulnerabilities that would exist would be those that people stumbled upon accidentally, which would be a relatively small number. But because at least some number of people did actively look for vulnerabilities and publicized them to the world, other people such as software companies had to look for vulnerabilities as well. This was a game-theoretic death spiral within which everyone became trapped.

Nation-states have a particular interest in zero-day vulnerabilities and a strong motivation to acquire them. A nation-state wants to acquire information from its rivals on the world stage, and zero-day vulnerabilities can be an effective tool against the substantial defenses that other countries can construct. Nation-states also have considerable resources that they can apply to the challenge of finding zero-day vulnerabilities.

In 2004, a nonprofit group named the Electronic Frontier Foundation (EFF) sued the US government to obtain information under the Freedom of Information Act regarding what zero-day vulnerabilities the government was holding.[34] On the eve of a court battle, the government released information that described how US intelligence agencies use vulnerabilities in support of their "offensive" mission, which includes spying and hacking into computers in foreign nations.[35] The acquisition and use of zero-day vulnerabilities by three-letter agencies such as the NSA and CIA was also revealed by a number of high-profile leaks. Beginning in August 2016, a hacker group calling themselves the Shadow Brokers made a series of posts online.[36] In those posts they claimed to have hacked a different hacking group called the Equation Group and stolen their "cyber weapons," meaning exploits for zero-day vulnerabilities.[37] The Shadow Brokers then stated that they would hold an online auction to sell the exploits to the highest bidder.[38] They wrote in broken English, "We hack Equation Group. We find many Equation Group cyber weapons. You see pictures. We give you some Equation Group files free, you see. This is good proof no? You enjoy!!! You break many things."[39] It is not clear whether the Shadow Brokers hacked a computer that was being used by the Equation Group and acquired the knowledge of the vulnerabilities from that computer, whether they simply happened upon the information, or whether the information was deliberately leaked to them.[40]

To prove the value of the information they were selling, the Shadow Brokers published some of the exploits they had acquired.[41] There were code words written into the source code for those exploits such as ETERNAL-BLUE, ETERNALROMANCE, and EXPLODINGCAN.[42] One of the exploits was a zero-day vulnerability in Microsoft Windows—a valuable prize. This information released by the Shadow Brokers meant that other hackers could now use the knowledge of those vulnerabilities. The ETERNALBLUE vulnerability was used to create an internet worm called WannaCry, which infected more than two hundred thousand computers across 150 countries.[43] WannaCry was ransomware that encrypted files on the infected computers and then displayed a message on the screen demanding that $300 be delivered within three days, or $6,000 within seven days, otherwise the encrypted files would be deleted.[44] Computers at the United Kingdom's National Health Service were infected by WannaCry, causing some hospitals to turn patients away.[45]

Within months a second malicious program began to spread using ETERNALBLUE.[46] NotPetya was so named because it resembled an existing ransomware program called Petya, but it soon became apparent that NotPetya was not designed to make money.[47] Although NotPetya presented as ransomware, its true purpose was to cause disruption.[48] NotPetya infected computers around the world but appears to have been designed to target computers primarily in Russia and Ukraine.[49] Organizations that provided key services in Ukraine were infected such as the state power company, the main airport in Kiev, and the Kiev metro system.[50] The computer systems at Ukraine's Chernobyl Nuclear Power Plant were also affected, causing site workers to revert to manual checking of radiation levels rather than computerized monitoring.[51]

The Shadow Brokers were mysterious, but even more puzzling was how the Equation Group had managed to develop such an extensive collection of zero-day vulnerability exploits. After examining the source code of the exploits written by the Equation Group, they were found to have a predilection for employing certain cryptographic algorithms, as well as having what was described as "extraordinary engineering skill" and apparently "unlimited resources."[52] The solution to this puzzle was that the Equation Group was almost certainly the Office of Tailored Access Operations (TAO) within the NSA.[53] The TAO is a unit that is focused on hacking foreign computers for the purpose of intelligence gathering.[54] It is said to employ hundreds of civilian hackers and supporting staff.[55] The ability of the TAO to develop the zero-day vulnerability exploits that were stolen by the Shadow Brokers was a result of the massive resources that it could bring to the task.

But as impressive as the capabilities of the TAO were, they were not without flaw. The attribution of the Equation Group as the TAO was possible due to the code words that were found inside the vulnerability exploits, and those code words had already been used elsewhere.[56] The TAO had also made the mistake of leaving the timestamps in their files.[57] Those timestamps showed that the code had been written by programmers working between the hours of 8:00 a.m. and 5:00 p.m. on the eastern side of the United States, the same time zone as the NSA headquarters in Fort Meade, Maryland.[58] Once the Equation Group exploits were revealed by the Shadow Brokers, it was also possible to determine some of the victims of previous hacking attacks that had employed those exploits, and those attacks appeared to favor targets in Iran, the Russian Federation, Pakistan, and Afghanistan.[59]

Like the NSA, the CIA suffered a breach of zero-day vulnerabilities. In March 2017, WikiLeaks published a tranche of more than eight thousand documents they called Vault 7.[60] WikiLeaks claimed that the documents had "circulated among former US government hackers and contractors in an unauthorized manner" and that within the documents were the details of several zero-day vulnerabilities including exploits for web browsers such as Google Chrome and Microsoft Edge, and for various operating systems such as Apple iPhone, Google Android, and Microsoft Windows.[61] Unlike the Shadow Brokers, WikiLeaks stated that they would not release the exploits themselves and that they were working with the affected vendors so that patches could be created. The Vault 7 leaks also revealed information regarding several CIA hacking tools. One tool with the CIA code name Weeping Angel had been jointly developed by the CIA and MI5, the counterintelligence security agency of the United Kingdom.[62] It exploited internet-enabled TVs manufactured by Samsung.[63] After being used against a TV, when the

TV appeared to be switched off it would in fact be listening to any conversations in the room, which it would record and send over the internet to CIA headquarters.[64] WikiLeaks described the Vault 7 leaks as demonstrating the need for a public debate about "whether the CIA's hacking capabilities exceeded its mandated powers" and "about the security, creation, use, proliferation and democratic control of cyberweapons"—by which they meant zero-day vulnerabilities and the hacking tools that incorporated them.[65]

The NSA and CIA would have no doubt preferred to avoid the disclosure of their zero-day exploits and the attribution of the materials that were leaked to their agencies. Some of the documents contained within the Vault 7 cache were pages from an internal CIA forum in which CIA employees discussed the mistakes that the NSA had made that enabled the Equation Group to be identified as the TAO, and how they might avoid making those same mistakes.[66]

The Shadow Brokers disclosed the zero-day vulnerabilities created by the NSA in an attempt to profit from that disclosure. WikiLeaks disclosed the zero-day vulnerabilities created by the CIA for the stated reason of beginning a public debate. But for white hat hackers, security researchers, and commercial security companies, the decision regarding whether to disclose zero-day vulnerabilities and how to do so was more complex. Disclosing a vulnerability to the software vendor would cause the software vendor to release a patch, but hackers could then use that patch to identify the vulnerability and create an exploit. Because organizations had difficulties with applying patches quickly and completely, hackers could use an exploit to hack organizations that had not yet applied the patch. But not disclosing the vulnerability to the software vendor would mean that there would never be a patch, and any hacker who discovered the vulnerability could exploit it. The question was whether it was better to have a larger number of hackers who possessed exploits for vulnerabilities for which patches existed or to have a smaller number of hackers who possessed exploits for vulnerabilities for which there was no patch. This was the question of disclosure, and there has been a long history of thinking on the topic within the field of information security.

In the late 1990s and early 2000s, the full disclosure approach to vulnerability disclosure was dominant. Hackers and vulnerability researchers would post the details of vulnerabilities to Bugtraq and to another mailing list named Full Disclosure.[67] The Bugtraq mailing list was created in 1993 and the Full Disclosure mailing list in 2002.[68] Full Disclosure, as its name implied, was dedicated to "unfettered and unmoderated discussions" regarding vulnerabilities.[69] Within a year of its creation, the Full Disclosure list was receiving more than one thousand new posts per month.[70]

The full disclosure approach represents a kind of initial conditions or foundation for the answer to the question of disclosure. Full disclosure is always possible since it is impossible to stop people from choosing to post information on the internet regarding vulnerabilities once they have acquired that knowledge. Full disclosure was in part a backlash against earlier secrecy around security vulnerabilities. From 1989 to 1991, participants on a restricted mailing list called Zardoz would discuss security vulnerabilities.[71] The actual name of the list was the Security Digest, but the list was given the informal name of Zardoz because that was the name of the computer used to send the emails to the list members. To become a member of the Zardoz list required a person to have a relevant job such as being the administrator of a large installation of computers, being an academic, or by being vetted by the other members of the list.[72] Because Zardoz contained information about zero-day vulnerabilities, it was a constant target of hackers who would try to find archives of the list on subscribers' computers.[73]

Full disclosure was described by some as a "necessary evil" but by others as being akin to the logic of US war planners during the Vietnam War, where "destroying the village was necessary in order to save it."[74] The public-shaming aspect of full disclosure was also unappealing to some, who described it as the equivalent of writing "WASH ME" in the dirt covering a person's car.[75] The full disclosure approach could even be seen as a kind of victim blaming, where public announcements were made regarding vulnerabilities in the products written by software vendors who perhaps did not have the resources to implement software security initiatives within their companies. Research also showed that there was only modest support at best for the claim that full disclosure made vendors issue patches for vulnerabilities more quickly than otherwise.[76] But even in the presence of these concerns, the prevailing view within the field of information security was that to be critical of people who disclosed vulnerabilities using full disclosure was shooting the messenger, that white hat hackers and security researchers who posted information regarding vulnerabilities and exploits to Bugtraq were "serving the greater good."[77]

White hat hackers and security researchers advocated for full disclosure during this period because it aligned with their self-interest. Full disclosure of vulnerabilities was dramatic and created a sense of urgency. The act of disclosing a zero-day vulnerability in a widely used piece of software could gain a person instant fame, and this was a powerful incentive.[78] The person who found and disclosed the vulnerability that was used by the Slammer worm told the *Washington Post* during an interview in the wake of the worm that he would "probably no longer publish such code" but the following month decided that he would return to practicing full disclosure.[79]

Full disclosure evolved into responsible disclosure. In responsible disclosure, the person who finds a zero-day vulnerability does not disclose it publicly.[80] Instead, she privately contacts the software vendor and informs them of the details.[81] This provides the vendor with the opportunity to fix the vulnerability and issue a patch before the larger world becomes aware.[82] The responsible disclosure approach removed the problem of black hat hackers using information regarding vulnerabilities to hack computers before a patch was made available.[83] In order to address the situation where a vendor received a notification regarding a vulnerability but sat on that knowledge and did not issue a patch, the responsible disclosure approach typically employed a scheme whereby the vendor was given a certain amount of time to produce a patch, such as ninety days. If the vendor did not produce a patch by the end of that time, the details of the vulnerability could be publicly released by the person who discovered it.[84]

A widely referenced codification of the informal rules around responsible disclosure was the "Full Disclosure Policy" document written by a security researcher with the pseudonym Rain Forest Puppy.[85] That policy sets basic rules for the two parties—the researcher and the vendor—such as the vendor having to reply to an emailed report of a vulnerability from a researcher within five days.[86]

Within the security community, responsible disclosure became viewed as The Right Thing To Do because it had fewer downsides than full disclosure. But part of the reason why responsible disclosure came to be the preferred approach was because it more effectively served the goals of both those who researched vulnerabilities and the goals of the software vendors. The incentive for white hat hackers, security researchers, and security companies to use responsible disclosure was that it enabled them to receive public credit for their work. When a software vendor announced a vulnerability alongside the availability of a patch, they typically credited the person who disclosed the vulnerability, and so responsible disclosure provided a public acknowl- edgment. The incentive for software vendors to use responsible disclosure was that it provided them with some amount of forewarning to fix vulner- abilities before information regarding those vulnerabilities became public knowledge. The experience for the customers of those software vendors was improved as a result. With full disclosure, customers would have to scram- ble to try and protect their systems against vulnerabilities for which no patch was available. But with responsible disclosure, customers received the patch before the information regarding the vulnerability was widely known and could install the patch to protect themselves in advance. Often a patch was made available without the details of the associated vulnerability ever being released.

Responsible disclosure replaced full disclosure as the preferred approach to disclosure, but responsible disclosure could only exist because the threat of full disclosure was lurking behind it. A software vendor knew that if they did not create and issue a patch after a security vulnerability had been re- ported to them, that the person who found the vulnerability could simply release the details of the vulnerability—essentially defaulting to full disclo- sure. Tensions emerged when the letter of responsible disclosure was followed but not the spirit. Some researchers and security companies chose to release working exploits for vulnerabilities within hours or even minutes of the soft- ware vendor issuing a patch, which created a race between hackers and organizations to see who could either patch or exploit the vulnerability first.[87]

Vulnerability researchers sometimes expressed frustration at the belief that vendors were sitting for too long on information regarding vulnerabilities that had been reported to them.[88] Vendors were also criticized for making excuses as to why they had not yet implemented patches.[89] For these reasons, some researchers became disquieted with the term *responsible disclosure*. They started to view it as emotionally loaded in that it implied that any other type of disclosure other than responsible disclosure was by definition irresponsi- ble.[90] In their opinion, responsible disclosure enabled the vendor to have too much of a say in who the researcher notified regarding the vulnerability and when.[91]

Responsible disclosure had created the situation for software companies where if an outside researcher were to find a vulnerability in one of the com- pany's products, the company was now on the researcher's schedule to fix the vulnerability and issue a patch. This led some large companies to create internal teams of bug hunters so that they could find vulnerabilities before outsiders did and not have to cede control over the timeline for creating the patch.[92] Those bug hunting teams were sometimes tasked with looking for vulnerabilities not just in their own company's software but also in other software.[93] That software might be open source software on which the company relied or just software that was commonly used by the general public. That work to find vulnerabilities in other people's software was often portrayed as an altruistic act that would protect consumers.[94] But companies with dedicated bug hunting teams that found critical vulnerabilities in other people's software sometimes disclosed those vulnerabilities in ways that appeared to serve two purposes: to not only highlight the existence of the vulnerability but also to promote the vulnerability-finding expertise of the company and thereby promote the company itself.[95] In this way, responsible disclosure was transformed by the large companies that funded their own vulnerability research into what could be described as promoted disclosure.

Companies whose bug hunting teams could find and disclose the most high-profile vulnerabilities would be rewarded by the popular press and by the security press with news coverage, and it was difficult to avoid the impression that on some occasions commercial considerations came into play.[96] Google's vulnerability hunting team, named Project Zero, found a vulnerability in Microsoft's Internet Explorer web browser and released the details of the vulnerability even after Microsoft had asked them not to release the information because a patch was not yet available.[97] On a different occasion, Project Zero disclosed a serious vulnerability in Microsoft Windows only ten days after reporting it to Microsoft.[98]

In April 2014, a vulnerability researcher working at Google discovered a vulnerability in code that was widely used to implement encrypted communications between web browsers and web servers.[99] This was a serious bug; around 17 percent of the web servers on the internet were believed to be vulnerable, with that percentage representing around half a million individual web servers.[100] In order to promote the vulnerability, it was given the name Heartbleed, a logo of a red heart dripping blood, and its own website.[101] The name Heartbleed came from the fact that the vulnerability was in the part of the software that dealt with the heartbeat of the program. The Heartbleed marketing exercise was praised for being emotionally provocative since the Heartbleed name was said to "sound serious" and "fatal."[102] But after Heartbleed was revealed and began to be promoted, hackers started to exploit the vulnerability. The Heartbleed vulnerability was used to compromise personal information stored by the Canadian government, causing the government to shut down its website for several days.[103] In August 2014, hackers used the Heartbleed vulnerability to compromise the security of four and a half million patient records from the second largest hospital chain in the United States.[104]

Other commercial companies have since tried to promote vulnerabilities that they have discovered with the same high-profile marketing approach as Heartbleed, using similarly provocative names such as Rampage, Shellshock, and Skyfall.[105]

Heartbleed created particular consternation for the NSA because they were accused of knowing about the vulnerability for at least two years prior to it being disclosed and using it as a zero-day vulnerability to hack into computers.[106] The NSA was in a unique position with regard to zero-day vulnerabilities because of its so-called dual mandate, which is not only the goal of obtaining intelligence from the United States' enemies and rivals but also the obligation to protect the security of computers within the country.[107] This dual mandate means that when the NSA discovers a zero-day vulnerability, it is faced with a dilemma. The vulnerability could be used in support of the NSA's goal of obtaining intelligence, but this would mean keeping it a secret, which would put computers within the homeland at risk. Alternatively, the NSA could choose to reveal the details of the vulnerability to the vendor of the software. This would enable US computers to be protected since the vendor would issue a patch, but the NSA would not then be able to use the zero-day vulnerability for the purpose of collecting intelligence.[108]

The dilemma hinges on how likely it is that another party such as a hacker or another foreign nation will also discover the same zero-day vulnerability. If it is unlikely, then in terms of the dual mandate it is more logical to not reveal the details of the vulnerability to the vendor and vice versa. This idea that a second party might discover the same zero-day vulnerability is called rediscovery.[109] If the rediscovery rate is high, zero-day vulnerabilities have less value because someone else is likely to also find them. US government agencies are likely to have a stockpile of the same zero-day vulnerabilities as the governments of other nations, and there is therefore little reason to not disclose them.[110] But if the rediscovery rate is low, then zero-day vulnerabilities have more value because it is unlikely that someone else will also discover them. US government agencies could assume that their stockpile of zero-day vulnerabilities was largely unique and would therefore lean more toward not disclosing them.[111] But calculating the rediscovery rate is not straightforward. One study estimates that zero-day vulnerabilities have quite a long average shelf life of seven years and that for a given set of zero-day vulnerabilities only 6 percent of them are likely to be discovered by an outside party after one year.[112] A different study estimates the rediscovery rate to be substantially higher at 13 percent.[113]

The debate concerning rediscovery and how to best serve the dual mandate was not new to the NSA. The agency has a long history of trying to break the encryption schemes used to secure communications so that the phone calls and other communications of foreign governments can be intercepted. That field of study, called communications security or COMSEC, had to confront many of the same dilemmas that now exist with zero-day vulnerabilities. This is because if the NSA finds a way to break the security of a particular kind of communications system, then the NSA could either use that knowledge to eavesdrop or propose a fix to make that communications system more secure.[114]

To address the accusation that they had known about Heartbleed before it was publicly disclosed, the NSA sent a tweet from its official Twitter account stating that "NSA was not aware of the recently identified Heartbleed vulnerability until it was made public."[115] Within weeks, the White House also published a blog post from the White House cybersecurity coordinator and special assistant to the president that said, "In the majority of cases, responsibly disclosing a newly discovered vulnerability is clearly in the national interest," but there are "legitimate pros and cons to the decision to disclose."[116] The White House blog post stated that the US government had "established a disciplined, rigorous and high-level decision-making process for vulnerability disclosure."[117]

That process was named the Vulnerabilities Equities Process (VEP).[118] It was developed by the Office of the Director of National Intelligence during 2008 and 2009, and it describes the process that the federal government uses to handle zero-day vulnerabilities—to make the choice about whether to notify the vendor so that a patch can be created or to keep the information secret so that the NSA and other US security agencies can use it.[119] The process requires government agencies that find or become aware of a zero-day vulnerability to notify the executive secretariat for the VEP, which is the NSA's Information Assurance Directorate.[120] A VEP board consisting of representatives from agencies such as the CIA, NSA, and Department of Defense then meet on a regular basis to review the list of vulnerabilities that have been submitted. The decision of the board as to whether to notify the affected vendor includes the consideration of whether the vulnerability has "operational value" for the purpose of supporting "intelligence collection, cyber operations, or law enforcement evidence collection" and whether the use of the vulnerability will provide "specialized operational value against cyber threat actors," among other criteria—in other words, whether the vulnerability will be useful for carrying out hacking.[121]

In 2015, the NSA made a statement that said that historically it had "released more than 91 percent of vulnerabilities that have gone through our internal review process and that are made and used in the United States."[122] But some organizations such as the EFF suggested that the statement provided a lot of wiggle room. There could conceivably have been vulnerabilities that were discovered by the US government but that were not put through the VEP or that were not "made and used in the United States." The NSA statement also does not say whether they first used the zero-day vulnerabilities to hack into computers and then entered them into the VEP.[123] These ambiguities caused some commentators to suggest that the VEP was created not as a triage mechanism but rather to serve the purpose of public relations.[124]

Zero-day vulnerabilities have value to the NSA and to others because of what can be accomplished by using them, and that value has been increasingly expressed in financial terms. During the full disclosure period, monetary compensation for finding vulnerabilities was eschewed. The Full Disclosure Policy created by Rain Forest Puppy stated that "monetary compensation . . . is highly discouraged."[125] But the idea of buying and selling zero-day vulnerabilities had been written about since 2000, and by 2002, commercial companies had begun to pay for information regarding zero-day vulnerabilities and for zero-day vulnerability exploits.[126]

In 2005, an enterprising hacker calling himself fearwall created a listing on the internet auction site eBay for the purpose of selling information regarding a zero-day vulnerability in Microsoft's Excel spreadsheet program.[127] The price on the site was bid up to around $1,200 before the listing was removed.[128] By the end of that year, a vulnerability exploit for Microsoft Windows was sold for $4,000 by Russian hackers.[129] The higher the perceived importance of the software that contained the vulnerability, the higher the price for an exploit became. When Microsoft released its Windows Vista operating system in January 2007, iDefense offered $8,000 for information on the first six zero-day vulnerabilities to be found and $4,000 more for each working exploit.[130] A vulnerability exploit for Windows Vista was later offered for sale at the price of $50,000.[131]

But even as the prices climbed higher and higher, the perception of some security researchers was that they were not being paid enough. In 2009, an ex-NSA employee who had become a commercial vulnerability researcher spearheaded a campaign called No More Free Bugs.[132] He and his colleagues argued that the market was unfair to vulnerability researchers, given the amount of time that researchers spent looking to find zero-day vulnerabilities.[133] This was a peculiar claim given that the researchers were not being forced to spend their days looking for zero-day vulnerabilities.[134] As talented programmers they could no doubt have obtained high-paying jobs. The difference would be that in those jobs they would not have been able to obtain the same "super geek fame" that finding vulnerabilities provided.[135]

The number of commercial companies participating in the market for zero-day vulnerabilities increased, and companies began to buy and sell information regarding zero-day vulnerabilities. Those companies included defense contractors such as Raytheon and Northrop Grumman and security companies such as Netragard and Endgame. Some of the executives at these companies were employed by both government and industry. The chairman of Endgame was the chief executive of In-Q-Tel, a venture capital firm set up at the request of the CIA to fund private companies that might benefit the intelligence community.[136]

The companies that were being established to buy, broker, and resell zero-day vulnerabilities believed that responsible disclosure was not rational because it left money on the table but that it was rational to sell zero-day vulnerabilities to the highest bidder.[137] This position created a backlash, with companies that bought and sold vulnerabilities being described as run by "ethically challenged opportunists" and "modern-day merchants of death" who were selling "the bullets for cyberwar."[138] Those who made these criticisms considered the commercial companies who bought and sold zero-day vulnerabilities to be, effectively, private arms manufacturers. The weapons that they bought and sold were the exploits for zero-day vulnerabilities, which could be used to hack other countries, private citizens, or used to carry out electronic crimes. Some of the companies attempted to mitigate those concerns by vowing to sell exploits for zero-day vulnerabilities only to NATO govern-ments.[139] But even with that restriction, the possibility existed for the informa-tion regarding those vulnerabilities to fall into the wrong hands, such as if a company that had purchased them was hacked.[140] In 2015, an Italian company named Hacking Team that sold "offensive security technologies" was hacked and hundreds of gigabytes of source code, internal emails, legal memos, and invoices were leaked onto the internet.[141] Inside those leaked files were exploits for zero-day vulnerabilities in software made by Adobe and Microsoft, includ-ing Microsoft Windows and Microsoft Internet Explorer.[142]

The market for zero-day vulnerabilities upended the norm of responsi-ble disclosure. White hat hackers and security researchers who would have previously reported vulnerabilities to the affected software vendor now had the option to sell that information, and it was unclear whether this was a net positive or a net negative for information security overall.[143] Money chang-ing hands in a commercial market could conceivably create perverse incen-tives, such as for a software developer to create vulnerabilities in their own products and then sell the knowledge of those vulnerabilities. Such a soft-ware developer could insert vulnerabilities into the code in a way that was plausibly deniable. The ability to write such code had already been proven by a competition called the Underhanded C Contest in which participants compete to create code written in the C programming language that appears to be benign but is actually malicious and that would look like a program-ming error or an oversight if discovered.[144] But these concerns were tram-pled by the virtual gold rush that was taking place. In the market for zero-day vulnerabilities, commercial companies were often outbid by governments who had larger purses.[145] Some of the largest spenders on zero-day vulner-abilities were the governments of Israel, the United Kingdom, Russia, India, and Brazil.[146] The NSA is known to have begun buying vulnerabilities in 2012, when they bought a subscription to a "zero-day service" from French security firm VUPEN.[147] The following year, the NSA was said to be the top purchaser of zero-day vulnerabilities in the world, and they bought them not for the purpose of being able to defend against them but to use for hack-ing.[148] Other US government agencies were also interested in purchasing zero-day vulnerabilities. The US Navy issued a proposal stating that it was seeking to obtain exploits for zero-day vulnerabilities in commercial software from vendors including Microsoft, IBM, and Apple.[149] In 2016, the FBI paid more than $1.3 million for an exploit for a zero-day vulnerability in Apple's iPhone.[150] Because of its security features, the iPhone had become a prize target that commanded the highest prices. A company named Zerodium announced that they would pay $1 million for zero-day vulnerabilities in iOS, which is the operating system that runs on Apple iPhones.[151] Zerodium later claimed that they did pay that price for just such a vulnerability but that they would resell the information "to US customers only" such as government agencies and "very big corporations."[152]

As the market for vulnerabilities grew, individual technology companies began to participate. These companies typically paid a standing fee or bounty for vulnerabilities that were found in their own products. The definition of what constituted a vulnerability was typically rather broad in these cases and would often encompass issues that were less significant than a zero-day. For example, a company might pay a person who found that an internet-facing computer owned by the company had a misconfiguration that could potentially cause a security issue.

Netscape Communications had offered a reward of $1,000 and a T-shirt for vulnerabilities found in their software in 1996, but it was not until the mid-2010s that a significant number of organizations began to establish bug bounty programs.[153] These programs enabled people who reported security vulnerabilities in the organization's products or website to receive a bounty, typically financial compensation. Major companies such as Apple, Google, Microsoft, and Facebook established bug bounty programs, as did some US government agencies such as the Department of Defense.[154] The organizations that established bug bounty programs often employed a broker in the form of a bug bounty company that would act as an intermediary. The bug bounty companies would work directly with the people who submitted bug reports on the front end, and also manage payouts on the back end. This model created an economy of scale in that the bug bounty companies could become proficient at handling the large numbers of people submitting bug reports across multiple organizations. By 2017, the leading bug bounty company had received $74 million in venture capital funding.[155] The CEO of that company stated that through bug bounties they were "empowering the world to build a safer internet," but the reality was not so simple.[156]

Bug bounty programs typically offer higher rewards for more important vulnerabilities and lower rewards for less important vulnerabilities. But because researchers get paid by a bug bounty program only when they find a vulnerability, this creates the incentive to look for only vulnerabilities that represent a good trade-off for the researcher in terms of the difficulty of finding a vulnerability versus the possible reward. The result is that an organization that offers a bug bounty might have many people looking for vulnerabilities that are relatively easy to find but relatively few people looking for vulnerabilities that are more difficult to find.[157] Vulnerability researchers also have the incentive to focus their time and effort on newly launched bug bounty programs and to switch to those new programs at the expense of existing programs.[158] The new programs represent fresh ground and a higher probability of finding a vulnerability that will provide a payoff.[159] This creates the situation where the goals of the bug bounty companies and their customers are not aligned. The bug bounty companies want to sign new customers, but by doing so they cannibalize the researchers working to find vulnerabilities for their existing customers.[160] A bug bounty program is by its very nature reactive; it attempts to address the presence of vulnerabilities that exist in code, but it does not address the more fundamental question of how those vulnerabilities came to be present in the code in the first place. Bug bounty programs do not therefore provide a solution to the systemic problems that cause vulnerabilities to exist. If a white hat hacker finds and reports a security vulnerability in a piece of software, this does nothing to address other vulnerabilities of that same type that will most likely be found in the software in the future.

Bug bounty programs appeared at first to be a mechanism by which the No More Free Bugs campaigners could potentially achieve their goals, but the financial return to security researchers from bug bounty programs would not be as lucrative as they might have hoped. In 2012, the largest bug bounty program was the Zero Day Initiative run by HP Tipping Point. Between 2005 and 2012, that program paid out $5.6 million in bounties, which amounted to $80,000 per year spread across every researcher who received a payout.[161] In 2016, the Facebook bug bounty program had paid $4.3 million to eight hundred bug hunters since its inception, a mathematical average of only around $5,000 per researcher.[162] The amount received by the average researcher would in reality be much smaller than that amount since a small elite of bug hunters take home most of the bounties.[163] The rationale put forward by one leading bug bounty company for not making large payouts was that they simply could not since software developers would leave their jobs and start working as bug hunters instead, and then "no one would be left to actually fix the bugs."[164] This was a ludicrous claim because if there were no software developers to write new code, then there would be no new code to examine for vulnerabilities. The claim was useful, however, in identifying the preferences of the commercial bug bounty companies. The bug bounty programs that they created for their corporate customers were intentionally regressive for the bug hunters—a scheme that was described as a way for "multi-national corporations to get hundreds of security researchers to do work for free."[165]

It quickly became apparent that finding vulnerabilities for the purpose of receiving rewards from bug bounty programs could not enable a person to obtain a salary that was comparable to a full-time job working in the field of information security.[166] Some vulnerability researchers complained that the amount of compensation paid by bug bounty programs was not high enough for researchers who had "mortgages and families."[167] The inability of all but a small number of vulnerability researchers to make a living from bug bounty programs began to influence the makeup of those who participated in the programs. People from developing countries began to participate in larger numbers because the money paid by the bug bounty programs had more purchasing power in their home countries.[168] Journalists found the idea of people from developing countries being paid to find vulnerabilities in the websites and software written by US companies intriguing, and a number of profiles of those individuals were published.[169] Those profiled in the articles were often young (in their twenties) and described themselves as either using bug bounties to support themselves until they could find a corporate job or planning to spend the money they made from bug bounties for the purpose of starting their own company.[170]

Another consideration for bug hunters was that participating in a bug bounty program was not necessarily a safe activity. In a 2015 incident, a bug hunter found a vulnerability in Instagram, which is a photo and video-sharing service owned by Facebook. After he reported the vulnerability using the Facebook bug bounty program, Alex Stamos, the chief security officer at Facebook, made a phone call to the CEO of the bug hunter's employer and threatened legal action.[171] Facebook felt that the bug hunter had gone too far in his testing.[172] The bug hunter felt that Alex Stamos had contacted his employer as an intimidation tactic.[173]

In some cases, bug bounty programs affected the healthy functioning of the financial markets. The ride-sharing service Uber suffered a security breach in 2016 in which the personal data of 57 million Uber users from around the world was compromised.[174] That information included names, email addresses, and phone numbers. But instead of disclosing the breach to regulators, the company used their bug bounty program to hide the fact that the breach occurred.[175] Uber paid the hackers $100,000 through the bug bounty program to destroy the information they had acquired and to keep the breach quiet.[176] The board of directors at Uber only discovered the breach after commissioning an investigation, and the chief security officer and one of his deputies who was an attorney were both subsequently fired because of the incident.[177]

The commercial markets that were created by the buying and selling of zero-day vulnerabilities and by the new bug bounty programs were the capitalistic endgame for the question of disclosure. The bug brokers—the middlemen who had inserted themselves between the buyers and sellers—believed that no other approach could be considered. They portrayed any alternative to their existence as "communism."[178] Bug bounty programs were in one sense a victory for the hackers because they represented a normalization of the idea of hacking as a social good. To the hackers, an invitation had been extended from the largest commercial companies to hack their software and to be paid for doing so. But this was also a commercialization of the hackers and their skills for finding vulnerabilities, and commercialization meant private control.

There was no romance to hacking now, no intellectual hedonism free of commercial concerns. The white hat hacker, now rebranded as a security researcher or a bug hunter, had become merely a cog in a machine that was larger than any single person and that was operated by corporations. Cash ruled everything around them, and that cash required secrecy. The person who sold a zero-day vulnerability could not disclose it publicly because it would rob the buyer that had purchased the vulnerability of their ability to use it. The buyer would also not disclose the vulnerability because they would want the information to retain its value for as long as possible. This arrangement removed the ability of white hat hackers, security researchers, and commercial security companies to promote themselves through disclosure and thereby gain status. They were trapped from both above and below. From above, they could no longer compete with the nation-states who were able to bring massive resources to the task of finding zero-day vulnerabilities. From below, the less severe vulnerabilities were being drained by software security initiatives within organizations and by bug bounty programs. They needed a new way to reclaim their status.

They invented stunt hacking.[179] This is the act of finding and publicizing security vulnerabilities in everyday technologies such as automobiles, airplanes, and medical devices.[180] Stunt hacking is a violent simplification of the world. It obviates any consideration for the role of economics or psychology in security failures and concentrates only on the technical aspects of hacking and vulnerabilities in which hackers hold expertise. The types of vulnerabilities that they pursued in their stunt hacking were those that they thought would generate the most publicity, no matter how esoteric the subject of their efforts. They hacked cargo container ships, multimillion-dollar superyachts, home thermostats, emergency sirens, wind farms, thermometers, and even electronic toilets.[181] This new focus for their security research created a kind of disaster tourism out of security vulnerabilities. In 2011, a security researcher presented the results of his research on the wireless hacking of insulin pumps, medical devices that help people with diabetes to stay alive.[182] The following year, a security researcher claimed that he could remotely hack a pacemaker inside a person's body and cause it to stop working, killing him.[183]

It was a dark and pessimistic vision. Everything was vulnerable, and by induction there was no hope for security. This was a message that many journalists were willing to embrace at face value. One *New York Times* article breathlessly reported on the stunt hacking of automobiles by asking the reader to "imagine driving on the freeway at sixty miles per hour and your car suddenly screeches to a halt, causing a pileup that injures dozens of people. Now imagine you had absolutely nothing to do with the accident because your car was taken over by hackers."[184] A second *New York Times* article suggested that "the only thing that stops a bad guy with a hack is a good guy with a hack."[185] Stunt hacking was warmly received by journalists and by readers perhaps because it satisfies a base human need—being told that the future will be awful is by some measure less distressing than merely suspecting it.

Stunt hacking was portrayed as a selfless act, a way to draw attention to dangerous vulnerabilities. What went unsaid was that stunt hacking was a means by which hackers and commercial security companies could promote themselves and their technical skill sets.[186] The broader security industry also benefited from stunt hacking because the promotion of vulnerabilities and security issues in the popular press led to a larger market for security products and services. Security conferences such as Black Hat and Defcon invited hackers with the most byline-friendly stunt hacking feats to speak.[187] This was a triumph for the hackers who saw themselves propelled to the forefront of attention. But what had begun as an exercise in self-promotion increasingly began to be seen as the truth. And sometimes, to their surprise, those who carried out stunt hacking did not receive the deference and gratitude that they expected.

In 2015, a security consultant was flying on a Boeing 737 plane from Denver to Chicago. During the flight he used the in-flight wireless networking to send a tweet stating that he had hacked one of the plane's computers. He asked, perhaps rhetorically, whether he should send a signal to the computer to activate the plane's oxygen masks.[188] As a result of sending that tweet he was arrested by the FBI.[189] When he was interviewed, he claimed to have used a network cable to connect to the electronics underneath his seat in the plane and to have done this on flights "approximately fifteen to twenty times."[190] He also claimed to have on one occasion issued a command to a plane that caused one of the airplane engines to climb, resulting in, as he put it, "lateral or sideways movement of the plane."[191] But this was abject self-delusion, the claim of a fantasist. The possibility that he had caused a Boeing 737 plane to move sideways was described by aviation experts as inconceivable.[192] Boeing also made a statement that the entertainment systems that are accessible from a seat are completely isolated from the systems that control the flight of the aircraft.[193]

The Boeing 737 stunt hacking incident illustrates the twin dangers of stunt hacking: that hacking for the purposes of generating publicity can create a make-believe idea of risk and can also drown out legitimate research.[194] Research on topics such as automobile security has been presented at refereed academic conferences and published in peer-reviewed academic journals.[195] But the existence of stunt hacking creates the situation where the popular press is much more likely to write articles about what one commentator has described as "avant-garde horrors such as the fact that pacemakers can be remotely controlled with a garage door opener and a Pringles can."[196] In turn, this reporting can cause the average person to develop an erroneous understanding of the level of risk that exists in everyday life.[197]

Stunt hacking was so successful at acquiring the attention of the mainstream press that the idea began to be projected outward. For those with the presupposition that hacking was an unalloyed good, it was logical to promote the act of hacking itself.[198] This belief led to the idea that every person, including children, should learn to "think like a hacker" and find vulnerabilities just like a hacker would.[199] At the Defcon conference in 2018, a workshop aimed to provide children between the ages of five and sixteen with "the opportunity to hack into exact replicas of the secretary of state election results websites for the thirteen presidential election battleground states, changing the vote tallies and thus the election results."[200] A former White House liaison for the Department of Homeland Security was quoted in a national US newspaper as saying that "these websites are so easy to hack we couldn't give them to adult hackers—they'd be laughed off the stage."[201] But for the average person, being told to "think like a hacker" was like being told to "think like a professional chef."[202] It is possible to learn how to hack computers, but that skill cannot be delivered via a catchphrase. Indeed, the Defcon workshop was revealed to be a sham. Instead of exact replicas, the children were coached to find vulnerabilities in look-alike websites created for the event.[203]

Stunt hacking promotes the idea that security vulnerabilities represent a dreadful danger to the common person, and through stunt hacking those with the darkest fears become the most powerful. But much of that story is a fantasy that has been exaggerated and distorted by hackers to serve their own interests. It is an illusion that has spread unquestioned, precisely because it benefits so many people.

# Chapter 8

# DATA BREACHES, NATION-STATE HACKING, AND EPISTEMIC CLOSURE

Today the field of information security bears three stigmata. These stigmata are the visible manifestation of history—the accretion of past decisions that have created the state of information security in the current day.

The first stigmata is data breaches that impact hundreds of millions of people.[1] After being compromised in a data breach, personal information such as financial records and health history is offered for sale on black markets.[2] Criminals buy that information and use it to commit crimes such as identity theft and fraud.[3] The people whose personal information is bought, traded, and abused in this way entrust their information to the companies and organizations with which they interact, because the alternative is to miss out on the online aspects of modern life.[4]

Perversely, the general public would know little about data breaches were it not for laws that have explicitly forced that information into the public domain. On July 1, 2003, California Senate Bill 1386 became law.[5] SB 1386 requires every company that conducts business in California to send a notification to "any resident of California whose unencrypted personal information was, or is reasonably believed to have been, acquired by an unauthorized person." This law led to an increasing number of data breaches being reported.[6] Other states followed California's lead and passed their own data breach notification laws. By 2016, forty-seven US states and the District of Columbia, Guam, Puerto Rico, and the US Virgin Islands had enacted data breach legislation.[7] Four US congressional hearings were also held to discuss data breach laws.[8]

Breach disclosure laws have two intended goals: to enable the people whose information has been compromised to become aware of that fact and to perform a kind of public shaming of the organization that experienced the breach.[9] The purpose of the latter is to prompt other organizations to take action to avoid suffering that public shaming themselves.[10] This is an old idea. In 1914, US Justice Louis D. Brandeis wrote that "publicity is justly commended as a remedy for social and industrial diseases. Sunlight is said to be the best disinfectant."[11] By highlighting security failures that result in a data breach, other organizations will have an incentive to disinfect themselves from bad security practices.[12] Data breach laws have been effective at bringing information about security incidents to light. However, data breach laws appear to have had a relatively small effect on reducing the amount of identity theft that has occurred as a result of data breaches.[13] This could be because much more identity theft occurs as a result of everyday crimes such as the theft of wallets and purses in proportion to the amount of identity theft that is caused by data breaches.[14]

In 2005, the US department store TJ Maxx suffered a serious security breach.[15] The hackers used an insecure wireless access point to access the internal TJ Maxx network and then acquired the debit and credit card information for more than one hundred million customers.[16] Because of the amount of debit and credit card information that was compromised, the TJ Maxx breach was called the "biggest card heist ever."[17] After acquiring the information, the hackers collaborated with other criminals around the world in order to enrich themselves.[18] Some were involved in the sale of the information on the black market, some carried out the subsequent credit card fraud, and some helped to launder the profits and transfer those funds back into the United States.[19] After investigating the hack, US federal prosecutors charged eleven people: three US citizens, one person from Estonia, three from Ukraine, two from China, one from Belarus, and one from parts unknown.[20]

The person who was charged with the initial hack of TJ Maxx was a US citizen from Miami named Albert Gonzalez.[21] With the proceeds of his crimes, he had built a lavish lifestyle. He owned a new BMW, stayed in luxury hotel suites, and reportedly spent $75,000 throwing a birthday party for himself.[22] Hacking had provided Gonzalez with so much money that on one occasion he complained to his friends about having to manually count twenty-dollar bills after his money counting machine had broken.[23] When federal agents arrested him on May 7, 2008, he was carrying $22,000 in cash and two laptop computers.[24] He would later lead federal agents to a barrel buried in his parents' backyard that contained $1.2 million in cash.[25]

Gonzalez had become interested in information security when, as a twelve-year-old, his computer had become infected with a virus.[26] By fourteen, he had reportedly hacked into NASA, which resulted in a visit to his school by FBI agents.[27] He then formed a black hat group that would deface websites and purchase clothes and CDs using credit card numbers the group had stolen by hacking.[28] After confessing to stealing credit card information from TJ Maxx and other companies, he was sentenced to twenty years in prison.[29] With regard to his motivations, he was unrepentant, saying that his loyalty "has always been to the black hat community."[30]

The TJ Maxx breach involved the theft of credit card numbers that were subsequently used to commit fraud, but credit cards have a built-in expiration date and can also be canceled. Credit card companies have improved their ability to detect fraudulent activity over time and have also implemented withdrawal limits.[31] These factors led criminals to look for other types of data that could be acquired through hacking.

On February 4, 2015, Anthem, one of the largest US health insurance companies, disclosed that hackers had acquired eighty million records from its computers. Those records contained the personal medical details of Anthem customers.[32] The Anthem breach was the first major example of many subsequent cases of data breaches affecting medical institutions.[33] The significance of breaches of medical information is that unlike a credit card, medical records cannot be canceled nor do they expire. Stolen medical information can be used for years after it has been compromised and used repeatedly. Medical records are also highly personal. A 2017 data breach of medical records from a cosmetic surgery clinic in Lithuania led to more than twenty-five thousand private photos from patients in sixty countries being leaked online, which included nude pictures.[34]

On July 8, 2015, the Obama administration announced that a data breach had occurred at the Office of Personnel Management (OPM).[35] The OPM is a US government agency that is responsible for managing civilian workers who work for the US federal government.[36] It creates policies and provides oversight for the health-care and retirement benefits for those workers. The OPM also has responsibility for carrying out background checks on any civilian who is applying for security clearance. The information that is required to be submitted by a person as part of that security clearance includes social security number, fingerprints, health records, and financial history.[37] To enable the background check to be performed, the person who is applying for security clearance must also submit information regarding her spouse and "people who know you well."[38] This is accomplished with the 127-page "standard form 86," which specifies that "they should be friends, peers, colleagues, college roommates, associates, etc."[39] The form requires that the full name, email address, telephone number, and home address of those people be included.[40] The fact that the OPM was responsible for gathering this information meant that it was stored within its computers. The information that was accessed by the hackers was not therefore only the personal information of the OPM workers but also the information that had been entered into the forms requesting security clearances, meaning people who ostensibly had no connection to the OPM.[41] In total, the OPM breach caused the personal details of twenty million people who had been subject to a government background check to be compromised, plus two million others whose information was contained in the forms.[42] Most organizations do not store the fingerprints of their workers, but because of the strict nature of the security clearance process, the OPM did, meaning that more than five million sets of fingerprints were also compromised in the security breach.[43]

Some companies have experienced a series of large data breaches. Yahoo!, a company that is well known for its web portal and its email service, suffered a breach in 2013 where information associated with its three billion user accounts was compromised.[44] (The population of planet Earth was around seven billion people at that time.) The next year, Yahoo! experienced another breach where the information associated with at least five hundred million user accounts was compromised.[45] The information that was acquired by the hackers included the answers to password reset questions.[46] If those Yahoo! users reused the same password reset questions and answers on other websites, their accounts on those other websites could also have become compromised as a result of the breach.

The TJ Maxx, Anthem, and OPM breaches are noteworthy because of their place on the timeline and because of the types of information that was compromised in each of those incidents, but many more breaches have occurred that have affected organizations of different sizes all over the world. Large data breaches have become so frequent that one study estimated that in 2016 more than one-quarter of all US adults—around sixty-four million people—had received a notification that their personal information had been compromised in a data breach.[47]

There are many ways that an organization might learn that they have suffered a breach. They might detect the evidence of hackers either during or after the act. A customer of the organization might notice that his personal information is being abused in some way, such as by seeing an unusual transaction on a bill or a financial statement, and then notify the organization. Or a law enforcement agency might discover a breach through the course of an investigation or by having it reported to them and then inform the organization that was breached.[48] A breach becomes public knowledge when the organization announces it or when they inform the affected customers, who can then put that information into the public domain. These cases represent the portion of the iceberg of data breaches that is visible above the waterline. The majority of the iceberg is hidden and comprises of the cases where a breach was detected by an organization but no breach notifications were sent and those occasions where a breach was not detected at all.[49]

Breaches harm both the organizations that experience them and the people whose information is compromised. The general public incur both tangible and intangible costs as a result of data breaches. These include not only the financial costs but also the opportunity costs for the time spent responding to the breach notification and the psychological costs that come from having personal information become compromised.[50] A 2016 study found that 6 percent of respondents to a survey on the topic of data breaches stated that they had each spent more than $10,000 recovering from a data breach.[51] The most costly cases were those that involved the compromise of credit card information or health records.[52] The identity theft that can result from a compromise of these types of information can be particularly damaging. The victims of identity theft have to take steps to prevent further harm, such as putting a freeze on credit files and reversing fraudulent transactions.[53] In the same study, 32 percent of respondents to the survey stated that they experienced no financial loss, but for those who did experience some loss, the median amount lost was estimated as $500.[54] A second study that was published a year later found that hospitals that suffered a data breach experienced a small but detectable increase of three-tenths of 1 percent in the mortality rate following a breach. Since 2011, the median mortality rate in hospitals has been decreasing by the same value, so if the finding in the study is correct, a hospital that experiences a security breach loses one year's worth of progress in reducing its mortality rate.[55]

Organizations that are breached sometimes offer to provide credit monitoring services to their customers. The purpose of this credit monitoring is to try and stop the compromised information from creating harm by highlighting when it is being used by criminals. Free credit monitoring is an olive branch extended from organizations to their customers, but it does not address all of the problems that a breach can create for those customers.[56] This is because the use of credit monitoring services might itself create new risks. After the OPM breach, free credit monitoring was offered to the victims, but a number of scams subsequently emerged that used phishing websites and social engineering phone calls to try and scam people by asking for personal information in order to "activate" that free credit monitoring.[57] The fact that free credit monitoring services are sold to organizations that have experienced data breaches and not directly to the victims of those breaches is telling because it reveals that the product provides more benefits to the organization that purchases it than to the end users.[58]

Information that is compromised in a data breach such as a social security number or a current address can be difficult to change. But medical information such as date of birth and health history is impossible to change. If a US secret agent had her fingerprint data compromised as part of the OPM breach, that person could be identified using those fingerprints even if she subsequently took on an entirely new identity.[59] Organizations often say that they have "no reason to believe" that the information compromised in a breach was used to commit crimes such as fraud, but in the case of information that cannot be changed such as someone's date of birth and place of birth, those organizations have no way to know that the information will not be used in the future—potentially decades after the breach occurred.[60]

The sheer number of well-publicized breaches has led to the general public having a low level of confidence that their personal information will be protected. A 2015 study found that only 6 percent of adults were "very confident" that credit card companies could maintain the security of their information.[61]

Perhaps surprisingly, the average customer attrition rate at organizations that experience a breach has been measured as only 11 percent.[62] That number must partly reflect the high costs involved with switching from an organization to a competitor, and it is not possible to switch at all if data are breached from a government entity or from an organization that has no viable competitors.

The plight of the common person with regard to security breaches is a sorry one. For organizations, the situation is also grim. Organizations that suffer a security breach experience two kinds of costs: direct and indirect.[63] Cleaning up after a breach and making sure that hackers have been purged from computers is an example of a direct cost.[64] Indirect costs are created by the loss of trust and goodwill in customers and in potential future customers.[65] Both kinds of cost can have a significant monetary value. Because of a 2012 breach at the South Carolina Department of Revenue that began with a phishing email, the state of South Carolina had to pay $12 million to provide credit monitoring services for the victims, $700,000 to notify out-of-state residents who had filed taxes in South Carolina of the breach, $500,000 to a consulting firm to investigate the breach, $500,000 to pay for security monitoring, $160,000 to a public relations firm, another $160,000 to install specialized security software, and $100,000 to a law firm for legal advice.[66]

Publicly traded companies can experience damage to their stock price as a consequence of a breach. The amount of the effect is unclear, but a 2017 study found the reduction to be relatively small—less than 1 percent on average on the day following the disclosure of a security breach.[67] An earlier study in 2006 found that there was a negative effect on stock price immediately after a breach, but that it was short lived.[68] The short-term hit to stock price is certainly small in comparison to the effect of a corporate scandal.[69] This can partly be explained by organizations bundling the announcement of a breach with positive news stories to balance or drown out the bad news that the breach represents.[70] Organizations have also been known to release the news of a breach during a time when there is a smaller than usual amount of negative news reports regarding the company.[71] This kind of gaming of the breach notification laws can occur because those laws typically provide a timeframe in which the breach must be reported to the victims, such as within two months.[72] That flexibility gives an organization the ability to schedule the announcement of the breach at a time that is convenient for them.

The US military has suffered a number of major data breaches. The most high-profile of these have been caused by insider threats where an insider exfiltrates data. Data breaches caused by malicious insiders are difficult to prevent because workers require access to information in order to carry out their jobs.[73] If a malicious insider is able to send emails, he can attempt to exfiltrate information by sending it outside the organization via email. Similarly, if a malicious insider can print documents, he can attempt to print out the information that he wishes to exfiltrate and simply carry it out of the building. The number of possible methods by which a malicious insider might be able to exfiltrate data is at least as large as the number of possible methods by which information can be communicated.[74] In the connected modern world, that number is very high. Instant messaging, social media, websites, and other forms of electronic communication all provide possible channels by which a malicious insider might attempt to exfiltrate data.

The nature of the information compromised in military data breaches has led to those incidents being widely reported. In 2010, a US soldier named Chelsea Manning leaked approximately seven hundred thousand US government documents to WikiLeaks.[75] Among the documents were 250 diplomatic cables and information on the wars in Iraq and Afghanistan.[76] Manning copied the documents onto a removable memory card in order to exfiltrate them and then transferred the files to the WikiLeaks computers in Sweden.[77] She was arrested in 2010 and sentenced to thirty-five years in prison in 2013.[78] Her sentence was commuted by President Barack Obama, and she was released in 2017.[79] In 2013, a CIA contractor named Edward Snowden leaked NSA information to a number of journalists after traveling to Hong Kong.[80] Exactly how many records were involved in the breach is unknown but has been estimated to be more than two hundred thousand.[81] The security controls that Snowden subverted in order to access and then exfiltrate the information have not been revealed, but he may have acquired more access than he was permitted by obtaining passwords from his coworkers.[82] In a supreme irony, Snowden had been accredited in 2010 as a Certified Ethical Hacker.[83]

It is easy to attribute the blame for security breaches to the organizations that experienced them, such as Yahoo!. After all, was it not the responsibility of Yahoo! and the other breached organizations to implement information security measures that would have prevented those breaches? This type of thinking led the satirical website The Onion to write a facetious history of Yahoo! that included the milestones "1994: Jerry Yang and David Filo decide to pursue their dream of creating a multipurpose web portal with easy-to-hack accounts" and "2017: Confirms a 2013 data breach had affected all three billion of its user accounts and all future user accounts."[84]

Blame is often directed at the organizations that are breached and often because a specific technical control was not in place that would have stopped the specific type of attack that was employed.[85] The absence of that specific technical control is frequently believed to be the deciding factor in the breach.[86] TJ Maxx was criticized for a lack of wireless encryption, and the OPM was criticized for not implementing two-factor authentication and encryption.[87] It is tempting to believe that a security breach can have such a single cause, because this enables an organization that suffers a breach to plug that hole and then tell their customers that the risk has been removed.[88] After the OPM breach, the director of the OPM, Katherine Archuleta, was quizzed by the US House of Representatives. She was asked to give herself a grade for her efforts and also asked whether she was "succeeding or failing" at leading the OPM with regard to information security. Her answer was that "cybersecurity problems are decades in the making. The whole of government is responsible, and it will take all of us to solve the issue and continue to work on them."[89] Her answer has been interpreted as an attempt to deflect blame from herself onto the larger government, which it might certainly have been.[90] She was, however, correct in saying that the root causes of the OPM data breach and other data breaches do run significantly deeper than a superficial analysis would suggest.[91]

The fact that hackers breached TJ Maxx by exploiting a vulnerability in wireless networking was somewhat immaterial, just as it was that the hackers who breached the OPM used vulnerabilities in two-factor authentication. Hackers could have exploited different vulnerabilities, or utilized phishing, or zero-day vulnerabilities, or any number of other hacking techniques to gain access.[92] In truth, the root causes of data breaches are legion, and both organizations and individuals face the same structural challenges. Both have to use software that contains vulnerabilities. Both have to use the internet protocols that underlie technologies such as email and the web that were not designed with security in mind. Both have to make security decisions, often without all of the relevant information. Security breaches will continue to impact both organizations and individuals because the causes have now become so diffuse.

The second stigmata is the harm caused by hacking carried out by nation-states. In 2009, a well-organized group was discovered to be hacking US businesses. Their goal appeared to be to steal intellectual property and to access the US-based email accounts of Chinese human rights activists.[93] The attacks were first publicized by Google in a blog post on January 12, 2010.[94] Google reported that they had been attacked alongside businesses in a wide range of industries that included finance, media, defense, shipping, aerospace, manufacturing, electronics, and software.[95] The information compromised by the hackers included the results of medical clinical trials, blueprints for products and manufacturing processes, and other confidential information.[96] To accomplish the attacks, the hackers primarily used phishing combined with a zero-day vulnerability in web browsers.[97] The hacking campaign was branded the Aurora attacks because that word was found inside one of the hacking tools used by the group.[98]

Over the following months, the hackers were traced to a twelve-story building in the Pudong area of Shanghai. That building is surrounded by businesses such as restaurants, massage parlors, and a wine importer, but the structure itself housed the offices of Unit 61398 of the People's Liberation Army of China.[99] Unit 61398 is a team of hackers that have been operating since at least 2006.[100] They are estimated to employ hundreds of hackers and other technical specialists, including people with English-language skills.[101] The group is thought to be the key player in Chinese computer espionage and to have carried out thousands of attacks.[102] Because of the scale of their hacking exploits, they have been given various names over time, including Elderwood, Byzantine Candor, and the Comment Crew.[103] The latter name is a result of their use of comments, meaning annotations, inside web pages, which they use as part of their hacking campaigns.[104]

These discoveries regarding Unit 61398 were made by a US-based information security company named Mandiant.[105] The attribution by Mandiant of the Aurora attacks to Unit 61398 was reported in the *New York Times*, to which the Chinese government offered a denial, saying that the Mandiant report was "unprofessional" and "annoying and laughable."[106] In response, a representative from Mandiant replied that "either [the attacks] are coming from inside Unit 61398, or the people who run the most-controlled, most-monitored internet networks in the world are clueless about thousands of people generating attacks from this one neighborhood."[107] The Mandiant spokesperson further stated that if it were not Unit 61398 carrying out the attacks, then it must be "a secret, resourced organization full of mainland Chinese speakers with direct access to Shanghai-based telecommunications infrastructure that is engaged in a multiyear enterprise-scale computer espionage campaign right outside of Unit 61398's gates."

The Aurora attacks were characterized by Mandiant as an "advanced persistent threat": advanced because the attackers used zero-day vulnerabilities, persistent because the attackers were well resourced and determined to succeed in their goal of hacking into the target companies and also because once they had successfully gained access, they would persist inside those computers for an extended timeframe.[108] On average, Unit 61398 would access the computers that they had hacked within an organization for an entire year. In one case, the hackers maintained access to an organization that they had hacked for almost five years.[109] Because the Aurora attacks led to the creation of the term *advanced persistent threat*, Unit 61398 was given the designation APT1.[110]

In May 2014, a US federal grand jury indicted five named members of Unit 61398 for charges relating to the theft of intellectual property from organizations in the United States.[111] This was largely a symbolic gesture on the part of the US government since it is unlikely that any of those individuals would be arrested unless they left mainland China and came within the reach of US law enforcement agencies. The indictments issued by the US government against members of Unit 61398 stemmed from the attacks against US businesses, but China had reportedly also stolen information from the US military. That information is reported to have included the plans for a system designed to shoot down ballistic missiles and the plans for military aircraft such as the V-22 Osprey, F-35 Joint Strike fighter, and Black Hawk helicopter.[112] In 2018, Chinese government hackers are believed to have hacked computers at a US government contractor and copied more than six hundred gigabytes of information regarding plans for a supersonic antiship missile code named Sea Dragon.[113] The 2016 data breach at the OPM was also subsequently attributed to China. This means that the sensitive information that was submitted as part of the background check process for federal employees was acquired by Chinese hackers and therefore by the Chinese government.[114] Hacking carried out by China has been so effective that just as they did with the data breaches suffered by Yahoo!, the satirical website The Onion lampooned US security failures with the headline "China Unable to Recruit Hackers Fast Enough to Keep Up with Vulnerabilities in US Security Systems."[115]

Like China, Russia is a nation-state that has invested substantial resources to develop its hacking capabilities. Fancy Bear is the name given to a major hacking group that is believed to be associated with the GRU, the military intelligence agency of Russia.[116] That attribution comes from the fact that some of the hacking tools associated with the group use the Russian language and because the hacking they have carried out has been observed to typically take place during Moscow working hours. Fancy Bear also focuses its hacking on topics that are of interest to the Russian government.[117] The group has demonstrated an interest in the state of Georgia, which Russia invaded in 2008, and in Eastern Europe generally.[118] Fancy Bear has targeted various member countries of the North Atlantic Treaty Organization (NATO) with the goal of promoting the Russian government's political interests.[119] Specific individuals that Fancy Bear has targeted include senior figures within NATO such as former US secretary of state Colin Powell and US Army general Wesley Clark, as well as US defense contractors such as Boeing, Lockheed Martin, and Raytheon.[120] An analysis of almost five thousand email accounts that were found to have been targeted by Fancy Bear showed that the group aimed to hack individuals and organizations in more than one hundred countries that oppose the Russian government, including the United States, Ukraine, Georgia, and Syria.[121]

The hacking capabilities of Fancy Bear are sufficiently developed that they have been categorized as an advanced persistent threat. As with APT1, Fancy Bear uses exploits for zero-day vulnerabilities and spear phishing as its primary hacking techniques.[122] But where APT1 gives the impression that they want their hacking to remain clandestine, Fancy Bear has shown little compunction to do the same.

In 2015, Fancy Bear pretended to be a hacking group that they invented called the CyberCaliphate.[123] Under the CyberCaliphate guise, Fancy Bear sent death threats to the wives of five US military personnel.[124] Later that year, Fancy Bear hacked into a French television network and interrupted the programs being broadcast on the company's eleven channels.[125] The disruption lasted for more than three hours, with the director of the station saying that the attack had "severely damaged" its systems.[126] The French government called the incident an "unacceptable attack on the freedom of information and expression."[127] During the attack, instead of the expected programming, the hackers broadcast logos from the Islamic State of Iraq and the Levant (ISIL) along with ISIL slogans in English, Arabic, and French.[128] At the same time, Fancy Bear posted messages on the Facebook page of the television station saying, "Soldiers of France, stay away from the Islamic State!

You have the chance to save your families, take advantage of it" and "Je suis IS."[129] A French television station might appear to be a peculiar target for Fancy Bear, but it might have been selected by the group as an experiment to determine how easily they could disrupt broadcasts from larger television stations in the future.

Beginning in 2016, Fancy Bear used phishing techniques to hack into the World Anti-Doping Agency, copying the drug-testing results of a number of Olympic athletes and then publishing them on a website with the brazen web address fancybear.net.[130] That website listed the compromised files and made the claim that "dozens of American athletes tested positive" for performance-enhancing drugs, even though those athletes had received approved exemptions for the drugs from the International Olympic Committee.[131]

The record of hacking carried out by Fancy Bear is long and rich, with one of the most notable and egregious instances being their interference in the 2016 US presidential election.[132] Their goal was to increase the probability that Donald Trump would be elected by harming the campaign of Hillary Clinton.[133] They began in March 2016 by sending phishing emails to members of the Clinton campaign and to members of the Democratic Party.[134] This enabled them to compromise the security of those computers and then copy tens of thousands of emails and other files.[135] In and around April 2016, they hacked computers belonging to the Democratic National Committee (DNC) and Democratic Congressional Campaign Committee.[136] An investigation by computer incident response companies determined that the hacking had been carried out not only by Fancy Bear but also by another Russian hacking group labeled Cozy Bear.[137] In the DNC hacks, Fancy Bear and Cozy Bear appeared to have been somewhat unaware of each other's presence, suggesting that they were operated by different Russian intelligence agencies.[138] John Podesta, the chairman of the Hillary Clinton presidential campaign, was then hacked using a phishing email that claimed to be alerting him to a security issue.[139] The email instructed him to change the password for his email account by clicking a web link, which sent him to a Russian-controlled server that enabled his account to be compromised.[140] The hackers were then able to access approximately sixty thousand of his emails.[141]

The materials that were compromised by the Russian hacking groups were released strategically over the three-month period prior to the presidential election.[142] Information was released on WikiLeaks, on a website the hackers created called DCLeaks, and through a fictitious hacker character they invented called Guccifer 2.0.[143] The timing of the releases left little doubt as to their motivations. One information dump took place within hours of the first report by the *Washington Post* regarding the so-called *Access Holly-wood* videotape in which Donald Trump could be heard making iniquitous remarks regarding women.[144] Another information dump involved the re-lease of over twenty thousand emails and other documents three days before the beginning of the Democratic National Convention.[145] The information released by Guccifer 2.0 was also found to have been connected to the most competitive races for the US House of Representatives, and there was no equivalent targeting of the Trump campaign or targeting of Republicans.[146]

Russia wields its hacking power in a brazen manner. In contrast, the United States attempts to keep its hacking secret, but it has not always been successful. The Snowden leaks described the global surveillance capabilities that have been created by the Five Eyes countries, the joint intelligence agen-cies of the United States, United Kingdom, Australia, Canada, and New Zealand. They also revealed details regarding the extraordinary hacking ca-pabilities of the US government—capabilities that "scared the daylights" out of seasoned information security professionals.[147]

The leaks revealed that the TAO—the Office of Tailored Access Opera-tions within the NSA had developed a hacking tool they named QUAN-TUM.[148] By listening to network traffic on the internet, QUANTUM can detect when a target's web browser is attempting to load a web page.[149] QUANTUM then quickly creates a copy of that specific web page but in-serts malicious code into it, and delivers it to the target's web browser before the real web server can respond. The malicious code then compromises the web browser to take control of the computer.[150] QUANTUM is able to win the race on the internet with the real web server because the NSA has placed servers strategically around the world to create a kind of shadow network.[151] This structural aspect makes QUANTUM much more difficult for a lone hacker or a non-nation-state group to implement.[152] QUANTUM is useful to the NSA because it does not require the target to make a wrong decision, such as by clicking a link in a phishing email. In the words of the NSA, "If we can get the target to visit us in some form of web browser, we can prob-ably own them."[153] (The phrase "to own someone" is hacker slang for com-promising the security of that person's computer.)

The Snowden leaks showed that the NSA was able to use QUANTUM to compromise the computers of people who visited the websites of Yahoo!,

LinkedIn, Facebook, Twitter, YouTube, and other popular websites.[154] The NSA documents also revealed that QUANTUM was used to hack into the Belgian telecommunications company Belgacom and the Organization of the Petroleum Exporting Countries (OPEC).[155] Government Communications Headquarters (GCHQ), the British equivalent of the NSA, described QUANTUM as "cool," and the NSA described QUANTUM as "the new exploit hotness."[156]

QUANTUM is an example of the NSA creating a hacking technique that can be used broadly. It can be employed to hack any person who uses a web browser to connect to a number of popular websites. But the NSA have also applied their hacking skills in a narrow way to attack very specific targets. In the 2000s, internet worms such as Slammer and Blaster ravaged the internet by infecting hundreds of thousands of computers. A worm that infects such a large number of computers in an indiscriminate way would be a poor choice for carrying out a targeted attack because it would be quickly discovered. But if a worm could be created that would infect only a small number of specific computers, it could fly under the radar and remain secret. The NSA created exactly such an internet worm in collaboration with the CIA and Israel.[157]

It was called Stuxnet. The goal of the project was to damage Iran's nuclear program, and so the worm was targeted at a specific Iranian nuclear facility.[158] Stuxnet was coded very carefully to infect only certain computers to such an extent that the targeting it employed was described as "a marksman's job."[159] To accomplish this, it would infect only industrial control systems that operated motors running at specific frequencies. This ensured that Stuxnet would infect the computers at the Iranian facility but not infect, say, an industrial control system operating a conveyor belt in a factory.[160] But rather than simply destroying the infected systems, Stuxnet was designed to introduce subtle errors.[161] Those errors would make it appear to the machine operators and the scientists working within the Iranian program that they did not understand their own technology.[162] This was achieved by changing the speed of the centrifuges used to create the nuclear material in a way that would introduce harmful vibrations to the equipment while simultaneously relaying false information to the control room to indicate that everything was normal.[163] In this way, Stuxnet was designed to delay the progress of the Iranian nuclear program and also to demoralize those people who worked on it.

Stuxnet was discovered in June 2010, but the main attack likely began a year earlier.[164] Stuxnet was successful, reportedly damaging one-fifth of Iran's nuclear centrifuges.[165] In the first half of 2009, the uranium enrichment facility at Natanz in Iran experienced a "serious nuclear accident" and had to shut down on several occasions in 2010 because of a series of major technical issues.[166] The number of centrifuge machines operated by Iran reached a peak of almost five thousand in May 2009 but then dropped 23 percent by August.[167]

To develop Stuxnet would have required substantial resources.[168] In order to infect the specific type of industrial equipment used at the Iranian facilities, the worm would have needed to be tested against that equipment, and that testing reportedly took place at the Dimona nuclear complex in Israel.[169] The effort to code the worm was estimated as being several person years' worth of work due to the fact that the worm implemented a number of technical innovations.[170] At their facility, the Iranians had implemented an air gap in an attempt to isolate the computers that controlled the industrial equipment from other computer networks.[171] This meant that the industrial equipment was on a completely separate network, and any files or data that were required would be transferred across the air gap using USB flash drives or other kinds of removable storage media. Theoretically, this approach would stop hacking attempts because there would be no way for a hacker or a worm to cross the air gap. But Stuxnet was written so that it would infect computers on the internet side of the air gap, then it would copy itself to any USB flash drives that were inserted into those computers. After being plugged into the computers on the other side of the air gap, Stuxnet would copy itself onto those computers, thereby jumping the gap.[172] Once inside the target network, Stuxnet employed an unprecedented four zero-day vulnerabilities in order to achieve the highest level of privilege on the computers that controlled the industrial equipment.[173] The authors of Stuxnet did not appear to know what version of Microsoft Windows was being used on those computers. Therefore, Stuxnet was programmed so that it would run on every single version of Windows that had been released in the last ten years.[174] After compromising those computers, Stuxnet hid itself by using two cryptographic certificates. Those certificates had previously been stolen from two separate companies in Taiwan.[175] Those companies were located in the same business park, suggesting that operatives from the NSA might have physically broken into the two facilities in order to steal the information.[176]

The attribution of Stuxnet to the NSA, CIA, and Israel is believed to be relatively clear, but the task of determining that a particular hacking incident was carried out by a particular nation-state can be a challenging task.[177] Hackers have long used the technique of laundering their activities through a chain of compromised computers in different countries in order to hide their true origin. In the case of APT1, an accumulation of relatively small operational errors led to their attribution as Unit 61398 of the People's Liberation Army. Nation-states are also faced with the conundrum that because their hacking activities are focused on specific goals, they might become identified simply through the pursuit of those goals.[178] Hackers working for China are very unlikely to attack companies in China but can be expected to attack companies in the United States. If information is compromised as a result of hacking and is subsequently used by the Russian government, it is unlikely to have been taken by Chinese hackers.[179]

Much has been written and hypothesized about the possible hacking of critical infrastructure such as the computers that control power grids, dams, transportation systems, and such like. That writing has sometimes employed language that is over the top. One article described Stuxnet as the "Hiroshima of Cyber War," and the phrase "cyber 9/11" has been used on an unfortunate number of occasions.[180] If a country were to experience a hacking attack against its critical infrastructure, that attack could be difficult to defeat, but from a pragmatic perspective it would still be preferable to being on the receiving end of bullets and bombs.[181] In that sense, the use of hacking by nation-states is less destructive than traditional war. If a nation-state can disable a target using hacking, then that would result in less loss of life than dropping a high-explosive bomb to destroy it. Instead of sending a spy into a foreign country where that spy might get arrested or killed, a nation-state can use hacking to acquire the same information that the spy would have attempted to steal. Wars are violent by their very nature, so hacking might in fact reduce violence.[182]

To accomplish the level of capability that China, Russia, and the United States have achieved has required a level of investment that only a nation-state could realistically make. The development of zero-day vulnerabilities, the large-scale development and operation of phishing campaigns, the creation of tools and technical infrastructure that enable massive amounts of data to be exfiltrated from compromised organizations, and the processing of those data once they have been exfiltrated all require substantial resources.

Fancy Bear, the TAO, and the other nation-state hacking groups must necessarily employ large teams of analysts and translators in addition to their hackers.[183] Like any large organization that has a specific goal, they have embraced the division of labor and employed individuals with specialized skills.[184] The TAO was said in 2013 to have more than six hundred hackers working in rotating shifts twenty-four hours a day, seven days a week.[185] The programmers and hackers working for the nation-state hacking groups are skilled and methodical. Their hacking tools are updated diligently and meticulously.[186] They create hacking tools with the intention of avoiding detection and complicating or slowing attribution if their tools are detected.[187]

The nation-states have become so accomplished at hacking that they have forced a restructuring of the entire field of information security. It has long been said that information security requires a balance of efforts across three distinct aspects: protection, detection, and response—that is, protect computers from hackers, detect hackers if they break through the protective measures, and respond by purging the hackers from the system. But the nation-states have so completely eclipsed the ability of the average organization to protect itself that the focus is now on detection and response. The reasonable assumption is that nation-state hackers have already broken in and the pressing task is to try and find them inside the organization and attempt to remove them.[188] In this way, the weaknesses of the conventional set of current-day security technologies have been laid bare. Installing patches, using antivirus programs and intrusion detection systems, and even incorporating an air gap are all expected to be ineffective when an organization is targeted by a nation-state.

Some organizations have responded to nation-state hacking by hiring hackers who previously worked for a nation-state organization such as the NSA and putting those people to work for the purpose of defense. This is the Ouroboros of Egyptian iconography—the snake eating its own tail. No matter how many ex-hackers an organization can hire, they cannot match the capabilities that the nation-states have developed and institutionalized. They have become like gods.

The nation-states will not stop using computer hacking to achieve their goals. Espionage is not against international law, and it seems unlikely that in the foreseeable future there will be an international law or strict norms established among nations that would cause a sea change in the use of hacking by nation-states.[189] After the Mandiant report on APT1 was released,

Chinese hacking operations went quiet for a while but then came back to the same level of activity. Officials from Mandiant have described Chinese hacking as the "new normal."[190] The nation-states can and will continue to use the hacking capabilities they have developed for the purpose of espionage, for the theft of intellectual property, and to interfere in elections.

The third stigmata is the opportunity costs that are created by the epistemic closure within the field of information security. The term *epistemic closure* was coined by political analysts who identified what they described as an alternate reality that had been created within the conservative movement in US politics.[191] This was the result of an interconnected cluster of television shows, books, radio programs, magazines, blogs, and other forms of media. Any material that contradicted the majority view that had been established within that echo chamber was instinctively pushed away because, ipso facto, if a source contradicted the majority view, it could not be trusted.[192] This is a profoundly dangerous state of affairs because the false reality that is constructed within such a community is unlikely to comport with the requirements of the real world.

Stunt hacking is a striking manifestation of the epistemic closure within the field of information security because it ignores the root causes of security failures and instead places the focus on the surface manifestation of those root causes. Stunt hacking forsakes the complex, real world and builds a simpler, fake world, and in doing so it creates a phantom enemy. Any victories won against that phantom enemy are false, an illusion, but because of epistemic closure they are rewarded. This is demonstrated by the hackers who are able to carry out the most spectacular stunt hacking being invited to present at the biggest security conferences and receiving press coverage from major news publications.[193]

The roots of this harmful inclination can be traced to the very beginning of the modern era. In 1974, the security evaluation of the Multics operating system described a new type of hack that could be carried out against compilers.[194] All programs have to be compiled in order to be transformed from their source code into a binary—that is, the program that can then be run on the computer. That transformation is performed by a special program called a compiler. The team that carried out the Multics security evaluation hypothesized that they could insert code into the compiler to modify it so that when it was compiling a program, it would insert a back door (what they called a trap door) into the resulting binary.[195] For example, if the modified compiler was being used to create a binary for a program that processed passwords, a back door could be inserted that would make that password program always accept a secret password. However, this could be detected relatively easily because the code for the back door would be visible to anyone who looked at the code of the compiler. The back door could be discovered, removed, and the compiler recompiled using a second compiler. To counter this, the team suggested going one step further and also modifying the *second* compiler so that it would recognize when it was being used to recompile the first compiler and insert the code that created the back door back into it. This created the situation where the only way to determine if a compiler did not have a back door was to find the source code for the compiler that created the compiler and then the source code for the compiler that created *that* compiler, and so on. It was "turtles all the way down"—a problem of infinite regress. When the US Air Force purchased the Multics operating system, they required the developers to provide them with the entire source code so that they could recompile the operating system if there was ever a bug or a security vulnerability that they wanted to fix.[196] But in reality, the air force could never be sure that they had removed a particular vulnerability if they had not also written their own compiler from scratch.[197]

In 1983, Ken Thompson, the cocreator of the Unix operating system, was awarded the Turing Award, which is known as the Nobel Prize of computing.[198] In his acceptance speech, Thompson coined the phrase *trusting trust* to refer to the hacking technique that had been identified in the Multics security evaluation.[199] He discussed the technique in the context of his work to develop the Unix operating system.[200] In his talk, Thompson also warned against what he described as "an explosive situation brewing" where "the press, television, and movies make heroes of vandals by calling them whiz kids."[201] He stated that "the act of breaking into a computer system has to have the same social stigma as breaking into a neighbor's house. The press must learn that the misguided use of a computer is no more amazing than drunk driving of an automobile."[202]

The Multics compiler hack is perhaps the platonic ideal of a hack. It does not take advantage of a particular vulnerability in a particular program. It is not simply another example of a buffer overflow. It is insidious and potentially pervasive. It causes the users of a computer to be suspicious of everything on the computer—even the computer programs that they have written with their own hands. After his talk, Thompson had to clarify that he himself had not introduced the backdoor technique into the Unix operating system that he had coauthored.[203]

It is a widely held view within the field of information security that when designing the security measures for a computer system the possible actions that an attacker might carry out should be considered as part of that design effort. The purpose of such a threat modeling exercise is to identify defenses that should be implemented within the system to protect against attacks. A person who thinks in this way is said to be employing the "security mindset."[204] In 2004, an editorial in a preeminent information security journal declared that "attacking systems is a good idea."[205] The editor's goal in making that statement was to promote the idea of discussing hacking techniques in the open so that they could be better understood. The editorial made the parallel to engineers in other fields learning from mistakes and failures and recommended that security professionals should embrace those same methods.[206] Balancing an understanding of offense and defense in this way is a pragmatic approach. But beginning with the Multics hack, the field of information security has developed a culture in which those who identify the most fantastic and obscurantist hacking techniques are both embraced and rewarded, and that impulse has led to bizarre and counterproductive situations.

In 2013, a well-known security researcher became convinced that his computers were infected with malware, meaning malicious programs created by hackers.[207] He claimed that malware on his computers was communicating even after the wireless networking on those computers had been turned off and while the computers were not physically connected to any kind of computer network.[208] He further claimed that the malware could infect three different types of operating system and that after reinstalling the operating system on his computers, the malware would quickly reinfect them again through some unknown mechanism.[209] His theory was that the malware could infect the BIOS on the computers, which is the lowest level of computer software. He also theorized that the malware was infecting the computers and communicating between them using high-frequency sound waves.[210] He believed that he had discovered something profound—a hidden and dangerous threat that lurked underneath the surface of everyday life and that was targeting him personally.

On social media, the default position for many members of the security community was to support his claims.[211] Alex Stamos, who would go on to become the chief security officer at Yahoo! and then at Facebook, sent a tweet saying that "everybody in security needs to . . . watch his analysis."[212] Jeff Moss, the founder of the Black Hat Briefings and Defcon security conferences, sent a tweet saying, "No joke it's really serious."[213] But the researcher's description of the supposed capabilities of the malware—high-frequency sound waves and all—appear similar to the claims of a person experiencing a psychotic episode, and no evidence for the existence of the malware was ever independently verified.[214] In response to other people being unable to find any evidence of the malware, the researcher claimed that the malware was able to recognize when a copy was being made to give to someone else and then erase itself.[215]

During the dot-com boom, the commercial security industry was propelled by security researchers and hackers acting as the "stimulant to the productive forces," as Karl Marx put it. But Marx's view of destruction and criminality as a creative force was wrong. The French economist Frédéric Bastiat wrote in his 1850 essay "Ce qu'on voit et ce qu'on ne voit pas" (That which is seen and that which is not seen) that the money spent on destruction does not in fact create a net benefit to society.[216] In his essay, he uses the example of a shopkeeper's son who accidentally breaks a window, causing the window to have to be replaced at the cost of six francs. The glazer earns six francs and so is thankful to the careless child. But the conclusion should not be that the broken window caused money to circulate and therefore acted as a stimulant to the economy. That was merely the part that was seen and did not take into account the part that was not seen. If the shopkeeper had not spent six francs replacing the window, he could have spent that money elsewhere. In other words, the money spent in one place means that it could not be spent somewhere else—somewhere potentially much more useful. In the same way, the epistemic closure within the field of information security that rewards activities such as stunt hacking and that rewards research into sensationalist hacking techniques has led to the creation of massive opportunity costs.

Today, newcomers to the field of information security tend to be attracted to the latest vulnerabilities and hacking exploits precisely because that is where the field of information security and the popular press tends to place its focus. Zero-day vulnerabilities and hacking are exciting because they represent the concerns of the moment. But those who have worked in the field for decades have come to see the endless parade of new vulnerabilities as creating a kind of hellish monotony—that the "hamster wheel of pain" created during the dot-com boom never stopped spinning. More recent initiatives such as bug bounty programs have only served to deepen these deleterious effects. Bug bounty programs are designed to reward solitary security practitioners working on a narrow range of problems, specifically security vulnerabilities in websites and computer software. But there is no bounty for attempting to solve the systemic underlying causes of those vulnerabilities. There is also no bounty for the purpose of rewarding those people who are researching problems in areas that are now known to be important to improving information security, such as the economics and psychology of security.

Some of this might be explained by the relevancy paradox in which people only seek out information that they perceive to be relevant to them. In a field that rewards stunt hacking and vulnerability research, people will naturally gravitate toward hacking and vulnerability research. Those people might not know that, for example, the economics of information security is relevant to their goals, so they do not consider it. But the relevancy paradox cannot serve as a blanket excuse because some of the most wasteful outcomes have occurred at the hands of experienced security professionals.

In 2016, a company named MedSec used eBay to purchase implantable medical devices from a number of different manufacturers.[217] They then disassembled and reverse engineered those devices with the goal of finding security vulnerabilities. The pacemakers manufactured by one company named St. Jude Medical appeared to contain a number of vulnerabilities. At that time, St. Jude Medical was one of the largest providers of medical devices such as pacemakers in the United States.[218] But instead of disclosing the vulnerabilities to St. Jude Medical, MedSec approached a Wall Street investment firm with a money-making proposal.[219] They suggested that the investment firm short the stock of St. Jude Medical, meaning take a position within the financial markets that would generate a profit if the value of the publicly traded stock of St. Jude Medical happened to fall.[220] They would then release the information showing that the medical devices could be hacked. If the stock market value of St. Jude Medical dropped, then both MedSec and the investment firm would be enriched through their short position.[221] The investment firm agreed to participate and issued a report that described the vulnerabilities MedSec believed they had found.[222] On the same day that the report was issued, the CEO of MedSec appeared on the business TV channel Bloomberg. In that appearance she claimed that there was a "complete absence of any security protections whatsoever in St. Jude Medical equipment."[223] She also made the claim in a separate TV appearance that "we can, remotely, cause the implants to cease to function," implying that hackers could kill people who were implanted with one of the devices.[224]

Their plan worked. The value of St. Jude Medical fell by almost 5 percent—the largest one-day fall for seven months.[225] The drop was so precipitous that trading in the stock was halted.[226] But within a few days, a team of researchers from the University of Michigan began to analyze the work carried out by MedSec.[227] That team included medical device researchers and a cardiologist, and their findings called into question the veracity of MedSec's claims.[228] MedSec had cited a number of error messages as evidence that a crash attack could be carried out against a home-monitored implantable cardiac defibrillator manufactured by St. Jude Medical.[229] However, those error messages would also be displayed if the device wasn't properly plugged in.[230] In a press release, the University of Michigan researchers wrote that "to the armchair engineer it may look startling, but to a clinician it just means you didn't plug it in. In layman's terms, it's like claiming that hackers took over your computer, but then later discovering that you simply forgot to plug in your keyboard." They politely suggested that the MedSec report was not necessarily wrong but that the evidence did not appear to support the report's conclusions.[231] St. Jude Medical then filed a defamation lawsuit against MedSec and the investment firm, which alleged that they had created a "malicious scheme to manipulate the securities markets for their own financial windfall through an unethical and unlawful scheme premised upon falsehoods and misleading statements."[232] Further, they tried to "frighten and confuse patients and doctors."[233] St. Jude Medical, since acquired by another company, did subsequently release software fixes for vulnerabilities in pacemakers, but it is not clear that the vulnerabilities that were patched were those that MedSec claimed to have found.[234]

The events that unfolded between MedSec and St. Jude Medical illustrate the massive opportunity costs that are created by the toxic combination of a focus on the most esoteric and dangerous types of stunt hacking, vulnerability research for profit, and promoted disclosure.

Epistemic closure takes place when a community retreats into itself, indifferent to the disparity between the world that they have created inside their protective bubble and the reality of the outside world. It would be naive to believe that individuals and groups do not benefit from the simplification and the feeling of correctness that the bubble provides. But dogmatism creates a trap into which the participants will inevitably fall and become ensnared, making it impossible for them to move on to a better kind of future.

Chapter 9

# The Wicked Nature of
# Information Security

The three stigmata exist because of path dependence, where the set of possible choices that are available in any given moment are limited by the choices that have been made in the past. RAND and the other early researchers set in motion the study of information security in the modern era, but they were unable to accomplish their goal of the protection of information through the primacy of technology. Their focus on approaches such as multilevel security and formal verification led the field of information security down a path that diverged from the future. When the new commercial markets emerged, a paradigm was created in which the field was forced to constantly react to new technologies. In a strange way, they did create the future of information security, but that future was profoundly different from their original objectives, merely a distant facsimile of their aspirations.

Being present at the beginning of the modern era of computing presented RAND and the other early researchers with a unique opportunity. But it was unlikely that they, or whoever had been present at that time, could have somehow quickly solved the challenge of delivering information security. It is as yet still an unsolved problem. It is also a "wicked problem."[1] The term comes from the field of social planning, with the word *wicked* being used not in the moral sense but rather to indicate difficulty and malignancy.[2] Wicked problems cross multiple domains, just as the study of information security can be seen to cross into economics, psychology, and other fields.[3] Wicked problems change over time, and for information security, that change is caused by new technologies and the shifting motivations of users.[4] Wicked problems inherently involve trade-offs, and this characteristic is present in important aspects of information security, such as in the apparent trade-off between security and usability.[5] Wicked problems are said to be unsolvable by approaching them in a sequential manner.[6] But this is precisely how the field of information security currently tends to operate, by attempting to address the latest security vulnerability with a new technology, a new signature, or some other new artifact of the moment.

The wicked nature of information security is compounded by the lack of basic definitions, such as what it means for something to be "secure." The absence of an agreed-upon definition has long been bemoaned, but the task is challenging because security is situational.[7] Something that is considered to be secure in one circumstance might not be considered to be secure in another. Security is not therefore a metaphysical property, where something can be said to be categorically "secure" or not. A better term to use might be high security, but even with this simplification there are complications. Modern computing environments are comprised of many different layers of technological elements, and those layers create a massive amount of abstraction. In contrast to the relatively straightforward scenario of a single program running on a single computer, a modern computer system might be constructed from an orchestrated set of microservices running in virtual machines on multiple physical computers inside cloud computing environments, which are themselves spread across multiple data centers on multiple continents. It is not clear that something can be considered to have a high level of security if it is constructed from elements that do not themselves each have a high level of security.[8] The same composition problem exists at the level of an organization. Given a normal distribution in ability to make good security decisions, a statistically significant proportion of employees will make decisions that jeopardize the security of the organization as a whole.[9]

But even if the assumption is made that "security" or "high security" can be defined in a meaningful and useful way, there exists an even more fundamental problem. The field of information security makes claims about what individuals and organizations should do in order to improve their security. An example of such a claim is that an organization must use a firewall to avoid being hacked. But such a claim is unfalsifiable.[10] Falsifiable means that the claim runs the risk of in some way being contradicted by empirical observation.[11] The scientific method emphasizes refutation of claims rather than confirmation of claims, and so the idea of falsifiability is a foundation of modern science.

Claims about security are unfalsifiable because a computer system with no known vulnerabilities might be secure, but it might also contain a vulnerability that has not yet been discovered.[12] A computer system can be declared to be insecure by observing a failure of security, but there is no observable outcome that can prove that a system is secure.[13] The claim that an organization must use a firewall to avoid being hacked cannot therefore be falsified.[14] If an organization does not use a firewall and is hacked, then this evidence supports the claim but does not definitively prove it. But if an organization does not use a firewall and is not hacked after a week, that fact does not falsify the claim because the organization might be hacked after a month or a year. This is a case of "heads I'm proved right, tails you've just been lucky so far."[15] If there is no empirical test for security then any claim that a particular condition is required to deliver security is unfalsifiable.[16] Any guidance given by security product vendors or by security practitioners that the use of a particular security technology, product, or practice is required for security is also unfalsifiable.[17]

This is the existential crisis lying in wait at the center of the field of information security. Whether people are aware of it or not, the practical effects are felt in the gigantic pile of security advice that has accumulated over the decades.[18] Because there is no way to determine which advice is effective, there is no method for discarding the advice that is ineffective, and so it gets added to the pile.[19] A security standard that is widely used by government agencies and companies is *Security and Privacy Controls for Information Systems and Organizations* by NIST. That single document is almost five hundred pages long and lists hundreds of security controls.[20] Some of the advice provided by the field of information security to organizations and individuals is undoubtedly useful, but which parts? John Wanamaker, the founder of the Wanamaker's chain of department stores in the 1880s, is reputed to have said that "half the money I spend on advertising is wasted; the trouble is I don't know which half." This is the same situation in which the field of information security currently finds itself.

The resulting confusion and inefficiency make it difficult for companies to maintain their security, even companies that specialize in information security. In 2011, the hacking group Anonymous hacked the security firm HBGary.[21] As well as posting sixty-eight thousand private emails and memos from the company online for anyone to see, they defaced its website with the message, "You have little to no security knowledge. . . . You're a pathetic gathering of media-whoring money-grabbing sycophants who want to reel in business for your equally pathetic company."[22] In 2018, the security company RSA offered a mobile application to the attendees of its RSA Conference, an information security conference that was attended by more than forty-two thousand people.[23] Unfortunately for those attendees, the mobile application contained a security hole that exposed all of their names.[24] Embarrassingly, this was the *second* time the RSA conference mobile application was discovered to contain a security flaw.[25] In 2014, a different security bug had exposed the name, last name, title, employer, and nationality of everyone who attended the conference that year.[26] A number of commercial security companies have even experienced security breaches during National Cyber Security Month.[27]

Security companies that are unable to deliver security for themselves and their customers are evidence of the massive underlying challenges that exist. Given this, the question can reasonably be asked why the internet has not yet suffered a destructive worst-case worm of the kind that was speculated about during the period when the Slammer, Blaster, Welchia, Sobig, and Sasser internet worms ran rampant. A worm that uses a zero-day vulnerability to infect a very large number of computers, spreads extremely quickly, and has a destructive payload would be highly damaging, especially if that worm was able to affect the infrastructure of the internet such as the routers that direct packets to their destinations.

A similar question was once posed to Steve Jobs, the computing pioneer and CEO of Apple.[28] In 1994, six years after the Morris worm, Jobs was interviewed in his offices and asked whether the internet was likely to experience a highly destructive worm. After the question was put to him, Jobs went silent and buried his face in his hands. He remained that way, motionless and silent. After several minutes had passed, the people in the room started to whisper to each about whether he was suffering a medical emergency and whether they should call a doctor. One touched his arm, but he did not respond.

But suddenly, just as they were about to leave the room to get help, Jobs came out of his trance and answered the question with a one-word reply: "No." Asked to elaborate, he explained, "Because they need it to do their work. The last thing they're going to do is shut off the means of doing their work."[29]

It is not the current set of security measures that prevents a worst-case worm. Jobs was likely correct that the reason there has not yet been such a worm is simply because it would not serve anyone's interests. In this case, as in many others, it is the consideration of the question from the perspective of the economics and psychology of information security that enables the key insight. A broader view of the problem space illuminates questions such as these, but the contrasting impulse also exists—to narrow the scope of inquiry.

In the compliance approach to security, an outside authority creates a written framework with a checklist that specifies various security measures. To achieve compliance with the framework requires an organization to implement the items on the checklist. For the organizations that participate, the checklist and the outside authority serve the purpose of defining the things they must do in order to be considered secure, which takes that responsibility off their shoulders.[30] If the organization is then asked by a customer or a regulator about their security efforts, they can provide the evidence that they have achieved compliance with the framework. The compliance approach serves a useful purpose where it helps organizations that have previously ignored information security to begin to implement security controls, because it helps them to structure those efforts.[31] An organization might also wish to become compliant with a particular framework in order to be allowed to perform certain activities. For example, compliance with the Payment Card Industry Data Security Standard (PCI DSS) enables organizations to process, store, and transmit payment card data.[32]

A problem with the compliance approach is that it can lead to a conflation of the map and the territory. The proscribed items in the checklist might deliver security or they might not—the organization has no way of knowing. Becoming compliant does not make an organization secure, and neither can an organization become compliant by becoming secure. Security and compliance are two different things.[33] For some organizations, this might not be a concern. Indeed, it might be considered a feature and not a bug. The organization's security might be ineffective, but they can receive top marks for their compliance paperwork.

Another issue with the compliance approach to security is that compliance frameworks are designed to apply to a variety of different organizations.[34] This is a deliberate choice by the authors of the frameworks in order to broaden the base of potential users to the greatest possible extent. However, there are numerous axes on which an organization might be different from the platonic form of organization that the authors of the framework envisioned. The organization might be highly centralized or highly distributed, it might be very small or very large, it might operate in a country with particular regulatory requirements or have no pressing regulatory requirements at all. Because of this, any organization that believes itself to be substantially different from the norm must be wary of the guidance provided in security compliance checklists.[35] The further an organization is from the general case that is assumed by the authors of the framework, the higher the probability that the value received from following its guidance shrinks to zero or even passes through zero and becomes negative.[36] In economics this is described as diminishing marginal utility. As an example, the guidance that employees within an organization should be trained to "confront people in the office you do not recognize" might be useful in a small or medium-size company but is completely impractical for an organization based in a downtown Manhattan office with a high amount of foot traffic and thousands of employees on various floors.[37]

These concerns are somewhat subtle, and the use of compliance frameworks has become commonplace. Security standards have also become widely used by organizations and within industry. Like compliance frameworks, the popularity of particular security standards tends to rise and fall over time. Security standards that become popular tend to follow a pattern where there is an initial steep rise in their popularity, followed by a peak in interest and then a long slide into disuse.[38]

A common goal for a security standard is to try and reduce the complexity of one aspect of information security and, by doing so, to render it more manageable. The Common Weakness Enumeration (CWE) project provides categories that enable security vulnerabilities to be categorized in various ways.[39] The Common Vulnerability Scoring System (CVSS) enables security vulnerabilities to be assigned a score between zero and ten so they can be more easily prioritized.[40] This is useful, but the process by which that simplification is carried out is typically subjective, at least to some degree. There is a danger, then, that this subjective aspect will be overlooked and the product of the standard interpreted as an objective representation of truth. A criticism that has been made of security standards such as CWE and CVSS is that they fall into the trap of "enumerating badness"—making a list of bad things such as vulnerabilities.[41] The problem is that the number of bad things is never ending, and so the act of counting and classifying them also has no end.[42] Counting and classifying vulnerabilities can also only ever help to address the underlying causes of vulnerabilities in an indirect, oblique manner.

A second way in which the field of information security has attempted to make the task of delivering security more tractable is through the application of risk management.[43] At the heart of risk management is an attractive calculus: that the security risk that exists in any given situation is a product of the threat and the vulnerability.[44] Performing such calculations should enable an objective and numbers-driven approach to security decision making. The idea of measuring risk and then making a decision on the basis of that measurement also has an intuitive appeal because it would appear to be a rational approach. Risk is often assumed within the field of information security to be a good metric, and NIST has developed and promoted its Cybersecurity Framework that is based on risk management.[45]

Risk management is already a well-established and proven approach in domains such as insurance. An insurance company is able to offer a person an insurance policy on a house because the insurance company can use actuarial data to calculate the risk of that house burning down or being destroyed by a hurricane, and so the company can price the insurance premiums appropriately. But this example reveals the current limitation of risk management when applied to information security: that high-quality actuarial data exist for house fires and hurricanes but not for security incidents.[46] In the 2000s, there was the hope that detailed information about data breaches would begin to be put into the public domain as a result of the data breach laws that were being passed such as California Senate Bill 1386.[47] This would have provided the data that could be used to usher in a "New School" of information security that could operate on the basis of that data.[48] Alas, the data breach laws that were passed did not require organizations to reveal a sufficient level of detail in the breach disclosures that would enable that analysis.[49]

Compliance frameworks, security standards, and risk management are nostrums that attempt to provide a way for organizations to approach information security without experiencing the existential dread that comes from considering the wicked nature of the problem space and the unfalsifiable nature of security claims. Where those prescriptions attempt to create a feeling of calm, a competing approach has the opposite intention. FUD—Fear, Uncertainty, and Doubt—emerged as a powerful force during the years of the dot-com boom. FUD was wielded flagrantly by commercial security vendors to sell security products and services, but as more and more organizations have experienced security breaches, the power of FUD has become somewhat diminished. Stunt hacking represents the most egregious modern-day example of FUD because it supplies misleading information in a hysterical way.[50] The use of FUD also enables grifters within the field of information security to pounce on the predictable security failures of the latest technologies and promote themselves as the cavalry arriving over the brow of the hill to save the day.

FUD is deliberately ostentatious in order to create an emotional response, but a more insidious strain of FUD uses bad statistics. Such statistics regarding information security might appear on the surface to be well researched, but in reality, they fall foul of a number of methodological errors or are simply wrong. In 2009, the chief security officer of AT&T testified to the US Congress that the annual profits made by cyber criminals was more than $1 trillion. That figure is implausible, given that $1 trillion was more than 7 percent of the gross domestic product of the United States at that time and larger than the entire information technology industry.[51]

The abuse of statistics within the field of information security is a long-running problem because there are systemic perverse incentives that reward making things seem worse than they actually are.[52] Many of the statistics that are available regarding information security within organizations come from surveys, but studies have found that those surveys can suffer from a range of issues. A 2003 study found that widely reported statistics from fourteen surveys on the state of information security practices and experiences were "in general fundamentally flawed."[53] A 2011 study with the compelling name "Sex, Lies, and Cyber-Crime Surveys" found that the majority of studies on the topic of security losses are affected by a bias whereby the results of the survey are dominated by as few as one or two of the survey responses.[54] This is the same error in reasoning as thinking that after Jeff Bezos walks into a bar, the average net worth of the bar's patrons becomes a billion dollars. The authors of the study also found that the statistical measures that could have been taken to prevent this type of error "have been universally ignored."[55]

They conclude their paper by asking the question, "Can any faith whatever be placed in the surveys we have?" To which they answer, "No, it appears not."[56]

Some might take the position that the exaggeration of security risks can be excused because security professionals have a built-in bias to defend their profession.[57] But it is difficult to think of a mature profession that has thrived on the basis of bad information. Good quality statistics and good quality surveys would increase the ability to make objective decisions, but in the absence of such information, the human tendency to make value judgments has made it impossible to escape subjective evaluations of the state of information security in the world. In 1972, the Anderson report lamented the ability of computers to resist penetration.[58] In 1984, the state of information security in government and business was described as "poor."[59] An employee of the NSA wrote that "among the sources of the difficulty are that responsibility is diffused, authority is sharply limited, commitment often seems half-hearted, vision is frequently short-sighted, and supporting technology has not been readily available."[60] In 1994, it was said that "in spite of repeated examples of the vulnerability of almost all computer systems to invasion and manipulation, very few people recognize the magnitude of the damage that can be done and even fewer have taken adequate steps to fix the problem."[61] In 1996, the state of security was said to be "dismal" and that "the same exposures keep recurring; we make no practically useful progress on the hard problems . . . and we are less and less able to adapt the . . . model to new technologies as they arise."[62] In 2004, the state of computer security was said to be such that "almost all the systems in service today [are] extremely vulnerable to attack."[63] In 2005, David Bell, the cocreator of the Bell-LaPadula model, wrote, "The general feeling . . . is that computer and network security is in decline."[64] The same year, Marcus Ranum wrote that there had been "zero progress for quite some time."[65] By 2009, computer security was said to be in "bad shape," and "people worry about it a lot and spend a good deal of money on it, but most systems are insecure."[66] In 2017, computer security was said to be "broken from top to bottom," and in 2018, "the trend is going the wrong way."[67]

These comments perhaps serve as good examples of the phenomenon described by George Bernard Shaw that "every person who has mastered a profession is a skeptic concerning it." But information security professionals should not minimize or diminish their collective accomplishments. The world would have worse and less security if it were not for their efforts. It is also useful to remember that information security is still a very young field.[68] Aristotle made the first use of the term *physics* in the fourth century BCE. More than two thousand years would pass until the work of Isaac Newton and a further 175 years until Maxwell's equations. Einstein's general theory of relativity would not be formulated for another fifty years—an event that is now more than one hundred years old. Physics, chemistry, and astronomy all have centuries-long histories. In sharp contrast, the modern era of information security that began with the creation of the first digital computers did not begin until the 1970s. In this regard, the uneven record of successes and failures might simply represent the growing pains of a nascent field. Indeed, in 1985 it was said that "the challenges of information security may well be with us for quite a while."[69]

Throughout history, many ideas and proposals have been put forward for what should be done to improve information security. Those suggestions have tended to relate to specific subject areas within the field, such as software security, network security, cryptography, and so on. This is to be expected given that the field of information security is a very wide and also a very deep field. There are many different areas of study, and each area is complex. During the 1970s and perhaps the 1980s, the common security practitioner could plausibly have read all of the research that was published each year, but since then, only the most dedicated person would be able to accomplish such a feat. This is actually beneficial since specialization enables division of labor, which is a far more efficient approach than if every security practitioner were to attempt to become a polymath. But because of specialization, each security practitioner has a relatively narrow view into the overall problem space. Without the ability to see the big picture, the mistaken belief can sometimes develop that some newly created security technology or approach that emerges from one particular subject area within the field is the panacea for security problems in the round. Such ideas inescapably slide into the trough of disillusionment over time. For centuries, alchemists believed they could find the philosopher's stone, a legendary substance that could transmute lead into gold. Those endeavors were pointless because the fundamental underlying rules of chemistry could not be changed. It has always been unlikely that there will be a breakthrough in any one specific area of information security that will solve the problems that exist across the entirety of the field. Any new security technology is unlikely to completely remove the security risks created by users, and likewise any new process or piece of educational training for users is unlikely to completely obviate the security risks created by new technologies, just as one factor.

An alternative approach has been to step outside the field of information security and examine information security problems from the perspective of other fields.[70] On the whole this has been a fruitful exercise that has generated many useful ideas: from the field of economics, the importance of externalities, the need to consider perverse incentives, and the idea of security as a public good; from agriculture, the concept of monoculture; from insurance, the notion of risk management and the value of actuarial data. But as useful as the multidisciplinary approach has proven to be, as yet no new insight from any other field has been able to create a radical improvement in information security.

It is possible that the best approach is not to look within the field or without but instead to take a step back and begin anew. A person who stands on the top of a hill can go no higher. In order to climb the highest mountain, the person must first descend that hill, and only then can they begin to climb up the foothills of the mountain. This will be a difficult task for the field to accomplish. The Dutch historian Jan Romein posited his "law of the handicap of a head start" in which he described how the culture within a group that makes its early successes possible works against any future success because this would require a different culture.[71] To make further progress will require the culture to be changed—a prodigious undertaking. It will also mean that in order for things to get better, they will probably have to first get worse. Given that a finite amount of resources is available, more time will have to be spent examining the causes of underlying problems rather than addressing the symptoms of those problems, and this could lead to more insecurity in the short term.

The security of every computer system depends on a myriad of factors, including the technologies that are employed, the incentives of the users, and the environment in which those technologies and users reside. This means that there is a limit to how much each discipline within the field of information security can contribute to improving the security of any system, whether it be software security, network security, user education, passwords, or cryptography. A computer system that has strong security in one area but weak security in any other area will be easily defeated because as Steve Bellovin has said, "You don't go through strong security, you go around it."[72]

The field of information security can itself be thought of as a system, with its own properties, strengths, and weaknesses. Some parts are stronger and more developed, other parts less so. Some parts draw the eye and the attention of researchers, whereas other parts lie moribund. There are strong incentives that pull researchers and practitioners down into focusing on individual pieces of the system, but wicked problems cannot be addressed by picking at them in a piecemeal way. Just as with the security of a computer system, there must be a consideration for the system as a whole.[73]

RAND invented systems analysis in the 1940s for exactly this purpose.[74] The analysts at RAND described systems analysis as a way to accomplish "a systematic examination of a problem" by the process of "question-raising and finding rational answers."[75] Systems analysis was employed for the purpose of ensuring that technology was used "in a constrained rather than a mindless way," and RAND employed the technique to good effect for the purpose of advising its paymasters in the US military.[76] By considering the history of information security in a similarly broad, sweeping way, certain themes can be seen to emerge. These are the cornerstones of the field that represent opportunities to improve information security in the long term.

The first leitmotif that becomes visible is that the challenge of delivering information security is in some sense a battle against complexity. Computers are complex, people are complex, and so complexity underlies information security. As early as 1985, information security was said to be "simply one way of contending with the problem of complexity."[77] Within the profession it is a widely held belief that the more complex a computer system, the more difficult it is to secure.[78]

RAND and the other early researchers had to respond to the complexity that was introduced to computing by the invention of time-sharing.[79] The Ware report predicted that as computers became ever-more complex, the abilities of their users would also increase, and this would make the difficulty of controlling users through the application of security measures ever-more difficult.[80] The Anderson report made a similar prediction, that security risk would increase with system complexity.[81] The efforts that followed the Ware and Anderson reports such as the development of the Bell-LaPadula model and the idea of provable security sought to bring order to the increasing complexity of computer operating systems.[82] The security technologies that emerged during the dot-com boom can likewise be viewed as attempts to manage complexity. A firewall reduces the complexity involved with managing the security of large numbers of individual computers and with the complexity of the possible interactions between those computers.[83] Marcus Ranum has described firewalls as being "deliberately placed between two areas that are incomprehensibly complex."[84]

More complex software is more likely to contain bugs, and some of those bugs will create security vulnerabilities.[85] In general, complexity is said to be the root cause of the "vast majority" of problems with software.[86] Larger and more complex systems are more difficult to understand and so are more difficult to design in such a way that they will fail in a manner that does not cause security problems.[87] Software has a tendency to become more complex over time because more code is added in order to deliver new features. A piece of software might also incorporate several other pieces of software, called modules or libraries, which can themselves be complex.

Certain categories of vulnerabilities in software exist because every program is essentially being programmed by the input that it receives.[88] The more complex that input, the more difficult it is to know what the effect on the program will be. If the input is a vulnerability exploit, the security of the system might become compromised as a result of processing that input. It has been half-jokingly said that in contrast to attempts to create secure programs, "for all other kinds of computing, being correct for normal inputs is sufficient."[89] Software security initiatives such as Microsoft's Trustworthy Computing initiative and the Security Development Lifecycle that Microsoft created can therefore be seen as structured approaches to attacking the problem of software complexity as it relates to the presence of security vulnerabilities in software.[90]

Complexity is also a challenge when considering the unit of an organization.[91] As the size of an organization grows, the challenges that it faces with regard to managing complexity appear to grow in an exponential rather than a linear manner. The computing environment within a large organization is characterized by a perpetual torrent of new people, computers, software, networking equipment, and connectivity to partners, customers, subsidiaries, and regulators. All of these create complexity, which in turn makes the task of delivering security more difficult.[92]

If complexity is one of the principle underlying root causes of security problems, then special efforts must be undertaken to understand it. The goal should not be to drive out all complexity, though. Antoine de Saint-Exupéry wrote that "perfection is achieved not when there is nothing more to add, but rather when there is nothing more to take away." This is a warning that if something is made overly simple, it will likely not be fit for purpose. The things that are important in everyday life, such as human relationships, the internet, and financial markets, all create value in part because of their complex nature.[93] How, then, is it possible to reduce complexity so that security can be improved but not remove too much complexity such that the system is no longer valuable?

The computer scientist Fred Brooks has distinguished between two types of complexity: essential complexity and accidental complexity.[94] Essential complexity is "real" complexity that cannot be escaped—it is required in order to solve the problem at hand.[95] But accidental complexity is "artificial" complexity that can be reduced by improving how the problem is approached.[96] The goal is therefore to reduce accidental complexity as much as possible.[97] A good example of a method for reducing accidental complexity within information security is the use of programming languages that are designed to eliminate entire classes of security vulnerabilities. A programmer that uses the C programming language must be careful not to introduce security vulnerabilities such as buffer overflows into the code, but code that is written in a language such as Rust or Microsoft's C# is unlikely to contain a buffer overflow.[98]

When examining the history of the field of information security, one of the most powerful ways in which accidental complexity has been successfully driven out is by removing decisions. The study of usable security that began in earnest with the "Why Johnny Can't Encrypt" paper focused on trying to help users make the correct security decisions.[99] That work had the propensity to assume that it was possible to equip users with sufficient knowledge such that they *could* make good decisions.[100] But this was revealed over time to be an unsafe assumption.[101] The very idea of improving information security by enabling people to make marginal improvements in their decision-making ability may well be flawed. This is because over a sufficiently long period, people are confronted with many security decisions, and it is very unlikely that they will make the correct decision on every occasion. A hacker needs them to make the wrong decision only once, which is commonly referred to as the asymmetric advantage of the attacker. The problem is compounded within organizations that have many employees who all need to make the right decisions all of the time.[102] Employees are not particularly motivated to learn about security because they view security as a secondary task that is separate to their main job responsibilities.[103] It is also difficult to teach employees how to identify security threats without also increasing their tendency to misjudge nonthreats as threats.[104]

The belief that users can make good security decisions has led in some cases to the worst possible outcomes. Web browsers attempt to improve security for users by presenting them with security warnings, such as in the case of a web browser that believes there is an issue with the security certificate of the website that a user is attempting to connect to. But almost 100 percent of such certificate errors are false positives, and this has led users to see warnings as a hindrance rather than a help.[105] It has also trained users to click reflexively to simply dismiss warnings.[106] Perversely, if a user connects to a phishing website, they are unlikely to ever see a certificate error because the hackers who run that site will likely have been careful enough to acquire a legitimate certificate, or they will run their site without a certificate, and the absence of a certificate does not typically generate any warning at all.[107]

The fundamental dilemma of computer security describes how people want security but are ill-equipped to make the decisions that would enable them to assess or improve their security.[108] Attempts to solve the fundamental dilemma by training users have been largely unsuccessful.[109] And so, rather than attempting to help users to make better choices, it is better to simply reduce their choices. When people enter an elevator, they do not worry that pushing the wrong button will send them plummeting to their death. A technology should expose only those aspects that allow the user to operate it and not require the user to make decisions that can endanger themselves and others. Microsoft embraced this philosophy to good effect with their strategy of "secure by design and secure by default." In more recent years Microsoft has continued to lead the way by making the installation of security patches automatic in their operating system products. When a person uses one of those computers, the choice of whether to install a security patch is simply no longer presented.

In addition to removing decisions from end users, there are many opportunities to remove decisions from technology practitioners, such as information security professionals. A 2004 paper investigated the task of deploying a public key infrastructure (PKI). This is an example of a piece of work that information security professionals might carry out as part of their duties. The paper found that even though the study participants were well educated in information security and the PKI technology was considered to be mature, the task of deploying a PKI was extremely difficult to complete. This was because thirty-eight separate steps were required, and every one of those steps required the person to make a decision.[110] A second study found a similar result for the task of deploying Hypertext Transfer Protocol Secure (HTTPS), the encrypted version of HTTP that uses TLS.[111]

It will clearly not be possible to simplify or eliminate every user decision, and in such cases, it might be useful to employ other techniques to minimize the possibility of user error. An example is the two-person rule, where two separate individuals are required to work together, reducing the possibility that any single person will make a damaging choice. The classical example of an implementation of the two-person rule is in permissive action link systems, such as those used in nuclear missile silos and nuclear submarines.[112] These systems require two separate individuals to perform certain actions simultaneously, such as each opening a separate safe to which they alone have the combination.[113] Implementing the two-person rule for all security decisions within an organization would be impractical, but it could be beneficial for important security decisions such as in government where the sensitivity of the information involved is very high.[114]

After complexity, a second theme that emerges is the importance of a collective effort. Academia, the community of information security practitioners, and the commercial information security industry all play a key role in improving information security, and no one group can be successful in isolation of the others. Academia creates ideas for new ways of working and new technologies. It also evaluates existing ideas and creates a robust intellectual framework for progress. Practitioners experience the practical realities of information security on a day-to-day basis and so hold information about security requirements and what approaches they find to be effective or ineffective. Industry creates products that deliver security capabilities to the people and organizations that purchase them. Because each group holds knowledge that the others require, an efficient and effective flow of information between the groups is crucial. Information sharing is widely believed to be useful, and so the exhortation to share information has been a common refrain for decades.[115]

Over time, businesses and other types of organization have improved their ability to share information between themselves, such as through participation in information-sharing forums. In the field of finance, the Financial Services Information Sharing and Analysis Center (FS-ISAC) facilitates information sharing between financial institutions.[116] These kinds of forums enable the participating organizations to share specific kinds of information relating to security, such as the tactics, techniques, and procedures used by hackers.[117] But even though the sharing of this type of information has become more robust, there is not yet broad sharing of information regarding why security fails. Other fields have accomplished this, and industries such as commercial air travel and nuclear power are by and large very safe today because they have shared and studied decades of information regarding accidents.[118] The sharing of detailed information on security failures would be enormously useful in the round, as would the sharing of information on near misses where a security measure failed but no security breach occurred.[119] This information sharing would enable a data set to be created that captured those details and that could then be analyzed.[120]

History shows that there is a particular weakness in the sharing of information between academia and both practitioners and industry. This gap creates significant opportunity costs since practitioners and industry could direct the research efforts of academia into the areas that appear to be the most practical and useful. The Orange Book is an example of an initiative that failed because it did not take into consideration the changes that were happening in the commercial market.[121] The reverse is also true in that the research produced within academia could help to identify fundamental problems with security technologies that are in the process of being developed by practitioners and industry. Practitioners could also adjust their use of the products created by industry based on research findings. Stefan Axelsson identified the problem with the base-rate fallacy and false alarms in intrusion detection systems long in advance of the subsequent billions of dollars spent on intrusion detection products.[122] If the finding by Axelsson had been more widely known, practitioners could have narrowed their use of intrusion detection systems to those situations where the false positive rate would not cause an operational issue. It was academia that identified the central importance of economics and psychology in obtaining a better understanding of information security, but the economics of information security and the psychology of security have not yet effectively penetrated the technology-focused mainstream of the field. A similar situation exists with policy makers working in government, who have been seen to draw the information they use for decision making from the popular press rather than from applicable academic research.[123]

Academia has already overcome many of the challenges that the field of information security has struggled with and continues to struggle with. The question of vulnerability disclosure has not yet been resolved to a satisfactory degree, but academia has learned how to safely share research that is much more explosive, literally, than zero-day vulnerabilities, namely the research into nuclear fission that began in the 1930s. Part of the reason for the disconnect is that practitioners can often be found working in the trenches managing security incidents, researching vulnerabilities, and installing patches of which there is a never-ending supply. The opportunity to read an academic paper requires having the time to be able to do so. Being able to understand an academic paper might also require knowledge of mathematics or academic jargon that the average practitioner might not possess. A useful service that would provide substantial value would produce summaries of published academic research on information security topics, organized by category such as network security or software security, and written in a way that a layperson could easily understand.

Conferences for information security practitioners do not frequently feature speakers from academia, and academic conferences do not typically feature speakers who are active information security practitioners.[124] This can be explained to some extent by academics wanting to present their work at academic conferences, the proceedings of which are published in academic journals. This makes it more likely that their work will receive citations from other academics, and the number of papers that an academic is able to publish and the number of citations that those papers receive can lead to better job positions or tenure. For practitioners, the peer review process employed by academic conferences might be perceived as intimidating or considered to be too high a bar to clear for anyone who is not an academic by training. There is therefore an in-built set of incentives that work against the cross-pollination of information between the two groups.

The problem could be alleviated somewhat if a material number of academics became practitioners and vice versa. But the number of academics that become practitioners is probably rather small, given that the number of universities that enable a person to receive a PhD in information security is itself small. The number of practitioners that become academics is probably also small. The average practitioner would likely have to accept a substantial reduction in their total financial compensation in order to join academia, and this likely dampens the number of people who might be interested in becoming an academic from doing so. The gap in effective information sharing between academia and both information security practitioners and the commercial information security industry is limiting the ability to improve information security. Unless that gap can be narrowed, there is a danger that there will be an ever-increasing amount of academic research with limited practical value and an ever-increasing number of fundamentally flawed security technologies and products.

A third important theme is the balance between offense and defense. Today it is easier to attack systems than to defend them. A single zero-day vulnerability is often all that is needed to compromise the security of a computer system, although it can be challenging to find a zero-day vulnerability or costly to acquire one. But if an attacker cannot successfully attack the technology, they can simply target the human user of the system with a technique such as phishing or social engineering. Organizations have to defend everywhere at all times, and nation-state hackers can outcompete almost all organizations because of their essentially unlimited resources.

There are only a small number of areas where defenders can be said to definitively have an advantage over hackers. One of these is encryption, where defenders can encrypt messages that hackers cannot decrypt unless they know the encryption key. But that guarantee flows from the mathematics that underpins the encryption algorithm, and so it only exists in a theoretical sense. A person who knows the encryption key can still be beaten with a rubber hose until he reveals it. A weakness in another part of the computer system might also make the presence of encryption irrelevant.

The weakness in defense has had the effect of creating a kind of learned helplessness, where new security products and services tend to forsake protection and focus instead on detection and response. But attempting to improve security by improving detection and response is incrementalism that can never create a secure system. Since the beginning of the dot-com boom, the siren song of the field of information security has been attempts to make incremental improvements, which has resulted in a mass of Band-Aids in the form of security patches, intrusion detection signatures, antivirus updates, and such like. These are all temporary bandages on the permanent wound that is the inability to provide protection.[125]

Defense was the focus of efforts within the field of information security during the earliest decades of the modern era. The work of Willis Ware, James P. Anderson, Jerry Saltzer and Michael Schroeder, and David Bell and Leonard LaPadula all concentrated largely on defense, but offense has since come to dominate hearts and minds. This has occurred in large part because of the promotion of stunt hacking and the constructed idolatry of hackers and their figurative and literal exploits. But the benefits of research into offensive are questionable. The discovery of a new instance of a known type of vulnerability does not provide any new insights into what defenders should do differently.[126] The tiger team security assessment of Multics reached this conclusion in 1974, but that finding has since been mostly forgotten.[127] In other fields, a mere observation, such as the fact that a particular piece of software contains a vulnerability, is not deemed sufficiently interesting to warrant publication.[128] Scientific research is expected to propose theories or generalizations resulting from observations, but in the case of vulnerability research that bar is rarely met.[129] Vulnerability research also creates a race to the bottom where the creation of new hacking techniques requires the creation of new defenses, but this in turn spurs the creation of new hacking techniques. Some might portray this as a virtuous cycle that improves the security of computers over time, but at the same time, it undeniably perfects methods of attack, which creates a road map for hackers that describes how to attack systems.[130] The numerous perverse incentives that have been created to spur and reward the discovery of new vulnerabilities increases the overall supply, assuming that the rediscovery rate is small.[131]

Contrary to claims, learning how to hack into computers will not provide a person with the ability to build a secure computer system. The field of information security has embraced the idea that security practitioners should "think like a hacker," but this assumes that the thinking of defenders should be similar to the way that attackers think, and it is questionable whether this is in fact true.[132] A person who only knows how to find vulnerabilities has a very narrow understanding of information security.[133] Gene Spafford is reputed to have

described this situation as tantamount to asserting that "the primary qualifi-
cation for an auto mechanic should be demonstrated excellence in putting
sugar in gas tanks."[134]

A more equitable balance must be struck in the allocation of resources between offense and defense, but it is not simply a matter of spending on any and
all kinds of defense. In 2013, a group of people working in the field of information security established an initiative to create educational content on information security topics. As part of that effort they proposed, apparently without
irony, to stage an opera by Joseph Martin Kraus, the "Swedish Mozart," in order to teach "the modern crime of identity theft and its consequences."[135] Some
academic researchers have also continued to labor on projects and technologies
that have effectively been proven to be impractical.[136]

A renewed emphasis on defense would create the opportunity to revisit
the fundamental goals of the field of information security as they are commonly understood. The goal that was prioritized by RAND and the other
early researchers was confidentiality. They wanted to enable the US military
to be able to store confidential information on multi-user time-sharing computers. Additional security requirements emerged over time. In their classic
paper "The Protection of Information in Computer Systems," Saltzer and
Schroeder provided their proposal for information security goals that combined confidentiality with integrity and availability, and so the CIA (confidentiality, integrity, and availability) triad was born.[137] Books on the topic of
information security that are intended for new security practitioners commonly place an emphasis on learning and using the CIA triad, and the CIA
triad has also been incorporated into the syllabus of professional certifications
that are intended for security practitioners.[138] As a result, the CIA triad has
become a kind of received wisdom and a rote answer to the question of what
the goals for security should be. But a piece of information can be kept confidential, have its integrity maintained, and be available but still be completely
wrong.[139] The CIA triad does not provide a good framework for addressing
the dangers of information pollution and misinformation.[140] These threats are
of particular concern if the incorrect information comes from a source that
is ordinarily considered to be trustworthy.

It is difficult to use the CIA triad to describe activities that are important to
security but that are not easily framed in terms of confidentiality, integrity, or
availability. An example is that when new employees join an organization,
they need to be given access to various computer systems in order to carry out

their job. As people move from role to role within the organization, they tend to accumulate these "entitlements" because their old access is not taken away when they transition into a new role. This means that they gain more and more entitlements over time, which creates security risks. When employees leave the organization, their entitlements can also remain in place even though they are no longer required. These entitlement problems are challenging, and it would be difficult to argue that they are not within the domain of information security, but they are not easily expressed using the CIA triad.

Jerry Saltzer himself described the CIA triad as an "arbitrary definition of security-related problems," and so academics have periodically revisited the CIA triad and suggested enhancements to it, such as by adding new terms.[141] But the larger field of information security has not exercised the same curiosity or initiative regarding these theoretical underpinnings.

A common dictum within the field of information security is that there can be "no security through obscurity." This phrase is widely used to express the belief that the security of a computer system should not rely on the defender needing to keep the details of the security measures secret from attackers. In other words, if the design for the security of the system were to fall into an attacker's hands, the security of the system would not immediately be compromised. But "no security by obscurity" has been used over time by information security professionals in a pejorative manner to suggest that any and all obscurity is undesirable.[142] Such a position ignores the historical context in which the phrase was first formulated. The Dutch cryptographer and linguist Auguste Kerckhoffs first made the statement in 1883, when discussing the design of a cryptographic system.[143] In such a system, the design of the encryption algorithm should be able to be published because it is the secret key—analogous to a password—that when combined with the algorithm provides the security. Outside of the design of such a cryptographic system, "no security through obscurity" does not necessarily apply.[144] A computer system should certainly be designed with the assumption that attackers know the technical details of the system, but there is no harm in working to keep those details secret.[145] This is self-evident since no organization would voluntarily publish the details of its security measures on its website for the world to see. Obscurity has value, such as by making attackers work to identify information that they do not yet have.[146]

"Defense in depth" is the idea that creating multiple barriers for a hacker to overcome benefits security.[147] An organization could be said to be using a defense-in-depth strategy if it uses a firewall but also works to secure the individual computers on its network, for example. If taken to its logical extreme, defense in depth can create a "more is better" mentality that can actually harm security. This is because implementing more and more security measures within an environment increases the complexity of that environment.[148] At some point, too many defenses becomes as dangerous as too few because of the additional complexity that is created and also because of risk homeostasis.[149] The partial meltdown of the nuclear reactor at Three Mile Island occurred in part because of the complexity created by safety and security measures.[150]

The field of information security has institutionalized the use of the CIA triad, "no security through obscurity," and "defense in depth" by codifying them in books, training materials, professional certifications, and elsewhere. This is pernicious because a newcomer might reasonably look to those resources in order to learn what is considered to be the body of knowledge within the field. But if newcomers are trained to think inside the same lines as those who came before them, this reduces the possibility that they will ever think outside of those lines. The CIA triad, "no security through obscurity," and "defense in depth" are not scientific or mathematical laws derived from first principles, nor are they inerrant. They are simply mantras and so can be recast.

A final theme that has played an important but subtle role throughout the history of information security is rationality: how it has been perceived, understood, and revealed over time. It was General Curtis LeMay who inculcated RAND with a focus on rationality.[151] His unemotional and analytical approach came to permeate the organization and ultimately led to the study of rationality by Kenneth Arrow.[152] The belief held by Arrow and other RAND researchers was that rationality could be evaluated in a mathematical manner—that by examining the probabilities associated with each course of action, a person's behavior could be predicted.[153] But over time it was found that behavior that was considered by some to be rational was perceived by others to be entirely irrational. The reasons why a person or an organization make a choice often only become clear later, when the surrounding events are better understood. As a company, Microsoft behaved rationally when it forsook security, but it also behaved rationally when it later embraced security.[154] The users who revealed their password in exchange for a bar of chocolate or who ignored security warnings appeared to security professionals to be acting irrationally. But Cormac Herley later showed that the rejection of security guidance by those users was in fact rational and that it is the field of information security that acts irrationally by expecting users to follow unrealistic security guidance.[155]

Rationality has been the focus of enormous research efforts involving economists, psychologists, philosophers, anthropologists, and experts from many disciplines.[156] Substantial gains in the ability to understand rationality have been made, but rationality still remains elusive. Throughout the history of information security, those who have worked in the field have consistently overestimated their ability to identify and predict what is rational behavior. The result has been a series of cascading errors, the effects of which were felt not in the moment but in the subsequent years and decades, where they have snowballed and multiplied.

The English philosopher Anthony Kenny has described rationality as the golden mean between excessive credulity and excessive skepticism.[157] The person who believes too completely will become gullible—his thoughts will contain too many falsehoods. But the person who believes too little will deprive himself of valuable information. An understanding of history is a prerequisite to striking a reasonable balance between credulity and skepticism, but a long view of the history of information security reveals that much of the modern-day thinking occurs in a profound ahistorical vacuum. The absence of historical knowledge in the present day is a great loss, because history is not a sunk cost. The author and Civil War veteran Ambrose Bierce described history as "a record of mistakes made in the past, so we shall know when we make them again."[158] Knowledge of the past can be used to better inform our understanding of the present and to improve our plans for the future.

The history of information security winds its way through space and time, creating a kind of hidden geography. What began in Santa Monica in the 1970s traveled to Cornell University in 1988, then Silicon Valley during the years of the dot-com boom, and Redmond, Washington at the beginning of the twenty-first century, all building toward some distant pinnacle as yet unseen. The future will always arrive, and it is easy to expect the future to deliver the answer to our problems. But in order to create the future we must first look to the past. There is much to learn and nowhere else to look.[159]

# Epilogue

## *The Past, Present, and a Possible Future*

The present is a product of the past, and the information security challenges of today will remain intractable until the past is better understood. Indeed, the three stigmata became manifest precisely because the past is so easy to overlook.

The first stigmata, data breaches, now affects billions of people each year.[1] The year 2019 was only four days old when the Marriott hotel group announced that hackers had been able to access the records of up to 383 million guests.[2] In February, a collection of 617 million website accounts that had been stolen by hackers from sixteen separate websites was put on sale for $20,000.[3] In March, a Russian-speaking hacking group called Fxmsp claimed to have breached three commercial antivirus companies. The hackers offered to sell access to computers in those companies and also offered to sell thirty terabytes of source code for antivirus products for the sum of $300,000.[4] The Fxmsp group had previously made more than $1 million by selling access to computers in organizations they had hacked.[5] In response to these reports, one of the three antivirus companies conceded that "unauthorized access" had been made to their computers, and a second vendor made a statement that did not deny they had been breached.[6] In May 2019, the personal information of 49 million Instagram users—an image and video-sharing website owned by Facebook—was reported to have been compromised.[7] Capital One, an American bank, released a statement the same month stating they had suffered a data breach of the confidential information of more than 100 million people in the United States and Canada.[8]

The number of records acquired by hackers in data breaches has climbed ever higher, reaching absurd levels. In September 2019, information on the entire population of Ecuador was leaked online, including every citizen's full name, place of birth, date of birth, home address, email addresses, national identification number, and other personal data.[9] In January 2020, a copy of a database containing the personal details of 56 million residents of the United States was found on the open internet, on a computer located in Hangzhou, China.[10]

It is the nature of the underlying structural issues that make it difficult to prevent data breaches. The internet, the World Wide Web, the Unix operating system, and the TCP/IP protocol suite were not designed with security in mind. It is difficult to write computer software in programming languages such as C that does not contain bugs and therefore does not also contain security vulnerabilities. Google spends massive amounts to secure its products, but in March 2019, the Google Chrome web browser suffered from a well-publicized zero-day vulnerability.[11] Chrome is written in the C++ programming language, and even with the resources that Google can bring to bear, the use of C++ creates the possibility of introducing security vulnerabilities.[12]

These structural issues lead to vulnerable computers that can be hacked using zero-day vulnerabilities or by simply exploiting known vulnerabilities that have not yet been patched. Hackers can also target the human users of computers by exploiting their human weaknesses and tendencies, such as with phishing and social engineering. For the field of information security, these two aspects—the computer and the user—are the two faces of Janus: the opposite sides of the same coin.

The use of computer hacking by nation-states—the second stigmata—has become unrelenting. The nation-states employ computer hacking for the purpose of stealing intellectual property, carrying out espionage, and attempting to sway elections.

In May 2019, two Chinese nationals were charged by the US Justice Department for the 2015 Anthem hack in which the personal medical information of eighty million people was compromised.[13] Just one month later, in an incident that was described as "massive espionage," an APT group believed to be based in China were discovered to have hacked into ten mobile phone networks around the world.[14] By carrying out these attacks, the group was able to acquire call records that enabled them to pinpoint the physical location of individuals.[15]

When the US Senate issued its report into Russian efforts to interfere in the 2016 US presidential election, it was revealed that Russian hackers had used SQL injection attacks to target election computer systems in all fifty US states.[16] As a result, the Russian hackers were able to access the voter files in at least two Florida counties.[17]

The nation-states are locked in a self-perpetuating arms race. The NSA created exploits for zero-day vulnerabilities so that they could hack into computers in other countries.[18] But those exploits were discovered by the Shadow Brokers in 2016, which led to the creation of the WannaCry internet worm.[19] It was subsequently reported that some of the NSA exploits had also been used by Chinese hackers prior to them being publicized.[20] It appears that the NSA had used the exploits against computers in China, and so Chinese hackers were able to reverse engineer them and employ them for their own ends.[21]

These kinds of interactions have an infinite horizon of unintended consequences. The mere fact that nation-states such as Russia, China, and the United States have developed such powerful hacking capabilities has incentivized other nations to attempt to do the same, including Iran and North Korea.[22]

The third stigmata—the epistemic closure within the field of information security—is a self-inflicted, enervating wound. Stunt hacking, promoted disclosure, and FUD are wielded to promote far-fetched hacking scenarios that appeal to the popular press. This in turn creates an amenable situation for hackers, security researchers, and commercial security companies to monetize their expertise.

In May 2019, the CEO of a commercial security company made the claim that personal information such as bank details could be stolen by hackers through internet-enabled coffee machines.[23] In December 2019, a different commercial security company promoted their research into children's smartwatches, claiming that hackers could hack those devices and then listen in to children's conversations.[24] Other efforts have targeted the emergency phones in elevators, smart light bulbs, construction cranes, and even remote control curtains.[25]

But as history reveals, these security failures are painfully predictable. The presence of a security vulnerability in a new technology that was not designed with a focus on security should not be a surprising finding. Even so, the popular press continues to act as a willing participant in the ecosystem of promoted disclosure. In March 2019, an information technology news website published a story regarding academic research that had been carried out at the University of Michigan.[26] In that research, mechanical hard drives were programmed to listen to nearby sound waves, enabling them to act as covert listening devices. But only toward the bottom of the article, far below the lede, did the author of the story note that in order to overhear and record speech, the volume of that speech would have to be at the same decibel level as a food blender or lawn mower.[27]

The teacher and author Clay Shirky has suggested that "institutions will try to preserve the problem to which they are the solution."[28] It is clear that commercial information security companies, security researchers, and the press have all contributed to myth making regarding information security risks and have done so to benefit themselves.

Given these challenges, there is the question of what should be done. The wicked nature of information security can obscure underlying causes behind a trammel of symptoms. It is a natural human response to attempt to alleviate those symptoms, but ultimately the underlying causes must be addressed. On a grand scale, the creation of yet another security technology, signature, or patch does little to contribute to that goal.

There must be a special effort to better understand how complexity affects information security and how that complexity can be managed. Modern programming languages that do not fall prey to certain kinds of security vulnerabilities are an example of a means by which accidental complexity can be reduced.[29] A second example is the removal of unnecessary security decisions from both end users and technology practitioners.[30]

Information security requires a collective effort. There must be more information sharing regarding failures and near misses. Complex industries such as aviation and nuclear power have successfully achieved information sharing at a level to which the field of information security must aspire. There is a particular weakness in information sharing between academia and both information security practitioners and the information security industry. This deficiency must be addressed to prevent the creation of further flawed security products and more quixotic academic research.

Incremental improvements to detection and response can never create a secure system. The balance between protection, detection, and response must be recalibrated, and as it did in the 1970s, the field of information security must again attempt to grasp the mantle of protection. As part of that effort, it will be necessary to revisit common mantras such as the CIA triad and "defense in depth," to determine if they meet the demands of the current day.

Last, it is a common assumption that computer users and organizations will act "rationally" with regard to their security. But beginning with the work carried out by RAND and the other early researchers in the 1960s and continuing through the intervening decades, it can be seen that rationality is enigmatic. The perspective that history provides often reveals that what was previously considered irrational can now be considered rational. This difficulty of understanding in the moment what is rational behavior must be incorporated into the manner in which the design of security measures is approached.

After the Napoleonic Wars, the Prussian general Carl von Clausewitz wrote a book on military strategy titled *On War*.[31] The book describes his view of the strategic theory of war, with the goal of giving the mind "insight into the great mass of phenomena and of their relationships, then leave it free to rise into the higher realms of action."[32] So it must be for the field of information security. The substantial must replace the superficial. The essential must eclipse the ephemeral.

# ACKNOWLEDGMENTS

Most importantly, I would like to thank Michael J. McGandy at Cornell University Press. Michael is the keystone of this book project. I would also like to thank Richard H. Immerman, Jeff Kosseff, and Ben Rothke for acting as readers. This book would not have been possible without Michael, Richard, Jeff, and Ben.

The materials published and archived by the Institute of Electrical and Electronics Engineers (IEEE), Association for Computing Machinery (ACM), and Advanced Computing Systems Association (USENIX) were crucial in the creation of the manuscript, as was the Security Mailing List Archive maintained by Gordon Lyon and the Security Digest Archives. The oral histories produced by the Charles Babbage Institute as part of their "Building an Infrastructure for Computer Security History" were also a key resource. In particular, Jeffery Yost has carried out a number of illuminating interviews.

Kirsty Leckie-Palmer provided expert feedback on the manuscript. The copy editor was Joyce Li. I would also like to thank my colleagues at Morgan

Stanley, in particular Jerry Brady, Grant Jonas, Mark Handy, Greg Gaskin, and Chip Ledford. Please note that my acknowledging these people here does not mean that they endorse the contents of this book.

Last but not least, a very special thank-you goes to my wife, Holly, and son, Tristan.

# Notes

## Introduction

1. Jason Pontin, "Secrets and Transparency: What Is WikiLeaks, and What Is Its Future?" *MIT Technology Review*, January 26, 2011, https://www.technologyreview.com/s/422521/secrets-and-transparency/.

2. Stuart Rintoul and Sean Parnell, "Julian Assange, Wild Child of Free Speech," *Australian*, December 10, 2010, https://www.theaustralian.com.au/in-depth/wikileaks/julian-assange-wild-child-of-free-speech/news-story/af356d93b25b28527eb106c255c942db; Suelette Dreyfus, *Underground: Tales of Hacking, Madness and Obsession on the Electronic Frontier* (Sydney: Random House Australia, 1997), http://underground-book.net/.

3. Rintoul and Parnell, "Julian Assange, Wild Child."

4. Fyodor [pseud.], "Info Security News Mailing List," SecLists.Org Security Mailing List Archive, last accessed July 24, 2019, https://seclists.org/isn/.

5. Fyodor [pseud.], "Info Security News Mailing List."

6. Julian Assange, "Re: The Paper That Launched Computer Security," SecLists.Org Security Mailing List Archive, last updated June 14, 2000, https://seclists.org/isn/2000/Jun/82.

7. Julian Assange, "Re: The Paper That Launched Computer Security."

8. Jennifer Lai, "Information Wants to Be Free, and Expensive," *Fortune*, July 20, 2009, https://fortune.com/2009/07/20/information-wants-to-be-free-and-expensive/.

9. Stuart Corner, "Billions Spent on Cyber Security and Much of It 'Wasted,'" *Sydney Morning Herald*, April 2, 2014, https://www.smh.com.au/technology/billions-spent-on-cyber-security-and-much-of-it-wasted-20140402-zqprb.html.

10. Ross Kerber, "Banks Claim Credit Card Breach Affected 94 Million Accounts," *New York Times*, October 24, 2007, https://www.nytimes.com/2007/10/24/technology/24iht-hack.1.8029174.html.

11. Robert McMillan and Ryan Knutson, "Yahoo Triples Estimate of Breached Accounts to 3 Billion," *Wall Street Journal*, October 3, 2017, https://www.wsj.com/articles/yahoo-triples-estimate-of-breached-accounts-to-3-billion-1507062804; Nicole Perlroth, "All 3 Billion Yahoo Accounts Were Affected by 2013 Attack," *New York Times*, October 3, 2017, https://www.nytimes.com/2017/10/03/technology/yahoo-hack-3-billion-users.html.

12. Kim Zetter, "How Digital Detectives Deciphered Stuxnet, the Most Menacing Malware in History," *Ars Technica*, July 11, 2011, https://arstechnica.com/tech-policy/2011/07/how-digital-detectives-deciphered-stuxnet-the-most-menacing-malware-in-history/; Thomas Rid, *Cyber War Will Not Take Place* (Oxford: Oxford University Press, 2017), 44.

13. David Drummond, "A New Approach to China," *Google* (blog), January 12, 2010, https://googleblog.blogspot.com/2010/01/new-approach-to-china.html.

14. "NSA-Dokumente: So knackt der Geheimdienst Internetkonten," *Der Spiegel*, last updated December 30, 2013, https://www.spiegel.de/fotostrecke/nsa-dokumente-so-knackt-der-geheimdienst-internetkonten-fotostrecke-105326-12.html.

15. James P. Anderson, *Computer Security Technology Planning Study* (Bedford, MA: Electronic Systems Division, Air Force Systems Command, United States Air Force, 1972), 64; Simson Garfinkel and Heather Richter Lipford, *Usable Security: History, Themes, and Challenges* (San Rafael, CA: Morgan & Claypool, 2014), 56; rain.forest.puppy [pseud.], "NT Web Technology Vulnerabilities," *Phrack* 8, no. 54 (1998), http://phrack.org/issues/54/8.html.

**1. A "New Dimension" for the Security of Information**

1. H. H. Goldstine and A. Goldstine, "The Electronic Numerical Integrator and Computer (ENIAC)," *IEEE Annals of the History of Computing* 18, no. 1 (1996): 10–16, https://doi.org/10.1109/85.476557.

2. Paul E. Ceruzzi, *A History of Modern Computing* (Cambridge, MA: MIT Press, 2003), 25.

3. Scott McCartney, *ENIAC: The Triumphs and Tragedies of the World's First Computer* (New York: Walker, 1999), 5; H. Polachek, "Before the ENIAC," *IEEE Annals of the History of Computing* 19, no. 2 (1997): 25–30, https://doi.org/10.1109/85.586069.

4. Ceruzzi, *History of Modern Computing*, 15.

5. Michael Swaine and Paul Freiberger, *Fire in the Valley: The Birth and Death of the Personal Computer* (Dallas: Pragmatic Bookshelf, 2014), 10; Alexander Randall, "Q&A: A Lost Interview with ENIAC Co-Inventor J. Presper Eckert," *Computerworld*, February 14,

2006, https://www.computerworld.com/article/2561813/q-a—a-lost-interview-with-eniac-co-inventor-j—presper-eckert.html.

6. Randall, "A Lost Interview."

7. W. B. Fritz, "The Women of ENIAC," *IEEE Annals of the History of Computing* 18, no. 3 (1996): 13–28, https://doi.org/10.1109/85.511940.

8. Meeri Kim, "70 Years Ago, Six Philly Women Became the World's First Digital Computer Programmers," *PhillyVoice*, February 11, 2016, https://www.phillyvoice.com/70-years-ago-six-philly-women-eniac-digital-computer-programmers/.

9. Simson L. Garfinkel and Rachel H. Grunspan, *The Computer Book: From the Abacus to Artificial Intelligence, 250 Milestones in the History of Computer Science* (New York: Sterling, 2018), 88.

10. L. R. Johnson, "Installation of a Large Electronic Computer" (presentation, ACM National Meeting, Toronto, 1952), https://doi.org/10.1145/800259.808998; Ceruzzi, *History of Modern Computing*, 27.

11. Ceruzzi, *History of Modern Computing*, 15.

12. Ceruzzi, *History of Modern Computing*, 27–28.

13. Johnson, "Large Electronic Computer"; Ceruzzi, *History of Modern Computing*, 27–28.

14. Peter Horner, "Air Force Salutes Project SCOOP," *Operations Research Management Science Today*, December 2007, https://www.informs.org/ORMS-Today/Archived-Issues/2007/orms-12-07/Air-Force-Salutes-Project-SCOOP.

15. Ceruzzi, *History of Modern Computing*, 35.

16. Ceruzzi, *History of Modern Computing*, 35.

17. Ceruzzi, *History of Modern Computing*, 154–155.

18. Willis H. Ware, *Security Controls for Computer Systems: Report of Defense Science Board Task Force on Computer Security* (Santa Monica, CA: RAND, 1970), https://www.rand.org/pubs/reports/R609-1/index2.html.

19. Ware, *Security Controls for Computer Systems*, xv.

20. Alex Abella, *Soldiers of Reason: The RAND Corporation and the Rise of the American Empire* (Boston: Mariner Books, 2009), 13, 203.

21. Abella, *Soldiers of Reason*, 13.

22. Willis H. Ware, *RAND and the Information Evolution: A History in Essays and Vignettes* (Santa Monica, CA: RAND, 2008), 6; Abella, *Soldiers of Reason*, 13.

23. Abella, *Soldiers of Reason*, 33.

24. Ware, *RAND and the Information Evolution*, 7.

25. Ware, *RAND and the Information Evolution*, 7.

26. Ware, *RAND and the Information Evolution*, 69.

27. Oliver Wainwright, "All Hail the Mothership: Norman Foster's $5bn Apple HQ Revealed," *Guardian*, November 15, 2013, https://www.theguardian.com/artanddesign/2013/nov/15/norman-foster-apple-hq-mothership-spaceship-architecture.

28. Ware, *RAND and the Information Evolution*, 34.

29. Ware, *RAND and the Information Evolution*, 7; Abella, *Soldiers of Reason*, 13–14.

30. Abella, *Soldiers of Reason*, 13.

31. Abella, *Soldiers of Reason*, 47.

32. Janet Abbate, *Inventing the Internet* (Cambridge, MA: MIT Press, 1999), 10; Abella, *Soldiers of Reason*, 13.

33. Abella, *Soldiers of Reason*, 18.

34. Thomas Schelling, *Arms and Influence* (New Haven, CT: Yale University Press, 1966); Fred Kaplan, "All Pain, No Gain: Nobel Laureate Thomas Schelling's Little-Known Role in the Vietnam War," *Slate*, October 11, 2005, https://slate.com/news-and-politics/2005/10/nobel-winner-tom-schelling-s-roll-in-the-vietnam-war.html.

35. Abella, *Soldiers of Reason*, 21.

36. Abella, *Soldiers of Reason*, 54.

37. Abella, *Soldiers of Reason*, 54–57.

38. Virginia Campbell, "How RAND Invented the Postwar World," *Invention & Technology*, Summer 2004, 53, https://www.rand.org/content/dam/rand/www/external/about/history/Rand.IT.Summer04.pdf; Abella, *Soldiers of Reason*, 57.

39. Abella, *Soldiers of Reason*, 57–63.

40. Ware, *RAND and the Information Evolution*, 53.

41. Ware, *RAND and the Information Evolution*, 53.

42. Ware, *RAND and the Information Evolution*, 56.

43. Abella, *Soldiers of Reason*, 147.

44. RAND Blog, "Willis Ware, Computer Pioneer, Helped Build Early Machines and Warned About Security Privacy," *RAND Blog*, November 27, 2013, https://www.rand.org/blog/2013/11/willis-ware-computer-pioneer-helped-build-early-machines.html.

45. McCartney, *ENIAC*, 94.

46. Abella, *Soldiers of Reason*, 147.

47. Abella, *Soldiers of Reason*, 49.

48. Kenneth J. Arrow, "Rational Choice Functions and Orderings," *Economica* 26, no. 102 (1959): 121–127. https://www.jstor.org/stable/i343698; Abella, *Soldiers of Reason*, 49.

49. Abella, *Soldiers of Reason*, 49–50.

50. Abella, *Soldiers of Reason*, 50.

51. Abella, *Soldiers of Reason*, 6.

52. Ware, *RAND and the Information Evolution*, 152.

## 2. The Promise, Success, and Failure of the Early Researchers

1. Willis H. Ware, interview by Nancy Stern, *Charles Babbage Institute*, January 19, 1981, 5, http://hdl.handle.net/11299/107699.

2. Willis H. Ware, interview by Jeffrey R. Yost, *Charles Babbage Institute*, August 11, 2003, 3, http://hdl.handle.net/11299/107703.

3. Ware, interview by Yost, 3.

4. Ware, interview by Yost, 3.

5. Ware, interview by Yost, 3.

6. Willis H. Ware, "Willis H. Ware," *IEEE Annals of the History of Computing* 33, no. 3 (2011): 67–73, https://doi.org/10.1109/MAHC.2011.60; Ware, interview by Yost, 4.

7. Ware, interview by Yost, 5.

8. Willis H. Ware, *RAND and the Information Evolution: A History in Essays and Vignettes* (Santa Monica, CA: RAND, 2008), 36; Ware, interview by Stern, 40; Ware, interview by Yost, 5.

9. Ware, "Willis H. Ware."

10. RAND, "Time Travelers," *RAND Review* 32, no. 2 (2008): 4; Willis H. Ware, "Future Computer Technology and Its Impact" (presentation, Board of Trustees, Air Force Advisory Group, November 1965), https://www.rand.org/pubs/papers/P3279 .html.

11. Ware, interview by Yost, 9.

12. Ware, interview by Yost, 12.

13. Ware, interview by Yost, 13.

14. Ware, interview by Yost, 14.

15. Ware, interview by Yost, 14.

16. Defense Science Board Task Force on Computer Security, *Security Controls for Computer Systems: Report of Defense Science Board Task Force on Computer Security— RAND Report R-60901* (Santa Monica, CA: RAND, February 11, 1970), https://www .rand.org/pubs/reports/R609-1/index2.html.

17. Defense Science Board, *Security Controls for Computer Systems*, xi–xii.

18. Defense Science Board, *Security Controls for Computer Systems*, v.

19. Steven J. Murdoch, Mike Bond, and Ross Anderson, "How Certification Systems Fail: Lessons from the Ware Report," *IEEE Security & Privacy* 10, no. 6 (2012): 40–44, https://doi.org/10.1109/MSP.2012.89.

20. Defense Science Board, *Security Controls for Computer Systems*.

21. Defense Science Board, *Security Controls for Computer Systems*, 2.

22. Defense Science Board, *Security Controls for Computer Systems*, 8.

23. Defense Science Board, *Security Controls for Computer Systems*, 8.

24. Defense Science Board, *Security Controls for Computer Systems*, vii.

25. Defense Science Board, *Security Controls for Computer Systems*, 19.

26. Alex Abella, *Soldiers of Reason: The RAND Corporation and the Rise of the American Empire* (Boston: Mariner Books, 2009), 82.

27. Abella, *Soldiers of Reason*, 82.

28. Kevin R. Kosar, *Security Classification Policy and Procedure: E.O. 12958, as Amended* (Washington, DC: Congressional Research Service, 2009), 5.

29. Elizabeth Goitein and David M. Shapiro, *Reducing Overclassification through Accountability* (New York: Brennan Center for Justice, 2011), 1.

30. Goitein and Shapiro, *Overclassification through Accountability*, 7.

31. Information Security Oversight Office, *2017 Report to the President* (Washington, DC: Information Security Oversight Office, 2018), 2.

32. Mike Giglio, "The U.S. Government Keeps Too Many Secrets," *Atlantic*, October 2019, https://www.theatlantic.com/politics/archive/2019/10/us-government-has-secrecy -problem/599380/.

33. Goitein and Shapiro, *Overclassification through Accountability*, 3.

34. Thomas Blanton, *Statement of Thomas Blanton to the Committee on the Judiciary, U.S. House of Representatives, Hearing on the Espionage Act and the Legal and Constitutional Implications of WikiLeaks* (Washington, DC: US House of Representatives, 2010), 3.

35. Ross Anderson, *Security Engineering: A Guide to Building Dependable Distributed Systems*, 2nd ed. (New York: Wiley, 2008), 277–278, https://www.cl.cam.ac.uk/~rja14/Papers/SEv2-c09.pdf.

36. Anderson, *Security Engineering*, 278.

37. Scott McCartney, *ENIAC: The Triumphs and Tragedies of the World's First Computer* (New York: Walker, 1999), 159–160.

38. McCartney, *ENIAC*, 159–160.

39. McCartney, *ENIAC*, 159–160.

40. Defense Science Board, *Security Controls for Computer Systems*, vi.

41. James P. Anderson, *Computer Security Technology Planning Study* (Bedford, MA: Electronic Systems Division, Air Force Systems Command, United States Air Force, 1972).

42. Roger R. Schell, interview by Jeffrey R. Yost, *Charles Babbage Institute*, May 1, 2012, 56, http://hdl.handle.net/11299/133439.

43. Schell, interview by Yost, 56.

44. "Passing of a Pioneer," Center for Education and Research in Information Assurance (CERIAS), Purdue University, last updated January 2, 2008, https://www.cerias.purdue.edu/site/blog/post/passing-of-a-pioneer.

45. "Passing of a Pioneer."

46. Steven B. Lipner, "The Birth and Death of the Orange Book," *IEEE Annals of the History of Computing* 37, no. 2 (2015): 19–31, https://doi.org/10.1109/MAHC.2015.27.

47. Schell, interview by Yost, 73.

48. Schell, interview by Yost, 73.

49. Anderson, *Planning Study*, 3.

50. Anderson, *Planning Study*, 14, 34, 89, 92.

51. Anderson, *Planning Study*, 1, 15.

52. Donald MacKenzie and Garrell Pottinger, "Mathematics, Technology, and Trust: Formal Verification, Computer Security, and the U.S. Military," *IEEE Annals of the History of Computing* 19, no. 3 (1997): 41–59, https://doi.org/10.1109/85.601735.

53. Anderson, *Planning Study*, 25.

54. Anderson, *Planning Study*, 55.

55. Anderson, *Planning Study*, 17.

56. Dieter Gollmann, *Computer Security* (New York: Wiley, 2011), 88.

57. Gollmann, *Computer Security*, 88; Anderson, *Planning Study*, 17.

58. Jerome H. Saltzer, "Protection and the Control of Information Sharing in Multics," *Communications of the ACM* 17, no. 7 (1974): 388–402, https://doi.org/10.1145/361011.361067.

59. "How the Air Force Cracked Multics Security," Multicians, Tom Van Vleck, last updated October 14, 2002, https://www.multicians.org/security.html.

60. Saltzer, "Protection and the Control."

61. Richard E. Smith, "A Contemporary Look at Saltzer and Schroeder's 1975 Design Principles," *IEEE Security & Privacy* 10, no. 6 (2012): 20–25, http://doi.org/10.1109/MSP.2012.85.

62. Jerome H. Saltzer and M. D. Schroeder, "The Protection of Information in Computer Systems," *Proceedings of the IEEE* 63, no. 9 (1975): 1278–1308, http://doi.org/10.1109/PROC.1975.9939; Smith, "A Contemporary Look."

63. Saltzer and Schroeder, "Protection of Information."

64. Adam Shostack, "The Security Principles of Saltzer and Schroeder," *Emergent Chaos* (blog), last accessed April 30, 2019, http://emergentchaos.com/the-security -principles-of-saltzer-and-schroeder.

65. Paul Karger and Roger R. Schell, *Multics Security Evaluation: Vulnerability Analysis* (Bedford, MA: Electronic Systems Division, Air Force Systems Command, United States Air Force, 1974).

66. David E. Bell, "Looking Back at the Bell-LaPadula Model" (presentation, 21st Annual Computer Security Applications Conference, Tucson, December 5–9, 2005), https://doi.org/10.1109/CSAC.2005.37.

67. MacKenzie and Pottinger, "Mathematics, Technology, and Trust," 45.

68. MacKenzie and Pottinger, "Mathematics, Technology, and Trust," 45; George F. Jelen, *Information Security: An Elusive Goal* (Cambridge, MA: Harvard University, 1995), II-70.

69. Bell, "Looking Back."

70. Paul Karger and Roger R. Schell, "Thirty Years Later: Lessons from the Multics Security Evaluation" (presentation, 18th Annual Computer Security Applications Conference, Las Vegas, December 9–13, 2002), https://doi.org/10.1109/CSAC.2002 .1176285; Karger and Schell, *Multics Security Evaluation.*

71. Karger and Schell, *Multics Security Evaluation.*

72. Karger and Schell, *Multics Security Evaluation.*

73. Roger R. Schell, "Information Security: Science, Pseudoscience, and Flying Pigs" (presentation, 17th Annual Computer Security Applications Conference, New Orleans, December 10–14, 2001), https://doi.org/10.1109/ACSAC.2001.991537; Bell, "Looking Back"; Karger and Schell, *Multics Security Evaluation.*

74. Karger and Schell, *Multics Security Evaluation.*

75. Karger and Schell, *Multics Security Evaluation.*

76. MacKenzie and Pottinger, "Mathematics, Technology, and Trust," 46.

77. David Elliot Bell, interview by Jeffrey R. Yost, *Charles Babbage Institute*, September 24, 2012, 8–9, http://hdl.handle.net/11299/144024.

78. Bell, interview by Yost, 11.

79. Bell, interview by Yost, 11.

80. Abella, *Soldiers of Reason*, 34.

81. Bell, interview by Yost, 13.

82. Bell, interview by Yost, 37.

83. Bell, interview by Yost, 14.

84. Bell, interview by Yost, 15.

85. Bell, interview by Yost, 16.

86. Bell, interview by Yost, 19.

87. Bell, interview by Yost, 20.

88. David Elliot Bell and Leonard J. LaPadula, *Secure Computer Systems: Mathematical Foundations* (Bedford, MA: Electronic Systems Division, Air Force Systems Command, United States Air Force, November 1973); David Elliot Bell and Leonard J. LaPadula, *Secure Computer System: Unified Exposition and Multics Interpretation* (Bedford, MA: Electronic Systems Division, Air Force Systems Command, United States Air Force, March 1976).

89. Bell and LaPadula, *Mathematical Foundations*, iv.

90. Bell and LaPadula, *Mathematical Foundations*, 22.

91. Bell, interview by Yost, 20.

92. Bell, interview by Yost, 20–21.

93. MacKenzie and Pottinger, "Mathematics, Technology, and Trust," 47.

94. Schell, interview by Yost, 128.

95. John D. McLean, interview by Jeffrey R. Yost, *Charles Babbage Institute*, April 22, 2014, 16–17, http://hdl.handle.net/11299/164989.

96. John McLean, "A Comment on the 'Basic Security Theorem' of Bell and La-Padula," *Information Processing Letters* 20, no. 2 (1985): 67–70, https://doi.org/10.1016/0020-0190(85)90065-1; McLean, interview by Yost, 18.

97. McLean, "A Comment."

98. John McLean, "The Specification and Modeling of Computer Security," *Computer* 23, no. 1 (1990): 9–16, https://doi.org/10.1109/2.48795.

99. McLean, "Specification and Modeling."

100. McLean, interview by Yost, 19–20.

101. McLean, interview by Yost, 20.

102. MacKenzie and Pottinger, "Mathematics, Technology, and Trust," 47.

103. MacKenzie and Pottinger, "Mathematics, Technology, and Trust," 47–48.

104. MacKenzie and Pottinger, "Mathematics, Technology, and Trust," 48.

105. MacKenzie and Pottinger, "Mathematics, Technology, and Trust," 48.

106. MacKenzie and Pottinger, "Mathematics, Technology, and Trust," 48.

107. MacKenzie and Pottinger, "Mathematics, Technology, and Trust," 48.

108. Butler W. Lampson, "A Note on the Confinement Problem," *Communications of the ACM* 16, no. 10 (1973): 613–615, https://doi.org/10.1145/362375.362389.

109. Lampson, "Confinement Problem."

110. Lampson, "Confinement Problem."

111. Jonathan Millen, "20 Years of Covert Channel Modeling and Analysis" (presentation, IEEE Symposium on Security and Privacy, Oakland, CA, May 14, 1999), https://doi.org/10.1109/SECPRI.1999.766906.

112. Alex Crowell, Beng Heng Ng, Earlence Fernandes, and Atul Prakash, "The Confinement Problem: 40 Years Later," *Journal of Information Processing Systems* 9, no. 2 (2013): 189–204, https://doi.org/10.3745/JIPS.2013.9.2.189.

113. MacKenzie and Pottinger, "Mathematics, Technology, and Trust," 51–52; Lipner, "Orange Book."

114. Lipner, "Orange Book."

115. Lipner, "Orange Book."

116. Department of Defense, *Department of Defense Trusted Computer System Evaluation Criteria* (Fort Meade, MD: Department of Defense, December 26, 1985).

117. Marvin Schaefer, "If A1 Is the Answer, What Was the Question? An Edgy Naif's Retrospective on Promulgating the Trusted Computer Systems Evaluation Criteria" (presentation, 20th Annual Computer Security Applications Conference, Tucson, December 6–10, 2004), https://doi.org/10.1109/CSAC.2004.22.

118. Lipner, "Orange Book"; Schaefer, "If A1 Is the Answer."

119. "How the Air Force Cracked Multics Security."

120. Department of Defense, *Evaluation Criteria*.

121. Department of Defense, *Evaluation Criteria*.

122. Department of Defense, *Evaluation Criteria*.

123. Lipner, "Orange Book."

124. MacKenzie and Pottinger, "Mathematics, Technology, and Trust," 52–53.

125. Gollmann, *Computer Security*, 4.

126. MacKenzie and Pottinger, "Mathematics, Technology, and Trust," 54.

127. Russ Cooper, "Re: 'Windows NT Security,'" *RISKS Digest* 20, no. 1 (1998), https://catless.ncl.ac.uk/Risks/20/01; MacKenzie and Pottinger, "Mathematics, Technology, and Trust," 56.

128. Schell, interview by Yost, 130.

129. Jelen, *An Elusive Goal*, III-37.

130. MacKenzie and Pottinger, "Mathematics, Technology, and Trust," 54.

131. Lipner, "Orange Book."

132. Schaefer, "If A1 Is the Answer."

## 3. The Creation of the Internet and the Web, and a Dark Portent

1. Yanek Mieczkowski, *Eisenhower's Sputnik Moment: The Race for Space and World Prestige* (Ithaca, NY: Cornell University Press, 2013), 13; NASA, "Sputnik and the Origins of the Space Age," NASA History, last accessed March 11, 2020, https://history.nasa.gov/sputnik/sputorig.html.

2. Katie Hafner and Matthew Lyon, *Where Wizards Stay Up Late: The Origins of the Internet* (New York: Simon & Schuster, 1996), 20.

3. Richard J. Barber, *The Advanced Research Projects Agency, 1958–1974* (Fort Belvoir, VA: Defense Technical Information Center, 1975), I-7, https://apps.dtic.mil/docs/citations/ADA154363.

4. Sharon Weinberger, *Imagineers of War* (New York: Vintage Books, 2017), 44; Hafner and Lyon, *Where Wizards Stay Up Late*, 20.

5. Janet Abbate, *Inventing the Internet* (Cambridge, MA: MIT Press, 1999), 38.

6. Johnny Ryan, *A History of the Internet and the Digital Future* (London: Reaktion Books, 2010), 25; Abbate, *Inventing the Internet*, 38.

7. Abbate, *Inventing the Internet*, 38; Ryan, *History of the Internet*, 27; Hafner and Lyon, *Where Wizards Stay Up Late*, 44.

8. Hafner and Lyon, *Where Wizards Stay Up Late*, 53.

9. Weinberger, *Imagineers of War*, 115; Abbate, *Inventing the Internet*, 10.

10. Hafner and Lyon, *Where Wizards Stay Up Late*, 56.

11. Hafner and Lyon, *Where Wizards Stay Up Late*, 57.

12. Hafner and Lyon, *Where Wizards Stay Up Late*, 58.

13. Hafner and Lyon, *Where Wizards Stay Up Late*, 58.

14. Ryan, *History of the Internet*, 15; Hafner and Lyon, *Where Wizards Stay Up Late*, 59–60.

15. Hafner and Lyon, *Where Wizards Stay Up Late*, 59–60.

16. Hafner and Lyon, *Where Wizards Stay Up Late*, 67.

17. Hafner and Lyon, *Where Wizards Stay Up Late*, 63.

18. Ryan, *History of the Internet*, 16–17; Hafner and Lyon, *Where Wizards Stay Up Late*, 62–64.

19. Hafner and Lyon, *Where Wizards Stay Up Late*, 64.

20. Abbate, *Inventing the Internet*, 44.

21. Abbate, *Inventing the Internet*, 56.

22. Abbate, *Inventing the Internet*, 56.

23. Abbate, *Inventing the Internet*, 56.

24. Hafner and Lyon, *Where Wizards Stay Up Late*, 75; Weinberger, *Imagineers of War*, 220.

25. Ryan, *History of the Internet*, 29; Hafner and Lyon, *Where Wizards Stay Up Late*, 79.

26. Hafner and Lyon, *Where Wizards Stay Up Late*, 80.

27. Hafner and Lyon, *Where Wizards Stay Up Late*, 81.

28. Hafner and Lyon, *Where Wizards Stay Up Late*, 81.

29. Ryan, *History of the Internet*, 29; Hafner and Lyon, *Where Wizards Stay Up Late*, 100.

30. Hafner and Lyon, *Where Wizards Stay Up Late*, 103.

31. Simson L. Garfinkel and Rachel H. Grunspan, *The Computer Book: From the Abacus to Artificial Intelligence, 250 Milestones in the History of Computer Science* (New York: Sterling, 2018), 224; Abbate, *Inventing the Internet*, 64.

32. Hafner and Lyon, *Where Wizards Stay Up Late*, 166.

33. Hafner and Lyon, *Where Wizards Stay Up Late*, 152.

34. Abbate, *Inventing the Internet*, 64.

35. Abbate, *Inventing the Internet*, 101.

36. Garfinkel and Grunspan, *Computer Book*, 312; Hafner and Lyon, *Where Wizards Stay Up Late*, 189.

37. Ryan, *History of the Internet*, 78; Abbate, *Inventing the Internet*, 69; Hafner and Lyon, *Where Wizards Stay Up Late*, 194.

38. Garfinkel and Grunspan, *Computer Book*, 292.

39. Brad Templeton, "Reaction to the DEC Spam of 1978," Brad Templeton's Home Page, last accessed April 30, 2019, https://www.templetons.com/brad/spamreact.html.

40. Templeton, "Reaction to the DEC Spam."

41. Garfinkel and Grunspan, *Computer Book*, 292; Templeton, "Reaction to the DEC Spam."

42. Templeton, "Reaction to the DEC Spam."

43. Hafner and Lyon, *Where Wizards Stay Up Late*, 144–145.

44. Hafner and Lyon, *Where Wizards Stay Up Late*, 144–145.

45. Hafner and Lyon, *Where Wizards Stay Up Late*, 144–145.

46. Internet Engineering Task Force, "RFC 1149 Standard for the Transmission of IP Datagrams on Avian Carriers," IETF Tools, last updated April 1, 1990, https://tools.ietf.org/html/rfc1149.

47. Abbate, *Inventing the Internet*, 130.

48. Hafner and Lyon, *Where Wizards Stay Up Late*, 226; Abbate, *Inventing the Internet*, 128.

49. Hafner and Lyon, *Where Wizards Stay Up Late*, 174.

50. Hafner and Lyon, *Where Wizards Stay Up Late*, 174.

51. Internet Engineering Task Force, "RFC 854 Telnet Protocol Specification," IETF Tools, last updated May 1983, https://tools.ietf.org/html/rfc854; Internet Engineering Task Force, "RFC 2577 FTP Security Considerations," IETF Tools, last updated May 1999, https://tools.ietf.org/html/rfc2577.

52. Internet Engineering Task Force, "RFC 1543 Instructions to RFC Authors," IETF Tools, last updated October 1993, https://tools.ietf.org/html/rfc1543.

53. Defense Advanced Research Projects Agency, *Memorandum for the Director* (Arlington, VA: DARPA, November 8, 1988).

54. Eugene H. Spafford, "A Failure to Learn from the Past" (presentation, 19th Annual Computer Security Applications Conference, Las Vegas, December 8–12, 2003), https://doi.org/10.1109/CSAC.2003.1254327; Geoff Goodfellow, "Re: 6,000 Sites," "Security Digest" Archives, last updated October 11, 1988, http://securitydigest.org/phage /archive/223.

55. Abbate, *Inventing the Internet*, 186.

56. Robert Morris (presentation, National Research Council Computer Science and Technology Board, September 19, 1988).

57. National Computer Security Center, *Proceedings of the Virus Post-Mortem Meeting* (Fort Meade, MD: NCSC, November 8, 1988).

58. Spafford, "A Failure."

59. Spafford, "A Failure."

60. Spafford, "A Failure."

61. Spafford, "A Failure."

62. Spafford, "A Failure."

63. Eugene H. Spafford, "The Internet Worm Program: An Analysis, Purdue University Report Number 88-823," *ACM SIGCOMM Computer Communication Review* 19, no. 1 (1989): 17–57, https://doi.org/10.1145/66093.66095.

64. National Computer Security Center, *Post-Mortem Meeting.*

65. National Computer Security Center, *Post-Mortem Meeting.*

66. National Computer Security Center, *Post-Mortem Meeting.*

67. M. W. Eichin and J. A. Rochlis, "With Microscope and Tweezers: An Analysis of the Internet Virus of November 1988" (presentation, IEEE Symposium on Security and Privacy, Oakland, CA, May 1–3, 1989), https://doi.org/10.1109/SECPRI.1989.36307.

68. Spafford, "A Failure."

69. Defense Advanced Research Projects Agency, "Memorandum for the Director."

70. Defense Advanced Research Projects Agency, "Memorandum for the Director."

71. National Computer Security Center, *Post-Mortem Meeting.*

72. Gene Spafford, "Phage List," "Security Digest" Archives, last accessed May 2, 2019, http://securitydigest.org/phage/.

73. Spafford, "A Failure."

74. National Computer Security Center, *Post-Mortem Meeting.*

75. National Computer Security Center, *Post-Mortem Meeting.*

76. United States General Accounting Office, *Virus Highlights Need for Improved Management* (Washington, DC: United States General Accounting Office, June 12, 1989).

77. Anon., "Phage #410," "Security Digest" Archives, last accessed May 2, 2019, http://securitydigest.org/phage/archive/410.

78. Eichin and Rochlis, "With Microscope and Tweezers."

79. Erik E. Fair, "Phage #047," "Security Digest" Archives, last accessed May 2, 2019, http://securitydigest.org/phage/archive/047.

80. Timothy B. Lee, "How a Grad Student Trying to Build the First Botnet Brought the Internet to Its Knees," *Washington Post*, November 1, 2013.

81. Lee, "How a Grad Student."

82. Ronald B. Standler, "Judgment in *U.S. v. Robert Tappan Morris*," rbs2.com, last updated August 14, 2002, http://rbs2.com/morris.htm.

83. John Markoff, "Computer Intruder Is Found Guilty," *New York Times*, January 23, 1990, https://www.nytimes.com/1990/01/23/us/computer-intruder-is-found-guilty.html; Standler, "Judgment in *U.S. v. Robert Tappan Morris*."

84. Josephine Wolff, *You'll See This Message When It Is Too Late: The Legal and Economic Aftermath of Cybersecurity Breaches* (Cambridge, MA: MIT Press, 2018), 212–213.

85. John Markoff, "Computer Intruder Is Put on Probation and Fined $10,000," *New York Times*, May 5, 1990, https://www.nytimes.com/1990/05/05/us/computer-intruder-is-put-on-probation-and-fined-10000.html.

86. "Computer Chaos Called Mistake, Not Felony," *New York Times*, January 10, 1990, https://www.nytimes.com/1990/01/10/us/computer-chaos-called-mistake-not-felony.html.

87. Mark W. Eichin, *The Internet Virus of November 3, 1988* (Cambridge, MA: MIT Project Athena, November 8, 1988), 5.

88. Lee, "How a Grad Student."

89. Eichin and Rochlis, "Microscope and Tweezers," 5.

90. Eichin and Rochlis, "Microscope and Tweezers," 3.

91. Spafford, "The Internet Worm Program," 21, 26.

92. Spafford, "The Internet Worm Program," 21.

93. Spafford, "The Internet Worm Program," 22.

94. James P. Anderson, *Computer Security Technology Planning Study* (Bedford, MA: Electronic Systems Division, Air Force Systems Command, United States Air Force, 1972), 64.

95. Spafford, "The Internet Worm Program," 23.

96. John Markoff, "Author of Computer 'Virus' Is Son of N.S.A. Expert on Data Security," *New York Times*, November 5, 1988, https://www.nytimes.com/1988/11/05/us/author-of-computer-virus-is-son-of-nsa-expert-on-data-security.html.

97. Robert Morris and Ken Thompson, "Password Security: A Case History," *Communications of the ACM* 22, no. 11 (1979): 594–597, https://doi.org/10.1145/359168.359172; Markoff, "Author of Computer 'Virus.'"

98. John Markoff, "Robert Morris, Pioneer in Computer Security, Dies at 78," *New York Times*, June 29, 2011, https://www.nytimes.com/2011/06/30/technology/30morris.html.

99. Hilarie Orman, "The Morris Worm: A Fifteen-Year Perspective," *IEEE Security & Privacy* 1, no. 5 (2003): 35–43, https://doi.org/10.1109/MSECP.2003.1236233.

100. Markoff, "Son of N.S.A. Expert."

101. Spafford, "The Internet Worm Program," 1.

102. Martin Campbell-Kelly, *From Airline Reservations to Sonic the Hedgehog* (Cambridge, MA: MIT Press, 2003), 144.

103. Eugene H. Spafford, *Unix and Security: The Influences of History* (West Lafayette, IN: Department of Computer Science, Purdue University, 1992), 2.

104. Ken Thompson and Dennis M. Ritchie, *The Unix Programmer's Manual*, 2nd ed. (Murray Hill, NJ: Bell Labs, June 12, 1972).

105. Spafford, "Unix and Security," 3; Paul E. Ceruzzi, *A History of Modern Computing* (Cambridge, MA: MIT Press, 2003), 247.

106. Campbell-Kelly, *From Airline Reservations*, 144.

107. Ceruzzi, *Modern Computing*, 283.

108. Defense Advanced Research Projects Agency, "ARPA Becomes DARPA," last accessed March 8, 2020, https://www.darpa.mil/about-us/timeline/arpa-name-change; Ceruzzi, *Modern Computing*, 284.

109. Campbell-Kelly, *From Airline Reservations*, 144.

110. Martin Minow, "Is Unix the Ultimate Computer Virus?" *Risks Digest* 11, no. 15 (1991), https://catless.ncl.ac.uk/Risks/11/15.

111. Dennis M. Ritchie, "The Development of the C Language" (presentation, 2nd ACM SIGPLAN on History of Programming Languages, Cambridge, MA, April 20–23, 1993), https://doi.org/10.1145/154766.155580; Ceruzzi, *Modern Computing*, 106.

112. Ceruzzi, *Modern Computing*, 106; Ritchie, "The C Language."

113. John Markoff, "Flaw in E-Mail Programs Points to an Industrywide Problem," *New York Times*, July 30, 1998, https://www.nytimes.com/1998/07/30/business/flaw-in-e-mail-programs-points-to-an-industrywide-problem.html.

114. Rob Diamond, "Re: Tony Hoar: 'Null References,'" *Risks Digest* 25, no. 55 (2009), https://catless.ncl.ac.uk/Risks/25/55.

115. Dennis M. Ritchie, *On the Security of Unix* (Murray Hill, NJ: Bell Labs, n.d.).

116. Spafford, "Unix and Security," 5.

117. Matt Bishop, "Reflections on Unix Vulnerabilities" (presentation, 2009 Annual Computer Security Applications Conference, Honolulu, December 7–11, 2009), https://doi.org/10.1109/ACSAC.2009.25.

118. Bishop, "Reflections."

119. Simson Garfinkel and Gene Spafford, *Practical Unix Security* (Sebastopol, CA: O'Reilly Media, 1991).

120. Shooting Shark [pseud.], "Unix Nasties," *Phrack* 1, no. 6 (1986), http://phrack.org/issues/6/5.html; Red Knight [pseud.], "An In-Depth Guide in Hacking Unix," *Phrack* 2, no. 22 (1988), http://phrack.org/issues/22/5.html; The Shining [pseud.], "Unix Hacking Tools of the Trade," *Phrack* 5, no. 46 (1994), http://phrack.org/issues/46/11.html.

121. Fyodor [pseud.], "Bugtraq Mailing List," SecLists.Org Security Mailing List Archive, last accessed May 2, 2019, https://seclists.org/bugtraq/.

122. Shooting Shark [pseud.], "Unix Trojan Horses," *Phrack* 1, no. 7 (1986), http://phrack.org/issues/7/7.html; Spafford, "Unix and Security," 1.

123. Steven M. Bellovin and William R. Cheswick, "Network Firewalls," *IEEE Communications Magazine* 32, no. 9 (1994): 50–57, https://doi.org/10.1109/35.312843.

124. William R. Cheswick and Steven M. Bellovin, *Firewalls and Internet Security: Repelling the Wily Hacker*, 2nd ed. (Boston: Addison-Wesley, 2003).

125. Cheswick and Bellovin, *Firewalls and Internet Security*.

126. Anderson, *Planning Study*, 89.

127. John Ioannidis, "Re: Ping Works, but ftp/telnet Get 'No Route to Host,'" comp.protocols.tcp-ip, July 22, 1992, http://securitydigest.org/tcp-ip/archive/1992/07.

128. Casey Leedom, "Is the Balkanization of the Internet Inevitable?" comp.protocols.tcp-ip, November 17, 1992, http://securitydigest.org/tcp-ip/archive/1992/11.

129. Steven Bellovin, "Re: Firewall Usage (Was: Re: Ping Works, but ftp/telnet Get 'No Route," comp.protocols.tcp-ip, July 24, 1992, http://securitydigest.org/tcp-ip/archive/1992/07.

130. Bill Cheswick, "The Design of a Secure Internet Gateway" (presentation, USENIX Summer Conference, 1990).

131. Cheswick, "Secure Internet Gateway."

132. Cheswick, "Secure Internet Gateway."

133. Cheswick, "Secure Internet Gateway."

134. Cheswick, "Secure Internet Gateway."

135. Steven M. Bellovin, "There Be Dragons" (presentation, 3rd USENIX Security Symposium, Berkeley, CA, September 14–16, 1992), https://doi.org/10.7916/D8V12BJ6.

136. Cheswick and Bellovin, *Firewalls and Internet Security*.

137. Rik Farrow, "Bill Cheswick on Firewalls: An Interview," *Login* 38, no. 4 (2013), https://www.usenix.org/publications/login/august-2013-volume-38-number-4/bill-cheswick-firewalls-interview.

138. Farrow, "Bill Cheswick on Firewalls."

139. Cheswick, "Secure Internet Gateway."

140. Avishai Wool, "The Use and Usability of Direction-Based Filtering in Firewalls," *Computers and Security* 23, no. 6 (2004), http://dx.doi.org/10.1016/j.cose.2004.02.003; Avishai Wool, "Architecting the Lumeta Firewall Analyzer" (presentation, 10th USENIX Security Symposium, Washington, DC, August 13–17, 2001).

141. Avishai Wool, "A Quantitative Study of Firewall Configuration Errors," *Computer* 37, no. 6 (2004): 62–67, https://doi.org/10.1109/MC.2004.2.

142. Avishai Wool, "Trends in Firewall Configuration Errors—Measuring the Holes in Swiss Cheese," *IEEE Internet Computing* 14, no. 4 (2010): 58, https://doi.org/10.1109/MIC.2010.29.

143. Garfinkel and Grunspan, *Computer Book*, 398.

144. Abbate, *Inventing the Internet*, 214; Garfinkel and Grunspan, *Computer Book*, 398.

145. Abbate, *Inventing the Internet*, 214.

146. Abbate, *Inventing the Internet*, 215.

147. Abbate, *Inventing the Internet*, 215.

148. Ryan, *History of the Internet*, 106–107.

149. Abbate, *Inventing the Internet*, 214.

150. Abbate, *Inventing the Internet*, 215.

151. Abbate, *Inventing the Internet*, 215; Abbate, *Inventing the Internet*, 216.

152. Abbate, *Inventing the Internet*, 216.

153. Abbate, *Inventing the Internet*, 216.

154. Ceruzzi, *Modern Computing*, 303; Garfinkel and Grunspan, *Computer Book*, 418.

155. Abbate, *Inventing the Internet*, 217.

156. John Cassidy, *Dot.con: The Greatest Story Ever Sold* (New York: Perennial, 2003), 51.

157. Abbate, *Inventing the Internet*, 217.

158. Abbate, *Inventing the Internet*, 217.

159. Ceruzzi, *Modern Computing*, 303.

160. Cheswick and Bellovin, *Firewalls and Internet Security*.

161. Rod Kurtz, "Has Dan Farmer Sold His Soul?" *Businessweek*, April 5, 2005.

162. "Elemental CTO Dan Farmer Recognized as a Technology Visionary by Info-World Magazine, Named an 'Innovator to Watch in 2006,'" *Help Net Security*, last accessed May 2, 2019, https://www.helpnetsecurity.com/2005/08/04/elemental-cto-dan-farmer-recognized-as-a-technology-visionary-by-infoworld-magazine-named-an-innovator-to-watch-in-2006/.

163. "Dan Farmer, Co-Founder and CTO, Elemental Security," *InformationWeek*, last accessed May 2, 2019, https://www.informationweek.com/dan-farmer-co-founder-and-cto-elemental-security/d/d-id/1041253.

164. Rik Farrow, "Interview with Dan Farmer," *Login* 39, no. 6 (2014): 33, https://www.usenix.org/publications/login/dec14/farmer.

165. Farrow, "Interview with Dan Farmer," 32.

166. Farrow, "Interview with Dan Farmer," 32.

167. Farrow, "Interview with Dan Farmer," 33.

168. "CERT Advisories 1988–2004," Software Engineering Institute, Carnegie Mellon University, last accessed May 2, 2019, https://resources.sei.cmu.edu/library/asset-view.cfm?assetID=509746.

169. Farrow, "Interview with Dan Farmer," 32–33.

170. Dan Farmer and Wietse Venema, "Improving the Security of Your Site by Breaking into It," comp.security.unix, December 2, 1993, http://www.fish2.com/security/admin-guide-to-cracking.html.

171. Farmer and Venema, "Improving the Security."

172. Wietse Venema, "SATAN (Security Administrator Tool for Analyzing Networks)," www.porcupine.org, last accessed May 2, 2019, http://www.porcupine.org/satan/.

173. "Company Timeline," ISS Timeline, IBM Internet Security Systems, last updated April 20, 2007, http://www.iss.net/about/timeline/index.html.

174. Farrow, "Interview with Dan Farmer," 33.

175. Farrow, "Interview with Dan Farmer," 33.

176. Farrow, "Interview with Dan Farmer," 33.

177. John Markoff, "Dismissal of Security Expert Adds Fuel to Internet Debate," *New York Times*, March 22, 1995, https://www.nytimes.com/1995/03/22/business/dismissal-of-security-expert-adds-fuel-to-internet-debate.html; Farrow, "Interview with Dan Farmer," 34.

178. Farrow, "Interview with Dan Farmer," 34.

179. Wietse Venema, "Quotes about SATAN," www.porcupine.org, last accessed May 2, 2019, http://www.porcupine.org/satan/demo/docs/quotes.html.

180. Anon., "A Possible 'Solution' to Internet SATAN: Handcuffs," *Risks Digest* 17, no. 4 (1995), https://catless.ncl.ac.uk/Risks/17/04.

181. "Info about SATAN," CERIAS—Center for Education and Research in Information Assurance and Security, Purdue University, last accessed May 2, 2019, http://www.cerias.purdue.edu/site/about/history/coast/satan.php.

182. Dan Farmer, "Shall We Dust Moscow? (Security Survey of Key Internet Hosts and Various Semi-Relevant Reflections)," December 18, 1996, http://www.fish2.com /survey/.

183. Farmer, "Dust Moscow."

184. Farmer, "Dust Moscow."

185. Farmer, "Dust Moscow."

186. Farmer, "Dust Moscow."

187. P. W. Singer and Allan Friedman, *Cybersecurity and Cyberwar: What Everyone Needs to Know* (Oxford: Oxford University Press, 2014), 20.

188. Cassidy, *Dot.con*, 110.

189. Farmer, "Dust Moscow."

190. Dan Farmer, "Your Most Important Systems Are Your Least Secure," *trouble .org* (blog), January 30, 2012, http://trouble.org/?p=262.

### 4. The Dot-Com Boom and the Genesis of a Lucrative Feedback Loop

1. John Cassidy, *Dot.con: The Greatest Story Ever Sold* (New York: Perennial, 2003), 4.

2. Cassidy, *Dot.con*, 25.

3. Cassidy, *Dot.con*, 85.

4. John Markoff, "Software Flaw Lets Computer Viruses Arrive via E-Mail," *New York Times*, July 29, 1998, www.nytimes.com/1998/07/29/business/software-flaw-lets -computer-viruses-arrive-via-e-mail.html; John Markoff, "Flaw in E-Mail Programs Points to an Industrywide Problem," *New York Times*, July 30, 1998, https://www.nytimes .com/1998/07/30/business/flaw-in-e-mail-programs-points-to-an-industrywide-problem .html.

5. Markoff, "Flaw in E-Mail Programs."

6. Markoff, "Flaw in E-Mail Programs."

7. Perry E. Metzger, "Ray Cromwell: Another Netscape Bug (and Possible Security Hole)," SecLists.Org Security Mailing List Archive, September 22, 1995, https://seclists .org/bugtraq/1995/Sep/77; Martin Hargreaves, "Is Your Netscape under Remote Control?" SecLists.Org Security Mailing List Archive, May 24, 1996, https://seclists.org /bugtraq/1996/May/82; Stevan Milunovic, "Internet Explorer 4 Buffer Overflow Security Bug Fixed," *Risks Digest* 19, no. 47 (1997), https://catless.ncl.ac.uk/Risks/19/46.

8. Georgi Guninski, "Netscape Communicator 4.5 Can Read Local Files," SecLists .Org Security Mailing List Archive, November 23, 1998, https://seclists.org/bugtraq /1998/Nov/258.

9. IEEE Computer Society, "Attacks, Flaws, and Penetrations," *Electronic Cipher* 25 (1997), https://www.ieee-security.org/Cipher/PastIssues/1997/issue9711/issue9711.txt.

10. David Kennedy, "YAAXF: Yet Another ActiveX Flaw," *Risks Digest* 19, no. 6 (1997), https://catless.ncl.ac.uk/Risks/19/06.

11. Dieter Gollmann, *Computer Security* (New York: Wiley, 2011), 395–400.

12. Ed Felten, "Java/Netscape Security Flaw," *Risks Digest* 17, no. 93 (1996), https:// catless.ncl.ac.uk/Risks/17/93; Ed Felten, "Java Security Update," *Risks Digest* 18, no. 32 (1996), https://catless.ncl.ac.uk/Risks/18/32.

13. Dirk Balfanz and Edward W. Felten, *A Java Filter—Technical Report 567–97* (Princeton, NJ: Department of Computer Science, Princeton University, 1997), 1, https://www.cs.princeton.edu/research/techreps/TR-567–97.

14. Balfanz and Felten, *A Java Filter*, 1.

15. Balfanz and Felten, *A Java Filter*, 1.

16. John Markoff, "Potentially Big Security Flaw Found in Netscape Software," *New York Times*, September 28, 1998, https://www.nytimes.com/1998/09/28/business /potentially-big-security-flaw-found-in-netscape-software.html.

17. DilDog [pseud.], "L0pht Advisory MSIE4.0(1)," SecLists.Org Security Mailing List Archive, January 14, 1998, https://seclists.org/bugtraq/1998/Jan/57; Georgi Guninski, "IE Can Read Local Files," SecLists.Org Security Mailing List Archive, September 5, 1998, https://seclists.org/bugtraq/1998/Sep/47; Georgi Guninski, "Netscape Communicator 4.5 Can Read Local Files," SecLists.Org Security Mailing List Archive, November 23, 1998, https://seclists.org/bugtraq/1998/Nov/258.

18. John Viega and Gary McGraw, *Building Secure Software: How to Avoid Security Problems the Right Way* (Boston: Addison-Wesley, 2001), 322–334.

19. Rain Forest Puppy [pseud.], "NT Web Technology Vulnerabilities," *Phrack* 8, no. 54 (1998), http://phrack.org/issues/54/8.html; OWASP Foundation, "Top 10 2007," OWASP.org, last accessed May 3, 2019, https://www.owasp.org/index.php/Top_10 _2007.

20. MITRE, "CWE-27: Path Traversal," MITRE Common Weakness Enumeration, last accessed May 3, 2019, https://cwe.mitre.org/data/definitions/27.html.

21. Eugene H. Spafford, "Quotable Spaf," Spaf's Home Page, last updated July 7, 2018, https://spaf.cerias.purdue.edu/quotes.html.

22. Tina Kelly, "A Consultant Reports a Flaw in eBay's Web Site Security," *New York Times*, May 20, 1999, https://www.nytimes.com/1999/05/20/technology/news-watch -a-consultant-reports-a-flaw-in-ebay-s-web-site-security.html; Aleph One [pseud.], "Re: Yahoo Hacked," SecLists.Org Security Mailing List Archive, December 10, 1997, https://seclists.org/bugtraq/1997/Dec/57; Tom Cervenka, "Serious Security Hole in Hotmail," SecLists.Org Security Mailing List Archive, August 24, 1998, https://seclists .org/bugtraq/1998/Aug/208.

23. Michael Janofsky, "New Security Fears as Hackers Disrupt 2 Federal Web Sites," *New York Times*, May 29, 1999, https://www.nytimes.com/1999/05/29/us/new -security-fears-as-hackers-disrupt-2-federal-web-sites.html.

24. "Defaced Commentary—Verisign Japan Defaced," attrition.org, last updated 2001, http://attrition.org/security/commentary/verisign.html; "Defaced Commentary— The SANS Institute Defaced," attrition.org, last updated 2001, http://attrition.org /security/commentary/sans.html.

25. CNN, "Hackers Put Racist, Anti-Government Slogans on Embassy Site," last updated September 7, 1999, http://www.cnn.com/TECH/computing/9909/07/embassy .hack/index.html.

26. Peter G. Neumann, "CIA Disconnects Home Page after Being Hacked," *Risks Digest* 18, no. 49 (1996), https://catless.ncl.ac.uk/Risks/18/49.

27. "Defaced Commentary—UNICEF Defaced for the Third Time," attrition.org, last updated 2001, http://attrition.org/security/commentary/unicef.html.

28. "TASC Defaced," attrition.org, last updated 2001, http://attrition.org/security /commentary/tasc1.html.

29. Declan McCullagh, "George W. Bush the Red?" *Wired*, October 19, 1999, https:// www.wired.com/1999/10/george-w-bush-the-red/.

30. McCullagh, "George W. Bush the Red?"

31. Phrack Staff [pseud.], "Phrack Pro-Philes on the New Editors," *Phrack* 7, no. 48 (1996), http://phrack.org/issues/48/5.html.

32. Phrack Staff, "Phrack Pro-Philes."

33. Phrack Staff [pseud.], "Introduction," *Phrack* 14, no. 67 (2010), http://www.phrack .org/issues/67/1.html.

34. Phrack Staff, "Phrack Pro-Philes."

35. Phrack Staff, "Phrack Pro-Philes."

36. Phrack Staff, "Phrack Pro-Philes."

37. Phrack Staff, "Phrack Pro-Philes."

38. Phrack Staff, "Phrack Pro-Philes."

39. Taran King [pseud.], "Introduction," *Phrack* 1, no. 1 (1985), http://www.phrack .org/issues/1/1.html.

40. Route [pseud.], "Project Neptune," *Phrack* 7, no. 48 (1996), http://phrack.org /issues/48/13.html.

41. Route, "Project Neptune."

42. Software Engineering Institute, *1996 CERT Advisories* (Pittsburgh, PA: Software Engineering Institute, Carnegie Mellon University, 1996), 21; Route, "Project Neptune."

43. Route, "Project Neptune."

44. Steven M. Bellovin, "Security Problems in the TCP/IP Protocol Suite," *ACM SIGCOMM Computer Communication Review* 19, no. 2 (April 1, 1989): 32–48, https://doi .org/10.1145/378444.378449; Robert T. Morris, *A Weakness in the 4.2BSD Unix TCP/IP Software* (Murray Hill, NJ: Bell Labs, February 25, 1985).

45. Steven M. Bellovin, "A Look Back at 'Security Problems in the TCP/IP Protocol Suite'" (presentation, 20th Annual Computer Security Applications Conference, Tucson, December 6–10, 2004), https://doi.org/10.1109/CSAC.2004.3.

46. William R. Cheswick and Steven M. Bellovin, *Firewalls and Internet Security: Repelling the Wily Hacker*, 2nd ed. (Boston: Addison-Wesley, 2003).

47. Cheswick and Bellovin, *Firewalls and Internet Security*, xiii.

48. Route, "Project Neptune."

49. Robert E. Calem, "New York's Panix Service Is Crippled by Hacker Attack," *New York Times*, September 14, 1996, https://archive.nytimes.com/www.nytimes.com/library /cyber/week/0914panix.html; John Markoff, "A New Method of Internet Sabotage Is Spreading," *New York Times*, September 19, 1996, https://www.nytimes.com/1996/09/19 /business/a-new-method-of-internet-sabotage-is-spreading.html.

50. Peter G. Neumann, "Major Denial-of-Service Attack on WebCom in San Francisco Bay Area," *Risks Digest* 18, no. 69 (1996), https://catless.ncl.ac.uk/Risks/18/69.

51. Daemon9 [pseud.], "Project Hades," *Phrack* 7, no. 49 (1996), http://phrack.org /issues/49/7.html.

52. Route, "Project Hades."

53. Daemon9 [pseud.], "Project Loki," *Phrack* 7, no. 49 (1996), http://phrack.org/issues/49/6.html.

54. Route, "Project Loki."

55. IETF, "RFC 770 Internet Control Message Protocol," IETF Tools, last updated April, 1981, https://tools.ietf.org/html/rfc792.

56. IETF, "RFC 770 Internet Control Message Protocol."

57. IETF, "RFC 770 Internet Control Message Protocol."

58. Route, "Project Loki."

59. IETF, "RFC 770 Internet Control Message Protocol."

60. IETF, "RFC 770 Internet Control Message Protocol."

61. Route, "Project Loki."

62. Daemon9 [pseud.], "Loki2 (The Implementation)," *Phrack* 7, no. 51 (1997), http://phrack.org/issues/51/6.html.

63. Route [pseud.], "Juggernaut," *Phrack* 7, no. 50 (1997), http://phrack.org/issues/50/6.html.

64. Software Engineering Institute, *1997 CERT Advisories* (Pittsburgh, PA: Software Engineering Institute, Carnegie Mellon University, 1997), 176.

65. Software Engineering Institute, *1997 CERT Advisories*, 176.

66. Software Engineering Institute, *1997 CERT Advisories*, 176–177; Microsoft, "Microsoft Security Bulletin MS13-065—Important," Microsoft Security Bulletins, last updated August 13, 2013, https://docs.microsoft.com/en-us/security-updates/securitybulletins/2013/ms13-065.

67. Richard Bejtlich, "Deflect Silver Bullets," *TaoSecurity* (blog), November 7, 2007, https://taosecurity.blogspot.com/2007/11/deflect-silver-bullets.html.

68. IBM Internet Security Systems, "Company Timeline," ISS Timeline, last updated April 20, 2007, http://www.iss.net/about/timeline/index.html; Cisco, "Cisco Scanner—Cisco," Products & Services, last accessed June 22, 2019, https://www.cisco.com/c/en/us/products/security/scanner/index.html.

69. Roger R. Schell, "Information Security: Science, Pseudoscience, and Flying Pigs" (presentation, 17th Annual Computer Security Applications Conference, New Orleans, December 10–14, 2001, https://doi.org/10.1109/ACSAC.2001.991537).

70. Defense Science Board Task Force on Computer Security, *Security Controls for Computer Systems: Report of Defense Science Board Task Force on Computer Security* (Santa Monica, CA: RAND, 1970), 41, https://www.rand.org/pubs/reports/R609-1/index2.html.

71. James P. Anderson, *Computer Security Technology Planning Study* (Bedford, MA: Electronic Systems Division, Air Force Systems Command, United States Air Force, 1972).

72. James P. Anderson, *Computer Security Threat Monitoring and Surveillance* (Fort Washington, PA: James P. Anderson Co., 1980).

73. Dorothy E. Denning and Peter G. Neumann, *Requirements and Model for IDES—A Real-Time Intrusion-Detection Expert System* (Menlo Park, CA: SRI International, 1985); Dorothy Denning, "An Intrusion-Detection Model," *IEEE Transactions on Software Engineering* 13, no. 2 (1987): 222–232, https://doi.org/10.1109/TSE.1987.232894.

74. Matt Bishop, *Computer Security: Art and Science* (Boston: Addison-Wesley, 2003), 733.

75. Bishop, *Computer Security*, 727.

76. Bishop, *Computer Security*, 765.

77. The President's National Security Telecommunications Advisory Committee, *Network Group Intrusion Detection Subgroup Report—Report on the NS/EDP Implications of Intrusion Detection Technology Research and Development* (Washington, DC: NSTAC Publications, 1997), 32–33, https://www.dhs.gov/publication/1997-nstac-publications.

78. Ellen Messmer, "Getting the Drop on Network Intruders," *CNN*, October 11, 1999, http://www.cnn.com/TECH/computing/9910/11/intrusion.detection.idg/index.html.

79. Ian Grigg, "The Market for Silver Bullets," March 2, 2008, http://iang.org/papers/market_for_silver_bullets.html.

80. Gollmann, *Computer Security*, 40.

81. Grigg, "The Market for Silver Bullets."

82. Spafford, "Quotable Spaf."

83. Frederick P. Brooks Jr., "No Silver Bullet: Essence and Accidents of Software Engineering," *Computer* 20, no. 4 (1987): 10–19, https://doi.org/10.1109/MC.1987.1663532.

84. Ross Anderson, "Why Information Security Is Hard: An Economic Perspective" (presentation, 17th Annual Computer Security Applications Conference, New Orleans, December 10–14, 2001), https://doi.org/10.1109/ACSAC.2001.991552.

85. Frank Willoughby, "Re: Firewalls/Internet Security—TNG," SecLists.Org Security Mailing List Archive, December 2, 1997, https://seclists.org/firewall-wizards/1997/Dec/20.

86. Thomas H. Ptacek and Timothy N. Newsham, *Insertion, Evasion, and Denial of Service: Eluding Network Intrusion Detection* (n.p.: Secure Networks, 1998); Secure Networks, "SNI-24: IDS Vulnerabilities," SecLists.Org Security Mailing List Archive, February 9, 1998, https://seclists.org/bugtraq/1998/Feb/41.

87. Ptacek and Newsham, "Insertion, Evasion."

88. Ptacek and Newsham, "Insertion, Evasion."

89. Mark Handley, Vern Paxson, and Christian Kreibich, "Network Intrusion Detection: Evasion, Traffic Normalization, and End-to-End Protocol Semantics" (presentation, 10th USENIX Security Symposium, Washington, DC, August 13–17, 2001), https://www.usenix.org/conference/10th-usenix-security-symposium/network-intrusion-detection-evasion-traffic-normalization; Ptacek and Newsham, "Insertion, Evasion."

90. Ptacek and Newsham, "Insertion, Evasion."

91. Ptacek and Newsham, "Insertion, Evasion."

92. Thomas H. Ptacek, "Important Comments re: Intrusion Detection," SecLists.Org Security Mailing List Archive, February 13, 1998, https://seclists.org/bugtraq/1998/Feb/61; Ptacek and Newsham, "Insertion, Evasion."

93. Mikko Sarela, Tomi Kyostila, Timo Kiravuo, and Jukka Manner, "Evaluating Intrusion Prevention Systems with Evasions," *International Journal of Communication Systems* 30, no. 16 (June 2017), https://onlinelibrary.wiley.com/doi/abs/10.1002/dac.3339.

94. Ptacek and Newsham, "Insertion, Evasion."

95. Dennis Fisher, "How I Got Here: Marcus Ranum," *Threatpost*, May 20, 2015, https://threatpost.com/how-i-got-here-marcus-ranum/112924/.

96. Fisher, "Marcus Ranum."

97. RAID—International Symposium on Research in Attacks, Intrusions and Defenses, "The Nature and Utility of Standards Organizations for the Intrusion Detection Community," RAID.org, last accessed May 6, 2019, http://www.raid-symposium.org/raid98/Prog_RAID98/Panels.html; IETF, "The Common Intrusion Detection Framework—Data Formats," IETF Tools, last updated September 18, 1998, https://tools.ietf.org/html/draft-staniford-cidf-data-formats-00.

98. Stefan Axelsson, "The Base-Rate Fallacy and Its Implications for the Difficulty of Intrusion Detection" (presentation, 2nd RAID Symposium, Purdue, IN, September 7–9, 1999).

99. Axelsson, "The Base-Rate Fallacy."

100. Axelsson, "The Base-Rate Fallacy."

101. Axelsson, "The Base-Rate Fallacy."

102. Axelsson, "The Base-Rate Fallacy."

103. Stephanie Mlot, "Neiman Marcus Hackers Set Off Nearly 60K Alarms," *PC Magazine*, February 23, 2014, https://www.pcmag.com/news/320948/neiman-marcus-hackers-set-off-nearly-60k-alarms.

104. Bill Home, "Umbrellas and Octopuses," *IEEE Security & Privacy* 13, no. 1 (2015): 3–5, https://doi.org/10.1109/MSP.2015.18.

105. Metzger, "Ray Cromwell: Another Netscape Bug (and Possible Security Hole)."

106. "Cisco to Acquire WheelGroup for about $124 Million in Stock," *Wall Street Journal*, February 18, 1998, https://www.wsj.com/articles/SB887844566548828000.

107. Ben Yagoda, "A Short History of 'Hack,'" *New Yorker*, March 6, 2014, https://www.newyorker.com/tech/annals-of-technology/a-short-history-of-hack.

108. Yagoda, "History of 'Hack.'"

109. Katie Hafner and Matthew Lyon, *Where Wizards Stay Up Late: The Origins of the Internet* (New York: Simon & Schuster, 1996), 189–190.

110. Yagoda, "History of 'Hack.'"

111. Erving Goffman, *The Presentation of Self in Everyday Life* (New York: Anchor, 1959).

112. Computer Fraud and Abuse Act of 1984, 18 U.S.C. § 1030 (2019).

113. "Computer Misuse Act 1990," legislation.gov.uk, National Archives (UK), last updated June 29, 1990, http://www.legislation.gov.uk/ukpga/1990/18/enacted.

114. Y Combinator, "*Phrack* Magazine (1985–2016)," Hacker News, last accessed May 6, 2019, https://news.ycombinator.com/item?id=18288767.

115. ISGroup, "The Greyhat Is Whitehat List," ush.it, last accessed May 6, 2019, http://www.ush.it/team/ush/mirror-phc_old/greyhat-IS-whitehat.txt; Charles Stevenson, "Greyhat Is Whitehat," SecLists.Org Security Mailing List Archive, September 19, 2002, https://seclists.org/fulldisclosure/2002/Sep/507.

116. Gabriella Coleman, "The Anthropology of Hackers," *Atlantic*, September 21, 2010, https://www.theatlantic.com/technology/archive/2010/09/the-anthropology-of-hackers/63308/.

117. Robert Lemos, "Script Kiddies: The Net's Cybergangs," *ZDNet*, July 13, 2000, https://www.zdnet.com/article/script-kiddies-the-nets-cybergangs/.

118. Lemos, "Script Kiddies."

119. Elias Levy, "Full Disclosure Is a Necessary Evil," *SecurityFocus*, August 16, 2001, https://www.securityfocus.com/news/238.

120. Andrew Zipern, "Technology Briefing: Privacy; Security Group to Sell Services," *New York Times*, April 20, 2001, https://www.nytimes.com/2001/04/20/business/technology -briefing-privacy-security-group-to-sell-services.html.

121. Daniel De Leon, "The Productivity of the Criminal," *Daily People*, April 14, 1905, http://www.slp.org/pdf/de_leon/eds1905/apr14_1905.pdf.

122. De Leon, "Productivity of the Criminal."

123. Andy Greenberg, "Symantec Scareware Tells Customers to Renew or 'Beg for Mercy,'" *Forbes*, October 4, 2010, https://www.forbes.com/sites/andygreenberg/2010/10/04 /symantec-scareware-tells-customers-to-renew-or-beg-for-mercy/.

124. CMP Media, "Black Hat USA 2019 Registration," Black Hat Briefings, last accessed May 6, 2019, https://www.blackhat.com/us-19/registration.html.

125. Jeff Moss, "The Black Hat Briefings, July 9–10, 1997," Black Hat Briefings, last accessed May 6, 2019, https://www.blackhat.com/html/bh-usa-97/info.html.

126. CMP Media, "Jeff Moss," Black Hat Briefings, last accessed May 6, 2019, https:// www.blackhat.com/us-18/speakers/Jeff-Moss.html.

127. Fisher, "Marcus Ranum."

128. Kelly Jackson Higgins, "Who Invented the Firewall?" *Dark Reading*, January 15, 2008, https://www.darkreading.com/who-invented-the-firewall/d/d-id/1129238; Marcus Ranum, "Who Is Marcus J. Ranum?" ranum.com, last accessed September 3, 2018, http://www.ranum.com/stock_content/about.html.

129. Marcus Ranum, "White House Tales—1," *Freethought Blogs*, September 16, 2018, https://freethoughtblogs.com/stderr/2018/09/16/the-white-house/.

130. Ranum, "White House Tales."

131. Ranum, "White House Tales."

132. Ranum, "White House Tales."

133. Ranum, "White House Tales."

134. Ranum, "White House Tales."

135. Marcus Ranum, "The Herd," ranum.com, last accessed September 3, 2018, http://ranum.com/fun/the_herd/index.html.

136. Marcus Ranum, "Soaps for Sale," ranum.com, last accessed September 3, 2018, http://ranum.com/fun/projects/soap/soap-sale.html; Marcus Ranum, "Ambrotypes and the Unique Process," ranum.com, last accessed September 3, 2018, http://ranum.com /fun/lens_work/ambrotypes/why.html.

137. Kelly Jackson Higgins, "Ranum's Wild Security Ride," *Dark Reading*, December 5, 2007, https://www.darkreading.com/vulnerabilities—threats/ranums-wild-security -ride/d/d-id/1129165; Marcus Ranum, "Do It Yourself Dealy," ranum.com, last accessed September 3, 2018, http://ranum.com/fun/bsu/diy-dealy/index.html; Marcus Ranum, "Safecracking 101," ranum.com, last updated July 7, 2005, http://ranum.com/fun/bsu /safecracking/index.html.

138. Marcus Ranum, "Script Kiddiez Suck" (presentation, Black Hat Briefings, Las Vegas, 2000, https://www.blackhat.com/html/bh-media-archives/bh-archives-2000.html.

139. Marcus Ranum, "The Six Dumbest Ideas in Computer Security," ranum.com, last updated September 1, 2005, http://ranum.com/security/computer_security/editorials/dumb/index.html.

140. Ranum, "Script Kiddiez Suck."

141. Ranum, "Script Kiddiez Suck."

142. Ranum, "Script Kiddiez Suck."

143. Ranum, "Script Kiddiez Suck."

144. Ranum, "Script Kiddiez Suck."

145. Marcus Ranum, "Dusty Old Stuff from the Distant Past," ranum.com, last accessed September 3, 2018, http://ranum.com/security/computer_security/archives/index.html.

146. Cassidy, *Dot.con*, 294.

147. Cassidy, *Dot.con*, 294.

## 5. Software Security and the "Hamster Wheel of Pain"

1. Andrew Jaquith, "Escaping the Hamster Wheel of Pain," *Markerbench* (blog), May 4, 2005, http://www.markerbench.com/blog/2005/05/04/Escaping-the-Hamster-Wheel-of-Pain/.

2. Peter A. Loscocco, Stephen D. Smalley, Patrick A. Muckelbauer, Ruth C. Taylor, S. Jeff Turner, and John F. Farrell, "The Inevitability of Failure: The Flawed Assumption of Security in Modern Computing Environments" (presentation, 21st National Information Systems Security Conference, Arlington, VA, October 8, 1998).

3. Loscocco et al., "The Inevitability of Failure."

4. Loscocco et al., "The Inevitability of Failure."

5. Software Engineering Institute, *2000 CERT Advisories* (Pittsburgh, PA: Software Engineering Institute, Carnegie Mellon University, 2000), https://resources.sei.cmu.edu/library/asset-view.cfm?assetID=496186; Software Engineering Institute, *2001 CERT Advisories* (Pittsburgh, PA: Software Engineering Institute, Carnegie Mellon University, 2001), https://resources.sei.cmu.edu/library/asset-view.cfm?assetID=496190; Software Engineering Institute, *2002 CERT Advisories* (Pittsburgh, PA: Software Engineering Institute, Carnegie Mellon University, 2002), https://resources.sei.cmu.edu/library/asset-view.cfm?assetID=496194.

6. Software Engineering Institute, *2000 CERT Advisories*; Software Engineering Institute, *2001 CERT Advisories*; Software Engineering Institute, *2002 CERT Advisories*.

7. David Litchfield, "Database Security: The Pot and the Kettle" (presentation, Black Hat Briefings Asia, Singapore, October 3–4, 2002), https://www.blackhat.com/html/bh-asia-02/bh-asia-02-speakers.html.

8. "Internet Exploder," *The Hacker's Dictionary*, Smart Digital Networks, last accessed May 11, 2019, http://www.hackersdictionary.com/html/entry/Internet-Exploder.html.

9. Steve Christey and Brian Martin, "Buying into the Bias: Why Vulnerability Statistics Suck" (presentation, Black Hat Briefings, Las Vegas, July 27–August 1, 2013), https://www.blackhat.com/us-13/briefings.html.

10. Christey and Martin, "Buying into the Bias."

11. Christey and Martin, "Buying into the Bias."

12. Brian Martin, "Our Straw House: Vulnerabilities" (presentation, RVASec, June 1, 2013), https://2013.rvasec.com/.

13. David Moore and Coleen Shannon, "The Spread of the Code-Red Worm (CRv2)," Center for Applied Internet Data Analysis, last updated March 27, 2019, https://www.caida.org/research/security/code-red/coderedv2_analysis.xml.

14. Moore and Shannon, "The Spread of the Code-Red Worm."

15. Moore and Shannon, "The Spread of the Code-Red Worm."

16. David Moore, Colleen Shannon, and Jeffery Brown, "Code-Red: A Case Study on the Spread and Victims of an Internet Worm" (presentation, 2nd ACM SIGCOMM Workshop on Internet Measurement, Marseille, France, November 6–8, 2002), https://doi.org/10.1145/637201.637244.

17. Moore and Shannon, "The Spread of the Code-Red Worm."

18. Moore and Shannon, "The Spread of the Code-Red Worm."

19. Moore et al., "Code-Red"; Moore and Shannon, "The Spread of the Code-Red Worm."

20. "Dynamic Graphs of Nimda," Center for Applied Internet Data Analysis, The Cooperative Association for Internet Data Analysis, last accessed May 11, 2019, http://www.caida.org/dynamic/analysis/security/nimda/.

21. Software Engineering Institute, *2001 CERT Advisories*.

22. "Nimda Virus 'on the Wane,'" *BBC News*, last updated September 20, 2001, http://news.bbc.co.uk/2/hi/science/nature/1554514.stm.

23. Software Engineering Institute, *2001 CERT Advisories*.

24. Software Engineering Institute, *2001 CERT Advisories*.

25. Software Engineering Institute, *2001 CERT Advisories*.

26. Software Engineering Institute, *2001 CERT Advisories*.

27. Mark Challender, "RE: Concept Virus (CV) V.5—Advisory and Quick Analysis," SecLists.Org Security Mailing List Archive, last updated September 18, 2001, https://seclists.org/incidents/2001/Sep/177.

28. "Nimda Virus 'on the Wane.'"

29. John Leyden, "Ten Years on from Nimda: Worm Author Still at Large," *Register*, September 17, 2011, https://www.theregister.co.uk/2011/09/17/nimda_anniversary/; "Nimda Virus 'on the Wane.'"

30. Microsoft Corporation, *Life in the Digital Crosshairs: The Dawn of the Microsoft Security Development Lifecycle* (Redmond, WA: Microsoft Press, 2014).

31. John Pescatore, *Nimda Worm Shows You Can't Always Patch Fast Enough* (Stamford, CT: Gartner, 2001).

32. Pescatore, *Nimda Worm*.

33. Diane Frank, "Security Shifting to Enterprise," SecLists.Org Security Mailing List Archive, last updated February 21, 2002, https://seclists.org/isn/2002/Feb/102.

34. Byron Acohido, "Air Force Seeks Better Security from Microsoft," *USA Today*, March 10, 2002, https://usatoday30.usatoday.com/life/cyber/tech/2002/03/11/gilligan.htm.

35. Acohido, "Air Force Seeks Better Security from Microsoft."

36. Jeremy Epstein, "UCSD Bans WinNT/2K—Will It Do Any Good?" *Risks Digest* 22, no. 31 (2002), https://catless.ncl.ac.uk/Risks/22/31; Tom Perrine, "Re: UCSD

Bans WinNT/2K—No, It Is UCSB," *Risks Digest* 22, no. 32 (2002), https://catless.ncl.ac
.uk/Risks/22/32.

37. Steve Ranger, "MS Outlook Booted Off Campus," SecLists.Org Security Mailing
List Archive, last updated May 23, 2002, https://seclists.org/isn/2002/May/146.

38. "Defaced Commentary—List of Defaced Microsoft Web Sites," attrition.org, last
accessed May 11, 2019, http://attrition.org/security/commentary/microsoft-list.html.

39. Susan Stellin, "Reports of Hackers Are on the Rise," *New York Times*, January 21,
2002, https://www.nytimes.com/2002/01/21/business/most-wanted-drilling-down-internet
-security-reports-of-hackers-are-on-the-rise.html.

40. Todd Bishop, "Should Microsoft Be Liable for Bugs?" *Seattle Post-Intelligencer*,
September 12, 2003.

41. Bishop, "Should Microsoft Be Liable?"

42. Rob Pegoraro, "Microsoft Windows: Insecure by Design," *Washington Post*, August 24, 2003.

43. Pegoraro, "Insecure by Design."

44. Ross Anderson, "Why Information Security Is Hard: An Economic Perspective"
(presentation, 17th Annual Computer Security Applications Conference, New Orleans, December 10–14, 2001), https://doi.org/10.1109/ACSAC.2001.991552.

45. Michael Swaine and Paul Freiberger, *Fire in the Valley: The Birth and Death of the
Personal Computer* (Dallas: Pragmatic Bookshelf, 2014), 30–31.

46. Swaine and Freiberger, *Fire in the Valley*, 30–31.

47. Swaine and Freiberger, *Fire in the Valley*, 30–31.

48. John Markoff, "Stung by Security Flaws, Microsoft Makes Software Safety a Top
Goal," *New York Times*, January 17, 2002, https://www.nytimes.com/2002/01/17/business
/stung-by-security-flaws-microsoft-makes-software-safety-a-top-goal.html.

49. Bill Gates, "Trustworthy Computing," *Wired*, January 17, 2002, https://www
.wired.com/2002/01/bill-gates-trustworthy-computing/.

50. Gates, "Trustworthy Computing."

51. Gates, "Trustworthy Computing."

52. Gates, "Trustworthy Computing."

53. Gates, "Trustworthy Computing."

54. Gates, "Trustworthy Computing."

55. Peter G. Neumann, "Another NT Security Flaw," *Risks Digest* 19, no. 2 (1997),
https://catless.ncl.ac.uk/Risks/19/02.

56. Michael Howard and David LeBlanc, *Writing Secure Code* (Redmond, WA:
Microsoft Press, 2002).

57. Gates, "Trustworthy Computing."

58. Microsoft Corporation, *Digital Crosshairs*.

59. Microsoft Corporation, *Digital Crosshairs*.

60. John Markoff, "Microsoft Programmers Hit the Books in a New Focus on Secure
Software," *New York Times*, April 8, 2002, https://www.nytimes.com/2002/04/08/business
/microsoft-programmers-hit-the-books-in-a-new-focus-on-secure-software.html.

61. Microsoft Corporation, *Digital Crosshairs*.

62. Robert Lemos, "Microsoft Developers Feel Windows Pain," *CNET News*, February 7, 2002.

63. Steve Lipner, "The Trustworthy Computing Security Development Lifecycle" (presentation, 20th Annual Computer Security Applications Conference, Tucson, December 6–10, 2004), https://doi.org/10.1109/CSAC.2004.41.

64. Lemos, "Microsoft Developers Feel Windows Pain."

65. Dennis Fisher, "Microsoft Puts Meat Behind Security Push," *eWeek*, September 30, 2002.

66. D. Ian Hopper and Ted Bridis, "Microsoft Announces Corporate Strategy Shift toward Security and Privacy," *Associated Press*, January 16, 2002.

67. Richard Grimes, "Preventing Buffer Overruns in C++," *Dr. Dobb's*, January 1, 2004, http://www.drdobbs.com/cpp/preventing-buffer-overruns-in-c/184405528.

68. Grimes, "Preventing Buffer Overruns in C++."

69. Crispin Cowan, Calton Pu, Dave Maier, Jonathan Walpole, Peat Bakke, Steve Beattie, Aaron Grier et al., "StackGuard: Automatic Adaptive Detection and Prevention of Buffer-Overflow Attacks" (presentation, 7th USENIX Security Symposium, San Antonio, TX, January 26–29, 1998).

70. Michael Howard and Steve Lipner, *The Security Development Lifecycle* (Redmond, WA: Microsoft Corporation, 2006), 31.

71. Microsoft Corporation, *Digital Crosshairs*.

72. David Moore, Vern Paxson, Stefan Savage, Colleen Shannon, Stuart Staniford, and Nicholas Weaver, "Inside the Slammer Worm," *IEEE Security & Privacy* 1, no. 4 (2003): 33–39, https://doi.org/10.1109/MSECP.2003.1219056.

73. Moore et al., "Inside the Slammer Worm."

74. Moore et al., "Inside the Slammer Worm."

75. Moore et al., "Inside the Slammer Worm."

76. Moore et al., "Inside the Slammer Worm."

77. Moore et al., "Inside the Slammer Worm."

78. Moore et al., "Inside the Slammer Worm."

79. Ted Bridis, "Internet Attack's Disruptions More Serious than Many Thought Possible," *Associated Press*, January 27, 2003; Katie Hafner with John Biggs, "In Net Attacks, Defining the Right to Know," *New York Times*, January 30, 2003, https://www.nytimes.com/2003/01/30/technology/in-net-attacks-defining-the-right-to-know.html.

80. Bridis, "Disruptions More Serious"; Hafner and Biggs, "In Net Attacks"; Moore et al., "Inside the Slammer Worm."

81. Bridis, "Disruptions More Serious."

82. Moore et al., "Inside the Slammer Worm."

83. John Leyden, "Slammer: Why Security Benefits from Proof of Concept Code," *Register*, February 6, 2003, https://www.theregister.co.uk/2003/02/06/slammer_why _security_benefits/.

84. Kirk Semple, "Computer 'Worm' Widely Attacks Windows Versions," *New York Times*, August 13, 2003, https://www.nytimes.com/2003/08/13/business/technology -computer-worm-widely-attacks-windows-versions.html.

85. Semple, "Computer 'Worm.'"

86. John Markoff, "Virus Aside, Gates Says Reliability Is Greater," *New York Times*, August 31, 2003, https://www.nytimes.com/2003/08/31/business/virus-aside-gates-says -reliability-is-greater.html.

87. John Leyden, "Blaster Variant Offers 'Fix' for Pox-Ridden PCs," *Register*, August 19, 2003, https://www.theregister.co.uk/2003/08/19/blaster_variant_offers_fix/.

88. "W32.Welchia.Worm," Symantec Security Center, Symantec, last updated August 11, 2017, https://www.symantec.com/security-center/writeup/2003-081815-2308-99; Leyden, "Blaster Variant."

89. John Schwartz, "A Viral Epidemic," *New York Times*, August 24, 2003, https://www.nytimes.com/2003/08/24/weekinreview/august-17-23-technology-a-viral-epidemic.html.

90. Elise Labott, "'Welchia Worm' Hits U.S. State Dept. Network," *CNN*, September 24, 2003, http://www.cnn.com/2003/TECH/internet/09/24/state.dept.virus/index.html.

91. "W32.Sobig.F@mm," Symantec Security Center, Symantec, last updated February 13, 2007, https://www.symantec.com/security-center/writeup/2003-081909-2118-99.

92. John Schwartz, "Microsoft Sets $5 Million Virus Bounty," *New York Times*, November 6, 2003, https://www.nytimes.com/2003/11/06/business/technology-microsoft-sets-5-million-virus-bounty.html.

93. Luke Harding, "Court Hears How Teenage Introvert Created Devastating Computer Virus in His Bedroom," *Guardian*, July 6, 2005, https://www.theguardian.com/technology/2005/jul/06/germany.internationalnews.

94. Harding, "Teenage Introvert."

95. NewsScan, "Sasser Creator Turned in for the Reward," *Risks Digest* 23, no. 37 (2004), https://catless.ncl.ac.uk/Risks/23/37.

96. "The Worm That Turned," *Sydney Morning Herald*, September 12, 2004, https://www.smh.com.au/world/the-worm-that-turned-20040912-gdjq5w.html.

97. Harding, "Teenage Introvert."

98. Harding, "Teenage Introvert."

99. Victor Homola, "'Sasser' Hacker Is Sentenced," *New York Times*, July 9, 2005, https://www.nytimes.com/2005/07/09/world/world-briefing-europe-germany-sasser-hacker-is-sentenced.html.

100. Nicholas Weaver and Vern Paxson, "A Worst-Case Worm" (presentation, 3rd Workshop on the Economics of Information Security, Minneapolis, May 2004), http://www.icir.org/vern/papers/worst-case-worm.WEIS04.pdf.

101. Stuart Staniford, Vern Paxson, and Nicholas Weaver, "How to Own the Internet in Your Spare Time" (presentation, 11th USENIX Security Symposium, San Francisco, August 5–9, 2002).

102. Staniford et al., "How to Own the Internet."

103. "Experts: Microsoft Security Gets an 'F,'" *CNN*, February 1, 2003, http://www.cnn.com/2003/TECH/biztech/02/01/microsoft.security.reut/.

104. "Microsoft and Dell Win $90M Homeland Security Contract," *Information Week*, last updated July 16, 2003, https://www.informationweek.com/microsoft-and-dell-win-$90m-homeland-security-contract/d/d-id/1019955; Greg Goth, "Addressing the Monoculture," *IEEE Security & Privacy* 1, no. 6 (2003): 8–10, https://doi.org/10.1109/MSECP.2003.1253561.

105. Jonathan Krim, "Microsoft Placates Two Foes," *Washington Post*, November 9, 2004.

106. Dan Geer, Rebecca Bace, Peter Gutmann, Perry Metzger, Charles P. Pfleeger, John S. Quarterman, and Bruce Schneier, *CyberInsecurity: The Cost of Monopoly* (Washington, DC: Computer & Communications Industry Association, 2003); Goth, "Addressing the Monoculture."

107. Geer et al., *The Cost of Monopoly.*

108. Geer et al., *The Cost of Monopoly*, 20.

109. Geer et al., *The Cost of Monopoly*, 12.

110. Geer et al., *The Cost of Monopoly*, 13.

111. Geer et al., *The Cost of Monopoly*, 17.

112. Geer et al., *The Cost of Monopoly*, 18.

113. Geer et al., *The Cost of Monopoly*, 5.

114. Geer et al., *The Cost of Monopoly*, 19.

115. Robert Lemos, "Academics Get NSF Grant for Net Security Centers," *ZDNet*, September 21, 2004, https://www.zdnet.com/article/academics-get-nsf-grant-for-net-security-centers/.

116. Dan Geer, "Monopoly Considered Harmful," *IEEE Security & Privacy* 1, no. 6 (2003): 14–17, https://doi.org/10.1109/MSECP.2003.1253563.

117. Geer et al., *The Cost of Monopoly*, 5; Goth, "Addressing the Monoculture."

118. John Schwartz, "Worm Hits Microsoft, Which Ignored Own Advice," *New York Times*, January 28, 2003, https://www.nytimes.com/2003/01/28/business/technology-worm-hits-microsoft-which-ignored-own-advice.html.

119. William A. Arbaugh, William L. Fithen, and John McHugh, "Windows of Vulnerability: A Case Study Analysis," *IEEE Computer* 33, no. 12 (2000), https://doi.org/10.1109/2.889093.

120. Arbaugh et al., "Windows of Vulnerability."

121. Eric Rescorla, "Security Holes . . . Who Cares?" (presentation, 12th USENIX Security Symposium, Washington, DC, August 4–8, 2003).

122. United States General Accounting Office, *Effective Patch Management Is Critical to Mitigating Software Vulnerabilities* (Washington, DC: United States Accounting Office, September 10, 2003).

123. Helen J. Wang, *Some Anti-Worm Efforts at Microsoft* (Redmond, WA: Microsoft Corporation, 2004), http://www.icir.org/vern/worm04/hwang.pdf; Steve Beattie, Seth Arnold, Crispin Cowan, Perry Wagle, Chris Wright, and Adam Shostack, "Timing the Application of Security Patches for Optimal Uptime" (presentation, 16th Large Installation System Administration Conference, Philadelphia, November 3–8, 2003), https://adam.shostack.org/time-to-patch-usenix-lisa02.pdf.

124. Ted Bridis, "Microsoft Pulls XP Update over Glitch," *Associated Press*, May 27, 2003; Brian Krebs, "New Patches Cause BSoD for Some Windows XP Users," *Krebs on Security* (blog), February 11, 2010, https://krebsonsecurity.com/2010/02/new-patches-cause-bsod-for-some-windows-xp-users/.

125. Beattie et al., "Security Patches."

126. Bishop, "Should Microsoft Be Liable?"

127. Martin LaMonica, "Microsoft Renews Security Vows," *CNET News*, June 3, 2003.

128. LaMonica, "Microsoft Renews Security Vows."

129. "Software: Microsoft Releases First Security Update," *New York Times*, October 16, 2003, https://www.nytimes.com/2003/10/16/business/technology-briefing-software-microsoft-releases-first-security-update.html; MSRC Team, "Inside the MSRC—The Monthly Security Update Releases," *MSRC* (blog), February 14, 2018, https://blogs.technet.microsoft.com/msrc/2018/02/14/inside-the-msrc-the-monthly-security-update-releases/.

130. "Microsoft Releases First Security Update."

131. MSRC Team, "Monthly Security Update Releases"; Christopher Budd, "Ten Years of Patch Tuesdays: Why It's Time to Move On," *GeekWire*, October 31, 2013, https://www.geekwire.com/2013/ten-years-patch-tuesdays-time-move/.

132. Ryan Naraine, "Exploit Wednesday Follows MS Patch Tuesday," *ZDNet*, June 13, 2007, https://www.zdnet.com/article/exploit-wednesday-follows-ms-patch-tuesday/.

133. Microsoft Corporation, *Digital Crosshairs*.

134. Microsoft Corporation, *Digital Crosshairs*.

135. Microsoft Corporation, *Digital Crosshairs*.

136. Microsoft Corporation, *Digital Crosshairs*.

137. Microsoft Corporation, *Digital Crosshairs*.

138. Microsoft Corporation, *Digital Crosshairs*.

139. Microsoft Corporation, *Digital Crosshairs*.

140. Microsoft Corporation, *Digital Crosshairs*.

141. Robert Lemos, "Microsoft Failing Security Test?" *ZDNet*, January 11, 2002, https://www.zdnet.com/article/microsoft-failing-security-test/.

142. Andy Oram and Greg Wilson, eds., *Making Software: What Really Works, and Why We Believe It* (Sebastopol, CA: O'Reilly Media, 2010).

143. Carol Sliwa, "Microsoft's Report Card," *Computerworld*, January 13, 2003.

144. Nick Wingfield, "Microsoft Sheds Reputation as an Easy Mark for Hackers," *New York Times*, November 17, 2015, https://www.nytimes.com/2015/11/18/technology/microsoft-once-infested-with-security-flaws-does-an-about-face.html; John Viega, "Ten Years of Trustworthy Computing: Lessons Learned," *IEEE Security & Privacy* 9, no. 5 (2011): 3–4, https://doi.ieeecomputersociety.org/10.1109/MSP.2011.143.

145. John Leyden, "10 Years Ago Today: Bill Gates Kicks Arse over Security," *Register*, January 15, 2012, https://www.theregister.co.uk/2012/01/15/trustworthy_computing_memo/; Jim Kerstetter, "Daily Report: Microsoft Finds Its Security Groove," *New York Times*, November 17, 2015, https://bits.blogs.nytimes.com/2015/11/17/daily-report-microsoft-finds-its-security-groove/.

146. Tom Bradley, "The Business World Owes a Lot to Microsoft Trustworthy Computing," *Forbes*, March 5, 2014.

147. Microsoft Corporation, *Digital Crosshairs*.

148. Stephen Foley, "Larry Ellison Owns a Fighter Jet, Yacht Racing Team and Supercars Galore, So What Did the Billionaire Buy Next? The Hawaiian Island of Lanai," *Independent* (UK), June 22, 2012, https://www.independent.co.uk/news/world/americas/larry-ellison-owns-a-fighter-jet-yacht-racing-team-and-supercars-galore-so-what-did-the-billionaire-7873541.html; Mark David, "Larry Ellison's Japanese Freak Out," *Variety*, January 3, 2007, https://variety.com/2007/dirt/real-estalker/larry-ellisons-japanese-freak-out-1201225604/; Emmie Martin, "Here's What It's Like to Stay on the

Lush Hawaiian Island Larry Ellison Bought for $300 Million," *CNBC*, November 15, 2017, https://www.cnbc.com/2017/11/14/see-lanai-the-hawaiian-island-larry-ellison-bought -for-300-million.html.

149. "A Decade of Oracle Security," attrition.org, last updated July 28, 2008, http:// attrition.org/security/rant/oracle01/; Andy Greenberg, "Oracle Hacker Gets the Last Word," *Forbes*, February 2, 2010, https://www.forbes.com/2010/02/02/hacker-litchfield -ellison-technology-security-oracle.html.

150. "Decade of Oracle Security."

151. "Decade of Oracle Security."

152. "Decade of Oracle Security."

153. Oracle Corporation, *Unbreakable: Oracle's Commitment to Security* (Redwood Shores, CA: Oracle Corporation, 2002).

154. Oracle Corporation, *Unbreakable*, 2.

155. Oracle Corporation, *Unbreakable*, 2.

156. Oracle Corporation, *Unbreakable*, 12.

157. Oracle Corporation, *Unbreakable*, 3.

158. Oracle Corporation, *Unbreakable*, 4.

159. David Litchfield, *Hackproofing Oracle Application Server* (Manchester, UK: NCC Group, 2013), https://www.nccgroup.trust/au/our-research/hackproofing-oracle -application-server/; Robert Lemos, "Guru Says Oracle's 9i Is Indeed Breakable," *CNET News*, March 2, 2002, https://www.cnet.com/news/guru-says-oracles-9i-is-indeed -breakable/.

160. Thomas C. Greene, "How to Hack Unbreakable Oracle Servers," *Register*, February 2, 2002, https://www.theregister.co.uk/2002/02/07/how_to_hack_unbreakable_oracle/.

161. Greene, "Unbreakable Oracle Servers."

162. "Decade of Oracle Security."

163. "Decade of Oracle Security."

164. "Decade of Oracle Security."

165. "Decade of Oracle Security."

166. David Litchfield, "Opinion: Complete Failure of Oracle Security Response and Utter Neglect of Their Responsibility to Their Customers," SecLists.Org Security Mailing List Archive, last updated January 6, 2005, https://seclists.org/bugtraq/2005/Oct/56.

167. Litchfield, "Opinion: Complete Failure of Oracle Security."

168. Munir Kotadia, "Oracle No Longer a 'Bastion of Security': Gartner," *ZDNet Australia*, January 24, 2006; "Decade of Oracle Security."

169. "Decade of Oracle Security."

170. Oracle Corporation, *Unbreakable*, 3.

171. Sean Michael Kerner, "Oracle Patches 301 Vulnerabilities in October Update," *eWeek*, October 18, 2018, https://www.eweek.com/security/oracle-patches-301-vulnerabilities -in-october-update.

172. "Oracle Agrees to Settle FTC Charges It Deceived Consumers about Java Software Updates," Federal Trade Commission, last updated December 21, 2015, https://www.ftc.gov/news-events/press-releases/2015/12/oracle-agrees-settle-ftc -charges-it-deceived-consumers-about-java; Sean Gallagher, "Oracle Settles with FTC over Java's 'Deceptive' Security Patching," *Ars Technica*, December 21, 2015, https://

arstechnica.com/information-technology/2015/12/oracle-settles-with-ftc-over-javas
-deceptive-security-patching/.

173. Gallagher, "Oracle Agrees to Settle."

174. Gallagher, "Oracle Agrees to Settle."

175. "Microsoft Security Intelligence Report," Microsoft Security, Microsoft Corporation, last accessed May 12, 2019, https://www.microsoft.com/securityinsights/; "Microsoft Security Guidance Blog," Microsoft TechNet, Microsoft Corporation, last accessed May 12, 2019, https://blogs.technet.microsoft.com/secguide/; "Microsoft Security Response Center," Microsoft Security Response Center, Microsoft Corporation, last accessed May 12, 2019, https://www.microsoft.com/en-us/msrc.

176. Howard and Lipner, *The Security Development Lifecycle*.

177. John Viega, J. T. Bloch, Tadayoshi Kohno, and Gary McGraw, "ITS4: A Static Vulnerability Scanner for C and C++ Code" (presentation, 16th Annual Computer Security Applications Conference, New Orleans, December 11–15, 2000), https://doi.org/10.1109/ACSAC.2000.898880.

178. "On the Record: The Year in Security Quotes," SearchEnterpriseDesktop, TechTarget, last updated December 29, 2004, https://searchenterprisedesktop.techtarget.com/news/1036885/On-the-record-The-year-in-security-quotes.

179. Ryan Singel, "Apple Goes on Safari with Hostile Security Researchers," *Wired*, June 14, 2007, https://www.wired.com/2007/06/researchersmeetsafari/.

180. Andy Greenberg, "Apples for the Army," *Forbes*, December 21, 2007, https://www.forbes.com/2007/12/20/apple-army-hackers-tech-security-cx_ag_1221army.html.

181. Gregg Keizer, "Apple Issues Massive Security Update for Mac OS X," *Computerworld*, February 12, 2009, https://seclists.org/isn/2009/Feb/48; Dan Goodin, "Apple Unloads 47 Fixes for iPhones, Macs and QuickTime," *Register*, September 11, 2009, https://www.theregister.co.uk/2009/09/11/apple_security_updates/.

182. Paul McDougall, "Apple iPhone Out, BlackBerry 8800 in at NASA," *InformationWeek*, July 31, 2007, https://seclists.org/isn/2007/Aug/1.

183. Charlie Miller, Jake Honoroff, and Joshua Mason, *Security Evaluation of Apple's iPhone* (Baltimore: Independent Security Evaluators, 2007), https://www.ise.io/wp-content/uploads/2017/07/exploitingiphone.pdf.

184. "Secure Enclave Overview," Apple Platform Security, Apple, last accessed March 10, 2020, https://support.apple.com/guide/security/secure-enclave-overview-sec59b0b31ff/web.

185. "Secure Enclave Overview."

186. Manu Gulati, Michael J. Smith, and Shu-Yi Yu, "Security Enclave Processor for a System on a Chip," US Patent US8832465B2, filed September 25, 2012, issued September 9, 2014, https://patents.google.com/patent/US8832465.

187. Simson Garfinkel, "The iPhone Has Passed a Key Security Threshold," *MIT Technology Review*, August 13, 2012, https://www.technologyreview.com/s/428477/the-iphone-has-passed-a-key-security-threshold/.

188. Apple, *Apple Platform Security* (Cupertino, CA: Apple, 2019), 53–54, https://manuals.info.apple.com/MANUALS/1000/MA1902/en_US/apple-platform-security-guide.pdf.

189. Devlin Barrett and Danny Yadron, "New Level of Smartphone Encryption Alarms Law Enforcement," *Wall Street Journal*, September 22, 2014, https://www.wsj.com/articles/new-level-of-smartphone-encryption-alarms-law-enforcement-1411420341.

190. Cyrus Farivar, "Judge: Apple Must Help FBI Unlock San Bernardino Shooter's iPhone," *Ars Technica*, February 16, 2016, https://arstechnica.com/tech-policy/2016/02/judge-apple-must-help-fbi-unlock-san-bernardino-shooters-iphone/.

191. Apple, "A Message to Our Customers," last updated February 16, 2016, https://www.apple.com/customer-letter/.

192. Cyrus Farivar and David Kravets, "How Apple Will Fight the DOJ in iPhone Backdoor Crypto Case," *Ars Technica*, February 18, 2016, https://arstechnica.com/tech-policy/2016/02/how-apple-will-fight-the-doj-in-iphone-backdoor-crypto-case/.

193. Gary McGraw, "From the Ground Up: The DIMACS Software Security Workshop," *IEEE Security & Privacy* 1, no. 2 (2003): 59–66, https://doi.org/10.1109/MSECP.2003.1193213.

194. Robert Lemos, "Re: The Strategic Difference of 0day," SecLists.Org Security Mailing List Archive, last updated June 15, 2011, https://seclists.org/dailydave/2011/q2/105; Dave Aitel, "Exploits Matter," SecLists.Org Security Mailing List Archive, last updated October 6, 2009, https://seclists.org/dailydave/2009/q4/2.

195. Jerry Pournelle, "Of Worms and Things," *Dr. Dobb's Journal*, December 2003.

## 6. Usable Security, Economics, and Psychology

1. Zinaida Benenson, Gabriele Lenzini, Daniela Oliveira, Simon Edward Parkin, and Sven Ubelacker, "Maybe Poor Johnny Really Cannot Encrypt: The Case for a Complexity Theory for Usable Security" (presentation, 15th New Security Paradigms Workshop, Twente, the Netherlands, September 8–11, 2015), https://doi.org/10.1145/2841113.2841120.

2. Tom Regan, "Putting the Dancing Pigs in Their Cyber-Pen," *Christian Science Monitor*, October 7, 1999, https://www.csmonitor.com/1999/1007/p18s2.html.

3. Bruce Sterling, *The Hacker Crackdown* (New York: Bantam, 1992), http://www.gutenberg.org/ebooks/101.

4. Sterling, *The Hacker Crackdown.*

5. Sterling, *The Hacker Crackdown.*

6. Steven M. Bellovin, Terry V. Benzel, Bob Blakley, Dorothy E. Denning, Whitfield Diffie, Jeremy Epstein, and Paulo Verissimo, "Information Assurance Technology Forecast 2008," *IEEE Security & Privacy* 6, no. 1 (2008): 16–23, https://doi.org/10.1109/MSP.2008.13.

7. Gary Rivlin, "Ideas & Trends: Your Password, Please; Pssst, Computer Users . . . Want Some Candy?" *New York Times*, April 25, 2004, https://www.nytimes.com/2004/04/25/weekinreview/ideas-trends-your-password-please-pssst-computer-users-want-some-candy.html.

8. Rivlin, "Your Password, Please."

9. Simson Garfinkel and Heather Richter Lipford, *Usable Security: History, Themes, and Challenges* (San Rafael, CA: Morgan & Claypool, 2014), 18.

10. Alma Whitten and J. D. Tygar, "Why Johnny Can't Encrypt: A Usability Evaluation of PGP 5.0" (presentation, 8th USENIX Security Symposium, Washington, DC, August 23–26, 1999).

11. Mary Ellen Zurko and Richard T. Simon, "User-Centered Security" (presentation, New Security Paradigms Workshop, Lake Arrowhead, CA, 1996).

12. Zurko and Simon, "User-Centered Security."

13. Jerome H. Saltzer and M. D. Schroeder, "The Protection of Information in Computer Systems," *Proceedings of the IEEE* 63, no. 9 (1975): 1278–1308, http://doi.org/10 .1109/PROC.1975.9939.

14. Saltzer and Schroeder, "Protection of Information."

15. Saltzer and Schroeder, "Protection of Information."

16. James Reason, *Human Error* (Cambridge: Cambridge University Press, 1990).

17. Zurko and Simon, "User-Centered Security."

18. Whitten and Tygar, "Why Johnny Can't Encrypt."

19. Whitten and Tygar, "Why Johnny Can't Encrypt."

20. "Encryption, Powered by PGP," Encryption Family, Symantec Corporation, last accessed May 14, 2019, https://www.symantec.com/products/encryption.

21. "Encryption, Powered by PGP."

22. Dieter Gollmann, *Computer Security* (New York: Wiley, 2011), 264.

23. Whitten and Tygar, "Why Johnny Can't Encrypt"; Garfinkel and Lipford, *Usable Security*, 15.

24. Whitten and Tygar, "Why Johnny Can't Encrypt."

25. Whitten and Tygar, "Why Johnny Can't Encrypt."

26. Whitten and Tygar, "Why Johnny Can't Encrypt."

27. Whitten and Tygar, "Why Johnny Can't Encrypt."

28. Whitten and Tygar, "Why Johnny Can't Encrypt."

29. Computing Research Association, *Four Grand Challenges in Trustworthy Computing* (Washington, DC: Computing Research Association, 2003).

30. Computing Research Association, *Four Grand Challenges*, 4.

31. "Symposium on Usable Privacy and Security," CyLab Usable Privacy and Security Laboratory, Carnegie Mellon University, last accessed May 14, 2019, http://cups.cs .cmu.edu/soups/.

32. Garfinkel and Lipford, *Usable Security*, 3.

33. Ka-Ping Yee, *User Interaction Design for Secure Systems* (Berkeley: University of California, 2002); Jakob Nielsen, "Security & Human Factors," Nielsen Normal Group, last updated November 26, 2000, https://www.nngroup.com/articles/security-and-human -factors/.

34. Whitten and Tygar, "Why Johnny Can't Encrypt."

35. Rogerio de Paula, Xianghua Ding, Paul Dourish, Kari Nies, Ben Pillet, David Redmiles, Jie Ren et al., "Two Experiences Designing for Effective Security" (presentation, Symposium on Usable Privacy and Security, Pittsburgh, PA, July 6–8, 2005), https:// doi.org/10.1145/1073001.1073004.

36. Lorrie Faith Cranor, "A Framework for Reasoning about the Human in the Loop' (presentation, 1st Conference on Usability, Psychology, and Security, San Francisco, April 14, 2008).

37. Cranor, "Human in the Loop."

38. Garfinkel and Lipford, *Usable Security*, 55.

39. Garfinkel and Lipford, *Usable Security*, 55.

40. David F. Gallagher, "Users Find Too Many Phish in the Internet Sea," *New York Times*, September 20, 2004, https://www.nytimes.com/2004/09/20/technology/users-find -too-many-phish-in-the-internet-sea.html; Garfinkel and Lipford, *Usable Security*, 55.

41. L. McLaughlin, "Online Fraud Gets Sophisticated," *IEEE Internet Computing* 7, no. 5 (2003): 6–8, http://dx.doi.org/10.1109/MIC.2003.1232512; Ronald J. Mann, *Regulating Internet Payment Intermediaries* (Austin: University of Texas, 2003), 699; Dinei Florencio, Cormac Herley, and Paul C. van Oorschot, "An Administrator's Guide to Internet Password Research" (presentation, 28th Large Installation System Administration Conference, Seattle, November 9–14, 2014).

42. Julie S. Downs, Mandy B. Holbrook, and Lorrie Faith Cranor, "Decision Strategies and Susceptibility to Phishing" (presentation, Symposium on Usable Privacy and Security, Pittsburgh, PA, July 12–14, 2006), https://doi.org/10.1145/1143120.1143131.

43. Garfinkel and Lipford, *Usable Security*, 56.

44. Garfinkel and Lipford, *Usable Security*, 56.

45. Ponnurangam Kumaraguru, Steve Sheng, Alessandro Acquisti, Lorrie Faith Cranor, and Jason Hong, "Teaching Johnny Not to Fall for Phish," *ACM Transactions on Internet Technology* 10, no. 2 (2010), https://doi.org/10.1145/1754393.1754396; Kyung Wha Hong, Christopher M. Kelley, Rucha Tembe, Emerson Murphy-Hill, and Christopher B. Mayhorn, "Keeping Up with the Joneses: Assessing Phishing Susceptibility in an Email Task," *Proceedings of the Human Factors and Ergonomics Society Annual Meeting* 57, no. 1 (2013): 1012–1016, https://doi.org/10.1177%2F1541931213571226; Ponnurangam Kumaraguru, Justin Cranshaw, Alessandro Acquisti, Lorrie Cranor, Jason Hong, Mary Ann Blair, and Theodore Pham, "School of Phish: A Real-World Evaluation of Anti-Phishing Training" (presentation, Symposium on Usable Privacy and Security, Mountain View, CA, July 15–17, 2009), https://doi.org/10.1145/1572532.1572536.

46. Andrew Stewart, "A Utilitarian Re-Examination of Enterprise-Scale Information Security Management," *Information and Computer Security* 26, no. 1 (2018): 39–57, https://doi.org/10.1108/ICS-03-2017-0012.

47. Stewart, "A Utilitarian Re-Examination."

48. Garfinkel and Lipford, *Usable Security*, 58–61.

49. Rachna Dhamija and J. D. Tygar, "The Battle against Phishing: Dynamic Security Skins" (presentation, Symposium on Usable Privacy and Security, Pittsburgh, PA, July 6–8, 2005), https://doi.org/10.1145/1073001.1073009.

50. Douglas Stebila, "Reinforcing Bad Behavior: The Misuse of Security Indicators on Popular Websites" (presentation, 22nd Conference of the Computer-Human Interaction Special Interest Group of Australia on Computer-Human Interaction, Brisbane, November 22–26, 2010), https://doi.org/10.1145/1952222.1952275.

51. Garfinkel and Lipford, *Usable Security*, 58.

52. Garfinkel and Lipford, *Usable Security*, 58.

53. Min Wu, Robert C. Miller, and Simson L. Garfinkel, "Do Security Toolbars Actually Prevent Phishing Attacks?" (presentation, SIGHCI Conference on Human

Factors in Computing Systems, Montreal, April 22–27, 2006); Rachna Dhamija, J. D. Tygar, and Marti Hearst, "Why Phishing Works" (presentation, SIGHCI Conference on Human Factors in Computing Systems, Montreal, April 22–27, 2006), https://doi.org /10.1145/1124772.1124861.

54. Wu et al., "Security Toolbars."

55. Kumaraguru et al., "School of Phish."

56. Ben Rothke, *Computer Security: 20 Things Every Employee Should Know* (New York: McGraw-Hill, 2003); Kumaraguru et al., "Teaching Johnny."

57. Garfinkel and Lipford, *Usable Security*, 55.

58. Cormac Herley, "Why Do Nigerian Scammers Say They Are from Nigeria?" (presentation, 11th Workshop on the Economics of Information Security, Berlin, June 25–26, 2012), https://www.microsoft.com/en-us/research/publication/why-do -nigerian-scammers-say-they-are-from-nigeria/.

59. Herley, "Nigerian Scammers."

60. Herley, "Nigerian Scammers."

61. Herley, "Nigerian Scammers."

62. Herley, "Nigerian Scammers."

63. Matt Bishop, *Computer Security: Art and Science* (Boston: Addison-Wesley, 2003), 309–310.

64. Bishop, *Computer Security*, 309–310.

65. Joe Bonneau, Cormac Herley, Paul C. van Oorschot, and Frank Stajano, "Passwords and the Evolution of Imperfect Authentication," *Communications of the ACM* 58, no. 7 (2015): 78–87, https://doi.org/10.1145/2699390.

66. Bonneau et al., "Evolution of Imperfect Authentication."

67. Bonneau et al., "Evolution of Imperfect Authentication."

68. Jerome H. Saltzer, "Protection and the Control of Information Sharing in Multics," *Communications of the ACM* 17, no. 7 (1974): 388–402, https://doi.org/10.1145 /361011.361067.

69. Robert Morris and Ken Thompson, "Password Security: A Case History," *Communications of the ACM* 22 no. 11 (1979): 594–597, https://doi.org/10.1145/359168.359172.

70. Morris and Thompson, "Password Security"; Bishop, *Computer Security*, 311.

71. Morris and Thompson, "Password Security"; Bishop, *Computer Security*, 311.

72. Bishop, *Computer Security*, 312.

73. Morris and Thompson, "Password Security."

74. Morris and Thompson, "Password Security."

75. Department of Defense, *Password Management Guideline* (Fort Meade, MD: Department of Defense, April 12, 1985); Bonneau et al., "Evolution of Imperfect Authentication."

76. Department of Defense, *Password Management Guideline*.

77. National Bureau of Standards, *Password Usage—Federal Information Processing Standards Publication 112* (Gaithersburg, MD: National Bureau of Standards, 1985), https://csrc.nist.gov/publications/detail/fips/112/archive/1985-05-01.

78. Bonneau et al., "Evolution of Imperfect Authentication."

79. Bonneau et al., "Evolution of Imperfect Authentication."

80. Dinei Florencio, Cormac Herley, and Paul C. van Oorschot, "Password Portfolios and the Finite-Effort User: Sustainably Managing Large Numbers of Accounts" (presentation, 23rd USENIX Security Symposium, San Diego, August 20–22, 2014).

81. Dinei Florencio and Cormac Herley, "A Large Scale Study of Web Password Habits" (presentation, 16th International Conference on World Wide Web, Banff, Canada, May 8–12, 2007), https://doi.org/10.1145/1242572.1242661.

82. Anupam Das, Joseph Bonneau, Matthew Caesar, Nikita Borisov, and XiaoFeng Wang, "The Tangled Web of Password Reuse" (presentation, San Diego, February 23–26, 2014), https://doi.org/10.14722/ndss.2014.23357.

83. Jianxin Yan, Alan Blackwell, Ross Anderson, and Alasdair Grant, *The Memorability and Security of Passwords—Some Empirical Results* (Cambridge: University of Cambridge, 2000).

84. Stuart Schechter, Cormac Herley, and Michael Mitzenmacher, "Popularity Is Everything; A New Approach to Protecting Passwords from Statistical-Guessing Attacks" (presentation, 5th USENIX Workshop on Hot Topics in Security, Washington, DC, August 11–13, 2010), https://www.microsoft.com/en-us/research/publication/popularity-is-everything-a-new-approach-to-protecting-passwords-from-statistical-guessing-attacks/.

85. Cynthia Kuo, Sasha Romanosky, and Lorrie Faith Cranor, "Human Selection of Mnemonic Phrase-Based Passwords" (presentation, Symposium on Usable Privacy and Security, Pittsburgh, PA, July 12–14, 2006), https://doi.org/10.1145/1143120.1143129.

86. Schechter et al., "Popularity Is Everything."

87. Dinei Florencio, Cormac Herley, and Baris Coskun, "Do Strong Web Passwords Accomplish Anything?" (presentation, 2nd USENIX Workshop on Hot Topics in Security, Boston, August 7, 2007).

88. Richard Shay, Saranga Komanduri, Patrick Gage Kelley, Pedro Giovanni Leon, Michelle L. Mazurek, Lujo Bauer, Nicolas Christin et al., "Encountering Stronger Password Requirements: User Attitudes and Behaviors" (presentation, Symposium on Usable Privacy and Security, Redmond, WA, July 14–16, 2010), https://doi.org/10.1145/1837110.1837113; Florencio et al., "An Administrator's Guide."

89. Garfinkel and Lipford, *Usable Security*, 40–43.

90. Joseph Bonneau, Cormac Herley, Paul C. van Oorschot, and Frank Stajano, "The Quest to Replace Passwords: A Framework for Comparative Evaluation of Web Authentication Schemes" (presentation, IEEE Symposium on Security and Privacy, San Francisco, May 20–23, 2012), https://doi.org/10.1109/SP.2012.44.

91. Garfinkel and Lipford, *Usable Security*, 46.

92. Garfinkel and Lipford, *Usable Security*, 43–25.

93. Cormac Herley and Paul van Oorschot, "A Research Agenda Acknowledging the Persistence of Passwords," *IEEE Security & Privacy* 10, no. 1 (2012): 28–36, https://doi.org/10.1109/MSP.2011.150.

94. Herley and van Oorschot, "A Research Agenda"; Bonneau et al., "Quest to Replace Passwords."

95. Bonneau et al., "Quest to Replace Passwords."

96. Herley and van Oorschot, "A Research Agenda."

97. Herley and van Oorschot, "A Research Agenda."

98. Herley and van Oorschot, "A Research Agenda."

99. Dinei Florencio and Cormac Herley, "Where Do Security Policies Come From?" (presentation, Symposium on Usable Privacy and Security, Redmond, WA, July 14–16, 2010), https://doi.org/10.1145/1837110.1837124; Florencio et al., "Strong Web Passwords."

100. Florencio et al., "An Administrator's Guide."

101. Florencio et al., "An Administrator's Guide."

102. Florencio et al., "Strong Web Passwords."

103. Bonneau et al., "Evolution of Imperfect Authentication."

104. Yinqian Zhang, Fabian Monrose, and Michael K. Reiter, "The Security of Modern Password Expiration: An Algorithmic Framework and Empirical Analysis" (presentation, 17th ACM Conference on Computer and Communications Security, Chicago, October 4–8, 2010), https://doi.org/10.1145/1866307.1866328.

105. Ross Anderson, "Ross Anderson's Home Page," University of Cambridge Computer Laboratory, last accessed May 15, 2019, https://www.cl.cam.ac.uk/~rja14/.

106. Ross Anderson, interview by Jeffrey R. Yost, *Charles Babbage Institute*, May 21, 2015, 5, http://hdl.handle.net/11299/174607.

107. Anderson, interview by Yost, 9.

108. Anderson, interview by Yost, 9.

109. Anderson, interview by Yost, 9.

110. Anderson, interview by Yost, 9, 10.

111. Anderson, interview by Yost, 32.

112. Gollmann, *Computer Security*, 284.

113. Anderson, interview by Yost, 37.

114. Anderson, interview by Yost, 37–38.

115. Ross Anderson, "Security Economics—A Personal Perspective" (presentation, 28th Annual Computer Security Applications Conference, Orlando, December 3–7, 2012), https://doi.org/10.1145/2420950.2420971.

116. Anderson, "Security Economics."

117. Anderson, interview by Yost, 39.

118. William Forster Lloyd, *Two Lectures on the Checks to Population* (Oxford: Oxford University Press, 1833).

119. Lloyd, *Two Lectures*.

120. Anderson, interview by Yost, 42; Anderson, "Security Economics."

121. Tyler Moore and Ross Anderson, *Economics and Internet Security: A Survey of Recent Analytical, Empirical and Behavioral Research* (Cambridge, MA: Harvard University, 2011).

122. Christian Kreibich, Chris Kanich, Kirill Levchenko, Brandon Enright, Geoff Voelker, Vern Paxson, and Stefan Savage, "Spamalytics: An Empirical Analysis of Spam Marketing Conversion" (presentation, ACM Conference on Computer and Communications Security, Alexandria, VA, October 27–31, 2008).

123. Kreibich et al., "Spamalytics."

124. Ross Anderson, "Why Information Security Is Hard—An Economic Perspective" (presentation, 17th Annual Computer Security Applications Conference, New Orleans, December 10–14, 2001), https://doi.org/10.1109/ACSAC.2001.991552.

125. Tyler Moore, Richard Clayton, and Ross Anderson, "The Economics of Online Crime," *Journal of Economic Perspectives* 23, no. 3 (2009): 3–20, https://www.aeaweb.org/articles?id=10.1257/jep.23.3.3.

126. Moore et al., "Economics of Online Crime."

127. Moore et al., "Economics of Online Crime."

128. Anderson, "Why Information Security Is Hard."

129. L. Jean Camp, *The State of Economics of Information Security* (Bloomington: Indiana University, 2006).

130. Benjamin Edelman, "Adverse Selection in Online 'Trust' Certifications and Search Results," *Electronic Commerce Research and Applications* 10, no. 1 (2011): 17–25, https://doi.org/10.1016/j.elerap.2010.06.001.

131. "The FTC's TRUSTe Case: When Seals Help Seal the Deal," Federal Trade Commission, last updated November 17, 2014, https://www.ftc.gov/news-events/blogs/business-blog/2014/11/ftcs-truste-case-when-seals-help-seal-deal.

132. Edelman, "Adverse Selection."

133. Edelman, "Adverse Selection."

134. Edelman, "Adverse Selection."

135. "TRUSTe Settles FTC Charges It Deceived Consumers through Its Privacy Seal Program," Federal Trade Commission, last updated November 17, 2014, https://www.ftc.gov/news-events/press-releases/2014/11/truste-settles-ftc-charges-it-deceived-consumers-through-its.

136. Hal R. Varian, "System Reliability and Free Riding" (presentation, 3rd Workshop on the Economics of Information Security, Minneapolis, 2004), https://doi.org/10.1007/1-4020-8090-5_1; Jack Hirshleifer, "From Weakest-Link to Best-Shot: The Voluntary Provision of Public Goods," *Public Choice* 41, no. 3 (1983): 371–386.

137. Ross Anderson and Tyler Moore: "Information Security: Where Computer Science, Economics and Psychology Meet," *Philosophical Transactions: Mathematical, Physical and Engineering Sciences* 367, no. 1898 (2009): 2717–2727, https://doi.org/10.1098/rsta.2009.0027.

138. Moore and Anderson, *Economics and Internet Security.*

139. Binyamin Appelbaum, "Nobel in Economics Is Awarded to Richard Thaler," *New York Times,* October 9, 2017, https://www.nytimes.com/2017/10/09/business/nobel-economics-richard-thaler.html.

140. Anderson, "Security Economics."

141. Nicolas Christin, Sally S. Yanagihara, and Keisuke Kamataki, "Dissecting One Click Frauds" (presentation, 17th ACM Conference on Computer and Communication Security, Chicago, October 4–8, 2010), https://doi.org/10.1145/1866307.1866310.

142. Christin et al., "Dissecting One Click Frauds."

143. Simson Garfinkel, "Cybersecurity Research Is Not Making Us More Secure" (presentation, University of Pennsylvania, Philadelphia, October 30, 2018), 63, https://simson.net/ref/2018/2018-10-31%20Cybersecurity%20Research.pdf.

144. Garfinkel, "Cybersecurity Research."

145. Steven Furnell and Kerry-Lynn Thomson, "Recognizing and Addressing Security Fatigue," *Computer Fraud & Security* 2009, no. 11 (2009): 7–11, https://doi.org/10.1016/S1361-3723(09)70139-3.

146. Brian Stanton, Mary F. Theofanos, Sandra Spickard Prettyman, and Susanne Furman, "Security Fatigue," *IT Professional* 18, no. 5 (2016): 26–32, http://dx.doi.org/10.1109/MITP.2016.84.

147. Emilee Rader, Rick Wash, and Brandon Brooks, "Stories as Informal Lessons about Security" (presentation, Symposium on Usable Privacy and Security, Washington, DC, July 11–13, 2012), https://doi.org/10.1145/2335356.2335364.

148. Emilee Rader and Rick Wash, "Identifying Patterns in Informal Sources of Security Information," *Journal of Cybersecurity* 1, no. 1 (2015): 121–144, https://doi.org/10.1093/cybsec/tyv008.

149. Rick Wash, "Folk Models of Home Computer Security" (presentation, Symposium on Usable Privacy and Security, Redmond, WA, July 14–16, 2010); Rader and Wash, "Identifying Patterns."

150. Wash, "Folk Models"; Rader and Wash, "Identifying Patterns."

151. Rader et al., "Stories as Informal Lessons."

152. Rader et al., "Stories as Informal Lessons."

153. Wash, "Folk Models."

154. Wash, "Folk Models."

155. Rader and Wash, "Identifying Patterns."

156. Rader and Wash, "Identifying Patterns."

157. Rader and Wash, "Identifying Patterns."

158. Andrew Stewart, "On Risk: Perception and Direction," *Computers & Security* 23, no. 5 (2004): 362–370, https://doi.org/10.1016/j.cose.2004.05.003.

159. Vic Napier, *Open Canopy Fatalities and Risk Homeostasis: A Correlation Study* (Monmouth: Department of Psychology, Western Oregon University, 2000).

160. Napier, *Open Canopy Fatalities.*

161. Napier, *Open Canopy Fatalities.*

162. John Adams, "Cars, Cholera, and Cows: The Management of Risk and Uncertainty," Cato Institute, last updated March 4, 1999, https://www.cato.org/publications/policy-analysis/cars-cholera-cows-management-risk-uncertainty.

163. Adams, "Cars, Cholera, and Cows."

164. Fridulv Sagberg, Stein Fosser, and Inger Anne Saetermo, "An Investigation of Behavioral Adaptation to Airbags and Antilock Brakes among Taxi Drivers," *Accident Analysis and Prevention* 29, no. 3 (1997): 293–302, http://dx.doi.org/10.1016/S0001-4575(96)00083-8.

165. Sagberg et al., "Investigation of Behavioral Adaptation."

166. M. Aschenbrenner and B. Biehl, "Improved Safety through Improved Technical Measures?" in *Challenges to Accident Prevention: The Issue of Risk Compensation Behavior* (Groningen, the Netherlands: Styx Publications, 1994), https://trid.trb.org/view/457353.

167. Aschenbrenner and Biehl, "Improved Safety."

168. John Ioannidis, "Re: Ping Works, but FTP/Telnet Get 'No Route to Host,'" comp.protocols.tcp-ip, July 22, 1992, http://securitydigest.org/tcp-ip/archive/1992/07.

169. Barry Glassner, *The Culture of Fear: Why Americans Are Afraid of the Wrong Things: Crime, Drugs, Minorities, Teen Moms, Killer Kids, Mutant Microbes, Plane Crashes, Road Rage, & So Much More* (New York: Basic Books, 2010).

170. Graham Lawton, "Everything Was a Problem and We Did Not Understand a Thing: An Interview with Noam Chomsky," *Slate*, March 25, 2012, https://slate.com /technology/2012/03/noam-chomsky-on-linguistics-and-climate-change.html.

171. Cormac Herley, "So Long, and No Thanks for the Externalities: The Rational Rejection of Security Advice by Users" (presentation, New Security Paradigms Workshop, Oxford, UK, September 8–11, 2009), https://doi.org/10.1145/1719030.1719050.

172. Benenson et al., "Maybe Poor Johnny Really Cannot Encrypt."

173. Herley, "So Long, and No Thanks."

174. Herley, "So Long, and No Thanks."

175. Dinei Florencio and Cormac Herley, "Is Everything We Know about Password-Stealing Wrong?" *IEEE Security & Privacy* 10, no. 6 (2012): 63–69, https:// doi.org/10.1109/MSP.2012.57.

176. Florencio and Herley, "Everything We Know."

177. Herley, "So Long, and No Thanks."

178. Herley, "So Long, and No Thanks."

179. Herley, "So Long, and No Thanks."

180. Herley, "So Long, and No Thanks."

181. Herley, "So Long, and No Thanks."

### 7. Vulnerability Disclosure, Bounties, and Markets

1. Freakonomics, "The Cobra Effect (Ep. 96): Full Transcript," *Freakonomics* (blog), October 11, 2012, http://freakonomics.com/2012/10/11/the-cobra-effect-full-transcript/.

2. John Diedrich and Raquel Rutledge, "ATF Sting in Milwaukee Flawed from Start," *Milwaukee Journal Sentinel*, September 12, 2016, https://www.jsonline.com /story/news/investigations/2016/09/12/atf-sting-milwaukee-flawed-start/90145044/; John Diedrich, "540: A Front," This American Life, last accessed May 19, 2019, https:// www.thisamericanlife.org/540/transcript; John Diedrich and Raquel Rutledge, "ATF Uses Rogue Tactics in Storefront Stings across Nation," *Milwaukee Journal Sentinel*, December 7, 2013, http://archive.jsonline.com/watchdog/watchdogreports/atf-uses -rogue-tactics-in-storefront-stings-across-the-nation-b99146765z1-234916641.html.

3. Steve McConnell, *Code Complete: A Practical Handbook of Software Construction*, 2nd ed. (Redmond, WA: Microsoft Press, 2004).

4. Leyla Bilge and Tudor Dumitras, "Investigating Zero-Day Attacks," *Login* 38, no. 4 (2013): 6–12, https://www.usenix.org/publications/login/august-2013-volume-38 -number-4/investigating-zero-day-attacks.

5. Bilge and Dumitras, "Investigating Zero-Day Attacks," 6.

6. Bilge and Dumitras, "Investigating Zero-Day Attacks," 6.

7. Trey Herr, Bruce Schneier, and Christopher Morris, *Taking Stock: Estimating Vulnerability Rediscovery* (Cambridge, MA: Harvard University, 2017), 6, https://www .belfercenter.org/publication/taking-stock-estimating-vulnerability-rediscovery.

8. Dave Aitel, "CIS VEP Panel Commentary," *CyberSecPolitics* (blog), November 23, 2016, https://cybersecpolitics.blogspot.com/2016/11/cis-vep-panel-commentary.html; Dave Aitel, "Do You Need 0days? What about Oxygen?" *CyberSecPolitics* (blog),

August 1, 2017, https://cybersecpolitics.blogspot.com/2017/08/do-you-need-0days-what-about-oxygen.html.

9. Dave Aitel, "Zero Day—Totally Gnarly," *CyberSecPolitics* (blog), January 7, 2017, https://cybersecpolitics.blogspot.com/2017/01/zero-daytotally-gnarly.html.

10. Dave Aitel, "Unboxing '0day' for Policy People," *CyberSecPolitics* (blog), November 28, 2016, https://cybersecpolitics.blogspot.com/2016/11/unboxing-0day-for-policy-people.html.

11. Bilge and Dumitras, "Investigating Zero-Day Attacks," 7.

12. Bilge and Dumitras, "Investigating Zero-Day Attacks," 7.

13. Bilge and Dumitras, "Investigating Zero-Day Attacks," 7.

14. Dave Aitel, "The Atlantic Council Paper," *CyberSecPolitics* (blog), January 17, 2017, https://cybersecpolitics.blogspot.com/2017/01/.

15. Dave Aitel, "The Atlantic Council Paper."

16. Sebastian Anthony, "The First Rule of Zero-Days Is No One Talks about Zero-Days (So We'll Explain)," *Ars Technica*, October 20, 2015, https://arstechnica.com/information-technology/2015/10/the-rise-of-the-zero-day-market/.

17. Anthony, "Zero-Days."

18. Riva Richmond, "The RSA Hack: How They Did It," *New York Times*, April 2, 2011, https://bits.blogs.nytimes.com/2011/04/02/the-rsa-hack-how-they-did-it/.

19. Richmond, "The RSA Hack."

20. John Markoff, "Security Firm Is Vague on Its Compromised Devices," *New York Times*, March 18, 2011, https://www.nytimes.com/2011/03/19/technology/19secure.html; Christopher Drew and John Markoff, "Data Breach at Security Firm Linked to Attack on Lockheed," *New York Times*, May 27, 2011, https://www.nytimes.com/2011/05/28/business/28hack.html; Christopher Drew, "Stolen Data Is Tracked to Hacking at Lockheed," *New York Times*, June 3, 2011, https://www.nytimes.com/2011/06/04/technology/04security.html.

21. Robert Graham and David Maynor, "A Simpler Way of Finding 0day" (presentation, Black Hat Briefings, Las Vegas, July 28–August 2, 2007), https://www.blackhat.com/presentations/bh-usa-07/Maynor_and_Graham/Whitepaper/bh-usa-07-maynor_and_graham-WP.pdf.

22. Graham and Maynor, "A Simpler Way."

23. Elias Levy, "Full Disclosure Is a Necessary Evil," *SecurityFocus*, last updated August 16, 2001, https://www.securityfocus.com/news/238; John Leyden, "Show Us the Bugs—Users Want Full Disclosure," *Register*, July 8, 2002, https://www.theregister.co.uk/2002/07/08/show_us_the_bugs_users/.

24. Levy, "Full Disclosure Is a Necessary Evil"; Leyden, "Show Us the Bugs."

25. Levy, "Full Disclosure Is a Necessary Evil"; Leyden, "Show Us the Bugs."

26. Marcus Ranum, "Script Kiddiez Suck: V2.0," ranum.com, last accessed May 19, 2019, https://www.ranum.com/security/computer_security/archives/script-kiddiez-suck-2.pdf; Marcus Ranum, "Vulnerability Disclosure—Let's Be Honest about Motives Shall We?" ranum.com, last accessed May 20, 2019, https://www.ranum.com/security/computer_security/editorials/disclosure-1/index.html.

27. Brian Martin, "A Note on Security Disclosures," *Login* 25, no. 8 (2000): 43–46, https://www.usenix.org/publications/login/december-2000-volume-25-number-8/note

-security-disclosures; William A. Arbaugh, William L. Fithen, and John McHugh, "Windows of Vulnerability: A Case Study Analysis," *IEEE Computer* 33, no. 12 (2000), https://doi.org/10.1109/2.889093.

28. Leyla Bilge and Tudor Dumitras, "Before We Knew It: An Empirical Study of Zero-Day Attacks in the Real World" (presentation, ACM Conference on Computer and Communications Security, Raleigh, NC, October 16–18, 2012), https://doi.org/10.1145/2382196.2382284.

29. Eric Rescorla, "Is Finding Security Holes a Good Idea?" *IEEE Security & Privacy* 3, no. 1 (2005): 14–19, https://doi.org/10.1109/MSP.2005.17.

30. Rescorla, "Finding Security Holes."

31. Rescorla, "Finding Security Holes."

32. Rescorla, "Finding Security Holes."

33. Andy Ozment, "The Likelihood of Vulnerability Rediscovery and the Social Utility of Vulnerability Hunting" (presentation, 4th Workshop on the Economics of Information Security, Cambridge, MA, June 1–3, 2005), http://infosecon.net/workshop/pdf/10.pdf.

34. Andrew Crocker, "It's No Secret that the Government Uses Zero Days for 'Offense,'" Electronic Frontier Foundation, last updated November 9, 2015, https://www.eff.org/deeplinks/2015/11/its-no-secret-government-uses-zero-days-offense.

35. Crocker, "It's No Secret that the Government Uses Zero Days for 'Offense.'"

36. Anon., "Equation Group—Cyber Weapons Auction," Pastebin, last updated August 15, 2016, https://archive.is/20160815133924/http://pastebin.com/NDTU5kJQ#selection-373.0-373.38; Scott Shane, "Malware Case Is Major Blow for the N.S.A.," *New York Times*, May 16, 2017, https://www.nytimes.com/2017/05/16/us/nsa-malware-case-shadow-brokers.html.

37. Anon., "Equation Group—Cyber Weapons Auction."

38. Anon., "Equation Group—Cyber Weapons Auction."

39. Anon., "Equation Group—Cyber Weapons Auction."

40. Scott Shane, Nicole Perlroth, and David E. Sanger, "Security Breach and Spilled Secrets Have Shaken the N.S.A. to Its Core," *New York Times*, November 12, 2017, https://www.nytimes.com/2017/11/12/us/nsa-shadow-brokers.html.

41. Dan Goodin, "NSA-Leaking Shadow Brokers Just Dumped Its Most Damaging Release Yet," *Ars Technica*, April 14, 2017, https://arstechnica.com/information-technology/2017/04/nsa-leaking-shadow-brokers-just-dumped-its-most-damaging-release-yet/; Selena Larson, "NSA's Powerful Windows Hacking Tools Leaked Online," *CNN*, April 15, 2017, https://money.cnn.com/2017/04/14/technology/windows-exploits-shadow-brokers/index.html.

42. Goodin, "NSA-Leaking Shadow Brokers."

43. Elizabeth Piper, "Cyber Attack Hits 200,000 in at Least 150 Countries: Europol," *Reuters*, May 14, 2017, https://www.reuters.com/article/us-cyber-attack-europol/cyber-attack-hits-200000-in-at-least-150-countries-europol-idUSKCN18A0FX.

44. Tanmay Ganacharya, "WannaCrypt Ransomware Worm Targets Out-of-Date Systems," *Microsoft Security* (blog), May 12, 2017, https://www.microsoft.com/security/blog/2017/05/12/wannacrypt-ransomware-worm-targets-out-of-date-systems/.

45. Eric Geller, "NSA-Created Cyber Tool Spawns Global Attacks—and Victims Include Russia," *Politico*, May 12, 2017, https://www.politico.com/story/2017/05/12/nsa

-hacking-tools-hospital-ransomware-attacks-wannacryptor-238328;    "Cyber-Attack: Europol Says It Was Unprecedented in Scale," *BBC News*, May 13, 2017, https://www .bbc.com/news/world-europe-39907965.

46. Dan Goodin, "A New Ransomware Outbreak Similar to WCry Is Shutting Down Computers Worldwide," *Ars Technica*, June 27, 2017, https://arstechnica.com /information-technology/2017/06/a-new-ransomware-outbreak-similar-to-wcry-is -shutting-down-computers-worldwide/.

47. Andy Greenberg, "The Untold Story of NotPetya, the Most Devastating Cyber-attack in History," *Wired*, August 22, 2018, https://www.wired.com/story/notpetya -cyberattack-ukraine-russia-code-crashed-the-world/; Kaspersky Global Research and Analysis Team, "Schrodinger's Pet(ya)," *SecureList* (blog), June 27, 2017, https://securelist .com/schroedingers-petya/78870/.

48. Dan Goodin, "Tuesday's Massive Ransomware Outbreak Was, in Fact, Something Much Worse," *Ars Technica*, June 28, 2017, https://arstechnica.com/information -technology/2017/06/petya-outbreak-was-a-chaos-sowing-wiper-not-profit-seeking -ransomware/.

49. Nicole Perlroth, Mark Scott, and Sheera Frenkel, "Cyberattack Hits Ukraine Then Spreads Internationally," *New York Times*, June 27, 2017, https://www.nytimes .com/2017/06/27/technology/ransomware-hackers.html.

50. "Global Ransomware Attack Causes Turmoil," *BBC News*, June 28, 2017, https:// www.bbc.com/news/technology-40416611.

51. Andrew Griffin, "'Petya' Cyber Attack: Chernobyl's Radiation Monitoring System Hit by Worldwide Hack," *Independent*, June 27, 2017; Perlroth et al., "Cyberat-tack Hits Ukraine."

52. Dan Goodin, "How 'Omnipotent' Hackers Tied to NSA Hid for 14 Years—and Were Found at Last," *Ars Technica*, February 16, 2015, https://arstechnica.com/information -technology/2015/02/how-omnipotent-hackers-tied-to-the-nsa-hid-for-14-years-and-were -found-at-last/.

53. Scott Shane, Matt Apuzzo, and Jo Becker, "Trove of Stolen Data Is Said to In-clude Top-Secret U.S. Hacking Tools," *New York Times*, October 19, 2016, https://www .nytimes.com/2016/10/20/us/harold-martin-nsa.html; Goodin, "How 'Omnipotent' Hackers."

54. Matthew M. Aid, "Inside the NSA's Ultra-Secret China Hacking Group," *Foreign Policy*, June 10, 2013, https://foreignpolicy.com/2013/06/10/inside-the-nsas-ultra -secret-china-hacking-group/.

55. Aid, "Ultra-Secret China Hacking Group."

56. Sam Biddle, "The NSA Leak Is Real, Snowden Documents Confirm," *Intercept*, August 19, 2016, https://theintercept.com/2016/08/19/the-nsa-was-hacked-snowden-docu ments-confirm/.

57. Dan Goodin, "New Smoking Gun Further Ties NSA to Omnipotent 'Equation Group' Hackers," *Ars Technica*, March 11, 2015, https://arstechnica.com/information -technology/2015/03/new-smoking-gun-further-ties-nsa-to-omnipotent-equation -group-hackers/.

58. Goodin, "New Smoking Gun."

59. Goodin, "How 'Omnipotent' Hackers."

60. Scott Shane, Matthew Rosenberg, and Andrew W. Lehren, "WikiLeaks Releases Trove of Alleged C.I.A. Hacking Documents," *New York Times*, March 7, 2017, https://www.nytimes.com/2017/03/07/world/europe/wikileaks-cia-hacking.html.

61. "Vault 7: CIA Hacking Tools Revealed," wikileaks.org, last updated March 7, 2017, https://wikileaks.org/ciav7p1/.

62. Shane et al., "Alleged C.I.A. Hacking Documents"; "Vault 7: CIA Hacking Tools Revealed."

63. Shane et al., "Alleged C.I.A. Hacking Documents"; "Vault 7: CIA Hacking Tools Revealed."

64. Shane et al., "Alleged C.I.A. Hacking Documents"; "Vault 7: CIA Hacking Tools Revealed."

65. "Vault 7: CIA Hacking Tools Revealed."

66. "What Did Equation Do Wrong, and How Can We Avoid Doing the Same?" wikiLeaks.org, WikiLeaks, last accessed May 19, 2019, https://wikileaks.org/ciav7p1/cms/page_14588809.html.

67. Fyodor [pseud.], "Full Disclosure Mailing List," SecLists.Org Security Mailing List Archive, last accessed May 19, 2019, https://seclists.org/fulldisclosure/.

68. Fyodor [pseud.], "Bugtraq Mailing List," SecLists.Org Security Mailing List Archive, last accessed May 19, 2019, https://seclists.org/bugtraq/; Fyodor [pseud.], "Full Disclosure Mailing List."

69. Len Rose, "New Security Mailing List Full-Disclosure," OpenSuse, last updated July 11, 2002, https://lists.opensuse.org/opensuse-security/2002-07/msg00259.html.

70. Fyodor [pseud.], "Full Disclosure Mailing List."

71. Fyodor [pseud.], "Zardoz 'Security Digest,'" The 'Security Digest' Archives, last accessed May 19, 2019, http://securitydigest.org/zardoz/.

72. Neil Gorsuch, "Zardoz Security Mailing List Status," Zardoz Security Mailing List, last updated December 20, 1988, https://groups.google.com/forum/#!msg/news.groups/p5rpZNAe5UI/ccJEtbQzJ2YJ.

73. Suelette Dreyfus, *Underground: Tales of Hacking, Madness and Obsession on the Electronic Frontier* (Sydney: Random House Australia, 1997), http://underground-book.net/.

74. Levy, "Full Disclosure Is a Necessary Evil"; Marcus J. Ranum, "The Network Police Blotter," *Login* 25, no. 6 (2000): 46–49, https://www.usenix.org/publications/login/october-2000-volume-25-number-6/network-police-blotter.

75. Robert Graham, "Vuln Disclosure Is Rude," *Errata Security* (blog), April 21, 2010, https://blog.erratasec.com/2010/04/vuln-disclosure-is-rude.html.

76. Ashish Arora and Rahul Telang, "Economics of Software Vulnerability Disclosure," *IEEE Security & Privacy* 3, no. 1 (2005): 20–25, https://doi.org/10.1109/MSP.2005.12.

77. Robert O'Harrow Jr. and Ariana Eunjung Cha, "Computer Worm Highlights Hidden Perils of the Internet," *Washington Post*, January 28, 2003; David Litchfield, "David Litchfield Talks about the SQL Worm in the *Washington Post*," SecLists.Org Security Mailing List Archive, last updated January 29, 2003, https://seclists.org/fulldisclosure/2003/Jan/365.

78. Simon Richter, "Re: Announcing New Security Mailing List," SecLists.Org Security Mailing List Archive, last updated July 11, 2002, https://seclists.org/fulldisclosure/2002/Jul/7.

79. O'Harrow and Cha, "Computer Worm Highlights Hidden Perils of the Internet"; Litchfield, "David Litchfield Talks about the SQL Worm in the *Washington Post*"; John Leyden, "Slammer: Why Security Benefits from Proof of Concept Code," *Register*, February 6, 2003, https://www.theregister.co.uk/2003/02/06/slammer_why_security_benefits/.

80. "Responsible Vulnerability Disclosure Process," IETF Tools, IETF, last updated February 2002, https://tools.ietf.org/html/draft-christey-wysopal-vuln-disclosure-00; Jon Lasser, "Irresponsible Disclosure," *Security Focus*, June 26, 2002, https://www.securityfocus.com/columnists/91.

81. "Responsible Vulnerability Disclosure Process."

82. "Responsible Vulnerability Disclosure Process."

83. "Responsible Vulnerability Disclosure Process."

84. "Responsible Vulnerability Disclosure Process."

85. Rain Forest Puppy [pseud.], "Full Disclosure Policy (RFPolicy) v2.0," Packet Storm Security, last accessed May 20, 2019, https://dl.packetstormsecurity.net/papers/general/rfpolicy-2.0.txt.

86. Rain Forest Puppy [pseud.], "Full Disclosure Policy (RFPolicy) v2.0."

87. Leif Nixon, "Re: Qualys Security Advisory," Openwall, last updated July 23, 2015, https://www.openwall.com/lists/oss-security/2015/07/23/17; Lasser, "Irresponsible Disclosure."

88. Brad Spengler, "Hyenas of the Security Industry," SecLists.Org Security Mailing List Archive, last updated June 18, 2010, https://seclists.org/dailydave/2010/q2/58.

89. Spengler, "Hyenas of the Security Industry."

90. Chris Evans, Eric Grosse, Neel Mehta, Matt Moore, Tavis Ormandy, Julien Tinnes, and Michal Zalewski, "Rebooting Responsible Disclosure: A Focus on Protecting End Users," *Google Security* (blog), July 20, 2010, https://security.googleblog.com/2010/07/rebooting-responsible-disclosure-focus.html; Spengler, "Hyenas of the Security Industry."

91. Spengler, "Hyenas of the Security Industry."

92. Chris Evans, "Announcing Project Zero," *Google Security* (blog), July 15, 2014, https://security.googleblog.com/2014/07/announcing-project-zero.html.

93. Evans, "Announcing Project Zero."

94. "Vulnerabilities—Application Security—Google," Google Application Security, Google, last accessed May 20, 2019, https://www.google.com/about/appsecurity/research/; Carl Franzen, "Google Created a Team to Stop the Worst Attacks on the Internet," *Verge*, July 15, 2014, https://www.theverge.com/2014/7/15/5902061/google-project-zero-security-team; Evans, "Announcing Project Zero."

95. Dave Aitel, "Remember the Titans," SecLists.Org Security Mailing List Archive, last updated July 31, 2015, https://seclists.org/dailydave/2015/q3/9.

96. Steve Dent, "Google Posts Windows 8.1 Vulnerability before Microsoft Can Patch It," *Engadget*, January 2, 2015, https://www.engadget.com/2015/01/02/google-posts-unpatched-microsoft-bug/; Liam Tung, "Google's Project Zero Exposes Unpatched Windows 10 Lockdown Bypass," *ZDNet*, April 20, 2018, https://www.zdnet.com/article/googles-project-zero-reveals-windows-10-lockdown-bypass/; Tom Warren, "Google Discloses Microsoft Edge Security Flaw before a Patch Is Ready," *Verge*, February 19, 2019,

https://www.theverge.com/2018/2/19/17027138/google-microsoft-edge-security-flaw
-disclosure.

97. Dan Goodin, "Google Reports 'High-Severity' Bug in Edge/IE, No Patch Available," *Ars Technica*, February 27, 2017, https://arstechnica.com/information-technology
/2017/02/high-severity-vulnerability-in-edgeie-is-third-unpatched-msft-bug-this
-month/.

98. Russell Brandom, "Google Just Disclosed a Major Windows Bug—and Microsoft Isn't Happy," *Verge*, October 31, 2016, https://www.theverge.com/2016/10/31/13481502
/windows-vulnerability-sandbox-google-microsoft-disclosure.

99. Ben Grubb, "Revealed: How Google Engineer Neel Mehta Uncovered the Heartbleed Security Bug," *Sydney Morning Herald*, October 9, 2014, https://www.smh
.com.au/technology/revealed-how-google-engineer-neel-mehta-uncovered-the
-heartbleed-security-bug-20141009-113kff.html.

100. Paul Mutton, "Half a Million Widely Trusted Websites Vulnerable to Heartbleed Bug," *Netcraft*, last updated April 8, 2014, https://news.netcraft.com/archives/2014
/04/08/half-a-million-widely-trusted-websites-vulnerable-to-heartbleed-bug.html.

101. "The Heartbleed Bug," heartbleed.com, Synopsis, last accessed May 20, 2019, http://heartbleed.com/; Patrick McKenzie, "What Heartbleed Can Teach the OSS Community about Marketing," *Kalzumeus* (blog), April 9, 2014, https://www.kalzumeus.com
/2014/04/09/what-heartbleed-can-teach-the-oss-community-about-marketing/.

102. McKenzie, "What Heartbleed Can Teach the OSS Community about Marketing."

103. Pete Evans, "Heartbleed Bug: RCMP Asked Revenue Canada to Delay News of SIN Thefts," *Canadian Broadcasting Corporation*, April 14, 2014, https://www.cbc.ca
/news/business/heartbleed-bug-rcmp-asked-revenue-canada-to-delay-news-of-sin
-thefts-1.2609192.

104. Sam Frizell, "Report: Devastating Heartbleed Flaw Was Used in Hospital Hack," *Time*, August 20, 2014, http://time.com/3148773/report-devastating-heartbleed
-flaw-was-used-in-hospital-hack/.

105. Victor van der Veen, "Rampage and Guardion," rampageattack.com, last accessed May 20, 2019, http://rampageattack.com/; Richard Bejtlich, "Lies and More Lies," *TaoSecurity* (blog), January 22, 2018, https://taosecurity.blogspot.com/2018/01/lies-and
-more-lies.html; Nicole Perlroth, "Security Experts Expect 'Shellshock' Software Bug in Bash to Be Significant," *New York Times*, September 25, 2014, https://www.nytimes
.com/2014/09/26/technology/security-experts-expect-shellshock-software-bug-to-be
-significant.html.

106. Michael Riley, "NSA Said to Have Used Heartbleed Bug, Exposing Consumers," *Bloomberg*, April 11, 2014, https://www.bloomberg.com/news/articles/2014-04-11
/nsa-said-to-have-used-heartbleed-bug-exposing-consumers; Kim Zetter, "Has the NSA Been Using the Heartbleed Bug as an Internet Peephole?" *Wired*, April 10, 2014, https://www.wired.com/2014/04/nsa-heartbleed/.

107. Andrea O'Sullivan, "NSA 'Cyber Weapons' Leak Shows How Agency Prizes Online Surveillance over Online Security," *Reason*, August 30, 2016, https://reason
.com/2016/08/30/shadow-brokers-nsa-exploits-leak.

108. O'Sullivan, "NSA 'Cyber Weapons' Leak."

109. Herr et al., "Estimating Vulnerability Rediscovery."

110. Lillian Ablon and Andy Bogart, *Zero Days, Thousands of Nights* (Santa Monica, CA: RAND, 2017), https://www.rand.org/pubs/research_reports/RR1751.html.

111. Ablon and Bogart, *Zero Days*.

112. Ablon and Bogart, *Zero Days*.

113. Herr et al., "Estimating Vulnerability Rediscovery."

114. Ryan Hagemann, "The NSA and NIST: A Toxic Relationship," *Niskanen Center* (blog), February 9, 2016, https://niskanencenter.org/blog/the-nsa-and-nist-a-toxic -relationship/.

115. NSA/CSS (@NSAGov), "Statement: NSA Was Not Aware of the Recently Identified Heartbleed Vulnerability until It Was Made Public," Twitter, April 11, 2014, 1:39 p.m., https://twitter.com/NSAGov/status/454720059156754434.

116. Michael Daniel, "Heartbleed: Understanding When We Disclose Cyber Vulnerabilities," White House, last updated April 28, 2014, https://obamawhitehouse.archives .gov/blog/2014/04/28/heartbleed-understanding-when-we-disclose-cyber -vulnerabilities; David E. Sanger, "White House Details Thinking on Cybersecurity Flaws," *New York Times*, April 28, 2014, https://www.nytimes.com/2014/04/29/us/white -house-details-thinking-on-cybersecurity-gaps.html.

117. Daniel, "Heartbleed: Understanding When We Disclose Cyber Vulnerabilities."

118. United States Government, *Vulnerabilities Equities Policy and Process for the United States Government* (Washington, DC: United States Government, 2017), https:// www.whitehouse.gov/sites/whitehouse.gov/files/images/External%20-%20Unclassi- fied%20VEP%20Charter%20FINAL.PDF.

119. Ari Schwartz and Rob Knake, *Government's Role in Vulnerability Disclosure: Creating a Permanent and Accountable Vulnerability Equities Process* (Cambridge, MA: Belfer Center for Science and International Affairs, 2016), https://www.belfercenter.org /publication/governments-role-vulnerability-disclosure-creating-permanent-and -accountable; United States Government, *Vulnerabilities Equities Policy*.

120. United States Government, *Vulnerabilities Equities Policy*.

121. United States Government, *Vulnerabilities Equities Policy*.

122. Joseph Menn, "NSA Says How Often, Not When, It Discloses Software Flaws," *Reuters*, November 6, 2015, https://www.reuters.com/article/us-cybersecurity-nsa-flaws -insight/nsa-says-how-often-not-when-it-discloses-software-flaws-idUSKCN0SV2 XQ20151107.

123. Andrew Crocker, "It's No Secret that the Government Uses Zero Days for 'Offense,'" Electronic Frontier Foundation, November 9, 2015, https://www.eff.org/deeplinks /2015/11/its-no-secret-government-uses-zero-days-offense.

124. Dave Aitel and Matt Tait, "Everything You Know about the Vulnerability Equities Process Is Wrong," *Lawfare*, August 18, 2016, https://www.lawfareblog.com/everything -you-know-about-vulnerability-equities-process-wrong; Dave Aitel, "The Tech Does Not Support the VEP," *CyberSecPolitics* (blog), September 5, 2016, https://cybersecpolitics .blogspot.com/2016/09/the-tech-does-not-support-vep.html.

125. Rain Forest Puppy [pseud.], "Full Disclosure Policy (RFPolicy) v2.0."

126. L. Jean Camp and Catherine D. Wolfram, "Pricing Security: Vulnerabilities as Externalities," *Economics of Information Security* 12 (2004), https://ssrn.com/abstract =894966; Anon., "iDefense Paying $$$ for Vulns," SecLists.Org Security Mailing List Archive, last updated August 7, 2002, https://seclists.org/fulldisclosure/2002/Aug/168.

127. sdse [pseud.], "Re: 0-Day for Sale on eBay—New Auction!" SecLists.Org Security Mailing List Archive, last updated December 12, 2005, https://seclists.org/fulldisclosure /2005/Dec/523; Jericho [pseud.], "Selling Vulnerabilities: Going Once . . . ," *OSVDB* (blog), December 8, 2005, https://blog.osvdb.org/2005/12/08/selling-vulnerabilities-going-once/.

128. Charlie Miller, "The Legitimate Vulnerability Market: Inside the Secretive World of 0-Day Exploit Sales" (presentation, 6th Workshop on the Economics of Information Security, Pittsburgh, PA, June 7–8, 2007), https://www.econinfosec.org/archive /weis2007/papers/29.pdf.

129. Brad Stone, "A Lively Market, Legal and Not, for Software Bugs," *New York Times*, January 30, 2006, https://www.nytimes.com/2007/01/30/technology/30bugs .html.

130. Stone, "A Lively Market."

131. Stone, "A Lively Market."

132. Michael S. Mimoso, "The Pipe Dream of No More Free Bugs," *TechTarget*, May 2009, https://searchsecurity.techtarget.com/The-Pipe-Dream-of-No-More-Free -Bugs; Robert Lemos, "No More Bugs for Free, Researchers Say," *SecurityFocus*, March 24, 2009, https://www.securityfocus.com/brief/933.

133. Charles Miller, "Re: No More Free Bugs (and WOOT)," SecLists.Org Security Mailing List Archive, last updated April 8, 2009, https://seclists.org/dailydave/2009/q2 /22; Mimoso, "The Pipe Dream of No More Free Bugs."

134. Dave Shackleford, "No More Free Bugs? Is Bullshit," *ShackF00* (blog), May 14, 2009, http://daveshackleford.com/?p=187.

135. Shackleford, "No More Free Bugs?"

136. Joseph Menn, "Special Report: U.S. Cyberwar Strategy Stokes Fear of Blowback," *Reuters*, May 10, 2013, https://www.reuters.com/article/us-usa-cyberweapons -specialreport/special-report-u-s-cyberwar-strategy-stokes-fear-of-blowback -idUSBRE9490EL20130510.

137. Menn, "U.S. Cyberwar Strategy."

138. Andy Greenberg, "Meet the Hackers Who Sell Spies the Tools to Crack Your PC (and Get Paid Six-Figure Fees)," *Forbes*, March 21, 2012, https://www.forbes.com /sites/andygreenberg/2012/03/21/meet-the-hackers-who-sell-spies-the-tools-to-crack -your-pc-and-get-paid-six-figure-fees/#7efd4fc41f74.

139. Greenberg, "Meet the Hackers."

140. Greenberg, "Meet the Hackers."

141. Mattathias Schwartz, "Cyberwar for Sale," *New York Times*, January 4, 2017, https://www.nytimes.com/2017/01/04/magazine/cyberwar-for-sale.html.

142. Jack Tang, "A Look at the OpenType Font Manager Vulnerability from the Hacking Team Leak," *Trend Micro Security Intelligence Blog*, July 7, 2015, https://blog .trendmicro.com/trendlabs-security-intelligence/a-look-at-the-open-type-font-manager -vulnerability-from-the-hacking-team-leak/.

143. P. W. Singer and Allan Friedman, *Cybersecurity and Cyberwar: What Everyone Needs to Know* (Oxford: Oxford University Press, 2014), 221.

144. "The Underhanded C Contest," Underhanded C Contest, last accessed May 22, 2019, http://underhanded-c.org/.

145. Robert Lemos, "Zero-Day Sales Not 'Fair'—to Researchers," *SecurityFocus*, June 1, 2007, https://www.securityfocus.com/news/11468.

146. Nicole Perlroth and David E. Sanger, "Nations Buying as Hackers Sell Flaws in Computer Code," *New York Times*, July 13, 2013, https://www.nytimes.com/2013/07/14/world/europe/nations-buying-as-hackers-sell-computer-flaws.html.

147. Matthew J. Schwartz, "NSA Contracted with Zero-Day Vendor Vupen," *Dark Reading*, September 17, 2013, https://www.darkreading.com/risk-management/nsa-contracted-with-zero-day-vendor-vupen/d/d-id/1111564.

148. Menn, "U.S. Cyberwar Strategy."

149. Michael Mimoso, "US Navy Soliciting Zero Days," *Threatpost*, June 15, 2015, https://threatpost.com/us-navy-soliciting-zero-days/113308/.

150. Eric Lichtblau and Katie Benner, "F.B.I. Director Suggests Bill for iPhone Hacking Topped $1.3 Million," *New York Times*, April 21, 2016, https://www.nytimes.com/2016/04/22/us/politics/fbi-director-suggests-bill-for-iphone-hacking-was-1-3-million.html.

151. Dan Goodin, "Security Firm Pledges $1 Million Bounty for iOS Jailbreak Exploits," *Ars Technica*, September 21, 2015, https://arstechnica.com/information-technology/2015/09/security-firm-pledges-1-million-bounty-for-ios-jailbreak-exploits/.

152. "Zerodium iOS 9 Bounty," Zerodium, last accessed May 22, 2019, https://www.zerodium.com/ios9.html; Lorenzo Franceschi-Bicchierai, "Somebody Just Claimed a $1 Million Bounty for Hacking the iPhone," *Motherboard*, November 2, 2015, https://www.vice.com/en_us/article/yp3mx5/somebody-just-won-1-million-bounty-for-hacking-the-iphone; Menn, "NSA Says How Often."

153. David Kennedy, "Another Netscape Bug US$1K," *Risks Digest* 18, no. 14 (1996), https://catless.ncl.ac.uk/Risks/18/14; Jim Griffith, "Company Blackmails Netscape for Details of Browser Bug," *Risks Digest* 19, no. 22 (1997), https://catless.ncl.ac.uk/Risks/19/22; Dancho Danchev, "Black Market for Zero Day Vulnerabilities Still Thriving," *ZDNet*, November 2, 2008, https://www.zdnet.com/article/black-market-for-zero-day-vulnerabilities-still-thriving/.

154. Nicky Woolf, "Bounty Hunters Are Legally Hacking Apple and the Pentagon—for Big Money," *Guardian*, August 22, 2016, https://www.theguardian.com/technology/2016/aug/22/bounty-hunters-hacking-legally-money-security-apple-pentagon; Joe Uchill, "3 Firms to Split DOD's $34 Million Bug Bounty Program," *Axios*, October 24, 2018, https://www.axios.com/pentagon-dod-bug-bounty-program-2e9be488-7943-465e-9a31-1fcd4ef2007c.html.

155. Charlie Osborne, "HackerOne Raises $40 Million to Empower Hacking Community," *ZDNet*, February 8, 2017, https://www.zdnet.com/article/hackerone-raises-40-million-to-empower-hacking-community/.

156. Marten Mickos, "Why I Joined HackerOne as CEO," *HackerOne* (blog), November 11, 2015, https://www.hackerone.com/blog/marten-mickos-why-i-joined-hackerone-as-ceo.

157. Thomas Maillart, Mingyi Zhao, Jens Grossklags, and John Chuang, "Given Enough Eyeballs, All Bugs Are Shallow? Revisiting Eric Raymond with Bug Bounty Programs," *Journal of Cybersecurity* 3, no. 2 (2017), 81–90, https://doi.org/10.1093/cybsec/tyx008.

158. Maillart et al., "Given Enough Eyeballs."

159. Maillart et al., "Given Enough Eyeballs."

160. Maillart et al., "Given Enough Eyeballs."

161. Kim Zetter, "With Millions Paid in Hacker Bug Bounties, Is the Internet Any Safer?" *Wired*, November 8, 2012, https://www.wired.com/2012/11/bug-bounties/.

162. Darren Pauli, "Facebook Has Paid $4.3m to Bug-Hunters since 2011," *Register*, February 15, 2016, https://www.theregister.co.uk/2016/02/15/facebook_bug_bounty_totals/.

163. Trent Brunson, "On Bounties and Boffins," *Trail of Bits Blog*, January 14, 2019, https://blog.trailofbits.com/2019/01/14/on-bounties-and-boffins/.

164. Katie Moussouris, "The Wolves of Vuln Street—The First System Dynamics Model of the 0day Market," *HackerOne* (blog), April 14, 2015, https://www.hackerone.com/blog/the-wolves-of-vuln-street.

165. Matthew Finifter, Devdatta Akhawe, and David Wagner, "An Empirical Study of Vulnerability Rewards Programs" (presentation, 22nd USENIX Security Symposium, Washington, DC, August 14–16, 2014), https://www.usenix.org/conference/usenixsecurity13/technical-sessions/presentation/finifter; Dennis Groves, "Re: The Monetization of Information Insecurity," SecLists.Org Security Mailing List Archive, last updated September 9, 2014, https://seclists.org/dailydave/2014/q3/39.

166. Arkadiy Tetelman, "Bug Bounty, 2 Years In," *Twitter Engineering* (blog), May 27, 2016, https://blog.twitter.com/engineering/en_us/a/2016/bug-bounty-2-years-in.html; amitku [pseud.], "Bug Bounty, Two Years In," Hacker News, last updated, June 1, 2016, https://news.ycombinator.com/item?id=11816527; Finifter et al., "An Empirical Study of Vulnerability Rewards Programs."

167. Charles Morris, "Re: We're Now Paying up to $20,000 for Web Vulns in Our Services," SecLists.Org Security Mailing List Archive, last updated April 24, 2012, https://seclists.org/fulldisclosure/2012/Apr/295.

168. Erin Winick, "Life as a Bug Bounty Hunter: A Struggle Every Day, Just to Get Paid," *MIT Technology Review*, August 23, 2018.

169. Josh Armour, "VRP News from Nullcon," *Google Security Blog*, March 2, 2017, https://security.googleblog.com/2017/03/vrp-news-from-nullcon.html; Winick, "Bug Bounty Hunter."

170. Winick, "Bug Bounty Hunter"; Kim Zetter, "Portrait of a Full-Time Bug Hunter," *Wired*, November 8, 2012, https://www.wired.com/2012/11/bug-hunting/.

171. Wesley Wineberg, "Instagram's Million Dollar Bug," Exfiltrated, last updated December 27, 2015, http://www.exfiltrated.com/research-Instagram-RCE.php.

172. Alex Stamos, "Bug Bounty Ethics," *Facebook* (blog), December 17, 2015, https://www.facebook.com/notes/alex-stamos/bug-bounty-ethics/10153799951452929; infosecau [pseud.], "Instagram's Million Dollar Bug (Exfiltrated.com)," Hacker News, last updated December 17, 2015, https://news.ycombinator.com/item?id=10754194.

173. infosecau [pseud.], "Instagram's Million Dollar Bug."

174. Mike Isaac, Katie Benner, and Sheera Frenkel, "Uber Hid 2016 Breach, Paying Hackers to Delete Stolen Data," *New York Times*, November 21, 2017, https://www.nytimes.com/2017/11/21/technology/uber-hack.html; Eric Newcomer, "Uber Paid Hackers to Delete Stolen Data on 57 Million People," *Bloomberg*, November 21, 2017, https://www.bloomberg.com/news/articles/2017-11-21/uber-concealed-cyberattack-that-exposed-57-million-people-s-data.

175. Isaac et al., "Uber Hid 2016 Breach"; Newcomer, "Uber Paid Hackers."

176. Isaac et al., "Uber Hid 2016 Breach"; Newcomer, "Uber Paid Hackers."

177. Isaac et al., "Uber Hid 2016 Breach"; Newcomer, "Uber Paid Hackers."

178. Andy Greenberg, "Shopping for Zero-Days: A Price List for Hackers' Secret Software Exploits," *Forbes*, March 23, 2012, https://www.forbes.com/sites/andygreenberg/2012/03/23/shopping-for-zero-days-an-price-list-for-hackers-secret-software-exploits/#4e9995e32660.

179. Dave Aitel, "Junk Hacking Must Stop!" *Daily Dave* (blog), September 22, 2014, https://lists.immunityinc.com/pipermail/dailydave/2014-September/000746.html; valsmith [pseud.], "Let's Call Stunt Hacking What It Is, Media Whoring," *Carnal0wnage* (blog), May 16, 2015, http://carnal0wnage.attackresearch.com/2015/05/normal-0-false-false-false-en-us-x-none.html; Andrew Plato, "Enough with the Stunt Hacking," *Anitian* (blog), July 22, 2015, https://www.anitian.com/enough-with-the-stunt-hacking/; Mattias Geniar, "Stunt Hacking: The Sad State of Our Security Industry," *Mattias Geniar* (blog), August 3, 2015, https://ma.ttias.be/stunt-hacking/.

180. Aitel, "Junk Hacking Must Stop!"; valsmith [pseud.], "Stunt Hacking"; Plato, "Stunt Hacking"; Geniar, "Stunt Hacking."

181. Ken Munro, "Sinking Container Ships by Hacking Load Plan Software," *Pen Test Partners* (blog), November 16, 2017, https://www.pentestpartners.com/security-blog/sinking-container-ships-by-hacking-load-plan-software/; Rupert Neate, "Cybercrime on the High Seas: The New Threat Facing Billionaire Superyacht Owners," *Guardian*, May 5, 2017, https://www.theguardian.com/world/2017/may/05/cybercrime-billionaires-superyacht-owners-hacking; Yier Jin, Grant Hernandez, and Daniel Buentello, "Smart Nest Thermostat: A Smart Spy in Your Home" (presentation, Black Hat Briefings, Las Vegas, August 6–7, 2014), https://www.blackhat.com/us-14/archives.html#smart-nest-thermostat-a-smart-spy-in-your-home; Michael Kassner, "IBM X-Force Finds Multiple IoT Security Risks in Smart Buildings," *TechRepublic*, February 13, 2016, https://www.techrepublic.com/article/ibm-x-force-finds-multiple-iot-security-risks-in-smart-buildings/; Andy Greenberg, "This Radio Hacker Could Hijack Citywide Emergency Sirens to Play Any Sound," *Wired*, April 10, 2018, https://www.wired.com/story/this-radio-hacker-could-hijack-emergency-sirens-to-play-any-sound/; Jason Staggs, "Adventures in Attacking Wind Farm Control Networks" (presentation, Black Hat Briefings, Las Vegas, July 22–27, 2017), https://www.blackhat.com/us-17/briefings.html#adventures-in-attacking-wind-farm-control-networks; Oscar Williams-Grut, "Hackers Once Stole a Casino's High-Roller Database through a Thermometer in the Lobby Fish Tank," *Business Insider*, April 15, 2018, https://www.businessinsider.com/hackers-stole-a-casinos-database-through-a-thermometer-in-the-lobby-fish-tank-2018-4; Kashmir Hill, "Here's What It Looks Like When a 'Smart Toilet' Gets Hacked," *Forbes*, August 15, 2013, https://www.forbes.com/sites/kashmirhill/2013/08/15/heres-what-it-looks-like-when-a-smart-toilet-gets-hacked-video/.

182. Jerome Radcliffe, "Hacking Medical Devices for Fun and Insulin: Breaking the Human SCADA System" (presentation, Black Hat Briefings, Las Vegas, August 3–4, 2011), https://www.blackhat.com/html/bh-us-11/bh-us-11-archives.html.

183. Jordan Robertson, "McAfee Hacker Says Medtronic Insulin Pumps Vulnerable to Attack," *Bloomberg*, February 29, 2012, https://www.bloomberg.com/news/articles/2012-02-29/mcafee-hacker-says-medtronic-insulin-pumps-vulnerable-to-attack; Arundhati Parmar, "Hacker Shows Off Vulnerabilities of Wireless Insulin Pumps," *MedCity News*, March 1, 2012, https://medcitynews.com/2012/03/hacker-shows-off-vulnerabilities-of-wireless-insulin-pumps/.

184. Nick Bilton, "Disruptions: As New Targets for Hackers, Your Car and Your House," *New York Times*, August 11, 2013, https://bits.blogs.nytimes.com/2013/08/11/taking-over-cars-and-homes-remotely/.

185. Kevin Roose, "A Solution to Hackers? More Hackers," *New York Times*, August 2, 2017, https://www.nytimes.com/2017/08/02/technology/a-solution-to-hackers-more-hackers.html.

186. Aitel, "Junk Hacking Must Stop!"; valsmith [pseud.], "Stunt Hacking"; Plato, "Stunt Hacking"; Geniar, "Stunt Hacking."

187. Billy Rios and Jonathan Butts, "Understanding and Exploiting Implanted Medical Devices" (presentation, Black Hat Briefings, Las Vegas, August 4–9, 2019), https://www.blackhat.com/us-18/briefings/schedule/#understanding-and-exploiting-implanted-medical-devices-11733; Jason Staggs, "Adventures in Attacking Wind Farm Control Networks" (presentation, Black Hat Briefings, Las Vegas, July 22–27, 2017), https://www.blackhat.com/us-17/briefings.html#adventures-in-attacking-wind-farm-control-networks; Colin O'Flynn, "A Lightbulb Worm?" (presentation, Black Hat Briefings, Las Vegas, August 3–4, 2016), https://www.blackhat.com/us-16/briefings.html; Marina Krotofil, "Rocking the Pocket Book: Hacking Chemical Plant for Competition and Extortion" (presentation, Black Hat Briefings, Las Vegas, August 5–6, 2015), https://www.blackhat.com/us-15/briefings.html#rocking-the-pocket-book-hacking-chemical-plant-for-competition-and-extortion; Kyle Wilhoit and Stephen Hilt, "The Little Pump Gauge That Could: Attacks against Gas Pump Monitoring Systems" (presentation, Black Hat Briefings, Las Vegas, August 5–6, 2015), https://www.blackhat.com/us-15/briefings.html#the-little-pump-gauge-that-could-attacks-against-gas-pump-monitoring-systems.

188. Chris Roberts (@Sidragon1), "Find Myself on a 737/800, Lets See Box-IFE-ICE-SATCOM,? Shall We Start Playing with EICAS Messages? 'PASS OXYGEN ON' Anyone?:)," Twitter, April 15, 2015, 1:08 p.m., https://twitter.com/Sidragon1/status/588433855184375808.

189. Rob Price, "People Are Having Serious Doubts about the Security Researcher Who Allegedly Hacked a Plane," *Business Insider*, May 18, 2015, https://www.businessinsider.com/doubts-grow-fbi-claims-chris-roberts-hacked-plane-mid-flight-2015-5; Evan Perez, "FBI: Hacker Claimed to Have Taken Over Flight's Engine Controls," *CNN*, May 18, 2015, https://www.cnn.com/2015/05/17/us/fbi-hacker-flight-computer-systems/index.html.

190. Price, "Serious Doubts"; Perez, "FBI: Hacker Claimed."

191. Price, "Serious Doubts."

192. Price, "Serious Doubts."

193. Price, "Serious Doubts."

194. Dinei A. F. Florencio, Cormac Herley, and Adam Shostack, "FUD: A Plea for Intolerance," *Communications of the ACM* 57, no. 6 (2014): 31–33, https://doi.org/10.1145/2602323; A. J. Burns, M. Eric Johnson, and Peter Honeyman, "A Brief Chronology of Medical Device Security," *Communications of the ACM* 59, no. 10 (2016): 66–72, https://cacm.acm.org/magazines/2016/10/207766-a-brief-chronology-of-medical-device-security/fulltext.

195. Karl Koscher, Alexei Czeskis, Franziska Roesner, Shwetak Patel, Tadayoshi Kohno, and Stephen Checkoway, et al., "Experimental Security Analysis of a Modern Automobile" (presentation, IEEE Symposium on Security and Privacy, Berkeley/Oakland, CA, May 16–19, 2010), https://doi.org/10.1109/SP.2010.34.

196. James Mickens, "This World of Ours," *Login*, January, 2014, https://www.usenix.org/publications/login-logout/january-2014-login-logout/mickens.

197. Andrew Stewart, "On Risk: Perception and Direction," *Computers & Security* 23, no. 5 (2004): 362–370, https://doi.org/10.1016/j.cose.2004.05.003.

198. Roose, "A Solution to Hackers?"

199. Roger A. Grimes, "To Beat Hackers, You Have to Think like Them," *CSO Magazine*, June 7, 2011, https://www.csoonline.com/article/2622041/to-beat-hackers—you-have-to-think-like-them.html; Steve Zurier, "5 Ways to Think like a Hacker," *Dark Reading*, June 24, 2016, https://www.darkreading.com/vulnerabilities—threats/5-ways-to-think-like-a-hacker-/d/d-id/1326043; Tony Raval, "To Protect Your Company, Think like a Hacker," *Forbes*, October 30, 2018, https://www.forbes.com/sites/forbestechcouncil/2018/10/30/to-protect-your-company-think-like-a-hacker/.

200. David Siders, "Hack an Election? These Kids Will Try," *Politico*, July 19, 2018, https://www.politico.com/story/2018/07/19/election-hacking-kids-workshop-las-vegas-734115.

201. Brett Molina and Elizabeth Weise, "11-Year-Old Hacks Replica of Florida State Website, Changes Election Results," *USA Today*, August 13, 2018, https://www.usatoday.com/story/tech/nation-now/2018/08/13/11-year-old-hacks-replica-florida-election-site-changes-results/975121002/.

202. Adam Shostack, "Think like an Attacker?" *Adam Shostack & Friends* (blog), September 17, 2008, https://adam.shostack.org/blog/2008/09/think-like-an-attacker/.

203. Lilia Chang, "No, a Teen Did Not Hack a State Election," *Pro Publica*, August 24, 2018, https://www.propublica.org/article/defcon-teen-did-not-hack-a-state-election; Dave Aitel, "Re: Voting Village at Defcon," SecLists.Org Security Mailing List Archive, last updated August 25, 2018, https://seclists.org/dailydave/2018/q3/14.

## 8. Data Breaches, Nation-State Hacking, and Epistemic Closure

1. Benjamin Edwards, Steven Hofmeyr, and Stephanie Forrest, "Hype and Heavy Tails: A Closer Look at Data Breaches," *Journal of Cybersecurity* 2, no. 1 (2016): 3–14, https://doi.org/10.1093/cybsec/tyw003.

2. Lillian Ablon, Martin C. Libicki, and Andrea M. Abler, *Hackers' Bazaar: Markets for Cybercrime Tools and Stolen Data* (Santa Monica, CA: RAND, 2014); Alvaro Cardenas, Svetlana Radosavac, Jens Grossklags, John Chuang, and Chris Jay Hoofnagle, "An Economic Map of Cybercrime" (presentation, Research Conference on Communications, Information and Internet Policy, Arlington, VA, September 26–27, 2009), https://papers.ssrn.com/sol3/papers.cfm?abstract_id=1997795.

3. Trey Herr and Sasha Romanosky, "Cyber Crime: Security under Scarce Resources," *American Foreign Policy Council Defense Technology Program Brief* no. 11 (2015), https://papers.ssrn.com/sol3/papers.cfm?abstract_id=2622683.

4. Edwards et al., "Hype and Heavy Tails."

5. "Law Section," California Legislative Information, State of California, last updated 2016, https://leginfo.legislature.ca.gov/faces/codes_displaySection.xhtml?lawCode=CIV&sectionNum=1798.29.

6. Henry Fountain, "Worry. But Don't Stress Out," *New York Times*, June 26, 2005, https://www.nytimes.com/2005/06/26/weekinreview/worry-but-dont-stress-out.html; Steve Lohr, "Surging Losses, but Few Victims in Data Breaches," *New York Times*, September 27, 2006, https://www.nytimes.com/2006/09/27/technology/circuits/27lost.html.

7. Lillian Ablon, Paul Heaton, Diana Catherine Lavery, and Sasha Romanosky, *Consumer Attitudes toward Data Breach Notifications and Loss of Personal Information* (Santa Monica, CA: RAND, 2016), 2, https://www.rand.org/pubs/research_reports/RR1187.html.

8. Sasha Romanosky, Rahul Telang, and Alessandro Acquisti, "Do Data Breach Disclosure Laws Reduce Identity Theft?" *Journal of Policy Analysis and Management* 30, no. 2 (2011): 256–286, https://papers.ssrn.com/sol3/papers.cfm?abstract_id=1268926.

9. Ablon et al., "Consumer Attitudes," ix, 2–3.

10. Ablon et al., "Consumer Attitudes," ix, 2–3.

11. Ablon et al., "Consumer Attitudes," ix.

12. Ablon et al., "Consumer Attitudes," ix, 2–3.

13. Romanosky et al., "Data Breach Disclosure Laws."

14. Romanosky et al., "Data Breach Disclosure Laws."

15. Ross Kerber, "Banks Claim Credit Card Breach Affected 94 Million Accounts," *New York Times*, October 24, 2007, https://www.nytimes.com/2007/10/24/technology/24iht-hack.1.8029174.html.

16. Brad Stone, "3 Indicted in Theft of 130 Million Card Numbers," *New York Times*, August 17, 2009, https://www.nytimes.com/2009/08/18/technology/18card.html.

17. Jenn Abelson, "Hackers Stole 45.7 Million Credit Card Numbers from TJX," *New York Times*, March 29, 2007, https://www.nytimes.com/2007/03/29/business/worldbusiness/29iht-secure.1.5071252.html.

18. Brad Stone, "11 Charged in Theft of 41 Million Card Numbers," *New York Times*, August 5, 2008, https://www.nytimes.com/2008/08/06/business/06theft.html.

19. Stone, "11 Charged."

20. Stone, "11 Charged."

21. Stone, "11 Charged."

22. James Verini, "The Great Cyberheist," *New York Times*, November 10, 2010, https://www.nytimes.com/2010/11/14/magazine/14Hacker-t.html; Kim Zetter, "TJX

Hacker Was Awash in Cash; His Penniless Coder Faces Prison," *Wired*, June 18, 2019, https://www.wired.com/2009/06/watt/.

23. Verini, "The Great Cyberheist."

24. Verini, "The Great Cyberheist."

25. Verini, "The Great Cyberheist."

26. Verini, "The Great Cyberheist."

27. Verini, "The Great Cyberheist."

28. Verini, "The Great Cyberheist."

29. Associated Press, "20-Year Sentence in Theft of Card Numbers," *New York Times*, March 25, 2010, https://www.nytimes.com/2010/03/26/technology/26hacker.html.

30. Verini, "The Great Cyberheist."

31. Josephine Wolff, *You'll See This Message When It Is Too Late: The Legal and Economic Aftermath of Cybersecurity Breaches* (Cambridge, MA: MIT Press, 2018), 57.

32. Reed Abelson and Matthew Goldstein, "Anthem Hacking Points to Security Vulnerability of Health Care Industry," *New York Times*, February 5, 2015, https://www.nytimes.com/2015/02/06/business/experts-suspect-lax-security-left-anthem-vulnerable-to-hackers.html; Edwards et al., "Hype and Heavy Tails."

33. Sung J. Choi and M. Eric Johnson, "Do Hospital Data Breaches Reduce Patient Care Quality?" (presentation, 16th Workshop on the Economics of Information Security, La Jolla, CA, June 26–27, 2017).

34. Alex Hern, "Hackers Publish Private Photos from Cosmetic Surgery Clinic," *Guardian*, May 31, 2017, https://www.theguardian.com/technology/2017/may/31/hackers-publish-private-photos-cosmetic-surgery-clinic-bitcoin-ransom-payments.

35. Julie Hirschfeld Davis, "Hacking of Government Computers Exposed 21.5 Million People," *New York Times*, July 9, 2015, https://www.nytimes.com/2015/07/10/us/office-of-personnel-management-hackers-got-data-of-millions.html.

36. Office of Personnel Management, "Our Mission, Role & History," OPM.gov, last accessed May 28, 2019, https://www.opm.gov/about-us/our-mission-role-history/what-we-do/.

37. Office of Personnel Management, "Questionnaire for National Security Positions," OPM.gov, last updated November 2016, https://www.opm.gov/Forms/pdf_fill/sf86.pdf.

38. Office of Personnel Management, "Questionnaire for National Security Positions."

39. Office of Personnel Management, "Questionnaire for National Security Positions."

40. Office of Personnel Management, "Questionnaire for National Security Positions."

41. C-SPAN, "Office of Personnel Management Data Breach," c-span.org, last updated June 24, 2015, https://www.c-span.org/video/?326767-1/opm-director-katherine-archuleta-testimony-data-security-breach; David E. Sanger, Nicole Perlroth, and Michael D. Shear, "Attack Gave Chinese Hackers Privileged Access to U.S. Systems," *New York Times*, June 20, 2015, https://www.nytimes.com/2015/06/21/us/attack-gave-chinese-hackers-privileged-access-to-us-systems.html; David E. Sanger, Julie Hirschfeld Davis, and Nicole Perlroth, "U.S. Was Warned of System Open to Cyberattacks," *New York Times*, June 5, 2015, https://www.nytimes.com/2015/06/06/us/chinese-hackers-may-be-behind-anthem-premera-attacks.html.

42. Davis, "Hacking of Government Computers."

43. Everett Rosenfeld, "Office of Personnel Mgmt: 5.6M Estimated to Have Fingerprints Stolen in Breach," *CNBC*, September 23, 2015, https://www.cnbc.com/2015/09/23/office-of-personnel-mgmt-56m-estimated-to-have-fingerprints-stolen-in-breach.html.

44. Robert McMillan and Ryan Knutson, "Yahoo Triples Estimate of Breached Accounts to 3 Billion," *Wall Street Journal*, October 3, 2017, https://www.wsj.com/articles/yahoo-triples-estimate-of-breached-accounts-to-3-billion-1507062804; Nicole Perlroth, "All 3 Billion Yahoo Accounts Were Affected by 2013 Attack," *New York Times*, October 3, 2017, https://www.nytimes.com/2017/10/03/technology/yahoo-hack-3-billion-users.html.

45. Nicole Perlroth, "Yahoo Says Hackers Stole Data on 500 Million Users in 2014," *New York Times*, September 22, 2016, https://www.nytimes.com/2016/09/23/technology/yahoo-hackers.html; Elizabeth Weise, "Are You a Yahoo User? Do This Right Now," *USA Today*, September 22, 2016, https://www.usatoday.com/story/tech/news/2016/09/22/yahoo-breach-500-million-what-to-do/90849498/.

46. Perlroth, "Hackers Stole Data."

47. Ablon et al., "Consumer Attitudes," ix.

48. Romanosky et al., "Data Breach Disclosure Laws."

49. Fabio Bisogni, Hadi Asghari, and Michel J. G. van Eeten, "Estimating the Size of the Iceberg from Its Tip" (presentation, 16th Workshop on the Economics of Information Security, La Jolla, CA, June 26–27, 2017).

50. Sasha Romanosky, David A. Hoffman, and Alessandro Acquisti, "Empirical Analysis of Data Breach Litigation," *Journal of Empirical Legal Studies* 11, no. 1 (2014): 74–104, https://doi.org/10.1111/jels.12035.

51. Ablon et al., "Consumer Attitudes," 32.

52. Ablon et al., "Consumer Attitudes," 35–36.

53. Romanosky et al., "Empirical Analysis."

54. Ablon et al., "Consumer Attitudes," xii.

55. Choi and Johnson, "Hospital Data Breaches."

56. Adam Shostack, "The Breach Response Market Is Broken (and What Could Be Done)," *New School of Information Security* (blog), October 12, 2016, https://newschoolsecurity.com/2016/10/the-breach-response-market-is-broken-and-what-could-be-done/.

57. Wolff, *You'll See This Message*, 123–124.

58. Shostack, "Breach Response Market."

59. Jose Pagliery, "OPM Hack's Unprecedented Haul: 1.1 Million Fingerprints," *CNN*, July 10, 2015, https://money.cnn.com/2015/07/10/technology/opm-hack-fingerprints/.

60. jkouns [pseud.], "Having 'Fun' with the Data Set," DataLossDB, last updated September 25, 2009, https://blog.datalossdb.org/2009/09/25/having-fun-with-the-data-set/.

61. Mary Madden and Lee Rainie, *Americans' Attitudes about Privacy, Security and Surveillance* (Washington, DC: Pew Research Center, 2015), https://www.pewinternet.org/2015/05/20/americans-attitudes-about-privacy-security-and-surveillance/.

62. Ablon et al., "Consumer Attitudes," 41.

63. Stefan Laube and Rainer Bohme, "The Economics of Mandatory Security Breach Reporting to Authorities," *Journal of Cybersecurity* 2, no. 1 (2016): 29, https://doi.org/10.1093/cybsec/tyw002.

64. Laube and Bohme, "Mandatory Security Breach Reporting," 29.

65. Laube and Bohme, "Mandatory Security Breach Reporting," 29.

66. Wolff, *You'll See This Message*, 43.

67. Sebastien Gay, "Strategic News Bundling and Privacy Breach Disclosures," *Journal of Cybersecurity* 3, no. 2 (2017): 91–108, https://doi.org/10.1093/cybsec/tyx009.

68. Alessandro Acquisti, Allan Friedman, and Rahul Telang, "Is There a Cost to Privacy Breaches? An Event Study" (presentation, 27th International Conference on Information Systems, Milwaukee, December 10–13, 2006).

69. Surendranath R. Jory, Thanh N. Ngo, Daphne Wang, and Amrita Saha, "The Market Response to Corporate Scandals Involving CEOs," *Journal of Applied Economics* 47, no. 17 (2015): 1723–1738, https://doi.org/10.1080/00036846.2014.995361.

70. Gay, "Strategic News Bundling."

71. Gay, "Strategic News Bundling."

72. Gay, "Strategic News Bundling."

73. Dawn M. Cappelli, Andrew P. Moore, and Randall F. Trzeciak, *The CERT Guide to Insider Threats* (Boston: Addison-Wesley, 2012).

74. Annarita Giani, Vincent H. Berk, and George V. Cybenko, "Data Exfiltration and Covert Channels" (presentation, Defense and Security Symposium, Kissimmee, FL, 2006), https://doi.org/10.1117/12.670123.

75. Ravi Somaiya, "Chelsea Manning, Soldier Sentenced for Leaks, Will Write for the Guardian," *New York Times*, February 10, 2015, https://www.nytimes.com/2015/02/11/business/media/chelsea-manning-soldier-sentenced-for-leaks-will-write-for-the-guardian.html.

76. Somaiya, "Chelsea Manning."

77. Kim Zetter, "Jolt in WikiLeaks Case: Feds Found Manning-Assange Chat Logs on Laptop," *Wired*, December 19, 2011, https://www.wired.com/2011/12/manning-assange-laptop/.

78. Charlie Savage and Emmarie Huetteman, "Manning Sentenced to 35 Years for a Pivotal Leak of U.S. Files," *New York Times*, August 21, 2013, https://www.nytimes.com/2013/08/22/us/manning-sentenced-for-leaking-government-secrets.html.

79. Charlie Savage, "Chelsea Manning to Be Released Early as Obama Commutes Sentence," *New York Times*, January 17, 2017, https://www.nytimes.com/2017/01/17/us/politics/obama-commutes-bulk-of-chelsea-mannings-sentence.html.

80. Robert Mackey, "N.S.A. Whistle-Blower Revealed in Video," *New York Times*, June 10, 2013, https://thelede.blogs.nytimes.com/2013/06/10/n-s-a-whistle-blower-revealed-in-video/.

81. Mark Hosenball, "NSA Chief Says Snowden Leaked up to 200,000 Secret Documents," *Reuters*, November 14, 2013, https://www.reuters.com/article/us-usa-security-nsa/nsa-chief-says-snowden-leaked-up-to-200000-secret-documents-idUSBRE9AD19B20131114.

82. Mark Hosenball and Warren Strobel, "Exclusive: Snowden Persuaded Other NSA Workers to Give Up Passwords—Sources," *Reuters*, November 7, 2013, https://www.reuters.com/article/net-us-usa-security-snowden/exclusive-snowden-persuaded-other-nsa-workers-to-give-up-passwords-sources-idUSBRE9A703020131108.

83. William Knowles, "Former NSA Contractor, Edward Snowden, Now Former EC-Council (C|EH)," *InfoSec News*, July 5, 2013, https://seclists.org/isn/2013/Jul/19.

84. Onion, "Yahoo! Turns 25," onion.com, last updated January 18, 2019, https://www.theonion.com/yahoo-turns-25-1831869954.

85. Wolff, *You'll See This Message*, 225–226.

86. Wolff, *You'll See This Message*, 225–226.

87. Wolff, *You'll See This Message*, 225–226.

88. Wolff, *You'll See This Message*, 21.

89. Wolff, *You'll See This Message*, 269.

90. Wolff, *You'll See This Message*, 134–135.

91. Wolff, *You'll See This Message*, 270.

92. Wolff, *You'll See This Message*, 24.

93. David Drummond, "A New Approach to China," *Google* (blog), January 12, 2010, https://googleblog.blogspot.com/2010/01/new-approach-to-china.html.

94. Drummond, "A New Approach."

95. "Industries Targeted by the Hackers," *New York Times*, last updated February 18, 2013, https://archive.nytimes.com/www.nytimes.com/interactive/2013/02/18/business/Industries-Targeted-by-the-Hackers.html.

96. David E. Sanger, David Barboza, and Nicole Perlroth, "Chinese Army Unit Is Seen as Tied to Hacking against U.S.," *New York Times*, February 18, 2013, https://www.nytimes.com/2013/02/19/technology/chinas-army-is-seen-as-tied-to-hacking-against-us.html.

97. Riva Richmond, "Microsoft Plugs Security Hole Used in Attacks on Google," *New York Times*, January 21, 2010, https://bits.blogs.nytimes.com/2010/01/21/microsoft-plugs-security-hole-used-in-december-attacks/; Sanger et al., "Chinese Army Unit."

98. George Kurtz, "Operation 'Aurora' Hit Google, Others by George Kurtz," *McAfee Blog Central*, January 14, 2010, https://web.archive.org/web/20120911141122/http://blogs.mcafee.com/corporate/cto/operation-aurora-hit-google-others.

99. Sanger et al., "Chinese Army Unit"; Mandiant, *APT1: Exposing One of China's Cyber Espionage Units* (Alexandria, VA: Mandiant, 2013), 3.

100. Mandiant, *APT1*, 2.

101. Mandiant, *APT1*, 3.

102. Sanger et al., "Chinese Army Unit."

103. Sanger et al., "Chinese Army Unit."

104. Sanger et al., "Chinese Army Unit."

105. Mandiant, *APT1*.

106. Sanger et al., "Chinese Army Unit"; Meng Yan and Zhou Yong, "Annoying and Laughable 'Hacker Case,'" SecLists.Org Security Mailing List Archive, last updated February 25, 2013, https://seclists.org/isn/2013/Feb/52.

107. Sanger et al., "Chinese Army Unit."

108. Mandiant, *APT1*, 2.

109. Sanger et al., "Chinese Army Unit."

110. Mandiant, *APT1*, 2.

111. Michael S. Schmidt and David E. Sanger, "5 in China Army Face U.S. Charges of Cyberattacks," *New York Times*, May 19, 2014, https://www.nytimes.com/2014/05/20/us/us-to-charge-chinese-workers-with-cyberspying.html; David E. Sanger, "With Spy Charges, U.S. Draws a Line that Few Others Recognize," *New York*

*Times*, May 19, 2014, https://www.nytimes.com/2014/05/20/us/us-treads-fine-line-in-fighting-chinese-espionage.html.

112. Alexander Abad-Santos, "China Is Winning the Cyber War because They Hacked U.S. Plans for Real War," *Atlantic*, May 28, 2013, https://www.theatlantic.com/international/archive/2013/05/china-hackers-pentagon/314849/.

113. Eric Walsh, "China Hacked Sensitive U.S. Navy Undersea Warfare Plans: *Washington Post*," *Reuters*, June 8, 2018, https://www.reuters.com/article/us-usa-china-cyber/china-hacked-sensitive-u-s-navy-undersea-warfare-plans-washington-post-idUSKCN1J42MM.

114. Sam Sanders, "Massive Data Breach Puts 4 Million Federal Employees' Records at Risk," *National Public Radio*, June 4, 2015, https://www.npr.org/sections/thetwo-way/2015/06/04/412086068/massive-data-breach-puts-4-million-federal-employees-records-at-risk.

115. "China Unable to Recruit Hackers Fast Enough to Keep Up with Vulnerabilities in U.S. Security Systems," *Onion*, last updated October 26, 2015, https://www.theonion.com/china-unable-to-recruit-hackers-fast-enough-to-keep-up-1819578374.

116. Melissa Eddy, "Germany Says Hackers Infiltrated Main Government Network," *New York Times*, March 1, 2018, https://www.nytimes.com/2018/03/01/world/europe/germany-hackers.html.

117. FireEye, *APT28: A Window into Russia's Cyber Espionage Operations?* (Milpitas, CA: FireEye, 2014), 5, 27.

118. FireEye, *APT28*, 6.

119. Raphael Satter, Jeff Donn, and Justin Myers, "Digital Hit List Shows Russian Hacking Went Well beyond U.S. Elections," *Chicago Tribune*, November 2, 2017, https://www.chicagotribune.com/nation-world/ct-russian-hacking-20171102-story.html.

120. Satter et al., "Russian Hacking."

121. Satter et al., "Russian Hacking."

122. FireEye, *APT28*, 6.

123. Ralph Satter, "Russian Hackers," *Talking Points Memo*, May 8, 2018, https://talkingpointsmemo.com/news/russian-hackers-isis-militant-posers-military-wives-threat.

124. Satter, "Russian Hackers."

125. Henry Samuel, "Isil Hackers Seize Control of France's TV5Monde Network in 'Unprecedented' Attack," *Telegraph*, April 9, 2015, https://www.telegraph.co.uk/news/worldnews/europe/france/11525016/Isil-hackers-seize-control-of-Frances-TV5Monde-network-in-unprecedented-attack.html.

126. Samuel, "Isil Hackers."

127. Samuel, "Isil Hackers."

128. Sam Thielman and Spencer Ackerman, "Cozy Bear and Fancy Bear: Did Russians Hack Democratic Party and If So, Why?" *Guardian*, July 29, 2016, https://www.theguardian.com/technology/2016/jul/29/cozy-bear-fancy-bear-russia-hack-dnc.

129. Thielman and Ackerman, "Cozy Bear and Fancy Bear."

130. Louise Matsakis, "Hack Brief: Russian Hackers Release Apparent IOC Emails in Wake of Olympics Ban," *Wired*, October 1, 2018, https://www.wired.com/story

/russian-fancy-bears-hackers-release-apparent-ioc-emails/; Reuters/AFP, "WADA Hacked by Russian Cyber Espionage Group Fancy Bear, Agency Says," *ABC News* (Australian Broadcasting Corporation), September 13, 2016, https://www.abc.net.au/news/2016-09 -14/doping-wada-systems-hacked-by-russian-cyber-espionage-group/7842644.

131. Josh Meyer, "Russian Hackers Post 'Medical Files' of Simone Biles, Serena Williams," *NBC News*, September 14, 2016, https://www.nbcnews.com/storyline/2016-rio -summer-olympics/russian-hackers-post-medical-files-biles-serena-williams-n647571.

132. David E. Sanger and Nick Corasaniti, "D.N.C. Says Russian Hackers Penetrated Its Files, Including Dossier on Donald Trump," *New York Times*, June 14, 2016, https://www.nytimes.com/2016/06/15/us/politics/russian-hackers-dnc-trump.html.

133. Damien Gayle, "CIA Concludes Russia Interfered to Help Trump Win Election, Say Reports," *Guardian*, December 10, 2016, https://www.theguardian.com/us -news/2016/dec/10/cia-concludes-russia-interfered-to-help-trump-win-election-report.

134. Autumn Brewington, Mikhaila Fogel, Susan Hennessey, Matthew Kahn, Katherine Kelley, Shannon Togawa Mercer, Matt Tait et al., "Russia Indictment 2.0: What to Make of Mueller's Hacking Indictment," *LawFare* (blog), July 13, 2018, https://www .lawfareblog.com/russia-indictment-20-what-make-muellers-hacking-indictment.

135. Brewington et al., "Russia Indictment 2.0."

136. David E. Sanger and Charlie Savage, "U.S. Says Russia Directed Hacks to Influence Elections," *New York Times*, October 7, 2016, https://www.nytimes.com/2016/10 /08/us/politics/us-formally-accuses-russia-of-stealing-dnc-emails.html.

137. Sanger and Corasaniti, "Russian Hackers."

138. Sanger and Corasaniti, "Russian Hackers."

139. Brewington et al., "Russia Indictment 2.0."

140. Brewington et al., "Russia Indictment 2.0."

141. Brewington et al., "Russia Indictment 2.0."

142. *United States of America v. Viktor Borisovish Netyksho et al.*, https://www.justice .gov/file/1080281/download.

143. David E. Sanger, Jim Rutenberg, and Eric Lipton, "Tracing Guccifer 2.0's Many Tentacles in the 2016 Election," *New York Times*, July 15, 2018, https://www.nytimes.com /2018/07/15/us/politics/guccifer-russia-mueller.html; *United States of America v. Viktor Borisovish Netyksho et al.*

144. David A. Graham, "The Coincidence at the Heart of the Russia Hacking Scandal," *Atlantic*, July 13, 2018, https://www.theatlantic.com/politics/archive/2018/07 /russia-hacking-trump-mueller/565157/.

145. *United States of America v. Viktor Borisovish Netyksho et al.*

146. Eric Lipton and Scott Shane, "Democratic House Candidates Were Also Targets of Russian Hacking," *New York Times*, December 13, 2016, https://www.nytimes.com /2016/12/13/us/politics/house-democrats-hacking-dccc.html.

147. Matt Blaze, "NSA Revelations: The 'Middle Ground' Everyone Should Be Talking About," *Guardian*, January 6, 2014, https://www.theguardian.com/commentisfree/2014 /jan/06/nsa-tailored-access-operations-privacy.

148. Spiegel Staff, "Documents Reveal Top NSA Hacking Unit," *Spiegel Online*, December 29, 2013, https://www.spiegel.de/international/world/the-nsa-uses-powerful -toolbox-in-effort-to-spy-on-global-networks-a-940969-3.html.

149. "Deep Dive into QUANTUM INSERT," fox-it.com, Fox IT, last updated April 20, 2015, https://blog.fox-it.com/2015/04/20/deep-dive-into-quantum-insert/.

150. "Deep Dive into QUANTUM INSERT."

151. Spiegel Staff, "Top NSA Hacking Unit."

152. Dave Aitel, "It Was Always Worms (in My Heart!)," *CyberSecPolitics* (blog), July 5, 2017, https://cybersecpolitics.blogspot.com/2017/07/it-was-always-worms.html.

153. "NSA Phishing Tactics and Man in the Middle Attacks," *Intercept*, last updated March 12, 2014, https://theintercept.com/document/2014/03/12/nsa-phishing-tactics-man-middle-attacks/.

154. "NSA-Dokumente: So knackt der Geheimdienst Internetkonten," *Der Spiegel*, last updated December 30, 2013, https://www.spiegel.de/fotostrecke/nsa-dokumente-so-knackt-der-geheimdienst-internetkonten-fotostrecke-105326-12.html.

155. Ryan Gallagher, "The Inside Story of How British Spies Hacked Belgium's Largest Telco," *Intercept*, December 12, 2014, https://theintercept.com/2014/12/13/belgacom-hack-gchq-inside-story/.

156. Electronic Frontier Foundation, "CSEC SIGINT Cyber Discovery: Summary of the Current Effort," eff.org, last updated November 2010, https://www.eff.org/files/2015/01/23/20150117-speigel-csec_document_about_the_recognition_of_trojans_and_other_network_based_anomaly_.pdf; "NSA Phishing Tactics and Man in the Middle Attacks."

157. William J. Broad, John Markoff, and David E. Sanger, "Israeli Test on Worm Called Crucial in Iran Nuclear Delay," *New York Times*, January 15, 2011, https://www.nytimes.com/2011/01/16/world/middleeast/16stuxnet.html.

158. Kim Zetter, "How Digital Detectives Deciphered Stuxnet, the Most Menacing Malware in History," *Ars Technica*, July 11, 2011, https://arstechnica.com/tech-policy/2011/07/how-digital-detectives-deciphered-stuxnet-the-most-menacing-malware-in-history/; Thomas Rid, *Cyber War Will Not Take Place* (Oxford: Oxford University Press, 2017), 44.

159. Broad et al., "Israeli Test on Worm."

160. Eric Chien, "Stuxnet: A Breakthrough," *Symantec* (blog), November 12, 2010, https://www.symantec.com/connect/blogs/stuxnet-breakthrough.

161. Ralph Langner, "Stuxnet's Secret Twin," *Foreign Policy*, November 19, 2013, https://foreignpolicy.com/2013/11/19/stuxnets-secret-twin/.

162. Ralph Langner, "Stuxnet's Secret Twin."

163. Ralph Langner, "Stuxnet's Secret Twin."

164. Jonathan Fildes, "Stuxnet Worm 'Targeted High-Value Iranian Assets,'" *BBC News*, September 23, 2010, https://www.bbc.com/news/technology-11388018; Rid, *Cyber War*, 43.

165. Michael B. Kelley, "The Stuxnet Attack on Iran's Nuclear Plant Was 'Far More Dangerous' than Previously Thought," *Business Insider*, November 20, 2013, https://www.businessinsider.com/stuxnet-was-far-more-dangerous-than-previous-thought-2013-11.

166. Yossi Melman, "Iran Pauses Uranium Enrichment at Natanz Nuclear Plant," *Haaretz*, November 23, 2010, https://www.haaretz.com/1.5143485; John Markoff, "A Silent Attack, but Not a Subtle One," *New York Times*, September 26, 2010, https://www.nytimes.com/2010/09/27/technology/27virus.html.

167. John Markoff and David E. Sanger, "In a Computer Worm, a Possible Biblical Clue," *New York Times*, September 29, 2010, https://www.nytimes.com/2010/09/30/world /middleeast/30worm.html.

168. Ralph Langner, "Stuxnet's Secret Twin."

169. Broad et al., "Israeli Test on Worm."

170. Kim Zetter, "Blockbuster Worm Aimed for Infrastructure, but No Proof Iran Nukes Were Target," *Wired*, September 23, 2010, https://www.wired.com/2010/09 /stuxnet-2/.

171. Kim Zetter, "An Unprecedented Look at Stuxnet, the World's First Digital Weapon," *Wired*, November 3, 2014, https://www.wired.com/2014/11/countdown-to -zero-day-stuxnet/.

172. Nicolas Falliere, Liam O. Murchu, and Eric Chien, *W32.Stuxnet Dossier* (Mountain View, CA: Symantec, 2011).

173. Fildes, "Stuxnet Worm."

174. P. W. Singer and Allan Friedman, *Cybersecurity and Cyberwar: What Everyone Needs to Know* (Oxford: Oxford University Press, 2014), 115.

175. Zetter, "Most Menacing Malware."

176. Zetter, "Most Menacing Malware."

177. Jeffrey Carr, *Inside Cyber Warfare, Second Edition* (Sebastopol, CA: O'Reilly Media, 2012), 47.

178. Rid, *Cyber War*, 188.

179. Dave Aitel, "An Old Dailydave Post on Cyber Attribution, and Some Notes," *CyberSecPolitics* (blog), September 12, 2016, https://cybersecpolitics.blogspot.com/2016/09 /an-old-dailydave-post-on-cyber.html.

180. Michael Joseph Gross, "A Declaration of Cyber-War," *Vanity Fair*, March 2011, https://www.vanityfair.com/news/2011/03/stuxnet-201104; H. Rodgin Cohen and John Evangelakos, "America Isn't Ready for a 'Cyber 9/11,'" *Wall Street Journal*, July 11, 2017, https://www.wsj.com/articles/america-isnt-ready-for-a-cyber-9-11-1499811450; Jeff John Roberts, "What a Cyber 9/11 Would Mean for the U.S.," *Fortune*, July 20, 2018, http:// fortune.com/2018/07/20/us-cyber-security-russia-north-korea/; Kate Fazzini, "Power Outages, Bank Runs, Changed Financial Data: Here Are the 'Cyber 9/11' Scenarios that Really Worry the Experts," *CNBC*, November 18, 2018.

181. Singer and Friedman, *Cybersecurity and Cyberwar*, 132.

182. Rid, *Cyber War*, 12–14.

183. Raphael Satter, Jeff Donn, and Justin Myers, "Digital Hit List," *Chicago Tribune*, May 29, 2019, https://www.chicagotribune.com/nation-world/ct-russian-hacking-20171102 -story.html.

184. Singer and Friedman, *Cybersecurity and Cyberwar*, 56.

185. Matthew M. Aid, "Inside the NSA's Ultra-Secret China Hacking Group," *Foreign Policy*, June 10, 2013, https://foreignpolicy.com/2013/06/10/inside-the-nsas-ultra -secret-china-hacking-group/.

186. Thielman and Ackerman, "Cozy Bear and Fancy Bear"; FireEye, *APT28*, 5.

187. FireEye, *APT28*, 5.

188. Singer and Friedman, *Cybersecurity and Cyberwar*, 94.

189. Singer and Friedman, *Cybersecurity and Cyberwar*, 189.

190. David E. Sanger and Nicole Perlroth, "Hackers from China Resume Attacks on U.S. Targets," *New York Times*, May 19, 2013, https://www.nytimes.com/2013/05/20/world/asia/chinese-hackers-resume-attacks-on-us-targets.html.

191. Julian Sanchez, "Frum, Cocktail Parties, and the Threat of Doubt," *Julian Sanchez* (blog), March 26, 2010, http://www.juliansanchez.com/2010/03/26/frum-cocktail-parties-and-the-threat-of-doubt/; Patricia Cohen, "'Epistemic Closure'? Those Are Fighting Words," *New York Times*, April 27, 2010, https://www.nytimes.com/2010/04/28/books/28conserv.html.

192. Sanchez, "Cocktail Parties."

193. Barnaby Jack, "Jackpotting Automated Teller Machines Redux" (presentation, Black Hat Briefings, Las Vegas, July 28–29, 2010), https://www.blackhat.com/html/bh-us-10/bh-us-10-archives.html#Jack; Kim Zetter, "Researcher Demonstrates ATM 'Jackpotting' at Black Hat Conference," *Wired*, August 28, 2010, https://www.wired.com/2010/07/atms-jackpotted/; William Alexander, "Barnaby Jack Could Hack Your Pacemaker and Make Your Heart Explode," *Vice*, June 25, 2013, https://www.vice.com/en_us/article/avnx5j/i-worked-out-how-to-remotely-weaponise-a-pacemaker.

194. Paul Karger and Roger R. Schell, *Multics Security Evaluation: Vulnerability Analysis* (Bedford, MA: Electronic Systems Division, Air Force Systems Command, United States Air Force, 1974), 51.

195. Karger and Schell, *Multics Security Evaluation*, 51.

196. Tom van Vleck, "How the Air Force Cracked Multics Security," Multicians, last updated October 14, 2002, https://www.multicians.org/security.html.

197. Van Vleck, "How the Air Force Cracked Multics Security."

198. Virginia Gold, "ACM's Turing Award Prize Raised to $250,000; Google Joins Intel to Provide Increased Funding for Most Significant Award in Computing," Association for Computing Machinery, last updated July 26, 2007, https://web.archive.org/web/20081230233653/http://www.acm.org/press-room/news-releases-2007/turing award/.

199. Ken Thompson, "Reflections on Trusting Trust," *Communications of the ACM* 27, no. 8 (1984): 761–763, https://doi.org/10.1145/358198.358210.

200. Thompson, "Reflections on Trusting Trust."

201. Thompson, "Reflections on Trusting Trust."

202. Thompson, "Reflections on Trusting Trust."

203. Jonathan Thornburg, "Backdoor in Microsoft Web Server," sci.crypt, April 18, 2000, https://groups.google.com/forum/#!msg/sci.crypt/PybcCHi9u6s/b-7U1y9Q BZMJ.

204. Vahab Pournaghshband, "Teaching the Security Mindset to CS 1 Students" (presentation, 44th ACM Technical Symposium on Computer Science Education, Denver, March 6–9, 2013), https://doi.org/10.1145/2445196.2445299.

205. Ivan Arce and Gary McGraw, "Guest Editors' Introduction: Why Attacking Systems Is a Good Idea," *IEEE Security & Privacy* 2, no. 4 (2004): 17–19, https://doi.org/10.1109/MSP.2004.46.

206. Arce and McGraw, "Guest Editors' Introduction."

207. Dan Goodin, "Meet badBIOS, the Mysterious Mac and PC Malware that Jumps Airgaps," *Ars Technica*, October 31, 2013, https://arstechnica.com/information

-technology/2013/10/meet-badbios-the-mysterious-mac-and-pc-malware-that-jumps
-airgaps/.

208. Goodin, "Meet badBIOS."

209. Goodin, "Meet badBIOS."

210. Goodin, "Meet badBIOS."

211. Goodin, "Meet badBIOS."

212. Goodin, "Meet badBIOS."

213. The Dark Tangent [pseud.] (@thedarktangent), "RT @alexstamos: Everybody in Security Needs to Follow @dragosr and Watch His Analysis of #badBIOS <- No Joke It's Really Serious," Twitter, October 25, 2013, 11:15 p.m., https://twitter.com/thedarktangent/status/393984201151627264; Goodin, "Meet badBIOS."

214. Roger A. Grimes, "4 Reasons BadBIOS Isn't Real," *CSO Magazine*, November 12, 2013, https://www.csoonline.com/article/2609622/4-reasons-badbios-isn-t-real.html; Roger A. Grimes, "NSA's Backdoors Are Real—but Prove Nothing about Bad-BIOS," *CSO Magazine*, January 14, 2014, https://www.csoonline.com/article/2609678/nsa-s-backdoors-are-real—-but-prove-nothing-about-badbios.html.

215. Roger A. Grimes, "New NSA Hack Raises the Specter of BadBIOS," *CSO Magazine*, March 3, 2015, https://www.csoonline.com/article/2891692/does-the-latest-nsa-hack-prove-badbios-was-real.html.

216. Frédéric Bastiat, "That Which Is Seen, and That Which Is Not Seen," bestiat.org, last accessed June 1, 2019, http://bastiat.org/en/twisatwins.html.

217. Jim Finkle and Dan Burns, "St. Jude Stock Shorted on Heart Device Hacking Fears: Shares Drop," *Reuters*, August 25, 2016, https://www.reuters.com/article/us-stjude-cyber-idUSKCN1101YV.

218. Michael Riley and Jordan Robertson, "In an Unorthodox Move, Hacking Firm Teams Up with Short Sellers," *Bloomberg*, August 25, 2016, https://www.bloombergquint.com/onweb/in-an-unorthodox-move-hacking-firm-teams-up-with-short-sellers.

219. Riley and Robertson, "Short Sellers."

220. Jordan Robertson and Michael Riley, "Carson Block's Attack on St. Jude Reveals a New Front in Hacking for Profit," *Bloomberg*, August 25, 2016, https://www.bloomberg.com/news/articles/2016-08-25/in-an-unorthodox-move-hacking-firm-teams-up-with-short-sellers.

221. Robertson and Riley, "Carson Block's Attack."

222. Muddy Waters Research, "MW Is Short St. Jude Medical (STJ:US)," muddywatersresearch.com, last updated August 25, 2016, https://www.muddywatersresearch.com/research/stj/mw-is-short-stj/.

223. "MedSec CEO Responds to Carson Block's St. Jude Comments," *Bloomberg*, last updated August 25, 2016, https://www.bloomberg.com/news/videos/2016-08-25/medsec-ceo-responds-to-carson-block-s-st-jude-medical-comments.

224. *St. Jude Medical, Inc., vs. Muddy Waters Consulting et al.*, https://regmedia.co.uk/2016/09/08/medsec_lawsuit.pdf.

225. Jim Finkle and Dan Burns, "St. Jude Stock Shorted on Heart Device Hacking Fears: Shares Drop," *Reuters*, August 25, 2016, https://www.reuters.com/article/us-stjude-cyber-idUSKCN1101YV.

226. Sean Gallagher, "Trading in Stock of Medical Device Paused after Hackers Team with Short Seller," *Ars Technica*, August 26, 2016, https://arstechnica.com/information-technology/2016/08/trading-in-stock-of-medical-device-paused-after-hackers-team-with-short-seller/.

227. University of Michigan, "Holes Found in Report on St. Jude Medical Device Security," University of Michigan News, last updated August 30, 2016, https://news.umich.edu/holes-found-in-report-on-st-jude-medical-device-security/.

228. University of Michigan, "Holes Found in Report on St. Jude Medical Device Security."

229. Muddy Waters Research, "MW Is Short St. Jude Medical."

230. University of Michigan, "Holes Found in Report on St. Jude Medical Device Security."

231. University of Michigan, "Holes Found in Report on St. Jude Medical Device Security."

232. *St. Jude Medical, Inc., vs. Muddy Waters Consulting et al.*

233. *St. Jude Medical, Inc., vs. Muddy Waters Consulting et al.*

234. Michael Erman, "Abbott Releases New Round of Cyber Updates for St. Jude Pacemakers," *Reuters*, August 28, 2017, https://www.reuters.com/article/us-abbott-cyber-idUSKCN1B921V.

## 9. The Wicked Nature of Information Security

1. Horst W. J. Rittel and Melvin M. Webber, "Dilemmas in a General Theory of Planning," *Policy Sciences* 4, no. 2 (1973): 155–169, https://doi.org/10.1007/BF01405730.

2. Rittel and Webber, "Dilemmas."

3. Rittel and Webber, "Dilemmas."

4. Rittel and Webber, "Dilemmas."

5. Rittel and Webber, "Dilemmas."

6. Rittel and Webber, "Dilemmas."

7. Simson L. Garfinkel, "The Cyber Security Mess," simson.net, last updated December 14, 2016, http://simson.net/ref/2016/2016-12-14_Cybersecurity.pdf.

8. Ben Laurie and Abe Singer, "Choose the Red Pill and the Blue Pill: A Position Paper" (presentation, 2008 New Security Paradigms Workshop, Lake Tahoe, CA, September 22–25, 2008), https://doi.org/10.1145/1595676.1595695; Shari Pfleeger and Robert Cunningham, "Why Measuring Security Is Hard," *IEEE Security & Privacy* 8, no. 4 (2010): 46–54, https://doi.org/10.1109/MSP.2010.60.

9. Andrew Stewart, "A Utilitarian Re-Examination of Enterprise-Scale Information Security Management," *Information and Computer Security* 26, no. 1 (2018), https://doi.org/10.1108/ICS-03-2017-0012.

10. Cormac Herley, "Unfalsifiability of Security Claims," *Proceedings of the National Academy of Sciences* 113, no. 23 (2016): 6415–6420, https://doi.org/10.1073/pnas.1517797113; Cormac Herley and P. C. van Oorschot, "SoK: Science, Security and the Elusive Goal of Security as a Scientific Pursuit" (presentation, IEEE Symposium on Security and Privacy, San Jose, CA, May 22–26, 2017), http://dx.doi.org/10.1109/SP.2017.38.

11. Herley, "Unfalsifiability of Security Claims"; Herley and van Oorschot, "Elusive Goal."

12. Herley, "Unfalsifiability of Security Claims"; Herley and van Oorschot, "Elusive Goal"; Pfleeger and Cunningham, "Measuring Security."

13. Herley, "Unfalsifiability of Security Claims"; Herley and van Oorschot, "Elusive Goal."

14. Herley, "Unfalsifiability of Security Claims"; Herley and van Oorschot, "Elusive Goal."

15. Herley, "Justifying Security Measures—A Position Paper" (presentation, 22nd European Symposium on Research in Computer Security, Oslo, September 11–15, 2017), https://cormac.herley.org/docs/justifyingSecurityMeasures.pdf.

16. Herley, "Unfalsifiability of Security Claims"; Herley and van Oorschot, "Elusive Goal."

17. Herley, "Unfalsifiability of Security Claims"; Herley and van Oorschot, "Elusive Goal."

18. Herley, "Unfalsifiability of Security Claims"; Herley and van Oorschot, "Elusive Goal."

19. Herley, "Unfalsifiability of Security Claims"; Herley and van Oorschot, "Elusive Goal."

20. National Institute of Standards and Technology, *Security and Privacy Controls for Information Systems and Organizations* (Gaithersburg, MD: NIST, 2017), https://csrc.nist.gov/publications/detail/sp/800-53/rev-5/draft.

21. P. W. Singer and Allan Friedman, *Cybersecurity and Cyberwar: What Everyone Needs to Know* (Oxford: Oxford University Press, 2014), 80–81.

22. Singer and Friedman, *Cybersecurity and Cyberwar.*

23. RSA Security, "RSA Conference 2018 Closes 27th Year Bringing Top Information Security Experts Together to Debate Critical Cybersecurity Issues," RSA Conference, last updated April 20, 2018, https://www.rsaconference.com/press/89/rsa-conference-2018-closes-27th-year-bringing-top.

24. Greg Otto, "RSA Conference App Leaks User Data," *Cyberscoop*, April 20, 2018, https://www.cyberscoop.com/2018-rsa-conference-app-leaks-user-data/.

25. Gunter Ollmann, "Beware Your RSA Mobile App Download," IOActive, last updated February 27, 2014, https://ioactive.com/beware-your-rsa-mobile-app-download/.

26. Ollmann, "Beware Your RSA Mobile App Download."

27. "Security Compromised at Security Companies—During Cyber Security Month," *Fox News*, October 8, 2013, https://www.foxnews.com/tech/security-compromised-at-security-companies-during-cyber-security-month.

28. Peter J. Denning, interview by Jeffrey R. Yost, *Charles Babbage Institute*, April 10, 2013, 67–68, http://hdl.handle.net/11299/156515.

29. Denning, interview by Yost, 67–68.

30. Adam Shostack and Andrew Stewart, *The New School of Information Security* (Upper Saddle River, NJ: Addison-Wesley, 2008), 107.

31. Ben Rothke and Anton Chuvakin, "PCI Shrugged: Debunking Criticisms of PCI DSS," *CSO Magazine*, April 16, 2009, https://www.csoonline.com/article/2123972/pci-shrugged—debunking-criticisms-of-pci-dss.html.

32. PCI Security Standards Council, "Securing the Future of Payments Together," Official PCI Security Standards Council Site, last accessed July 14, 2019, https://www .pcisecuritystandards.org/.

33. Klaus Julish, "Security Compliance: The Next Frontier in Security Research" (presentation, New Security Paradigms Workshop, Lake Tahoe, CA, September 22–25, 2008), https://doi.org/10.1145/1595676.1595687.

34. Andrew Stewart, "A Utilitarian Re-Examination of Enterprise-Scale Information Security Management," *Information and Computer Security* 26, no. 1 (2018), https:// doi.org/10.1108/ICS-03-2017-0012.

35. Stewart, "A Utilitarian Re-Examination."

36. Stewart, "A Utilitarian Re-Examination."

37. Stewart, "A Utilitarian Re-Examination."

38. "By Organization Name," Making Security Measurable, MITRE Corporation, last accessed July 14, 2019, http://makingsecuritymeasurable.mitre.org/directory /organizations/index.html.

39. "Common Weakness Enumeration (CWE)," The Bugs Framework, National Institute of Standards and Technology, last accessed July 14, 2019, https://samate.nist .gov/BF/Enlightenment/CWE.html.

40. "Common Vulnerability Scoring System SIG," first.org, Global Forum of Incident Response and Security Teams, last accessed July 17, 2019, https://www.first.org/cvss/.

41. Marcus Ranum, "The Six Dumbest Ideas in Computer Security" ranum.com, last accessed July 14, 2019, https://www.ranum.com/security/computer_security/editorials /dumb/.

42. Ranum, "The Six Dumbest Ideas in Computer Security."

43. Andrew Stewart, "On Risk: Perception and Direction," *Computers & Security* 23, no. 5 (2004): 362–370, https://doi.org/10.1016/j.cose.2004.05.003.

44. Stewart, "On Risk."

45. Vilhelm Verendel, *A Prospect Theory Approach to Security* (Gothenburg, Sweden: Gothenburg University, 2008); National Institute of Standards and Technology, *Framework for Improving Critical Infrastructure Cybersecurity* (Gaithersburg, MD: NIST, April 16, 2018), https://www.nist.gov/cyberframework/framework.

46. Marc Donner, "Insecurity through Obscurity," *IEEE Security & Privacy* 4, no. 5 (2006), https://doi.ieeecomputersociety.org/10.1109/MSP.2006.123; Stewart, "On Risk."

47. Shostack and Stewart, *The New School.*

48. Shostack and Stewart, *The New School.*

49. Adam Shostack, "The Breach Response Market Is Broken (and What Could Be Done)," *New School of Information Security* (blog), October 12, 2016, https:// newschoolsecurity.com/2016/10/the-breach-response-market-is-broken-and-what -could-be-done/.

50. Dinei A. F. Florencio, Cormac Herley, and Adam Shostack, "FUD: A Plea for Intolerance," *Communications of the ACM* 57, no. 6 (2014): 31–33, https://doi.org/10.1145 /2602323.

51. Tyler Moore and Ross Anderson, *Economics and Internet Security: A Survey of Recent Analytical, Empirical, and Behavioral Research* (Cambridge, MA: Harvard University, 2011), 7, http://nrs.harvard.edu/urn-3:HUL.InstRepos:23574266.

52. Tyler Moore, Richard Clayton, and Ross Anderson, "The Economics of Online Crime," *Journal of Economic Perspectives* 23, no. 3 (2009): 3–20, https://www.aeaweb.org/articles?id=10.1257/jep.23.3.3; Ross Anderson, Rainer Bohme, Richard Clayton, and Tyler Moore, *Security Economics and the Internal Market* (n.p.: European Network and Information Security Agency, 2008), https://www.enisa.europa.eu/publications/archive/economics-sec/; Dan Barrett, "Abuse of Statistics about Computer Crime," *Risks Digest* 18, no. 4 (1996), https://catless.ncl.ac.uk/Risks/18/04; "Errata—Statistics," attrition.org, last updated 2011, http://attrition.org/errata/statistics/index.html.

53. Julie J. C. H. Ryan and Theresa I. Jefferson, "The Use, Misuse, and Abuse of Statistics in Information Security Research" (presentation, American Society for Engineering Management, Saint Louis, MO, October 15–18, 2003), http://citeseerx.ist.psu.edu/viewdoc/summary?doi=10.1.1.203.5387.

54. Dinei Florencio and Cormac Herley, "Sex, Lies, and Cyber-Crime Surveys," in *Economics of Information Security and Privacy III*, ed. Bruce Schneier (New York: Springer, 2013), https://doi.org/10.1007/978-1-4614-1981-5_3.

55. Florencio and Herley, "Cyber-Crime Surveys."

56. Florencio and Herley, "Cyber-Crime Surveys."

57. Ryan and Jefferson, "Misuse and Abuse."

58. James P. Anderson, *Computer Security Technology Planning Study* (Bedford, MA: Electronic Systems Division, Air Force Systems Command, United States Air Force, 1972).

59. George F. Jelen, *Information Security: An Elusive Goal* (Cambridge, MA: Harvard University, 1995), III-32.

60. Jelen, *An Elusive Goal*, III-32.

61. Peter G. Neumann, "Computer Insecurity," *Issues in Science and Technology* 11, no. 1 (1994): 50–54, https://www.jstor.org/stable/43310933; Garfinkel, "The Cyber Security Mess," 27.

62. Bob Blakley, "The Emperor's Old Armor" (presentation, New Security Paradigms Workshop, Lake Arrowhead, CA, September 17–20, 1996), https://doi.org/10.1145/304851.304855.

63. Butler W. Lampson, "Computer Security in the Real World," *Computer* 37, no. 6 (2004): 37–47, https://doi.org/10.1109/MC.2004.17.

64. David E. Bell, "Looking Back at the Bell-LaPadula Model" (presentation, 21st Annual Computer Security Applications Conference, Tucson, December 5–9, 2005), https://doi.org/10.1109/CSAC.2005.37.

65. Federico Biancuzzi, "Interview with Marcus Ranum," *SecurityFocus*, June 21, 2005, https://www.securityfocus.com/columnists/334.

66. Butler Lampson, "Usable Security: How to Get It," *Communications of the ACM* 52, no. 11 (2009): 25–27, https://doi.org/10.1145/1592761.1592773.

67. "Computer Security Is Broken from Top to Bottom," *Economist*, April 8, 2017, https://www.economist.com/science-and-technology/2017/04/08/computer-security-is-broken-from-top-to-bottom; Angus Loten, "NSA Cyber Chief Says Companies Are Losing Ground against Adversaries," *Wall Street Journal*, December 11, 2018, https://www.wsj.com/articles/nsa-cyber-chief-says-companies-are-losing-ground-against-adversaries-11544548614.

68. John D. McLean, "On the Science of Security," *IEEE Security & Privacy* 16, no. 3 (2018): 6–10, https://doi.ieeecomputersociety.org/10.1109/MSP.2018.2701158.

69. Jelen, *An Elusive Goal*, IV-60.

70. Shari Lawrence Pfleeger, "Learning from Other Disciplines," *IEEE Security & Privacy* 13, no. 4 (2015): 10–11, https://doi.ieeecomputersociety.org/10.1109/MSP.2015.81.

71. Jan Romein, *De dialectiek van de vooruitgang* (n.p., 1937).

72. Steven M. Bellovin, "Security as a Systems Property," *IEEE Security & Privacy* 7, no. 5 (2009): 88, https://doi.org/10.1109/MSP.2009.134.

73. Steven M. Bellovin, "Security Is a System Property," *SMBlog* (blog), September 1, 2017, https://www.cs.columbia.edu/~smb/blog//2017-09/2017-09-01.html.

74. Alex Abella, *Soldiers of Reason: The RAND Corporation and the Rise of the American Empire* (Boston: Mariner Books, 2009).

75. Malcolm W. Hoag, *An Introduction to Systems Analysis* (Santa Monica, CA: RAND Corporation, 1956), https://www.rand.org/pubs/research_memoranda/RM1678.html; Jack Stockfisch, *The Intellectual Foundations of Systems Analysis* (Santa Monica, CA: RAND Corporation, 1987), https://www.rand.org/pubs/papers/P7401.html.

76. Stockfisch, *Systems Analysis*; Abella, *Soldiers of Reason*.

77. Jelen, *An Elusive Goal*, III-50.

78. Eugene H. Spafford, "Complexity Is Killing Us: A Security State of the Union with Eugene Spafford of CERIAS" (presentation, CERIAS Symposium, Purdue University, West Lafayette, IN, March 3, 2011), https://www.cerias.purdue.edu/site/news/view/complexity_is_killing_us_a_security_state_of_the_union_with_eugene_spafford/; Marcus Ranum, "Teaching an Old Dog New Tricks: The Problem Is Complexity," ranum.com, last accessed July 16, 2019, http://ranum.com/security/computer_security/editorials/codetools/index.html; Thomas Dullien, "Security, Moore's Law, and the Anomaly of Cheap Complexity" (presentation, 10th International Conference on Cyber Conflict, Tallinn, Estonia, May 29–June 1, 2018), https://www.youtube.com/watch?v=q98foLaAfX8; John Viega and Gary McGraw, *Building Secure Software: How to Avoid Security Problems the Right Way* (Boston: Addison-Wesley, 2001).

79. Willis H. Ware, *Security Controls for Computer Systems: Report of Defense Science Board Task Force on Computer Security* (Santa Monica, CA: RAND Corporation, 1970), https://www.rand.org/pubs/reports/R609-1/index2.html.

80. Ware, *Security Controls*.

81. James P. Anderson, *Computer Security Technology Planning Study* (Bedford, MA: Electronic Systems Division, Air Force Systems Command, United States Air Force, 1972).

82. Donald MacKenzie and Garrell Pottinger, "Mathematics, Technology, and Trust: Formal Verification, Computer Security, and the U.S. Military," *IEEE Annals of the History of Computing* 19, no. 3 (1997): 41–59, https://doi.org/10.1109/85.601735.

83. Marcus Ranum, "The Network Police Blotter," *Login* 25, no. 1 (2000), https://www.usenix.org/publications/login/february-2000-volume-25-number-1.

84. Ranum, "The Network Police Blotter."

85. Michael Howard and David LeBlanc, *Writing Secure Code* (Redmond, WA: Microsoft Press, 2002); Steve McConnell, *Code Complete: A Practical Handbook of Software Construction*, 2nd ed. (Redmond, WA: Microsoft Press, 2004); Michael Howard and Steve Lipner, *The Security Development Lifecycle* (Redmond, WA: Microsoft Press, 2006).

86. Ben Moseley and Peter Marks, "Out of the Tar Pit," n.p., February 6, 2006.

87. Martyn Thomas, "Complexity, Safety, and Computers," *Risks Digest* 10, no. 31 (1990), https://catless.ncl.ac.uk/Risks/10/31; Moseley and Marks, "Out of the Tar Pit."

88. Sergey Bratus, Trey Darley, Michael Locasto, Meredith L. Patterson, Rebecca Shapiro, and Anna Shubina, "Beyond Planted Bugs in 'Trusting Trust': The Input-Processing Frontier," *IEEE Security & Privacy* 12, no. 1 (2014), https://ieeexplore.ieee.org/document/6756892.

89. Crispin Cowan, "Turning around the Security Problem: Why Does Security Still Suck?" n.p., August 3, 2006.

90. Howard and LeBlanc, *Writing Secure Code*; Howard and Lipner, *The Security Development Lifecycle*.

91. Bill Horne, "Humans in the Loop," *IEEE Security & Privacy* 12, no. 1 (2014): 3–4, https://doi.ieeecomputersociety.org/10.1109/MSP.2014.5; Stewart, "A Utilitarian Re-Examination."

92. Stewart, "A Utilitarian Re-Examination."

93. Phil Venables, "Information Security & Complexity," n.p., 2004.

94. Frederick P. Brooks Jr., "No Silver Bullet: Essence and Accidents of Software Engineering," *Computer* 20, no. 4 (1987): 10–19, https://doi.org/10.1109/MC.1987.1663532.

95. Brooks, "No Silver Bullet."

96. Brooks, "No Silver Bullet."

97. Brooks, "No Silver Bullet."

98. Gavin Thomas, "A Proactive Approach to More Secure Code," Microsoft Security Response Center, last updated July 16, 2019, https://msrc-blog.microsoft.com/2019/07/16/a-proactive-approach-to-more-secure-code/.

99. Alma Whitten and J. D. Tygar, "Why Johnny Can't Encrypt: A Usability Evaluation of PGP 5.0" (presentation, 8th USENIX Security Symposium, Washington, DC, August 23–26, 1999), https://people.eecs.berkeley.edu/~tygar/papers/Why_Johnny_Cant_Encrypt/OReilly.pdf.

100. Zinaida Benenson, Gabriele Lenzini, Daniela Oliveira, Simon Edward Parkin, and Sven Ubelacker, "Maybe Poor Johnny Really Cannot Encrypt: The Case for a Complexity Theory for Usable Security" (presentation, 15th New Security Paradigms Workshop, Twente, the Netherlands, September 8–11, 2015), https://doi.org/10.1145/2841113.2841120.

101. Benenson et al., "Poor Johnny."

102. Stewart, "A Utilitarian Re-Examination."

103. Ponnurangam Kumaraguru, Steve Sheng, Alessandro Acquisti, Lorrie Faith Cranor, and Jason Hong, "Teaching Johnny Not to Fall for Phish," *ACM Transactions on Internet Technology* 10, no. 2 (2010), https://doi.org/10.1145/1754393.1754396.

104. Kumaraguru et al., "Teaching Johnny."

105. Cormac Herley, "So Long, and No Thanks for the Externalities: The Rational Rejection of Security Advice by Users" (presentation, New Security Paradigms Workshop, Oxford, UK, September 8–11, 2009), https://doi.org/10.1145/1719030.1719050.

106. Herley, "So Long."

107. Herley, "So Long."

108. Dieter Gollmann, *Computer Security* (New York: Wiley, 2011), 40.

109. Simson Garfinkel and Heather Richter Lipford, *Usable Security: History, Themes, and Challenges* (San Rafael, CA: Morgan & Claypool, 2014); Benenson et al., "Poor Johnny."

110. Dirk Balfanz, Glenn Durfee, Rebecca E. Grinter, and D. K. Smetters, "In Search of Usable Security: Five Lessons from the Field," *IEEE Security & Privacy* 2, no. 5 (2004): 19–24, https://doi.org/10.1109/MSP.2004.71.

111. Katharina Krombholz, Wilfried Mayer, Martin Schmiedecker, and Edgar Weippl, "'I Have No Idea What I'm Doing': On the Usability of Deploying HTTPS" (presentation, 26th USENIX Conference on Security Symposium, Vancouver, August 16–18, 2017), https://dl.acm.org/citation.cfm?id=3241293.

112. Steven M. Bellovin, "Permissive Action Links," Department of Computer Science, Columbia University, last accessed July 17, 2019, https://www.cs.columbia.edu/~smb/nsam-160/pal.html.

113. Bellovin, "Permissive Action Links."

114. Shaya Potter, Steven M. Bellovin, and Jason Nieh, "Two-Person Control Administration: Preventing Administration Faults through Duplication" (presentation, 23rd Conference on Large Installation System Administration, Baltimore, November 1–6, 2009), https://dl.acm.org/citation.cfm?id=1855700.

115. National Research Council, *Computers at Risk: Safe Computing in the Information Age* (Washington, DC: National Academy Press, 1991); Richard Forno, "Re: Nation's Cybersecurity Suffers from a Lack of Information Sharing," *InfoSec News*, March 5, 2010, https://seclists.org/isn/2010/Mar/21; Horne, "Humans in the Loop."

116. Financial Services Information Sharing and Analysis Center (FS-ISAC), "Reducing Cyber-Risk for Financial Services Institutions," fsisac.com, last accessed July 17, 2019, https://www.fsisac.com/who-we-are.

117. FS-ISAC, "Reducing Cyber-Risk for Financial Services Institutions."

118. Steven M. Bellovin and Adam Shostack, *Input to the Commission on Enhancing National Cybersecurity* (n.p.: September 2016), https://www.cs.columbia.edu/~smb/papers/Current_and_Future_States_of_Cybersecurity-Bellovin-Shostack.pdf.

119. Jonathan Bair, Steven M. Bellovin, Andrew Manley, Blake Reid, and Adam Shostack, "That Was Close! Reward Reporting of Cybersecurity 'Near Misses,'" *Colorado Technology Law Journal* 16, no. 2 (2018): 327–364, https://ssrn.com/abstract=3081216.

120. Bair et al., "That Was Close!"

121. Steven B. Lipner, "The Birth and Death of the Orange Book," *IEEE Annals of the History of Computing* 37, no. 2 (2015): 19–31, https://doi.org/10.1109/MAHC.2015.27.

122. Stefan Axelsson, "The Base-Rate Fallacy and Its Implications for the Difficulty of Intrusion Detection," (presentation, 2nd RAID Symposium, Purdue University, West Lafayette, IN, September 7–9, 1999).

123. Mara Tam, "Re: 'Clickbait Policy-Making,'" Dailydave, July 29, 2016, https://seclists.org/dailydave/2016/q3/23.

124. Teresa F. Lunt, interview by Jeffrey R. Yost, *Charles Babbage Institute*, June 4, 2013, 27, http://hdl.handle.net/11299/162378.

125. *Mad Men*, episode 13, season 5, "The Phantom," directed by Matthew Weiner, written by Jonathan Igla and Matthew Weiner, aired June 10, 2012, https://www.amc.com/shows/mad-men/season-5/episode-13/the-phantom.

126. Herley and van Oorschot, "SoK."

127. Paul Karger and Roger R. Schell, *Multics Security Evaluation: Vulnerability Analysis* (Bedford, MA: Electronic Systems Division, Air Force Systems Command, United States Air Force, 1974); Tom van Vleck, "How the Air Force Cracked Multics Security," Multicians, last updated October 14, 2002, https://www.multicians.org/security .html.

128. Herley and van Oorschot, "SoK."

129. Herley and van Oorschot, "SoK."

130. Adrian Stone, Josh Shaul, and Matt Watchinski, "Panel Discussion: The Value (and Danger) of Offensive Security Research" (presentation, Virus Bulletin, Dallas, September 26–28, 2012), https://www.virusbulletin.com/conference/vb2012/abstracts /panel-discussion-value-and-danger-offensive-security-research/; Ryan Naraine, "Offensive Security Research Community Helping Bad Guys," *ZDNet*, February 7, 2012, https://www.zdnet.com/article/offensive-security-research-community-helping-bad -guys/.

131. Ashish Arora and Rahul Telang, "Economics of Software Vulnerability Disclosure," *IEEE Security & Privacy* 3, no. 1 (2005): 20–25, https://doi.org/10.1109/MSP.2005.12.

132. Arne Padmos, "Against Mindset" (presentation, New Security Paradigms Workshop, Windsor, UK, August 28–31, 2018), https://doi.org/10.1145/3285002.3285004.

133. Marcus Ranum, "Are the Skills of a Hacker Necessary to Build Good Security?" ranum.com, last accessed July 17, 2019, http://www.ranum.com/security/computer _security/editorials/skillsets/index.html; Ranum, "The Six Dumbest Ideas in Computer Security."

134. Rebecca G. Bace, interview by Jeffrey R. Yost, *Charles Babbage Institute*, July 31, 2012, 48, http://hdl.handle.net/11299/144022.

135. "Initiatives," The Analogies Project, last accessed July 17, 2019, http:// theanalogiesproject.org/initiatives/.

136. Butler Lampson, interview by Jeffrey R. Yost, *Charles Babbage Institute*, December 11, 2014, 19, http://hdl.handle.net/11299/169983.

137. Jerome H. Saltzer and M. D. Schroeder, "The Protection of Information in Computer Systems," *Proceedings of the IEEE* 63, no. 9 (1975): 1278–1308, http://doi.org/10 .1109/PROC.1975.9939; Gollmann, *Computer Security*, 34.

138. Michael E. Whitman and Herbert J. Mattord, *Principles of Information Security*, 5th ed. (Boston: Cengage Learning, 2014), 10–16. David Kim and Michael G. Solomon, *Fundamentals of Information Systems Security* (Burlington, MA: Jones & Bartlett Learning, 2016), 16–17; Adam Gordon, *Official (ISC)2 Guide to the CISSP CBK* (Boca Raton, FL: Auerbach, 2015); Shon Harris and Fernando Maymi, *CISSP All-in-One Exam Guide*, 8th ed. (New York: McGraw-Hill, 2018).

139. Phil Venables, "21st Century InfoSec Management and Beyond," *Information Security Bulletin*, February 2000.

140. Venables, "21st Century InfoSec Management."

141. Jerome H. Saltzer, "Repaired Security Bugs in Multics," in *Ancillary Reports: Kernel Design Project*, MIT Laboratory for Computer Science Technical Memo MIT/LCS/ TM-87, 1977, 1–4, http://web.mit.edu/Saltzer/www/publications/pubs.html; Donn B.

Parker, *Fighting Computer Crime: A New Framework for Protecting Information* (New York: Wiley, 1998); Spyridon Samonas and David Coss, "The CIA Strikes Back: Redefining Confidentiality, Integrity and Availability in Security," *Journal of Information System Security* 10, no. 3 (2014): 21–45, http://www.jissec.org/Contents/V10/N3/V10N3-Samonas.html.

142. Thomas Rid, *Cyber War Will Not Take Place* (Oxford: Oxford University Press, 2017), 73.

143. Auguste Kerckhoffs, "La cryptographie militaire," *Journal des sciences militaires* 9 (1883): 5–38, 161–191.

144. Rid, *Cyber War*, 73.

145. Steven M. Bellovin, "Re: Security through Obscurity," *Risks Digest* 25, no. 71 (2009), https://catless.ncl.ac.uk/Risks/25/71.

146. Bellovin, "Re: Security through Obscurity."

147. "Defense-in-Depth," Computer Security Resource Center, NIST, last accessed July 17, 2019, https://csrc.nist.gov/glossary/term/defense_in_depth.

148. Josephine Wolff, *You'll See This Message When It Is Too Late: The Legal and Economic Aftermath of Cybersecurity Breaches* (Cambridge, MA: MIT Press, 2018), 86–87, 236–237.

149. Josephine Wolff, "Perverse Effects in Defense of Computer Systems: When More Is Less" (presentation, 49th Hawaii International Conference on System Sciences, Koloa, March 10, 2016), https://doi.org/10.1109/HICSS.2016.598; Don Norman, "Why Adding More Security Measures May Make Systems Less Secure," *Risks Digest* 23, no. 63 (2004), https://catless.ncl.ac.uk/Risks/23/63.

150. Charles Perrow, *Normal Accidents: Living with High-Risk Technologies* (Princeton, NJ: Princeton University Press, 1999).

151. Abella, *Soldiers of Reason*.

152. Abella, *Soldiers of Reason*.

153. Abella, *Soldiers of Reason*.

154. Ross Anderson, "Why Information Security Is Hard—An Economic Perspective" (presentation, 17th Annual Computer Security Applications Conference, New Orleans, December 10–14, 2001), https://doi.org/10.1109/ACSAC.2001.991552.

155. Herley, "So Long."

156. Richard Samuels, Stephen Stich, and Luc Faucher, "Reason and Rationality," in *Handbook of Epistemology*, ed. I. Niiniluoto, Matti Sintonen, and Jan Wolenski (Dordrecht: Springer Netherlands, 2004), https://www.researchgate.net/publication/286299529_Reason_and_Rationality.

157. "Aristotle's Ethics," *Stanford Encyclopedia of Philosophy*, last updated June 15, 2018, https://plato.stanford.edu/entries/aristotle-ethics/; Aristotle, *The Eudemian Ethics*, trans. Anthony Kenny (Oxford: Oxford World's Classics, 2011).

158. Matt Bishop, "A Taxonomy of UNIX System and Network Vulnerabilities," n.p., May 1995.

159. James Burke, *Connections*, dir. Mick Jackson (United Kingdom: BBC, 1978).

**Epilogue**

1. Davey Winder, "Data Breaches Expose 4.1 Billion Records in First Six Months of 2019," *Forbes*, August 20, 2019, https://www.forbes.com/sites/daveywinder/2019/08/20/data-breaches-expose-41-billion-records-in-first-six-months-of-2019/; "2019 Data Breaches: 4 Billion Records Breached So Far," Emerging Threats, Norton, last accessed March 4, 2020, https://us.norton.com/internetsecurity-emerging-threats-2019-data-breaches.html.

2. Alfred Ng, "Marriott Says Hackers Stole More Than 5 Million Passport Numbers," *CNET*, January 4, 2019, https://www.cnet.com/news/marriott-says-hackers-stole-more-than-5-million-passport-numbers/.

3. Chris Williams, *Register*, February 11, 2019, https://www.theregister.co.uk/2019/02/11/620_million_hacked_accounts_dark_web/.

4. Sean Gallagher, "Hackers Breached 3 US Antivirus Companies, Researchers Reveal," *Ars Technica*, May 2019, https://arstechnica.com/information-technology/2019/05/hackers-breached-3-us-antivirus-companies-researchers-reveal/.

5. Dell Cameron, "Antivirus Makers Confirm, and Deny, Getting Breached by Hackers Looking to Sell Stolen Data," *Gizmodo*, May 13, 2019, https://gizmodo.com/antivirus-makers-confirm-and-deny-getting-breached-afte-1834725136/.

6. Ionut Ilascu, "Fxmsp Chat Logs Reveal the Hacked Antivirus Vendors, AVs Respond," *BleepingComputer*, May 13, 2019, https://www.bleepingcomputer.com/news/security/fxmsp-chat-logs-reveal-the-hacked-antivirus-vendors-avs-respond/.

7. Mark Bridge, "Biggest Instagram Leak Exposes Data of 49 Million Users," *Times*, May 22, 2019, https://www.thetimes.co.uk/article/biggest-instagram-leak-exposes-data-of-50-million-users-m8dsnh7xd/.

8. "Information on the Capital One Cyber Incident," *Capital One*, last updated September 23, 2019, https://www.capitalone.com/facts2019/.

9. Jessie Yeung, "Almost Entire Population of Ecuador Has Data Leaked," *CNN*, September 17, 2019, https://www.cnn.com/2019/09/17/americas/ecuador-data-leak-intl-hnk-scli/index.html; Catalin Cimpanu, "Database Leaks Data on Most of Ecuador's Citizens, Including 6.7 Million Children," *ZDNet*, September 16, 2019, https://www.zdnet.com/article/database-leaks-data-on-most-of-ecuadors-citizens-including-6-7-million-children/.

10. Shaun Nichols, "Why Is a 22GB Database Containing 56 Million US Folks' Personal Details Sitting on the Open Internet Using a Chinese IP Address? Seriously, Why?" *Register*, January 9, 2020, https://www.theregister.com/2020/01/09/checkpeoplecom_data_exposed/.

11. Naked Security, "Serious Chrome Zero-Day," *Naked Security* (blog), March 6, 2019, https://nakedsecurity.sophos.com/2019/03/06/serious-chrome-zero-day-google-says-update-right-this-minute/.

12. "Analysis of a Chrome Zero Day: CVE-2019-5786," McAfee Labs, McAfee, last updated March 20, 2019, https://www.mcafee.com/blogs/other-blogs/mcafee-labs/analysis-of-a-chrome-zero-day-cve-2019-5786/.

13. Eric Geller, "Chinese Nationals Charged for Anthem Hack, 'One of the Worst Data Breaches in History,'" *Politico*, May 9, 2019, https://www.politico.com/story/2019/05/09/chinese-hackers-anthem-data-breach-1421341/.

14. Zack Whittaker, "Hackers Are Stealing Years of Call Records from Hacked Cell Networks," *TechCrunch*, June 24, 2019, https://techcrunch.com/2019/06/24/hackers-cell-networks-call-records-theft/.

15. Whittaker, "Stealing Years of Call Records."

16. United States Senate, *Report of the Select Committee on Intelligence on Russian Active Measures Campaigns and Interference in the 2016 Election* (Washington, DC: United States Senate, September 25, 2019), https://www.intelligence.senate.gov/sites/default/files/documents/Report_Volume1.pdf; David E. Sanger, "Russia Targeted Election Systems in All 50 States, Report Finds," *New York Times*, September 25, 2019, https://www.nytimes.com/2019/07/25/us/politics/russian-hacking-elections.html.

17. Gary Fineout, "Russians Hacked 2 Florida Voting Systems; FBI and DeSantis Refuse to Release Details," *Politico*, May 14, 2019, https://www.politico.com/states/florida/story/2019/05/14/russians-hacked-2-florida-voting-systems-fbi-and-desantis-refuse-to-release-details-1015772/.

18. Sam Biddle, "The NSA Leak Is Real, Snowden Documents Confirm," *Intercept*, August 19, 2016, https://theintercept.com/2016/08/19/the-nsa-was-hacked-snowden-documents-confirm/.

19. Elizabeth Piper, "Cyber Attack Hits 200,000 in at Least 150 Countries: Europol," *Reuters*, May 14, 2017, https://www.reuters.com/article/us-cyber-attack-europol/cyber-attack-hits-200000-in-at-least-150-countries-europol-idUSKCN18A0FX/.

20. Nicole Perlroth, "How Chinese Spies Got the N.S.A.'s Hacking Tools, and Used Them for Attacks," *New York Times*, May 6, 2019, https://www.nytimes.com/2019/05/06/us/politics/china-hacking-cyber.html.

21. Dan Goodin, "Stolen NSA Hacking Tools Were Used in the Wild 14 Months before Shadow Brokers Leak," *Ars Technica*, May 6, 2019, https://arstechnica.com/information-technology/2019/05/stolen-nsa-hacking-tools-were-used-in-the-wild-14-months-before-shadow-brokers-leak/.

22. Orion Rummler and Rebecca Falconer, "Iranian Cyberattacks against the U.S. Are on the Rise," *Axios*, June 23, 2019, https://www.axios.com/iranian-cyberattacks-against-the-us-are-on-the-rise-46e2f3a2-7c4d-4589-b006-4d90a4dd6d0b.html; Tim Starks, "Security Firms See Spike in Iranian Cyberattacks," *Politico*, June 21, 2019, https://www.politico.com/story/2019/06/21/us-iran-cyberattacks-3469447/; Michelle Nichols, "North Korea Took $2 Billion in Cyberattacks to Fund Weapons Program: U.N. Report," *Reuters*, August 5, 2019, https://www.reuters.com/article/us-northkorea-cyber-un/north-korea-took-2-billion-in-cyberattacks-to-fund-weapons-program-u-n-report-idUSKCN1UV1ZX/.

23. Jamie Nimmo, "Now Hackers Can Steal Your ID and Bank Details from a Coffee Machine! Cyber Security Guru Also Warns People from Using WhatsApp and Smart TVs," *Mail on Sunday*, May 18, 2019, https://www.dailymail.co.uk/news/article-7045105/Now-hackers-steal-ID-bank-details-coffee-machine.html/.

24. Alfred Ng, "These Kids' Smartwatches Have Security Problems as Simple as 1-2-3," *CNET*, December 11, 2019, https://www.cnet.com/news/these-kids-smartwatches-have-security-problems-as-simple-as-1-2-3/.

25. WillC [pseud.], "Phreaking Elevators" (presentation, Defcon, Las Vegas, NV, August 9, 2019), https://www.youtube.com/watch?v=NoZ7ujJhb3k; Daniel Oberhaus, "This Hacker Showed How a Smart Lightbulb Could Leak Your Wi-Fi Password," *Vice*,

January 31, 2019, https://www.vice.com/en_us/article/kzdwp9/this-hacker-showed-how-a-smart-lightbulb-could-leak-your-wi-fi-password/; Trend Micro Research, *Attacks against Industrial Machines via Vulnerable Radio Remote Controllers: Security Analysis and Recommendations* (Tokyo: Trend Micro, 2019); Patrick Clark, "The Hotel Hackers Are Hiding in the Remote Control Curtains," *Bloomberg Businessweek*, June 26, 2019, https://www.bloomberg.com/news/features/2019-06-26/the-hotel-hackers-are-hiding-in-the-remote-control-curtains/.

26. Thomas Claburn, "From Hard Drive to Over-Heard Drive: Boffins Convert Spinning Rust into Eavesdropping Mic," *Register*, March 7, 2019, https://www.theregister.co.uk/2019/03/07/hard_drive_eavesdropping/.

27. Claburn, "From Hard Drive."

28. Kevin Kelly, "The Shirky Principle," *Technium* (blog), April 2, 2010, https://kk.org/thetechnium/the-shirky-prin/.

29. "A Proactive Approach to More Secure Code," Microsoft Security Response Center, Gavin Thomas, last updated July 16, 2019, https://msrc-blog.microsoft.com/2019/07/16/a-proactive-approach-to-more-secure-code/.

30. Dirk Balfanz, Glenn Durfee, Rebecca E. Grinter, and D. K. Smetters, "In Search of Usable Security: Five Lessons from the Field," *IEEE Security & Privacy* 2, no. 5 (2004): 19–24, https://doi.org/10.1109/MSP.2004.71; Katharina Krombholz, Wilfried Mayer, Martin Schmiedecker, and Edgar Weippl, "'I Have No Idea What I'm Doing': On the Usability of Deploying HTTPS" (presentation, 26th USENIX Conference on Security Symposium, Vancouver, August 16–18, 2017), https://dl.acm.org/citation.cfm?id=3241293.

31. Carl von Clausewitz, *On War*, ed. Michael Howard and Peter Paret (Princeton, NJ: Princeton University Press, 1989).

32. Clausewitz, *On War*, 578.

# Select Bibliography

Abbate, Janet. *Inventing the Internet*. Cambridge, MA: MIT Press, 1999.

Abella, Alex. *Soldiers of Reason: The RAND Corporation and the Rise of the American Empire*. Boston: Mariner Books, 2009.

Anderson, James P. *Computer Security Technology Planning Study*. Bedford, MA: Electronic Systems Division, Air Force Systems Command, United States Air Force, 1972.

Anderson, Ross. "Why Information Security Is Hard: An Economic Perspective." Paper presented at the 17th Annual Computer Security Applications Conference, New Orleans, December 10–14, 2001. https://doi.org/10.1109/ACSAC.2001.991552.

Axelsson, Stefan. "The Base-Rate Fallacy and Its Implications for the Difficulty of Intrusion Detection." Paper presented at the 2nd RAID Symposium, Purdue, IN, September 7–9, 1999.

Bell, David Elliot, and Leonard J. LaPadula. *Secure Computer System: Unified Exposition and Multics Interpretation*. Bedford, MA: Electronic Systems Division, Air Force Systems Command, United States Air Force, March 1976.

———. *Secure Computer Systems: Mathematical Foundations*. Bedford, MA: Electronic Systems Division, Air Force Systems Command, United States Air Force, November 1973.

Bellovin, Steven M. "Security Problems in the TCP/IP Protocol Suite." *ACM SIGCOMM Computer Communication Review* 19, no. 2 (April 1, 1989): 32–48. https://doi.org/10.1145/378444.378449.

Bellovin, Steven M., and William R. Cheswick. "Network Firewalls." *IEEE Communications Magazine* 32, no. 9 (1994): 50–57. https://doi.org/10.1109/35.312843.

Bishop, Matt. "A Taxonomy of UNIX System and Network Vulnerabilities." N.p.: May 1995.

———. *Computer Security: Art and Science*. Boston: Addison-Wesley, 2003.

Calem, Robert E. "New York's Panix Service Is Crippled by Hacker Attack." *New York Times*, September 14, 1996. https://archive.nytimes.com/www.nytimes.com/library/cyber/week/0914panix.html.

Campbell-Kelly, Martin. *From Airline Reservations to Sonic the Hedgehog: A History of the Software Industry*. Cambridge, MA: MIT Press, 2003.

Ceruzzi, Paul E. *A History of Modern Computing*. Cambridge, MA: MIT Press, 2003.

Cheswick, William R. "The Design of a Secure Internet Gateway." Paper presented at USENIX Summer Conference, 1990.

Cheswick, William R., and Steven M. Bellovin, *Firewalls and Internet Security: Repelling the Wily Hacker*, 2nd ed. Boston: Addison-Wesley, 1994.

Computer Fraud and Abuse Act of 1984, 18 U.S.C. § 1030 (2019).

De Leon, Daniel. "The Productivity of the Criminal." *Daily People*, April 14, 1905. http://www.slp.org/pdf/de_leon/eds1905/apr14_1905.pdf.

Denning, Dorothy E. "An Intrusion-Detection Model." *IEEE Transactions on Software Engineering* 13, no. 2 (1987): 222–232. https://doi.org/10.1109/TSE.1987.232894.

Department of Defense. *Department of Defense Trusted Computer System Evaluation Criteria*. Fort Meade, MD: Department of Defense, December 26, 1985.

Edelman, Benjamin. "Adverse Selection in Online 'Trust' Certifications and Search Results." *Electronic Commerce Research and Applications* 10, no. 1 (2011): 17–25. https://doi.org/10.1016/j.elerap.2010.06.001.

Eichin, M. W., and J. A. Rochlis. "With Microscope and Tweezers: An Analysis of the Internet Virus of November 1988." Paper present at IEEE Symposium on Security and Privacy, Oakland, CA, May 1–3, 1989. https://doi.org/10.1109/SECPRI.1989.36307.

Farmer, Dan. "Shall We Dust Moscow? (Security Survey of Key Internet Hosts and Various Semi-Relevant Reflections)." December 18, 1996. http://www.fish2.com/survey/.

Florencio, Dinei, and Cormac Herley. "Sex, Lies, and Cyber-Crime Surveys." In *Economics of Information Security and Privacy III*, ed. Bruce Schneier. New York: Springer, 2013. https://doi.org/10.1007/978-1-4614-1981-5_3.

Fyodor [pseud.]. "Bugtraq Mailing List." SecLists.Org Security Mailing List Archive. Last accessed May 19, 2019. https://seclists.org/bugtraq/.

———. "Full Disclosure Mailing List." SecLists.Org Security Mailing List Archive. Last accessed May 19, 2019. https://seclists.org/fulldisclosure/.

———. "Zardoz 'Security Digest.'" The "Security Digest" Archives. Last accessed May 19, 2019. http://securitydigest.org/zardoz/.

Garfinkel, Simson, and Heather Richter Lipford. *Usable Security: History, Themes, and Challenges*. San Rafael, CA: Morgan & Claypool, 2014.

Garfinkel, Simson, and Gene Spafford. *Practical Unix Security*. Sebastopol, CA: O'Reilly Media, 1991.

Gates, Bill. "Trustworthy Computing." *Wired*, January 17, 2002. https://www.wired.com/2002/01/bill-gates-trustworthy-computing/.

Geer, Dan, Rebecca Bace, Peter Gutmann, Perry Metzger, Charles P. Pfleeger, John S. Quarterman, and Bruce Schneier. *CyberInsecurity: The Cost of Monopoly*. Washington, DC: Computer & Communications Industry Association, 2003.

Goffman, Erving. *The Presentation of Self in Everyday Life*. New York: Anchor, 1959.

Gollmann, Dieter. *Computer Security*. New York: Wiley, 2011.

Grigg, Ian. "The Market for Silver Bullets." March 2, 2008. http://iang.org/papers/market _for_silver_bullets.html.

Hafner, Katie, and Matthew Lyon. *Where Wizards Stay Up Late: The Origins of the Internet*. New York: Simon & Schuster, 1996.

Herley, Cormac. "So Long, and No Thanks for the Externalities: The Rational Rejection of Security Advice by Users." Paper presented at the New Security Paradigms Workshop, Oxford, UK, September 8–11, 2009. https://doi.org/10.1145/1719030 .1719050.

———. "Unfalsifiability of Security Claims." *Proceedings of the National Academy of Sciences* 113, no. 23 (2016): 6415–6420. https://doi.org/10.1073/pnas.1517797113.

Herley, Cormac, and Paul Van Oorschot. "A Research Agenda Acknowledging the Persistence of Passwords." *IEEE Security & Privacy* 10, no. 1 (2012): 28–36. https://doi .org/10.1109/MSP.2011.150.

———. "SoK: Science, Security and the Elusive Goal of Security as a Scientific Pursuit." Paper presented at the IEEE Symposium on Security and Privacy, San Jose, CA, May 22–26, 2017. http://dx.doi.org/10.1109/SP.2017.38.

Howard, Michael, and David LeBlanc. *Writing Secure Code*. Redmond, WA: Microsoft Press, 2002.

Howard, Michael, and Steve Lipner. *The Security Development Lifecycle*. Redmond, WA: Microsoft Press, 2006.

Jelen, George F. *Information Security: An Elusive Goal*. Cambridge, MA: Harvard University Press, 1995.

Karger, Paul, and Roger R. Schell. *Multics Security Evaluation: Vulnerability Analysis*. Bedford, MA: Electronic Systems Division, Air Force Systems Command, United States Air Force, 1974.

Kerckhoffs, Auguste. "La cryptographie militaire." *Journal des sciences militaires* 9 (1883): 5–38, 161–191.

Lampson, Butler. "A Note on the Confinement Problem." *Communications of the ACM* 16, no. 10 (1973): 613–615. https://doi.org/10.1145/362375.362389.

Levy, Elias. "Full Disclosure Is a Necessary Evil." *SecurityFocus*, August 16, 2001. https:// www.securityfocus.com/news/238.

Lipner, Steve. "The Birth and Death of the Orange Book." *IEEE Annals of the History of Computing* 37, no. 2 (2015): 19–31. https://doi.org/10.1109/MAHC.2015.27.

Loscocco, Peter A., Stephen D. Smalley, Patrick A. Muckelbauer, Ruth C. Taylor, S. Jeff Turner, and John F. Farrell. "The Inevitability of Failure: The Flawed Assumption of Security in Modern Computing Environments." Paper presented at the 21st National Information Systems Security Conference, Arlington, VA, October 8, 1998.

MacKenzie, Donald, and Garrell Pottinger. "Mathematics, Technology, and Trust: Formal Verification, Computer Security, and the U.S. Military." *IEEE Annals of the History of Computing* 19, no. 3 (1997): 41–59. https://doi.org/10.1109/85.601735.

Mandiant. *APT1: Exposing One of China's Cyber Espionage Units*. Alexandria, VA: Mandiant, 2013.

McCartney, Scott. *ENIAC: The Triumphs and Tragedies of the World's First Computer*. New York: Walker, 1999.

McLean, John. "A Comment on the 'Basic Security Theorem' of Bell and LaPadula." *Information Processing Letters* 20, no. 2 (1985): 67–70. https://doi.org/10.1016/0020-0190(85)90065-1.

———. "The Specification and Modeling of Computer Security." *Computer* 23, no. 1 (1990): 9–16. https://doi.org/10.1109/2.48795.

Moore, David, Vern Paxson, Stefan Savage, Colleen Shannon, Stuart Staniford, and Nicholas Weaver. "Inside the Slammer Worm." *IEEE Security & Privacy* 1, no. 4 (2003): 33–39. https://doi.org/10.1109/MSECP.2003.1219056.

Morris, Robert T. *A Weakness in the 4.2BSD Unix TCP/IP Software*. Murray Hill, NJ: Bell Labs, February 25, 1985.

Morris, Robert, and Ken Thompson. "Password Security: A Case History." *Communications of the ACM* 22, no. 11 (1979): 594–597. https://doi.org/10.1145/359168.359172.

National Archives (UK). "Computer Misuse Act 1990." legislation.gov.uk. Last updated June 29, 1990. http://www.legislation.gov.uk/ukpga/1990/18/enacted.

National Bureau of Standards. *Password Usage—Federal Information Processing Standards Publication 112*. Gaithersburg, MD: National Bureau of Standards, 1985. https://csrc.nist.gov/publications/detail/fips/112/archive/1985-05-01.

Oracle Corporation. *Unbreakable: Oracle's Commitment to Security*. Redwood Shores, CA: Oracle, 2002.

Ptacek, Thomas H., and Timothy N. Newsham. *Insertion, Evasion, and Denial of Service: Eluding Network Intrusion Detection*. N.p.: Secure Networks, 1998.

Rain Forest Puppy [pseud.]. "NT Web Technology Vulnerabilities." *Phrack* 8, no. 54 (1998). http://phrack.org/issues/54/8.html.

Ranum, Marcus. "Script Kiddiez Suck." Paper presented at Black Hat Briefings, Las Vegas, NV, 2000. https://www.blackhat.com/html/bh-media-archives/bh-archives-2000.html.

Route [pseud.]. "Project Neptune." *Phrack* 7, no. 48 (1996). http://phrack.org/issues/48/13.html.

Ryan, Julie J. C. H., and Theresa I. Jefferson. "The Use, Misuse, and Abuse of Statistics in Information Security Research." Paper presented at the American Society for Engineering Management, Saint Louis, MO, October 15–18, 2003. http://citeseerx.ist.psu.edu/viewdoc/summary?doi=10.1.1.203.5387.

Saltzer, Jerome H., and M. D. Schroeder. "The Protection of Information in Computer Systems." *Proceedings of the IEEE* 63, no. 9 (1975): 1278–1308. http://doi.org/10.1109/PROC.1975.9939.

Schaefer, Marvin. "If A1 Is the Answer, What Was the Question? An Edgy Naif's Retrospective on Promulgating the Trusted Computer Systems Evaluation Criteria." Paper presented at the 20th Annual Computer Security Applications Conference, Tucson, AZ, December 6–10, 2004. https://doi.org/10.1109/CSAC.2004.22.

Schell, Roger R. "Information Security: Science, Pseudoscience, and Flying Pigs." Paper presented at the 17th Annual Computer Security Applications Conference, New Orleans, December 10–14, 2001. https://doi.org/10.1109/ACSAC.2001.991537.

Spafford, Eugene H. "The Internet Worm Program: An Analysis—Purdue University Report Number 88-823." *ACM SIGCOMM Computer Communication Review* 19, no. 1 (1989): 17–57. https://doi.org/10.1145/66093.66095.

Templeton, Brad. "Reaction to the DEC Spam of 1978." Brad Templeton's home page. Last accessed April 30, 2019. https://www.templetons.com/brad/spamreact.html.

Thompson, Ken. "Reflections on Trusting Trust." *Communications of the ACM* 27, no. 8 (1984): 761–763. https://doi.org/10.1145/358198.358210.

Van Vleck, Tom. "How the Air Force Cracked Multics Security." Multicians. Last updated October 14, 2002. https://www.multicians.org/security.html.

Ware, Willis H. *Security Controls for Computer Systems: Report of Defense Science Board Task Force on Computer Security*. Santa Monica, CA: RAND, 1970. https://www.rand.org/pubs/reports/R609-1/index2.html.

Whitten, Alma, and J. D. Tygar. "Why Johnny Can't Encrypt: A Usability Evaluation of PGP 5.0." Paper presented at the 8th USENIX Security Symposium, Washington, DC, August 23–26, 1999.

WikiLeaks. "Vault 7: CIA Hacking Tools Revealed." wikiLeaks.org. Last updated March 7, 2017. https://wikileaks.org/ciav7p1/.

Wool, Avishai. "A Quantitative Study of Firewall Configuration Errors." *Computer* 37, no. 6 (2004): 62–67. https://doi.org/10.1109/MC.2004.2.

# INDEX